Praise from Readers and Reviewers

Here's what critics and readers have said about Eric Tyson and his previous national best-selling personal finance guides:

"Personal Finance For Dummies is the perfect book for people who feel guilty about inadequately managing their money but are intimidated by all of the publications out there. It's a painless way to learn how to take control. My college-aged daughters even enjoyed reading it!"
— Karen Tofte, producer, National Public Radio's *Sound Money*

"I own many finance and investment books — this is <u>by</u> <u>far</u> the best!"
— Mike Dodge, Baltimore, MD

"Among my favorite financial guides are . . . Eric Tyson's *Personal Finance For Dummies.*"
— Jonathan Clements, *The Wall Street Journal*

"The book was well-written, concise, inspirational, excellent for common folk, and doesn't send you running for a dictionary."
— Brian O'Connor, Bogota, NJ

"Smart advice for dummies . . . skip the tomes . . . and buy *Personal Finance For Dummies,* which rewards your candor with advice and comfort."
— Temma Ehrenfeld, *Newsweek*

"Superb reference! Led to my being offered a job as a mortgage originator. [The] bank said I was the 'most informed buyer' they ever sat with!!!"
— K.A. Carney, Greensburg, PA

"Eric Tyson is doing something important — namely, helping people at all income levels to take control of their financial futures. This book is a natural outgrowth of Tyson's vision that he has nurtured for years. Like Henry Ford, he wants to make something that was previously accessible only to the wealthy accessible to middle-income Americans."
— James C. Collins, coauthor of the national bestseller *Built to Last;* Lecturer in Business, Stanford Graduate School of Business

"Eric Tyson took a subject — finances — which has always intimidated me and made it manageable. Thanks!"
— Margaret Holtje, North Sebago, ME

"Eric Tyson . . . seems the perfect writer for a ...*For Dummies* book. He doesn't tell you what to do or consider doing without explaining the why's and how's — and the booby traps to avoid — in plain English. . . . It will lead you through the thickets of your own finances as painlessly as I can imagine."
    — Clarence Peterson, *Chicago Tribune*

"The best book I've ever bought!"
    — David Clarke, Chicago, IL

"*Personal Finance For Dummies* is, by far, the best book I have read on financial planning. It is a simplified volume of information that provides tremendous insight and guidance into the world of investing and other money issues."
    — Althea Thompson, producer, "PBS Nightly Business Report"

". . . amazingly you were even able to add humor to such a topic."
    — Steve Stachling, Wausau, WI

"This book provides easy-to-understand personal financial information and advice for those without great wealth or knowledge in this area. Practitioners like Eric Tyson, who care about the well-being of middle-income people, are rare in today's society."
    — Joel Hyatt, founder, Hyatt Legal Services, one of the nation's largest general-practice personal legal service firms

". . . very understandable, informative and enjoyable. . . . This should be required reading for every senior!"
    — Barbara Greub, River Falls, WI

"*Personal Finance For Dummies* is a sane and useful guide that will be of benefit to anyone seeking a careful and prudent method of managing their financial world."
    — John Robbins, founder of EarthSave, author of *May All Be Fed*

"Very informative, lighthearted. . . . I read it cover to cover."
    — Lou Furry, Northampton, PA

by Eric Tyson and Ray Brown

IDG Books Worldwide, Inc.
An International Data Group Company

Foster City, CA ♦ Chicago, IL ♦ Indianapolis, IN ♦ Braintree, MA ♦ Southlake, TX

Home Buying For Dummies™

Published by
IDG Books Worldwide, Inc.
An International Data Group Company
919 E. Hillsdale Blvd.
Suite 400
Foster City, CA 94404

Library of Congress Catalog Card No.: 96-76346

ISBN: 1-56884-385-2

Printed in the United States of America

10 9 8 7 6 5 4 3 2 1

1A/TQ/QV/ZW/IN

Distributed in the United States by IDG Books Worldwide, Inc.

Distributed by Macmillan Canada for Canada; by Computer and Technical Books for the Caribbean Basin; by Contemporanea de Ediciones for Venezuela; by Distribuidora Cuspide for Argentina; by CITEC for Brazil; by Ediciones ZETA S.C.R. Ltda. for Peru; by Editorial Limusa SA for Mexico; by Transworld Publishers Limited in the United Kingdom and Europe; by Al-Maiman Publishers & Distributors for Saudi Arabia; by Simron Pty. Ltd. for South Africa; by IDG Communications (HK) Ltd. for Hong Kong; by Toppan Company Ltd. for Japan; by Addison Wesley Publishing Company for Korea; by Longman Singapore Publishers Ltd. for Singapore, Malaysia, Thailand, and Indonesia; by Unalis Corporation for Taiwan; by WS Computer Publishing Company, Inc. for the Philippines; by WoodsLane Pty. Ltd. for Australia; by WoodsLane Enterprises Ltd. for New Zealand.

For general information on IDG Books Worldwide's books in the U.S., please call our Consumer Customer Service department at 800-762-2974. For reseller information, including discounts and premium sales, please call our Reseller Customer Service department at 800-434-3422.

For information on where to purchase IDG Books Worldwide's books outside the U.S., contact IDG Books Worldwide at 415-655-3021 or fax 415-655-3295.

For information on translations, contact Marc Jeffrey Mikulich, Director, Foreign & Subsidiary Rights, at IDG Books Worldwide, 415-655-3018 or fax 415-655-3295.

For sales inquiries and special prices for bulk quantities, write to the address above or call IDG Books Worldwide at 415-655-3200.

For information on using IDG Books Worldwide's books in the classroom, or ordering examination copies, contact the Education Office at 800-434-2086 or fax 817-251-8174.

For authorization to photocopy items for corporate, personal, or educational use, please contact Copyright Clearance Center, 222 Rosewood Drive, Danvers, MA 01923, or fax 508-750-4470.

is a trademark under exclusive license to IDG Books Worldwide, Inc., from International Data Group, Inc.

About the Authors

Eric Tyson, MBA

Eric Tyson is a nationally recognized personal financial writer, lecturer, and counselor. He is dedicated to teaching people to manage their personal finances better. Eric is a former management consultant to Fortune 500 financial service firms. Over the past two decades, he has successfully invested in securities as well as in real estate, started and managed several businesses, and earned a bachelor's degree in economics at Yale and an M.B.A. at the Stanford Graduate School of Business.

An accomplished freelance personal finance writer, Eric is the author of four national best-sellers in the . . .*For Dummies* series: *Personal Finance For Dummies, Investing For Dummies, Mutual Funds For Dummies,* and *Taxes For Dummies* (co-author). Eric is also a columnist and an award-winning journalist for the *San Francisco Examiner.* His work has been featured and praised in hundreds of national and local publications, including *Newsweek, Kiplinger's, The Wall Street Journal, Money, Los Angeles Times, Chicago Tribune,* and on NBC's *Today Show,* PBS's *Nightly Business Report,* CNN, *The Oprah Winfrey Show,* ABC, CNBC, Bloomberg Business Radio, CBS National Radio, and National Public Radio.

Eric has counseled thousands of clients on a variety of personal finance, investment, and real estate quandaries and questions. In addition to maintaining a financial counseling practice, he is a lecturer of the Bay Area's most highly attended financial management course at the University of California, Berkeley.

Ray Brown

Ray Brown is a veteran of the real estate profession with more than two decades of hands-on experience. A former manager for Coldwell Banker Residential Brokerage Company and McGuire Real Estate and founder of his own real estate firm, the Raymond Brown Company, Ray is currently a writer, consultant, and public speaker on residential real estate topics.

Ray knows that most people are pretty darn smart. When they have problems, it's usually because they don't know the right questions to ask to get the information they need to make good decisions themselves. He always wanted to write a book that focused on what you need to know to make sound home-buying decisions — a book that kept people from manipulating you by exploiting your ignorance. This, *at last,* is that book!

On his way to becoming an real estate guru, Ray worked as the real estate analyst for KGO-TV (ABC's affiliate in San Francisco), a syndicated real estate columnist for *The San Francisco Examiner,* and he still hosts a weekly radio program, *Ray Brown on Real Estate* for KNBR. In addition to his work for ABC, Ray has appeared as a real estate expert on CNN, NBC, CBS, and in *The Wall Street Journal* and *Time.*

That's all fine and good. Ray's three proudest achievements, however, are Jeff and Jared, his two extraordinary sons, and more than 30 years of nearly always wedded bliss to the always wonderful Annie B.

ABOUT IDG BOOKS WORLDWIDE

Welcome to the world of IDG Books Worldwide.

IDG Books Worldwide, Inc., is a subsidiary of International Data Group, the world's largest publisher of computer-related information and the leading global provider of information services on information technology. IDG was founded more than 25 years ago and now employs more than 7,700 people worldwide. IDG publishes more than 250 computer publications in 67 countries (see listing below). More than 70 million people read one or more IDG publications each month.

Launched in 1990, IDG Books Worldwide is today the #1 publisher of best-selling computer books in the United States. We are proud to have received 8 awards from the Computer Press Association in recognition of editorial excellence and three from Computer Currents' First Annual Readers' Choice Awards, and our best-selling ...For Dummies® series has more than 19 million copies in print with translations in 28 languages. IDG Books Worldwide, through a joint venture with IDG's Hi-Tech Beijing, became the first U.S. publisher to publish a computer book in the People's Republic of China. In record time, IDG Books Worldwide has become the first choice for millions of readers around the world who want to learn how to better manage their businesses.

Our mission is simple: Every one of our books is designed to bring extra value and skill-building instructions to the reader. Our books are written by experts who understand and care about our readers. The knowledge base of our editorial staff comes from years of experience in publishing, education, and journalism — experience which we use to produce books for the '90s. In short, we care about books, so we attract the best people. We devote special attention to details such as audience, interior design, use of icons, and illustrations. And because we use an efficient process of authoring, editing, and desktop publishing our books electronically, we can spend more time ensuring superior content and spend less time on the technicalities of making books.

You can count on our commitment to deliver high-quality books at competitive prices on topics you want to read about. At IDG Books Worldwide, we continue in the IDG tradition of delivering quality for more than 25 years. You'll find no better book on a subject than one from IDG Books Worldwide.

John J. Kilcullen

John Kilcullen
President and CEO
IDG Books Worldwide, Inc.

IDG Books Worldwide, Inc., is a subsidiary of International Data Group, the world's largest publisher of computer-related information and the leading global provider of information services on information technology. International Data Group publishes over 250 computer publications in 67 countries. Seventy million people read one or more International Data Group publications each month. International Data Group's publications include: **ARGENTINA:** Computerworld Argentina, GamePro, Infoworld, PC World Argentina; **AUSTRALIA:** Australian Macworld, Client/Server Journal, Computer Living, Computerworld, Digital News, Network World, PC World, Publishing Essentials, Reseller; **AUSTRIA:** Computerwelt, PC TEST; **BELARUS:** PC World Belarus; **BELGIUM:** Data News; **BRAZIL:** Annuário de Informática, Computerworld Brazil, Connections, Super Game Power, Macworld, PC World Brazil, Publish Brazil, SUPERGAME; **BULGARIA:** Computerworld Bulgaria, Networkworld/Bulgaria, PC & MacWorld Bulgaria; **CANADA:** CIO Canada, ComputerWorld Canada, InfoCanada, Network World Canada, Reseller World; **CHILE:** Computerworld Chile, GamePro, PC World Chile; **COLUMBIA:** Computerworld Colombia, GamePro, PC World Colombia; **COSTA RICA:** PC World Costa Rica/Nicaragua; **THE CZECH AND SLOVAK REPUBLICS:** Computerworld Czechoslovakia, Elektronika Czechoslovakia, PC World Czechoslovakia; **DENMARK:** Communications World, Computerworld Danmark, Macworld Danmark, PC World Danmark, PC World Danmark Supplements, TECH World; **DOMINICAN REPUBLIC:** PC World Republica Dominicana; **ECUADOR:** PC World Ecuador, GamePro; **EGYPT:** Computerworld Middle East, PC World Middle East; **EL SALVADOR:** PC World Centro America; **FINLAND:** MikroPC, Tietoverkko, Tietoviikko; **FRANCE:** Distributique, Golden, Info PC, Le Guide du Monde Informatique, Le Monde Informatique, Reseaux & Telecoms; **GERMANY:** Computer Business, Computerwoche, Computerwoche Extra, Computerwoche Focus, Electronic Entertainment, GamePro, I/M Information Management, Macwelt, PC Welt; **GREECE:** GamePro, Macworld & Publish; **GUATEMALA:** PC World Centro America; **HONDURAS:** PC World Centro America; **HONG KONG:** Computerworld Hong Kong, PCWorld Hong Kong, Publish in Asia; **HUNGARY:** ABCD CD-ROM, Computerworld Szamitastechnika, PC & Mac World Hungary, PC-X Magazine; **INDIA:** Computerworld India, PC World India, Publish in Asia; **INDONESIA:** InfoKomputer PC World, Komputek Computerworld, Publish in Asia; **IRELAND:** ComputerScope, PC Live!; **ISRAEL:** PC World 32 BIT, People & Computers; **ITALY:** Computerworld Italia, Computerworld Italia Special Editions, Lotus Italia, Macworld Italia, Networking Italia, PC Shopping, PC World Italia; **JAPAN:** Macworld Japan, Nikkei Personal Computing, SunWorld Japan, Windows World Japan; **KENYA:** East African Computer News; **KOREA:** Hi-Tech Information/Computerworld, Macworld Korea, PC World Korea; **MACEDONIA:** PC World Macedonia; **MALAYSIA:** Computerworld Malaysia, PC World Malaysia, Publish in Asia; **MEXICO:** Computerworld Mexico, GamePro, Macworld, PC World Mexico; **MYANMAR:** PC World Myanmar; **NETHERLANDS:** Computable, Computer! Totaal, LAN Magazine, Macworld, Net Magazine; **NEW ZEALAND:** Computer Buyer, Computerworld New Zealand, MTB, Network World, PC World New Zealand; **NICARAGUA:** PC World Costa Rica/Nicaragua; **NIGERIA:** PC World Africa; **NORWAY:** Computerworld Norge, Computerworld Privat, CW Rapport Klient/Tjener, CW Rapport Nettverk & Telecom, CW Rapport Offentlig Sektor, IDG's KURSGUIDE, Macworld Norge, Multimedia World, PC World Ekspress, PC World Nettverk, PC World Norge, PC World's Produktguide, Windows Spesial; **PAKISTAN:** Computerworld Pakistan, PC World Pakistan; **PANAMA:** GamePro, PC World Panama; **PARAGUAY:** PC World Paraguay; **P. R. OF CHINA:** China Computerworld, China Infoworld, Computer & Communication, Electronic Product World, Electronics Today, Game Camp, PC World China, Popular Computer Week, Software World, Telecom Product World; **PERU:** Computerworld Peru, GamePro, PC World Profesional Peru, PC World Peru; **POLAND:** Computerworld Poland, Computerworld Special Report, Macworld, Networld, PC World Komputer; **PHILIPPINES:** Computerworld Philippines, PC Digest, Publish in Asia; **PORTUGAL:** Cerebro/PC World, Correio Informático/Computerworld, Mac•In/PC•In Portugal; **PUERTO RICO:** PC World Puerto Rico; **ROMANIA:** Computerworld Romania, PC World Romania, Telecom Romania; **RUSSIA:** Computerworld Rossiya, Network World Russia, PC World Russia; **SINGAPORE:** Computerworld Singapore, PC World Singapore, Publish in Asia; **SLOVENIA:** MONITOR; **SOUTH AFRICA:** Computing S.A., Network World S.A., Software World; **SPAIN:** Computerworld España, COMUNICACIONES WORLD, Dealer World, Macworld España, PC World España; **SWEDEN:** CAP&Design, Computer Sweden, Corporate Computing, MacWorld, Maxi Data, MikroDatorn, Nätverk & Kommunikation, PC/Aktiv, PC World, Windows World; **SWITZERLAND:** Computerworld Schweiz, Macworld Schweiz, PCtip; **TAIWAN:** Computerworld Taiwan, Macworld Taiwan, PC World Taiwan, Publish Taiwan, Windows World; **THAILAND:** Thai Computerworld, Publish in Asia; **TURKEY:** Computerworld Monitör, MACWORLD Turkiye, PC WORLD Turkiye; **UKRAINE:** Computerworld Kiev, Computers & Software Magazine, PC World Ukraine; **UNITED KINGDOM:** Acorn User, Amiga Action, Amiga Computing, Amiga, Appletalk, CD Powerplay, CD-ROM Now, Computing, Connexion, GamePro, Lotus Magazine, Macaction, Macworld, Open Computing, Parents and Computers, PC Home, PC Works, The WEB; **UNITED STATES:** Cable in the Classroom, CD Review, CIO Magazine, Computerworld, Computerworld Client/Server Journal, Digital Video Magazine, DOS World, Electronic, InfoWorld, I-Way, Macworld, Maximize, MULTIMEDIA WORLD, Network World, PC World, PUBLISH, SWATPro Magazine, Video Event, WebMaster; **URUGUAY:** PC World Uruguay; **VENEZUELA:** Computerworld Venezuela, GamePro, PC World Venezuela; and **VIETNAM:** PC World Vietnam. 10/17/95b

Dedications

This book is hereby and irrevocably dedicated to my family and friends, as well as to my counseling clients and customers, who ultimately have taught me everything I know about how to explain financial terms and strategies so that all of us may benefit. – Eric Tyson

This book is lovingly dedicated to my real estate pals who taught me how the game is played, to my clients and friends who honor me with their trust and loyalty, to my brother Steve and best buddy Ben Colwell who made RBCo a reality, to Bruce Koon and Corrie Anders who taught me the dubious joy of writing, to Warren Doane and Dennis Tarmina who encouraged me to follow this dream, to both brother Daves and Bob Agnew for being there, and, saving the best for last, to Annie B., Jeff, and Jared who have cheerfully (most of the time anyhow) put up with the "Ray way" all these years. – Ray Brown

Authors' Acknowledgments

Many, many people at IDG helped to make this book possible and (we hope in your opinion) good. They include John Kilcullen, Milissa Koloski, Kathy Welton, and Project Editor Shannon Ross. Thanks also to Diana Conover for all her fine copy editing, to Andy Lewandowski for additional editorial and research help, and to the fine folks in Production for making this book look great! Thanks also to Stacy Collins and Kathy Day for all their sound work behind the scenes, and to everyone else at IDG Books who contributed to getting this book done and done right.

Extraordinary acclamation, copious praise, and profound gratitude is due our brilliant technical reviewers who toiled long hours to ensure that we did not write something that wasn't quite right. These good folks include Kip Oxman, McGuire Real Estate, Dolph Meyerson, Meyerson Residential, and Lynnea Key, Lynnea Key Realty — three extraordinary real estate professionals. Thank you one and all!

We also owe a huge debt of gratitude to Jeff Hershberger of the California Association of Realtors for helping us obtain the real estate purchase contract included in Appendix A and the counteroffer used in Chapter 10; Warren Camp, Camp Brothers Inspection Services, Inc., for providing the exemplary inspection report included in Appendix B; Robert Jackson, BayCal Financial, for supplying additional forms; and Brian Felix, Old Republic Title Company, who generously allowed us to pick his Einstein-like brain about the complexities of title insurance and escrows.

Publisher's Acknowledgments

We're proud of this book; please send us your comments about it by using the Reader Response Card at the back of the book or by e-mailing us at feedback/dummies@idgbooks.com. Some of the people who helped bring this book to market include the following:

Acquisitions, Development, & Editorial

Project Editor: Shannon Ross

Executive Editor: Sarah Kennedy

Copy Editor: Diana Conover

Technical Reviewers: Lynnea Key, Dolph Meyerson, and Kip Oxman

Editorial Manager: Kristin A. Cocks

Editorial Assistants: Chris H. Collins and Ann Miller

Special Help

Diane Steele, Mike Kelly, and Milissa Koloski

Production

Project Coordinator: Cindy L. Phipps

Layout and Graphics: E. Shawn Aylsworth, Brett Black, Linda M. Boyer, Cheryl Denski, Julie Forey, Todd Klemme, Kate Snell, Michael Sullivan, Gina Scott, Angela F. Hunckler

Proofreaders: Christine Meloy Beck, Nancy Price, Dwight Ramsey, Carl Saff, Robert Springer, Karen York

Indexer: David Heiret

General & Administrative

IDG Books Worldwide, Inc.: John Kilcullen, President & CEO; Steven Berkowitz, COO & Publisher

Dummies, Inc.: Milissa Koloski, Executive Vice President & Publisher

Dummies Technology Press & Dummies Editorial: Diane Graves Steele, Associate Publisher; Judith A. Taylor, Brand Manager; Myra Immell, Editorial Director

Dummies Trade Press: Kathleen A. Welton, Vice President & Publisher; Stacy S. Collins, Brand Manager

IDG Books Production for Dummies Press: Beth Jenkins, Production Director; Cindy L. Phipps, Supervisor of Project Coordination; Kathie S. Schnorr, Supervisor of Page Layout; Shelley Lea, Supervisor of Graphics and Design

Dummies Packaging & Book Design: Erin McDermitt, Packaging Coordinator; Kavish+Kavish, Cover Design

◆

The publisher would like to give special thanks to Patrick J. McGovern, without whom this book would not have been possible.

◆

Contents at a Glance

Table of Contents

Introduction

Welcome to *Home Buying For Dummies* — the one and only, absolutely essential real estate book that you can't live without!

Okay, maybe we're being a bit melodramatic. We know that this book isn't quite on the same level as food, water, and the air you breathe. However, for about the cost of a couple of movie tickets or dining out, you can quickly and easily discover how to save thousands, perhaps even tens of thousands, of dollars the next time you buy a home.

How can we make such a claim? Easy. Between the two of us, we've spent nearly 40 years personally advising thousands of people like you about home purchases and other important personal financial decisions. We've seen how ignorance of basic concepts and practices translates into money-draining mistakes. We know that many of these mistakes are both needless and avoidable.

No one is born knowing how to buy a home. Everyone who'd like to buy a home must learn how to do it. Unfortunately, too many people get a crash course in the school of hard knocks — and learn by making costly mistakes at their own expense.

We know that you're not a dummy. You've already demonstrated an interest in learning by picking up this book, which can help you make a lot of smart moves and avoid financial land mines.

If you're still wondering whether to use your discretionary dollars to buy either this book or the next several issues of the *National Enquirer,* allow us a moment, please, to make our case. First, the O.J. trial is over; and second, Michael Jackson's marriage has dissolved. Seriously, though, buying a home will probably be the largest purchase that you'll ever make. If you're like most people, buying a home can send shock waves through your personal finances and may even cause a sleepless night or two. Buying a home is a major financial step and a life event for most people. It certainly was for us when we bought our first homes. You owe it to yourself to do things right.

The Eric Tyson/Ray Brown Difference

We know that many real estate books are competing for your attention. If the fact that our families are counting on you to purchase this book doesn't sway you, here are several other compelling reasons why this is the best book for you:

- ✔ **It's in English.** Because we're still working with real people and answering real questions (Eric, through his financial counseling, teaching, and writing — Ray, through his radio show, real estate consulting, and writing), our information is current, and we have a great deal of experience at explaining things. This experience can put you firmly in control of the home-buying process (rather than having *it* control *you*).

- ✔ **It's objective.** We're not trying to sell you an expensive newsletter or some real estate product that you don't need. Our goal is to make you as knowledgeable as possible before you purchase a home. We even explain why you may *not* want to buy a home. We're not here to be real estate cheerleaders.

- ✔ **It's holistic.** When you purchase a home, that purchase affects your ability to save money and accomplish other important financial goals. We help you to understand how best to fit your home acquisition into the rest of your personal-finance puzzle.

- ✔ **It's a reference.** You can read this book from cover to cover if you want. However, we know that you're busy and that you likely don't desire to become a real estate expert, so each portion of the book stands on its own. You can read it piecemeal to address your specific questions and immediate concerns.

The Road Map

So you're ready to buy a home. Or maybe you know that you're not ready, but you see a home purchase somewhere in the not-too-distant horizon. This book starts with the premise that many important things should fall into place *before* you sign a contract to buy a home. Even after the deal is done, you'll have questions. Fear not! Our book covers everything you need to know.

Part I: Home Economics

Perplexed about whether or not to buy a home? Concerned that your financial house isn't as neat and tidy as it should be? Don't know what you can afford or how you'll pay for it? This section is for you! Many prospective homebuyers make the mistake of putting the cart (buying) before the horse (understanding their financial options and the home-buying process). As an added bonus, we explain real estate market economics and tell you how to spot a buyer's market (good values) and avoid the perils of a seller's market (inflated prices).

Part II: Financing 101

One of the most challenging and important parts of the home-buying process is choosing a mortgage. Although not quite as jargon-prone as an Internal Revenue Service auditor, most mortgage lenders do have a penchant for using terminology — such as *negative amortization* and *points* — you likely don't use in your daily life. In this important part, we explain the different types of mortgages and cut through all that jargon to help you select the type of mortgage that matches your needs. In addition to explaining how to get the best deal that you can on a mortgage, we also navigate you through the morass of paperwork required to apply for and obtain your loan.

Part III: Property, Players, and Prices

After you've decided that you're ready to buy, and you know how much you can really afford (given your budget and other financial objectives), you're ready to explore how the home-buying game is played. In this part, we introduce you to the various types of property you may consider buying and the people you may hire to help you buy a home. In addition to steering you towards winning strategies and winning players, we help you avoid loser properties and people. We close this section by giving you a crash course on how to distinguish good buys from overpriced turkeys so that you won't overpay (and may even get a very good deal) when you purchase your dream home.

Part IV: Let the Game Begin

In this part, we get down to brass tacks — how to negotiate a super deal and how to get your home inspected from roof to foundation so that you know whether it's in perfect shape or riddled with expensive defects. Because you can't close the purchase until you get homeowners insurance, we explain what, where, and how to buy it right. Finally, we describe some of the legal and tax ramifications of your purchase along with ways to make sure that your deal closes smoothly and without unnecessary costs.

Part V: The Part of Tens

In this part, we tackle shorter topics that didn't seem to fit elsewhere in this book. Here, we list the ten financial musts after you buy, the ten things to know when investing in real estate, and the ten things to consider when selling your house.

Part VI: Appendixes

Appendixes are usually not very interesting. And, although you aren't going to want to peruse them before you've read most of the rest of the book, skipping these documents could be a mistake. In addition to showing you what a good home inspection report looks like, we also provide a sample home-buying contract so that these documents won't look Greek to you when you see them in your purchase.

Those Silly Little Icons

Sprinkled throughout this book are cute little icons to help reinforce and draw attention to key points or to flag stuff that you can skip over.

This bull's-eye notes key strategies that can improve your real estate deal and, in some cases, save you lots of moola. Think of these as helpful little paternalistic hints we would whisper in your ear if we were close enough to do so!

Numerous land mines await novice as well as experienced homebuyers. This explosive symbol marks those mines and tells you how to sidestep them.

Occasionally, we suggest that you do more research or homework. Don't worry: We tell you exactly what you need to do.

Unfortunately, as is the case in all parts of the business world, some people and companies are more interested in short-term profits than in meeting your needs and concerns. We warn you how, when, and where you may be fleeced and, where appropriate, show you how to de-fleece yourself!

"If I've told you once, I've told you a thousand times. . . ." Remember good old Mom and Dad? Okay, we don't talk to you that way; but we do, from time to time, tell you something quite important and perhaps repeat ourselves. Just so you don't forget the point, this icon serves as a little nag to bring back those childhood memories.

Some of you are curious and have time to spare. Others of you are busy and just want to know the essentials. This geeky icon points out tidbits and information that you don't really *have* to know, but knowing this stuff can make you more self-confident and proud!

This stamp of approval highlights the best resources available to help you find, secure, and pay for your home.

Part I
Home Economics

In this part . . .

1s home buying for you? Is now the right time? How much can you afford to spend on a home? These questions aren't meant to throw you into a panic. If you don't know how to answer them (and perhaps even if you think that you do) this part is for you! Many people assume that they need to buy a home (or that they don't) without taking a good look at their overall personal financial situation. Don't make that mistake! Read this part to see how a home purchase should fit into your financial puzzle and to understand how and why home prices do what they do.

Chapter 1

To Buy or Not to Buy, That Is the Question

*E*very month, week, and day, we buy things: lunch, coffee, a magazine or newspaper, a new pair of shoes, and every now and then, a car.

Most people buy things without doing much comparison shopping, but instead draw upon their past experiences. If the counter help at Starbuck's Coffee was friendly and you liked their espresso, you'll probably go back for more the next time you need your caffeine fix. And some purchases lead you by association to related purchases. You get coffee, and buying a pastry or cookie naturally follows. You buy Ed McCarthy's and Mary Ewing-Mulligan's *Wine For Dummies* and spend some time imbibing, and that perhaps arouses your interest in Dr. Ruth Westheimer's *Sex For Dummies*.

You end up being really happy with some items you purchase. Others fall short of your expectations . . . or worse. If the items in question don't cost you much, it's no big deal. Perhaps you return them or simply don't buy more in the future. But when it comes to buying a home, that kind of sloppy shopping can lead to disaster.

If you're not willing to invest time, and if you don't work with and heed the advice of the best people, you could end up overpaying for a home you hate. Our goals in this book are simple — to ensure that you're happy with the home you buy, that you get the best deal you can, and that owning the home helps you to accomplish your financial goals.

The Realities of Home Ownership

Nearly everyone seems to have an opinion about buying a home. Most people in the real estate business — including agents, lenders, property inspectors, and other related people — endorse home ownership. Of course, why wouldn't they? Their livelihoods depend upon it. The more people who buy homes, the more money they make! Therein lies one fundamental problem of nearly all home-buying books written by people who have a vested interest in convincing their readers to buy a home.

Home ownership is not for everyone. One of our objectives in this chapter is to help you determine whether or not home buying is right for you.

Some people who buy homes shouldn't. Consider the case of Peter, who thought that owning a home was the best financial move he could make. What with tax write-offs and living in a place while it made money for him, how could he lose? Peter envied his investment-banking colleagues who'd seemingly made piles of money with property they bought in the 1980s. Peter was a busy man and didn't have time to research other ways to invest his money.

Unfortunately, Peter bought a place that stretched his budget and required lots of attention and maintenance. Adding insult to injury, Peter went to graduate school clear across the country (something he knew he was likely to do at the time he bought) three years after he purchased. During these three years of his ownership, home prices dropped 10 percent in Peter's neighborhood. So, after paying the expenses of sale and closing costs, Peter ended up losing his entire down payment when he sold.

Conversely, some people who continue to rent should buy. In her twenties, Melody didn't want to buy a home because she didn't like the idea of settling down. Her monthly rent seemed so cheap compared to the sticker prices on homes for sale.

As it always does, time passed. Her twenties turned into thirties, which melted into forties and then fifties, and Melody was still renting. Her rent was now eight times what it was when she first started renting — that insignificant $125 monthly rent was now over $1,000 per month. But now, home prices really seemed out of sight. She fearfully looked ahead to escalating rental rates in the decades when she hoped to be retired.

Ownership advantages

Most people should eventually buy homes, but not everyone and not at every point in their lives. To decide whether now's the time for you to a buy a house, consider the advantages of buying and whether they apply to you.

Owning should be less expensive than renting

You probably didn't appreciate it growing up, but in addition to the thousands of diaper changes, patience during potty training, help with homework, bandaging bruised knees, and countless meals, your folks made sure that you also had a roof over your head. Most of us take shelter for granted, unless we don't have it or are confronted for the first time with paying for it ourselves.

Remember your first apartment when you graduated from college or when your folks finally kicked you out? That place probably made you appreciate the free or lower cost rent you enjoyed elsewhere — even those cramped college dormitories may not have seemed so bad anymore!

But even if you pay several hundred to a thousand dollars or more per month in rent, that expense may not seem so steep if you happen to peek at a home for sale. In most parts of the United States, we're talking about a big number — $50,000, $100,000, $200,000 or more for the sticker price. (Of course, if you're a medical doctor, lawyer, management consultant, or investment banker, you probably think that you can't find a habitable place to live for less than a quarter- or half-million dollars.)

Here's a *rule of thumb* that may change the way you view your seemingly cheap monthly rent. In order for you to see how expensive a home you could afford to buy and have the *same* approximate monthly cost as your current rent, simply do the following calculation:

Take your monthly rent	multiply by	200	=	purchase price of home
$ _____ per month	×	200	=	$ _____
Example: $ 500	×	200	=	$100,000

So, in the preceding example, if you're paying rent of $500 per month, you would pay approximately the same amount per month to own a $100,000 home (factoring in tax savings). Now your monthly rent doesn't sound quite so cheap compared to the cost of buying a home, does it? (Note that in Chapter 3 we show you how to accurately calculate the total costs of owning a home.)

Even more important than the cost *today* of buying versus renting, what about the cost in the *future*? As a renter, your rent is fully exposed to increases in the cost of living, also known as *inflation*. A reasonable expectation for annual increases in your rent is 4 percent per year. Figure 1-1 shows what happens to a $500 monthly rent at just 4 percent annual inflation.

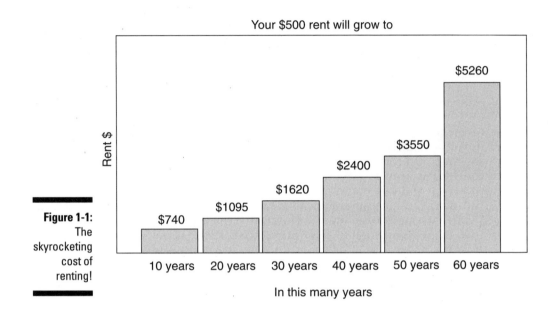

Your $500 rent will grow to

$5260

$3550

$2400

$1620

$1095

$740

Rent $

Figure 1-1:
The skyrocketing cost of renting!

10 years   20 years   30 years   40 years   50 years   60 years

In this many years

If you're in your 20s or 30s, you may not now be thinking or caring about your golden years, but look what will happen to your rent over the decades ahead with just modest inflation! Then remember that paying $500 rent per month now is the equivalent of buying a home for $100,000. Well, in 40 years with 4 percent inflation per year, your $500 per month rent will balloon to $2,400 per month. That's like buying a house for $480,000!

If you're middle-aged or retired, you may not be planning on having 40 to 60 years ahead of you. On the other hand, don't underestimate how many more years of housing you'll need. U.S. health statistics indicate that, if you make it to age 50, you have a life expectancy of nearly 30 more years, and at age 65, nearly 20 more years.

Although the cost of purchasing a home generally increases over the years, once you purchase a particular home, the bulk of your housing costs are not exposed to inflation — if you use a fixed-rate mortgage to finance the purchase. As we explain in Chapter 5, a *fixed-rate mortgage* means that your mortgage payment is locked in and level (as opposed to an adjustable-rate mortgage payment that fluctuates in value with changes in interest rates). Therefore, the much smaller property taxes, insurance, and maintenance expenses are the only housing costs you will have that will increase over time with inflation. (In Chapter 3, we cover in excruciating detail what buying and owning a home costs.)

You're always going to need a place to live. And, over the long term, inflation has almost always been around. Even if you must stretch a little to buy a home today, in the decades ahead, you should be glad that you did. The financial danger with renting long term is that all of your housing costs (rent) will increase with inflation over time. We're not saying that everyone should buy because of inflation, but we are suggesting that, if you're not going to buy, you should be careful to plan your finances accordingly. We discuss the pros and cons of renting later in the chapter.

Making your house your own

Think back to all the places you ever rented, including the rental in which you may currently be living. For each unit, make a list of all the things you didn't like that you could have changed if the property were yours: ugly carpeting, yucky exterior paint job, outdated appliances that don't work well, and so on.

Uses for the wealth you build up in your home

Over the many years that you are likely to own it, your home should become an important part of your financial *net worth* — that is, the difference between your *assets* (financial things of value that you own) and your *liabilities* (debts). Why?

Because homes generally increase in value over the decades while you're paying down your loan (mortgage debt) used to buy the home.

Even if you're one of those rare people who owns a home but doesn't see much *appreciation* (increase in the home's value) over the decades of your adult ownership, you will benefit from the monthly forced savings that results from paying down the remaining balance due on your mortgage. Retirees will tell you that one financial joy of retirement is owning a home free and clear of a mortgage.

All that *home equity* (which is the difference between the market value of a home and the outstanding loan on the home) can help your personal and financial situation in a number of ways. If, like most people, you hope to someday retire, but (also like most people) saving doesn't come easily, your home's equity can help

supplement your other sources of retirement income.

How can you tap into your home's equity? Some people choose to *trade down* — that is, to move to a less costly home in retirement. Sell your home for $200,000, replace it with one costing $100,000, and you've freed up $100,000. If you sell your home after age 55, you can trade down without paying tax on up to $125,000 of your profits (see Chapter 15 to find out more about this home-ownership tax break).

Another way to tap your home's equity is through borrowing. Your home's equity may be an easily tapped and low-cost source of cash (the interest you pay is generally tax-deductible — see Chapter 3). Some retirees also consider what's called a *reverse mortgage*. Under this arrangement, the lender sends you a monthly check you can spend however you want. Meanwhile, a debt balance (that will be paid off when the property is finally sold) is built up against the property.

What can you do with all this home equity? Help pay for your children's college education, start your own business, remodel your home, or whatever!

Although we know some tenants who actually do some work to their own apartments, we don't generally endorse this approach because it takes your money and time, but financially benefits the owner of the building. If, through persistence and nagging, you can get your landlords to make the improvements and repairs at their expense, great! If not, you're out of luck.

When you own your own place, however, you can do whatever you want to it. Want hardwood floors instead of ugly, green shag carpeting? Tear it out. Love neon-orange carpeting and pink exterior paint? You can add it!

In your zest and enthusiasm to buy a place and make it your own, you should be careful of two things.

- ✔ **Don't make the place too weird.** You'll probably want or need to sell your home someday, and the more outrageous you've made it, the fewer the buyers it will appeal to — and the lower the price it will likely fetch. If you don't mind throwing money away, or are convinced that you can find a future buyer with similarly (ahem) sophisticated tastes, be as weird as you want. Heck, even invite Howard Stern over if you like! If you do make improvements, focus on those that add value: for example, skylights, a deck addition for outdoor living area, updating kitchens and bathrooms, and so on.

- ✔ **Beware of running yourself into financial ruin.** Changing, improving, remodeling, or whatever you want to call it costs money. We know many homebuyers who have neglected other important financial goals (such as saving for retirement and gaining the tax benefits of doing so) in order to endlessly renovate their homes. Others have racked up significant debts that hang like financial weights over their heads. In the worst cases, homes become money pits that cause owners to build up high-interest consumer debt as a prelude to bankruptcy.

Avoiding unpleasant landlords

A final (and not inconsequential) benefit of owning your own home is that you don't have to subject yourself to the whims of an evil landlord. Much is made among real estate investors of the challenges of finding good tenants. If you're a tenant, perhaps you've already discovered that finding a good landlord isn't easy, either.

The fundamental problem with some landlords is that they are slow to fix problems and make improvements. The best (and smartest) landlords realize that being responsive and keeping the building ship-shape help attract and keep good tenants and maximize rents and profits. But to some landlords, like Leona Helmsley, maximizing profits means being stingy with repairs and improvements. (Although quite a large number of Leona's tenants ganged up on her and took her to court for her excessive thriftiness.)

If you own your home, the good news is that you're in control — you can get your stopped-up toilet fixed or your ugly walls painted whenever and however you like. No more hassling with unresponsive, obnoxious landlords. The bad news is that you're responsible for paying for and ensuring completion of the work. Even if you hire someone else to do it, you still must find competent contractors and oversee their work, neither of which is an easy responsibility.

Another risk of renting is that landlords may decide to sell the building and put you out on the street. You should ask your prospective landlords whether they have plans to sell. Some landlords won't give you a truthful answer, but the question is worth asking, if this issue is a concern to you.

One way to avoid being jilted by a wayward landlord is to request that the lease contract guarantee you the right to renew your annual lease for a certain number of years, even with a change in building ownership. Unless landlords are planning on selling, and perhaps want to be able to boot you out, they should be delighted with a request that shows you're interested in staying a while. Also, by knowing if and when a landlord desires to sell, you may be able to be the buyer!

Renting advantages

Buying and owning a home throughout most of your adult life makes good financial and personal sense for most people — but not all people and not at all times. Renting works better for some people. The benefits of renting are many:

- **Simplicity:** Yes, searching for a rental unit that meets your needs can take more than a few evenings or weekend days, but it should be a heck of lot easier than finding a place to buy. When you buy, you must line up financing, conduct inspections, and deal with myriad other issues that renters never have to face. If you do it right, finding and buying a good home can be a time consuming pain in the posterior.

- **Convenience:** After you find and move into your rental, your landlord is the one who must be responsible for the never-ending task of property maintenance and upkeep. Buildings and appliances age, and bad stuff happens. Fuses blow, plumbing backs up, heaters break in the middle of winter, roofs spring leaks during record breaking rainfalls, trees come crashing down during windstorms. The list goes on and on and on. As a renter, you can kick back in the old recliner with your feet up, a glass of wine in one hand and the remote control in the other and say, "Ahhhhh, the joys of *not* being part of the landed gentry!"

- **Flexibility:** If you're the footloose and fancy-free type, you dislike feeling tied down. With a rental, so long as your lease allows (and most leases don't run longer than a year), you can move on. As a homeowner, if you want to move, you must deal with the significant chores of selling your home or finding a tenant to rent it.

✔ **Increased liquidity:** Unless you are the beneficiary of a large inheritance or work at a high-paying job, odds are you'll be financially stretched when you buy your first home. Coming up with the down payment and closing costs usually cleans out most people's financial reserves. In addition, when you buy a home, you must also meet your monthly mortgage payments, property taxes, insurance, and maintenance and repair expenses. As a renter, you can keep your extra cash to yourself and budgeting is also easier without the upkeep expense surprises.

You don't need to buy a home to cut your taxes. If you have access to a retirement account such as a 401(k), 403(b), SEP-IRA, or Keogh plan (see Chapter 2), you can slash your taxes while you save and invest your extra cash *as a renter.* So saving on taxes should not be a sufficient motivation for you to buy a home.

✔ **Better diversification:** Many homeowners who are financially stretched have the bulk of their wealth tied up in their homes. As a renter, you can invest your money in a variety of sound investments such as stocks, bonds, and perhaps your own small business. You can even invest a small amount of money in real estate through stocks or mutual funds if you wish (see Chapter 14). Over the long term, the stock market has produced comparable rates of return to investing in the real estate market. So don't feel that you'll be missing out on good investments if you can't or don't want to purchase real estate.

✔ **Maybe lower cost:** If you live in an area where home prices have rocketed ahead much faster than rental rates, real estate may be overpriced and not a good buy. In Chapter 4, we explain how to compare the cost of owning to the cost of renting in your area and how to spot an overpriced real estate market.

Renting should also be cheaper than buying if you expect to move soon. Buying and selling property costs big bucks. With real estate agent commissions, loan fees, title insurance, inspections, and all sorts of other costs, your property must appreciate approximately 15 percent just for you to break even and recoup these costs. Therefore, buying property that you don't expect to hold onto for at least three (and preferably five or more) years doesn't make much economic sense for you. Although you may sometimes experience appreciation in excess of 15 percent over a year or two, most of the time, you won't. If you're counting on such high appreciation, you're setting yourself up for disappointment.

Ten Pitfalls of the Rent-versus-Buy Decision

When you're considering purchasing a home, you can do lots of reflecting, crunch lots of numbers, and conduct lots of research to help you with your decision. We encourage these activities and show you how to do them in later chapters.

In reality, we know that many people are tempted to jump into making a decision about buying or continuing to rent without dotting all their "i"s and crossing all their "t"s. We know that you fear not having a life and lacking the time to keep up with *Seinfeld, Friends, The X-Files,* and Congressional deficit reduction talks on C-Span. So, at a minimum, we want to keep you from making the common, costly mistakes that many before you have fallen prey to. Here are ten biggies to avoid.

Continuing to rent because it seems cheaper than buying

As we discuss earlier in this chapter, in the long run, owning should save you money compared to renting a comparable abode. But come on, we're Americans, after all, and we live on — nay, thrive on — instant gratification. We're not long-term thinkers — we live for today. Well, when you go out to look at homes on the market *today,* the sticker prices will be in the tens if not hundreds of thousands of dollars. Your monthly rent seems dirt cheap by comparison.

You must compare the *monthly* cost of home ownership to the monthly cost of renting. And you must factor in the tax saving you will realize from home-ownership tax deductions. (We show you how to make these calculations in Chapter 3.) But you must also think about the future. Just as your educational training affects your career prospects and income-earning ability for years to come, your rent-versus-buy decision affects your housing costs not just this year but for years and decades to come.

Fretting too much over job security

Being insecure about your job is natural. Most people are — even corporate chief executives, superstar athletes, and movie stars. And buying a home seems like such a permanent things to do. Job-loss fears can easily make you feel a financial noose tightening around your neck when you sit down to sign a contract to purchase a home.

Although a few people have real reason to worry about losing their jobs, the reality is that the vast majority of people shouldn't worry about job loss. We don't mean to say that you *can't* lose your job — almost anyone can, in reality. Just remember that, within a reasonable time, your skills and abilities will allow you to land back on your feet in a new, comparable position. We're not career experts, but we've witnessed thousands of people bounce back in just this way.

If losing your job is a high likelihood, and especially if you would have to relocate for a new job, consider postponing the purchase of a home until your employment situation stabilizes. (If you've not demonstrated a recent history of stable employment, most mortgage lenders won't want to lend you money anyway — see Chapters 5 and 6.) If you must move to find an acceptable or desirable job, selling your home and then buying another one can cost you thousands, if not tens of thousands, of dollars in transaction fees.

Buying when you expect to move soon

People move for many reasons other than job loss. You may want to move soon to advance your career, to be nearer to (or farther from!) family, to try living somewhere new, or just to get away from someplace old. Unless you're planning to hold onto your home and convert it into a rental when you move, buying a home rarely makes sound financial sense when you expect to move within three years. Ideally, you should stay put in the home you buy for at least five years.

Letting people with vested interests push you to buy

When you buy a house, you're the one who will be coming home to it day after day — and you're the one who will be on the hook for all the expenses. Don't ever forget these facts when you plunge into the thick of purchasing a home.

Many people involved in home-buying transactions have a vested interest in getting you to buy. They may push you to buy sooner (and buy more than) you intended to or can afford, given your other financial goals and obligations. The reasons: Many people who make their living in the real estate trade get paid only if and when you buy, and the size of their earnings depends upon how much you spend. In Chapter 8, we show you how to put together the best team to assist you in making a decision, rather than push you into making a deal. You had better be as sure as possible before you commit to buying a home; if you have lingering doubts, apply the brakes.

Ignoring logistics

Sometimes, when looking at homes, you can lose your perspective on big-picture issues. After months of searching, Frederick finally found a home that met his needs for both space and cost. He bought the home and moved in on a Saturday. Come Monday morning, Frederick hopped in his car and spent the next hour commuting. At the end of his workday, it was the same thing coming home. He was tired and grumpy when he arrived home Monday evening, and, after making dinner for himself, he soon had to hit the hay to rise early enough to do it all over again on Tuesday.

Initially, Frederick hoped that the trying traffic was an aberration that would go away — but no such luck. In fact, on many days, his commute was worse than an hour each way. Frederick grew to hate his car, his commute, his job, and his new home.

When you buy a home, you're also buying the commute, the neighborhood, its amenities, and all the other stuff that comes along for the literal and figurative ride. Understand these issues *before* you buy. In the end, after 18 months of commuter hell, Frederick sold his home and went back to renting. Forgetting to consider what the commute from a home to his job would entail was an expensive lesson for Frederick. Don't make the same mistake Frederick made; take your time and consider all the important factors about the home you're thinking about purchasing.

Overbuying

Many first-time homebuyers discover that their desires outstrip their budgets. Nelson and his wife Laura had good jobs in the computer industry and together made in excess of $100,000 per year. They got used to buying whatever they desired — they ate out at fancy restaurants, took luxury vacations, and otherwise indulged themselves.

When it came time to purchase a home, they spent the maximum amount and borrowed the maximum amount that the mortgage person told them they could. After the home purchase, Laura got pregnant and eventually left her job to spend more time at home. With the high home-ownership expenses, kid costs, and reduced household income, Nelson and Laura soon found themselves struggling to pay their monthly bills and started accumulating significant credit card debts. Ultimately, they ended up filing personal bankruptcy.

Either you own the home, or it owns you. Get your finances in order and understand how much you can truly afford to spend on a home before you buy (see Chapters 2 and 3).

Underbuying

Remember in the story, "Goldilocks and the Three Bears," how Goldilocks had difficulty finding porridge to her liking? In one case, it was too cold and in another, too hot. Well, just as you can overbuy when selecting a home, you can also underbuy. That's what Nathan and Rebecca did when they bought their first home. They believed in living within their means — a good thing — but they took it to an extreme.

Nathan and Rebecca bought a home whose cost was far below the maximum amount they could have afforded. They borrowed $70,000 when they could have afforded to borrow three times that amount. They knew when they bought the home that they would want to move to a bigger home within just a few years. Although this made the real estate agents and lenders happy, all the costs of buying and then selling soon after gobbled a huge chunk of Nathan and Rebecca's original down payment.

Buying because it's the grown-up thing to do

Peer pressure can be subtle or explicit. Some people even impose pressure on themselves. Buying a home is a major milestone and a tangible display of financial maturity and success. If your friends, siblings, and coworkers all seem to be homeowners, you may sometimes feel as though you're being a tad juvenile by not jumping on the same train.

Be strong! Be independent! Everyone has different needs; not everyone should own a home and certainly not at every point in their adult lives. Besides, although they're loath to admit it, some home-owning friends and colleagues are jealous of you and other financially footloose and fancy-free renters.

A study even supports the notion that the life of a typical renter is, in some respects, better than that of the average homeowner. Peter Rossi and Eleanor Weber of the University of Massachusetts' Social and Demographic Research Institute conducted a survey of thousands of people. Here are some of their survey findings:

- Homeowners are less social, on average, than renters — spending less time with friends, neighbors, and coworkers.
- Homeowners spend more time on household chores.
- Perhaps for the preceding reasons, renters have more sex, less marital discord, and cope better with parenting than homeowners do!

Buying because you're afraid that escalating prices will lock you out of the market forever

From time to time, particular local real estate markets experience rapidly escalating prices. During such times, some prospective buyers literally panic, often with encouragement from those with vested interests in converting prospective renters into buyers. Escalating housing prices make some renters feel left out of the party. Booming housing prices make it on the front page of the newspaper and onto the local television news. And gloating homeowners clucking over their equity doesn't help, either.

Never in the history of the real estate business have prices risen so high as to price vast numbers of people out of the market. In fact, patient buyers who can wait out a market that has increased sharply in value are often rewarded with steadying and, in some cases, declining prices. Although you won't be locked out of the market forever, you should keep in mind that, if you postpone buying for many years, you will likely be able to buy less home for your money thanks to home prices increasing faster than the rate of inflation.

Not understanding what you can really afford

When you make a major decision, be it personal or financial, it's perfectly natural and human to feel uncomfortable if you're flying by the seat of your pants and don't have enough background. With a home purchase, if you haven't considered and examined your overall financial situation and goals, you're just guessing how much you should be spending on a home.

Again, the vested-interest folks won't generally bring this issue to your attention — partly because of their agenda and motivations but also because it's not what they are trained and expert at doing. Look in the mirror to see the person who can help you with these important issues. And don't worry — we won't leave you stranded. The next chapter walks you through all the important personal financial considerations you should explore before you set out on your buying expedition.

Chapter 2

Getting Your Financial House in Order

. . . .

In This Chapter

▶ Analyzing your budget and spending

▶ Calculating your savings needs and planning for retirement

▶ Protecting yourself and your assets

. . . .

"*P*ut on your shoes before you go out and play."

"Brush your teeth before you go to bed."

"Tie your shoelaces before you trip and destroy the thousand of dollars we've spent on orthodontia work."

Although you may have thought that *your* parents were the only ones who persistently said such things for 18 or more years, our informal survey of children-turned-adults suggests otherwise. Sometimes, you rejected your parents' advice just to prove to them (and yourself) that the sun would still rise each day and your teeth wouldn't start falling out in your teens if you didn't do as they said.

This chapter has a similar paternalistic edge to it. Please don't take offense and please don't skip to another chapter to assert your independence. When you're shopping for a home, no one else can look out for your overall interests the way that you can . . . with our help. The people involved in typical real estate deals (such as real estate agents, bankers, loan brokers, and the like) are there to get the job done. It's *not* within their realm of responsibility to worry about how the real estate purchase fits with the rest of your personal finances and how best to arrange your finances before and after purchasing a home. This chapter explains how you can address these important issues.

Now, time for a parental warning: Skip this chapter at your own peril. In the great history of home buying, many people have bought real estate without first getting their finances in order, setting some goals, and dealing with problems and oversights — and they have often paid dearly for this oversight. What are the consequences of plunging headlong into a home purchase before you're financially ready? For starters, you could end up paying tens of thousands of dollars more in taxes and interest over the years ahead. In the worst cases, we've witnessed the financial ruin of intelligent, hardworking people who end up over their heads in debt (and in some situations, even in bankruptcy). We want you to be happy and financially successful in your home — *so please don't skip this chapter!*

Survey Your Spending

Even if your income and spending fluctuates, you may have unknowingly developed a basic spending routine. Every month, you earn a particular income and then spend most of, all of, or perhaps even more than you earn on the necessities (and the not-so-necessary things) of life. The average American saves less than 5 percent of his or her take-home (after-tax) income. (Note that this is far less than the average amount saved by people in most similarly industrialized countries.)

If you want to buy a home, saving is one area where it pays to be "above average." Consistently saving more than 5 percent of your income can help turn you from a renter into a financially able and successful homeowner. Why? For two important reasons:

- ✔ First, in order to purchase a home, you need to accumulate a decent chunk of money for the down payment and closing costs. True, wealthy relatives may help you out, but counting on their generosity is dangerous. The attached strings may make such a gift or loan undesirable.

- ✔ Second, after you buy a home, your total monthly expenses will probably increase. So, if you had trouble saving before the purchase, your finances are really going to be squeezed post-purchase. This will further handicap your ability to accomplish other important financial goals, such as accumulating money for retirement. If you don't take advantage of tax-sheltered retirement accounts, you'll miss out on thousands (if not tens of thousands) of dollars in valuable tax benefits. We discuss the importance and value of funding retirement accounts later in this chapter.

Get the data

One of the single most important things that you can and should do *before* you head out to purchase a home is to examine where (and on what) you are currently spending your money. Completing these financial calisthenics enables you to see what portion of your current income you are saving. Having a handle on your current budget also enables you to see how a given home purchase will fit within or destroy it!

Collect your spending data for at least a three-month span to determine how much you spend in a typical month on various things — such as for rent, clothing, income taxes, haircuts, and everything else (see Table 2-1). If your spending fluctuates greatly throughout the year, you may need to analyze and average for six (or even twelve) months to get an accurate sense of your spending behavior and shenanigans.

Financial software packages, such as Quicken and Microsoft Money, can help with the task of tracking and analyzing your spending; but old-fashioned paper and pencil work fine, too. What you need to do is assemble information that shows what you typically spend your money on. Get out your checkbook register, credit- and charge-card bills, your pay stub, and your most recent tax return.

Whether you use our handy-dandy table or your own software isn't important. What does matter is that you capture the bulk of your spending. But you don't need to account for 100 percent of your spending, and detail where every last penny (or even every dollar) went. You're not designing an airplane or performing a financial audit for a major accounting firm here!

As you collect your spending data and consider your home purchase, think about how that purchase will affect and change your spending and ability to save. For example, as a homeowner, if you live farther away from your job than you did when you rented, how much will your transportation expenses increase? Also note that, in the next chapter, we walk you through estimating home-ownership expenses, such as property taxes, insurance, maintenance, and the like.

Table 2-1	Your Spending, Now and After Purchasing a Home	
Item	*Current Monthly Average ($)*	*Expected Monthly Average with Home Purchase ($)*
Income		
Taxes		
Social Security		
Federal		
State and local		
Housing Expenses		
Rent		n/a
Mortgage	n/a	
Property taxes	n/a	
Gas/electric/oil		
Water/garbage		
Phone		
Cable TV		
Furniture/appliances		
Maintenance/repairs		
Food and Eating		
Supermarket		
Restaurants and takeout		
Transportation		
Gasoline		
Maintenance/repairs		
State registration fees		
Tolls and parking		
Bus or subway fares		
Appearance		
Clothing		
Shoes		
Jewelry (watches, earrings)		
Dry cleaning		
Haircuts		
Makeup		
Other		
Debt Repayments		
Credit/charge cards		
Auto loans		
Student loans		
Other		

Item	Current Monthly Average ($)	Expected Monthly Average with Home Purchase ($)
Fun Stuff		
Entertainment (movies, concerts)	_____	_____
Vacation and travel	_____	_____
Gifts	_____	_____
Hobbies	_____	_____
Pets	_____	_____
Health club or gym	_____	_____
Other	_____	_____
Advisors		
Accountant	_____	_____
Attorney	_____	_____
Financial advisor	_____	_____
Health Care		
Physicians and hospitals	_____	_____
Drugs	_____	_____
Dental and vision	_____	_____
Therapy	_____	_____
Insurance		
Homeowners/renters	_____	_____
Auto	_____	_____
Health	_____	_____
Life	_____	_____
Disability	_____	_____
Educational Expenses		
Courses	_____	_____
Books	_____	_____
Supplies	_____	_____
Kids		
Day care	_____	_____
Toys	_____	_____
Child support	_____	_____
Charitable Donations	_____	_____
Other		
_____	_____	_____
_____	_____	_____
_____	_____	_____
_____	_____	_____
_____	_____	_____
Total Spending	_____	_____
Amount Saved	_____	_____
(subtract from income on previous page)		

Trimming the fat from your budget

If you're like most people planning to buy a home, you need to reduce your spending in order to accumulate enough money to pay for the down payment and closing cost and create enough slack in your budget to afford the extra costs of homeownership. (Increasing your income is another strategy, but that is usually more difficult to do.) Where you decide to make cuts in your budget is a matter of personal preference — but, unless you're independently wealthy or a spendthrift, cut you must.

First, get rid of any and all consumer debt — such as that on credit cards and auto loans. Ridding yourself of such debt as soon as possible is vital to your long-term financial health. Consumer debt is as harmful to your financial health as smoking is to your personal health. Borrowing through consumer loans encourages you to live beyond your means and do the opposite of saving — call it "dis-saving" (or *deficit financing,* as those in Washington D.C. say). The interest rates on consumer debt are high; and, unlike the interest on a mortgage, the interest on consumer debt is not tax-deductible, so you bear the full brunt of its cost.

If you have accessible savings to pay down your consumer debts, by all means use those savings. You're surely paying a higher interest rate on the debt than you're earning from interest on your savings. Plus, interest on your savings is taxable. Just be sure that you have access to sufficient emergency money through family or other means.

If you lack the savings to make your high-cost debts disappear, start by refinancing your high-cost credit card debt onto cards with lower-interest-rates. Then work at reducing your spending in order to free up cash to pay down these debts as quickly as possible. And, if you've had a tendency to run up credit card balances, consider getting rid of your credit cards and obtaining a VISA or MasterCard debit card. These debit cards look like credit cards and are accepted the same as credit cards by merchants, but they function like checks. When you make a purchase with a debit card, the money is deducted from your checking account within a day or two.

Trim the non-necessities from your budget. Even if you're not a high-income earner, some of the things you spend your money on are non-necessities. Although everyone needs food, shelter, clothing, and health care, people spend a great deal of additional money on luxuries and non-essentials. Even some of what we spend on the "necessity" categories is partly for luxury.

Purchase products and services that offer value. High quality doesn't have to cost more. In fact, higher-priced products and services are sometimes inferior to lower-cost alternatives.

And, finally, buy in bulk. Most items are cheaper per unit when you buy them in larger sizes or volumes. Wholesale superstores such as Costco and Wal-Mart offer family sizes and competitive pricing.

What to do with your spending numbers

Tabulating your spending is only half the battle on the path to fiscal fitness and a financially successful home purchase. (After all, our federal government knows where it spends our money, yet that knowledge hasn't helped the government close its vast deficit and reduce its debt.) You must *do* something with the personal spending information that you collect.

Here, in order of likelihood, are the possible outcomes of your spending analysis:

- ✔ **You spend too much.** When most people examine their spending for the first time, they are somewhat horrified at *how much* they are spending overall and *for what* specific things they are spending their money. Perhaps you had no idea that your café latté addiction is setting you back $100 per month or that you spend $400 per month on eating out.

  Your challenge is to decide where to make reductions or cutbacks. (Check out the nearby sidebar, "Trimming the fat from your budget.") Everybody who has enough discretionary income to buy this book has fat in his or her budget, some much more than others. In order for most people to reach their financial goals, they must save at least 10 percent of their pre-tax income. But how much *you* should be saving depends upon what your goals are and how aggressive and successful an investor you are. If, for example, you want to retire early and don't have much put away yet, you may need to save much more than 10 percent per year to reach your goal.

- ✔ **You save just right.** You may be one of those people who has mapped out a financial path and is right on track. Great! However, just as a cue ball sends a neatly racked set of billiard balls into disarray, buying a home disrupts even the most organized and on-track budgets.

  Reviewing what your budget may look like with a home in the picture is important. So, if you haven't already done so, be sure to complete Table 2-1 to analyze your current spending and project how it may look after a home purchase.

- ✔ **You save a lot.** If you're one of those rare sorts who saves more than necessary, you may not only be able to skip doing a budget but you may also be able to stretch the amount you spend and borrow when buying a home. But, even if you've made your financial plans and are saving more than enough, you still may want to complete Table 2-1 to ensure that your financial train doesn't get derailed.

Reckoning Your Savings Requirements

"How much should I be saving?"

If you're asking that question, you're not alone. If you've never seriously asked yourself this question, you're most definitely not alone. Not only do most people not know how much they are currently saving, even more people don't know how much they should be saving. You should know these amounts *before* you buy a home.

How much you should be saving likely differs from how much your neighbors and coworkers should be saving. Why? Because each person has a different situation, different resources, and different goals.

The wise use of credit

Just because borrowing on credit cards bears a high cost doesn't mean that all credit is bad for you. Borrowing money for long-term purposes can make sense if you borrow for sound, wealth-building investments. Borrowing money for a real estate purchase, for a small business, or for education can pay dividends down the road.

When you borrow for investment purposes, you may earn tax benefits as well. With a home purchase, for example, home mortgage interest and property taxes are generally tax deductible (as we discuss in Chapter 3). When fixed-rate mortgages go for around 7 percent, for example, the effective after-tax cost of borrowing money is just 4.6 percent for a moderate-income earner who is paying approximately 35 percent in federal and state income taxes.

If you own a business, you may deduct the interest expenses on loans that you take out for business purposes. Interest incurred through borrowing against your security investments (through so-called *margin loans*) is deductible against your investment income for the year.

In fact, you can even make wise use of short-term credit on your credit cards to make your money work harder for you. For example, you can use your credit cards for the convenience that they offer, not for their credit feature. If you pay your bill in full and on time during each monthly billing cycle, you've had free use of the money that you owed from the credit card charges that you made during the previous month. If you had paid for the previous month's credit card purchases by cash or check, you would have had to part with your money sooner.

Setting some goals

Most people find it enlightening to see how much they need to save in order to accomplish particular goals. Wanting to retire someday is a common goal. The challenge is that, in your 20s and 30s, it's difficult to have more clearly defined goals — such as knowing that you want to retire at age 58 and move to New Mexico where you'll join a shared-housing community and buy a home that currently costs $200,000. Not to worry; you don't need to know exactly when, where, and how you want to retire.

But you do want to avoid nasty surprises. When Peter and Nancy hit their 40s, they came to the painful realization that retirement was a long way off because they were still working off consumer debts and trying to initiate a regular savings program. Now they are confronted with a choice: having to work into their 70s to achieve their retirement goals or settling for a much less comfortable lifestyle in retirement.

If retirement is not one of your goals, terrific! If you want (and are able) to continue working throughout your 60s, 70s, and 80s, you won't need to accumulate the vast savings that others must in order to be lollygagging during those golden years. But counting on being able to keep working throughout your lifetime is risky — you don't know what the job market or your personal health may be like later in life.

Retirement savings accounts and a dilemma

Prior years' tax reforms took away many of the previously available tax write-offs, except for one of the best and most available write-offs: funding a retirement-savings plan. Money that you contribute to an employer-based retirement plan — such as a 401(k) or a 403(b) — or to a self-employed plan — such as an SEP-IRA or a Keogh — is generally tax deductible, thus saving you both federal and state income taxes in the year for which the contribution is made. Additionally, all of your money in these accounts compounds over time without taxation. These tax-reduction accounts are one of the best ways to save your money and make it grow.

Take the case of a 40-year-old person who is in a moderate tax bracket (paying approximately 35 percent in federal and state income tax). Suppose that this person can afford to contribute $4,000 per year to a retirement account — for example, a 401(k). In 25 years (at age 65), this person's retirement account balance will have grown to $393,388. With a retirement account, taxes are deferred until the money is withdrawn. So if the person pays taxes on this $393,388 balance at the same rate (35 percent) upon withdrawal in retirement, the after-tax value of the retirement account will be $255,702.

Contrast this amount with $153,108 (over $100,000 less), which is how much would be available if this person had saved the $4,000 each year and invested it *outside* the tax-sheltered retirement account. Why so much less if you save and invest outside a retirement account? Because more of your money is siphoned off sooner to pay taxes, rather than compounding for you. (This example assumes a 10 percent annual investment return.)

If you're concerned that you'll be worse off saving inside retirement accounts because you think that your tax rate may be higher when you reach retirement age, you probably shouldn't worry so much. In order for a person to be worse off by saving in a retirement account, the person's retirement tax rate (in the previous example) would have to exceed 61 percent!

The challenge for most people is keeping their spending down to a level that allows them to save enough to contribute to these terrific tax-reduction accounts. Suppose that you're currently spending all of your income (a very American thing to do) and that you want to be able to save 10 percent of your income. If you are able to cut your spending by just 7.5 percent and put that savings into a tax-deductible retirement account, you'll actually be able to reach your 10-percent target. How? With the tax savings that you'll net from funding your retirement account.

More ways to slash your taxes

Funding retirement accounts is the best first step to reducing your taxes, both today and in the years ahead. When investing your money, it pays to learn the other numerous methods to legally and permanently reduce your tax burden.

Pay particular attention to taxes when investing money *outside* of tax-sheltered retirement accounts. Interest, dividends, and *capital gains* (the profits that you realize from selling an investment at a higher price than you bought it) are all subject to taxation. So, for example, if you're in a higher-tax bracket, consider using tax-free money market funds and tax-free bonds instead of taxable ones.

When possible, make capital gains *long-term* — that is, hold the investment more than one year. The federal income tax rate on long-term capital gains is capped at a maximum of 28 percent. On the other hand, investments sold within 12 months are taxed at your ordinary income tax rate, which may range as high as 39.6 percent.

Another way to reduce your taxes is to itemize deductions on Schedule A of your Form 1040. Homeownership, along with its deductions for mortgage interest and property taxes, makes itemizing possible for millions of taxpayers. Peruse Schedule A to identify what other deductible expenses you may have — such as large medical and dental expenses, state and local income taxes, charitable contributions, and unreimbursed employee expenses.

If you're self-employed, definitely take the time to understand the myriad deductible expenses that you can take for your business. For example, self-employed people can deduct 30 percent of their health insurance premiums. To find out more about the wonderful world of taxes and how to keep more money in your wallet, pick up a copy of *Taxes For Dummies*.

Generally speaking, when you contribute money to a retirement account, the money is not accessible to you unless you pay a penalty. So, if you're accumulating down-payment money for the purchase of a home, putting that money into a retirement account is generally a bad idea. Why? Because when you withdraw money from a retirement account, you not only owe current income taxes, but you also owe hefty penalties (10 percent of the amount withdrawn must go to the IRS; plus you must pay whatever penalty your state assesses).

So the dilemma is that you can save outside of retirement accounts and have access to your down-payment money but pay much more in taxes. Or you can fund your retirement accounts and gain tax benefits, but lack access to the money for your home purchase.

One exception that a small number of people can take advantage of offers the best of both worlds. Some employers' retirement-savings plans allow borrowing privileges. Under such arrangements, you can fund the account, slash your taxes, and borrow your own money to use as a down payment to boot. If your employer's account has such a provision, be sure that you understand the repayment rules so that you won't be tripped up and forced to treat the withdrawal as a taxable distribution.

Because most of us have limited discretionary dollars, we must decide what our priorities are. Saving for retirement and reducing your taxes are important; but when you're trying to save to purchase a home, some or most of your savings need to be outside a tax-sheltered retirement account. Putting your retirement savings on the back burner for a short time in order to build up your down-payment cushion is okay. Be careful, though, to purchase a home that offers enough slack in your budget to fund your retirement accounts after the purchase. You *gotta* do the budget exercise in Table 2-1, earlier in this chapter.

Other reasons to save

Wanting to have the financial resources to retire someday is hardly the only reason to save. Most people have several competing reasons to squirrel away money. Here are some other typical financial objectives or goals that motivate people (or should be motivating them) to save money. We tell you how to fit each goal into your home-purchasing desires and your overall personal financial situation:

- ✔ **Emergency reserve:** Whether random bad things happen isn't so much the issue as *when* they happen. You simply can't predict what impact a job loss, death in the family, accident, or unexpectedly large expense may have on you and your family. That's why it's a good idea to have an easily accessible and safe reservoir of money that you can tap should the need arise.

  Make sure that you have access to at least three months worth of expenses (if you have a highly unstable job and volatile income, perhaps even six months worth). Ideally, you should keep this money in a money market fund because such funds offer you both high yields and liquidity. The major mutual fund companies (such as Vanguard, Fidelity, and T. Rowe Price) offer money funds with competitive yields, check-writing privileges, and access to other good investments. (See Chapter 3 to find out more about these funds and how you can use them for investing your down-payment money.) Alternatively, a bank savings account will do, but it will likely offer a lower yield. If you have benevolent relatives who will fork over some dough in a flash, they could serve as your emergency reserve as well.

- ✔ **Educational expenses:** If you have little cherubs at home, it's natural to want the best for them, and that typically includes a good college education. So, when the first cash gifts start rolling in from Grandma and Grandpa, many a new parent establishes an investment account in the child's name.

Your best intentions could come back to haunt you, however, when junior applies to enter college. All things being equal, the more you have available in your nonretirement accounts and in your child's name, the less financial aid your child will qualify for. (By *financial aid,* we mean all types of assistance, including grants and loans that are not based on need.) Unless you're wealthy or are sure that you can afford to pay for the full cost of a college education for your kids, think long and hard before putting money in your child's name. Although it may sound selfish, you actually do yourself and your child a financial favor by taking full advantage of opportunities to fund your retirement accounts. Remember, too, that one of the advantages of being a homeowner is that you can borrow against your home's equity to help pay for your child's college expenses.

✔ **Start a business:** Another reason to save money is if you hope to start or purchase a business someday. If you have sufficient equity in your home, you can borrow against that equity to fund the business. But you may desire to accumulate a separate investment pool to fund your business.

No matter what your personal and financial goals are, you're likely going to need to save a decent amount of money to achieve them. Consider what your goals are and how much you need to save to accomplish those goals, especially for retirement. Get your finances in order *before* you decide how much you can really afford to spend on a home. Otherwise, you may end up being a financial prisoner to your home.

Protecting Yourself, Your Dependents, and Your Assets

One of the more potentially disastrous things you can do to both yourself and your dependents is not carry proper insurance. We're not talking about homeowners insurance here. (Heck, we haven't even explained how to find a home or get a loan yet! We get to homeowners insurance in Chapter 11.)

You need proper insurance protection for yourself, personally, as well as for your assets. Sure, you can take your chances and hope and expect that you won't contract a dreaded disease, get into a horrible auto accident, or suffer some other misfortune or bad luck. But misfortune and bad luck usually come knocking without a warning.

Trust us when we say that we're optimistic, positive thinkers. However — and this is a big *however* — we know more than a few folks who have gotten themselves (or their families or both) into major financial trouble after purchasing a home, because they neglected to obtain proper insurance:

✔ Steve bought a home and then learned from his doctor that he had multiple sclerosis. Steve had to cut back dramatically on work, and because he lacked proper long-term disability insurance, he was forced to sell his home at a large loss due to his lowered work income.

✔ Mary owned a home in California and, despite the known risk of earth-quakes, didn't purchase earthquake coverage. "It's so expensive; and besides, the insurance companies won't be able to meet the claims in a major quake. Government assistance will help," she said. Mary's home was a total loss in an earthquake; and, although the government made a loan, it did not *pay for* the loss — ultimately, the money came out of Mary's pocket.

✔ Maggie and Donald were living a charmed life in the New England country-side with their two children, a white farmhouse, and a dog and a cat — until Maggie came down with cancer. She left her job, which placed some strain on the family finances. After much treatment, Maggie died. Donald and the kids were forced to move because Maggie lacked proper life insurance.

✔ Michelle had a walkway in disrepair. Unfortunately, one day an older man tripped and severely injured himself. To make a long story short, after lengthy legal proceedings, the settlement in favor of the man was signifi-cant enough to force Michelle to sell her home. A good chunk of the settlement money came out of Michelle's pocket because she lacked sufficient liability insurance.

Now we're not about to try and tell you that insurance would have made these situations come out fine. Insurance generally can't prevent most major medical problems, keep a person from dying, or stop someone from suing you. However, proper insurance can protect you and your family from the adverse and severe financial consequences of major problems. The right kind of insurance can make the difference between keeping versus losing your home, and it can help you and your family maintain your standard of living.

Wanting to skip insurance is tempting and a natural human tendency. After all, insurance costs you your hard-earned, after-tax dollars, and (unlike a meal out, a vacation, or a new stereo) insurance has no up-front, tangible benefit.

You hope that you won't need to use insurance; but if you need it, you're glad it's there to protect you and, in some cases, your dependents. Of course, insurance is not free — if it were, you might buy unlimited amounts of it. Insurance costs money and takes time to purchase. On the other hand, if you buy too little insurance, it won't protect you and yours against a real catastro-phe. So you need the right amount of coverage that balances good protection against cost.

Insuring yourself

Before you buy a home, get your insurance protection (for yourself *and* for your valuable assets) in order. Not doing so is the financial equivalent of driving down the highway in an old subcompact car at 90 miles per hour without a seat belt. You should purchase sufficient protection to prevent a financial catastrophe.

Disability insurance

Your ability to produce income should be insured. During your working years, your future income-earning ability is likely your most valuable asset — far more valuable than a car or even your home.

Long-term disability insurance replaces a portion of your lost income in the event that a disability, such as multiple sclerosis, prevents you from working. Even if you don't have dependents, you probably need disability coverage. Unless you're quite wealthy and no longer need to work for income, aren't *you* dependent on your paycheck? Although many larger companies offer long-term disability insurance, many small-company employees and self-employed people have no coverage — a situation that's risky.

Life insurance

If you have dependents, you may also need life insurance protection. The question to ask yourself and your family is how they would fare financially if you died and they no longer had your income coming in. If your family is dependent upon your income and you want them to be able to maintain their current standard of living in your absence, you need life insurance.

Term life insurance, like most other forms of insurance, is pure insurance protection and is the best type of insurance for the vast majority of people. The amount of coverage you buy should be based upon how many years *worth* of your income you desire to provide your family with in the event of your passing.

Insurance brokers love to sell *cash-value life insurance* (also known as *whole* or *universal* life insurance) because of the hefty commissions that they can earn by selling this type of insurance. (These commissions, of course, come out of your pocket.) Some mortgage lenders lobby you to buy the mortgage life insurance that they sell. Skip both these options. Mortgage life insurance is simply overpriced term insurance, and cash-value life insurance generally combines overpriced life insurance with a low-return investment account.

Health insurance

In addition to evaluating your need for disability and life insurance, everyone should have a comprehensive health insurance policy. Even if you're in good health, you never know when an accident or illness can happen. Medical bills can mushroom into tens or hundreds of thousands of dollars in no time. Don't be without comprehensive health insurance.

Wills, living trusts, and estate planning

Although some of us don't like to admit or even think about it, we are all mortal. Because of the way our legal and tax systems work, it's often beneficial to have legal documents in place specifying important details such as what should be done with your assets (including your home) when you die.

A *will* is the most basic of such documents and, for most people, particularly those who are younger or don't have great assets, the only critical one. Through a will, you can direct to whom your assets will go upon your death as well as who will serve as guardian for your minor children. In the absence of a will, state law dictates these important issues.

Along with your will, also consider signing a *living will* and a *medical power of attorney.* These documents help your doctor and family members make important decisions regarding your health care, should you be unable to make those decisions for yourself.

Even a will and supporting medical and legal documents may not be enough to get your assets to your desired heirs, as well as minimize taxes and legal fees. If you hold significant assets (such as a home and business) outside tax-sheltered retirement accounts, in most states, those assets must be *probated* — which is the

court-administered process for implementing your will. Establishing and placing your home and other assets in a *living trust* can eliminate much of the hassle and cost of probate. Attorneys' probate fees can run quite high — up to 5 percent of the value of the probated assets.

Finally, if your *net worth* (assets minus liabilities) exceeds $600,000 upon your death, the federal (and perhaps your state's) government will levy significant estate taxes. Estate planning can help minimize the portion of your estate subject to such taxation. One simple but powerful estate-planning strategy is to *gift* (give) money to your desired heirs in order to reduce your taxable estate. (If your relatives are in the fortunate position of having great wealth, they may gift, free of tax, up to $10,000 each to as many recipients as they want. If they gift you $10,000, you can use this money toward your home's down payment.)

Wills, living trusts, and estate planning are nothing more than forms of insurance. Remember that it takes both time and money to generate these documents, and the benefits may be a long time off, so don't get carried away with doing too many of these things before you're older and have significant assets. Read *Taxes For Dummies* to find out more about estate planning.

Insuring your assets

As your wealth builds over the years (hopefully, at least in part, due to the increasing value of the home that we help you buy), so, too, does the risk of losing — or facing a lawsuit arising from — your valuable assets. For example, you should have comprehensive insurance on your home and car(s). If your home burns to the ground, a comprehensive homeowners insurance policy should pay for the cost of rebuilding the home. Likewise, if your car is totaled in an accident, auto insurance should pay to replace the car.

With all types of insurance that you purchase, take the highest deductible that you can comfortably afford. The *deductible* represents the amount of money that you must pay out of your own pocket if you have a loss for which you file a claim. High deductibles help keep the cost of your coverage low and also eliminate the hassle associated with filing small claims.

Along with buying insurance to cover the replacement costs for loss of or damage to your valuable assets, you can (and should) purchase adequate liability insurance for those assets. Both homeowners insurance and auto insurance come with liability protection. Make sure that you carry liability coverage for at least twice the value of your *net worth* (assets minus liabilities).

In addition to the liability protection that comes with auto and homeowners insurance, you may purchase a supplemental liability insurance policy known as an *umbrella* or *excess liability policy.* Purchased in increments of $1,000,000, this coverage can protect people with larger net worth. Note that this coverage does not protect against lawsuits arising from your work.

Invest in Yourself

Last but not least, in your zest to build your financial empire and buy ever bigger and more expensive homes, don't forget your best investment: you. Don't run your life and body into the ground by working horrendous hours just to afford a big, fat box of lumber, nails, and paint.

In addition to investing in your health, your family, and your friends, invest in educating yourself and taking charge of your finances. If you need more help with assessing your current financial health, reducing your spending, your taxes, and your debts, and mapping out an overall financial plan (including dealing with your investments and insurance), be smart and pick up a copy of *Personal Finance For Dummies.*

Chapter 3

What Can You Afford to Buy?

*I*f you walk into an auto showroom, one of the first questions the salespeople ask (after you pry them off you) is, "What is your budget?" or "How much can you afford to spend on a car?" Of course, they hope that a large number rolls off your tongue. If you're like many car buyers, you may be likely to say something along the lines of, "I'm not really sure."

Lenders Can't Tell You What You Can Afford

Many car buyers today finance the purchase — so they allow a banker or other lender to determine how much car they can afford. Such determinations are based upon the buyers' income and other debt obligations.

But here's where many people get confused. If the lender says that you qualify to borrow, say, $20,000 for a car purchase, this doesn't mean that you can *afford* to spend that much on a car. What the lender is effectively saying to you is, "Based on what little I know about your situation and the fact that I can't control your future behavior, this is the maximum amount that I think is a prudent risk for my organization to be lending you."

The lending organization normally requires a certain down payment to protect itself against the possibility that you may default on the loan. If you default on an auto loan, for example, the lender has to send the repo man out to take away and sell your car. This process takes time and money, and the lender will surely get less for the car than the amount that you paid for it.

Ultimately, the lending firm doesn't care about you, your financial situation, or your other needs, so long as it has protected its financial interests. The lender doesn't know or care whether, for example, you're

- ✔ Behind in saving for retirement
- ✔ Wanting to save money for other important financial goals, such as starting or buying your own small business
- ✔ Parenting an army of kids
- ✔ Lacking proper personal insurance protection

And therein lies the problem of making your decision about how much home (or car) you can afford to buy on the basis of how much money a lender is willing to lend you. That's what Walter and Susan did. They set out to purchase a home when Walter's business was booming. They were making in excess of $200,000 per year — more than the President of the United States!

Walter and Susan really wanted to buy the biggest and best house that they could afford. When they met with their friendly neighborhood banker, the banker was more than willing to show them how they could borrow $900,000 by getting an adjustable-rate mortgage. (You can read all about these mortgages in Chapter 5. We'll simply tell you here that, because some adjustable mortgages start out at an artificially low "teaser" interest rate, they enable you to qualify to borrow a good deal more than would be the case with a traditional, fixed-rate mortgage.)

Walter and Susan bought their million-dollar-plus dream home with an adjustable-rate $900,000 mortgage. Within a few years, Walter and Susan's dream home turned into the Nightmare on Oak Street. Their mortgage became a financial noose around their necks.

Now blessed with young children, Walter and Susan didn't want to work crazy hours anymore; yet they were forced to do so in order to meet their gargantuan mortgage payments. The initial payments on their adjustable mortgage were high, but they ballooned gigantically as the loan's interest rate increased.

The financial strain led to personal strain as Walter and Susan began to get into frequent arguments about money and child care. We know of others who stretched themselves the same way that Walter and Susan did. Many of them continue slaving away long hours in jobs that they don't like and making other unnecessary sacrifices, such as limiting the time they spend with family, in order to make their housing payments. Some end up divorcing, due (in part) to the financial strains. Others default on their loan and lose their homes and their good credit.

People at all income levels, even the affluent, can get into trouble and over-extend themselves by purchasing more house than they can afford and taking on more debt than they can comfortably handle. Just because a lender or real estate agent says that you're eligible for, or can qualify for, a certain-size loan doesn't mean that's what you can afford in your personal financial situation. Lenders *can't* tell you what you can afford — they can *only* tell you the maximum that they will allow you to borrow.

The Cost of Buying and Owning a Home

Before you set out in search of your dream home, one of the single most important questions you need to answer is, "What can I afford to spend on a home?" In order to answer that question intelligently, you first need to understand what your financial goals are, what it will take to achieve them, and where you are today. If you haven't yet read Chapter 2, now's the time (unless you're 100-percent sure that your personal finances are in tip-top shape).

Without further ado, dig into the costs of buying and owning a home.

Mortgage payments

In Chapter 5, we discuss selecting the best type of mortgage that fits with your particular circumstances. In the meantime, you must still confront mortgages (with our assistance), because mortgages undoubtedly constitute the biggest component of the total cost of owning a home.

Start with the basics: What is a mortgage? A *mortgage* is nothing more than a loan you take out to buy a home. A mortgage allows you to purchase a $150,000 home even though you yourself have far less money than that to put towards the purchase.

With few exceptions, mortgage loans in the U.S. are typically repaid over a 15- or 30-year time span. Almost all mortgages require monthly payments. Here's how a mortgage works. Suppose that you are purchasing a $150,000 home and that (following our sage advice, appearing later in this chapter) you have diligently saved until you accumulated a 20-percent ($30,000 in this example) down payment. Thus, you are in the market for a $120,000 mortgage loan.

You sit down with a mortgage lender who asks you to complete a volume of paperwork (we navigate you through that morass in Chapter 6) that dwarfs the stack required for your annual income tax return. Just when you think the worst is over (after the paperwork blizzard subsides), the lender proceeds to give you an even bigger headache by talking about the literally hundreds of mortgage permutations and options.

Don't worry — we can help you cut through the clutter! Imagine, for a moment, a simple world where the mortgage lender offers you only two mortgage options: a 15-year fixed-rate mortgage and a 30-year fixed-rate mortgage (*fixed-rate* simply means that the interest rate on the loan stays fixed and level over the life of the loan). Here's what your monthly payment would be under each mortgage option:

$120,000, 15-year mortgage @ 7.00 percent = $1,079 per month

$120,000, 30-year mortgage @ 7.25 percent = $ 819 per month

As we discuss in Chapter 5, the interest rate is typically a little bit lower on a 15-year mortgage versus a 30-year mortgage because shorter-term loans are a little less risky for lenders. Note how much higher the monthly payment is on the 15-year mortgage than it is on the 30-year mortgage. Your payments must be higher for the 15-year mortgage because you're paying off the same size loan 15 years faster.

But don't let the higher monthly payments on the 15-year loan cause you to forget that, at the end of 15 years, your mortgage payments disappear; whereas, with the 30-year mortgage, you still have 15 more years worth of monthly payments to go. So, although you do have a higher required monthly payment with the 15-year mortgage, check out the difference in the total payments and interest on the two mortgage options:

Mortgage Option	*Total Payments*	*Total Interest*
15-year mortgage	$ 194,147	$ 74,147
30-year mortgage	$ 294,700	$ 174,700

Note: In case you're curious about how we got the total interest amount, we simply subtracted the amount of the loan repaid ($120,000) from the "Total Payments." Also, the monthly payment numbers previously cited as well as these total payments and interest numbers are rounded off, so if you try multiplying 180 or 360 by the monthly payment numbers, you won't get the answers above.

With the 30-year mortgage (compared to the 15-year mortgage), because you're borrowing the money over 15 additional years, it shouldn't come as a great surprise that (with a decent-sized mortgage loan like this one) you end up paying more than $100,000 additional interest. The 30-year loan is not necessarily inferior, for example, if its lower payments better allow you to accomplish other important financial goals, such as saving in a tax-deductible retirement account. (See Chapter 5 for more information about 15-year versus 30-year mortgages.)

In the early years of repaying your mortgage, nearly all of your mortgage payment goes towards paying interest on the money that you borrowed. Not until the later years of your mortgage do you begin to rapidly pay down your loan balance, as shown in Figure 3-1.

As interest rates increase, so does the time required to pay off half the loan. For example, at 10-percent interest, paying off half the loan takes almost 24 years of the loan's 30-year term; and at 14-percent interest, paying off half the loan takes over 25 years of the loan's 30-year life.

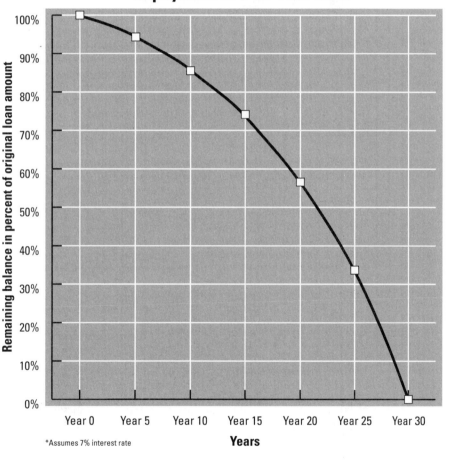

Figure 3-1:
It takes many years into a mortgage to begin to make real progress at repaying the amount originally borrowed. In this case, paying off half the loan balance takes nearly 22 years.

Repayment of a 30-Year Loan*

*Assumes 7% interest rate

Years

Remaining balance in percent of original loan amount

Lender's limits

Because we have personally seen the financial consequences of people borrowing too much (yet still staying within the boundaries of what mortgage lenders allow), you won't hear us saying in this section that lenders can tell you the amount that you can afford to spend on a home. They can't.

All that mortgage lenders can do is tell you their criteria for approving and denying mortgage applications and calculating the maximum that you're eligible to borrow.

Most, but by no means all, mortgage lenders follow similar loan-evaluation criteria because they actually sell the mortgage loans they originate in the financial markets to picky investors. Government agencies — such as *Fannie Mae* (FNMA: the Federal National Mortgage Association) and *Ginnie Mae* (GNMA: the Government National Mortgage Association) — will guarantee the repayment of principal and interest on such loans so long as the bank that originates the mortgage adheres to certain specific criteria for accepting or rejecting the mortgage loan. Perhaps, in the often-confusing world of investments, you've heard of *Ginnie Maes*. Well, when you invest in these mortgage-backed securities, what you're basically buying are bonds which are mortgages, perhaps even yours!

A mortgage lender tallies up your monthly *housing expense,* the components of which they consider to be

	Mortgage payment	(PI for *p*rincipal and *i*nterest)
	Property taxes	(T for *t*axes)
+	Insurance	(I for *i*nsurance)
	Lender's definition of *housing expense*	(PITI is the common acronym)

For a given property that you are considering buying, a mortgage lender calculates the housing expense and normally requires that it not exceed 33 percent of your monthly before-tax (*gross*) income. (Some lenders allow the percentage to go a bit higher). So, for example, if your monthly gross income is $6,000, your lender will not allow your expected monthly housing expense to exceed $2,000. If you're self-employed and complete IRS Form 1040, Schedule C, mortgage lenders use your after-expenses (*net*) income, from the bottom line of Schedule C.

Now, if you've been paying attention thus far in this chapter, you should smell something terribly wrong with such a simplistic, one-number-fits-all approach. This housing expense ratio completely ignores almost all your other financial goals, needs, and obligations. It also ignores maintenance and remodeling expenses, which can suck up a lot of homeowner's dough.

About the only other financial considerations a lender takes into account (besides your income) are your other debts. Specifically, mortgage lenders examine the required monthly payments for other debts you may have, such as student loans, an auto loan, and credit card bills. In addition to the 33 percent of your income lenders allow for housing expenses, lenders typically allow an additional 5 percent of your monthly income to go towards other debt repayments. Thus, your monthly housing expense and monthly repayment of nonhousing debts can total up to, but generally no more than, 38 percent.

If you have consumer debt, be sure to read Chapter 2. Suffice it to say here that you should get out (and stay out) of consumer debt. Consumer debt has a high cost and, unlike the interest on a mortgage loan, the interest on consumer debt is not tax-deductible. And consumer debt handicaps your ability to qualify for and pay back your mortgage. *Consumer debt is the financial equivalent of cancer.*

Stretching more than lenders allow

Sometimes, prospective homebuyers feel that they can handle more debt than lenders will allow. Such homebuyers may seek to borrow more money from family or fib on their mortgage application about their income. (Self-employed people have the greatest opportunity to do this.) Such behavior is not unlike the shenanigans of some teenagers who drive above the speed limit, drink and smoke forbidden things, or stay out past curfew and sneak in the back door.

Although some teenagers get away with such risky behavior, others end up in trouble academically or psychologically. Some even die. The same is true of homeowners who stretch themselves financially thin to buy a more costly property. Some survive just fine, but others end up in financial and emotional trouble.

And, increasingly, homebuyers who lie on their mortgage applications are getting caught. How? When you're ready to close on your loan, lenders can (and often do) ask you to sign a form authorizing them to request a copy of your income tax return from the IRS. This allows the lender to validate your income. (See Chapter 6 for more details.)

So, although we've said that the lender's word isn't the gospel as to how much home you can truly afford, we will go on record as saying that telling the truth on your mortgage application is the only way to go (and prevents you from committing perjury and fraud). Telling the truth is not only honest but it also helps keep you from getting in over your head. Bankers don't want you to default on your loan, and you shouldn't want to do so either.

Figuring the size of your mortgage payments

Calculating the size of your mortgage payment, after you know the amount you want to borrow, is a piece of a cake. The hard part for most people is determining how much they can afford to borrow. Start by reading Chapter 2, if you haven't yet done so.

If you already know how large a monthly mortgage payment you can afford, terrific! Go to the head of the class. Suppose that you worked through your budget in Chapter 2 (Table 2-1) and calculated that you can afford to spend $1,500 per month on housing. Determining the exact size of mortgage that allows you to stay within this boundary is a little challenging because the housing cost you figure that you can afford ($1,500, in our example) is made up of several components. Lucky for you, we cover each of these components in this chapter, including mortgage payments, property taxes, insurance, and maintenance. (Note that, although lenders don't care about maintenance expenses in figuring what you can afford to buy, you shouldn't overlook this very real and not-insignificant expense.)

As you change the amount that you're willing to spend on a home, the size of the mortgage you choose to take out also usually changes; but so, too, do the other property cost components, which generally increase. So you will likely have to play with the numbers a bit to get them to work out just right. You may pick a certain-priced home and then figure the property taxes, insurance, maintenance, and the like. When you tally everything up, you may find that the total comes in above or below your desired target ($1,500, in our example). Obviously, if you come out a little high, you need to cut back a bit and choose a slightly less-costly property and smaller mortgage.

Using Table 3-1, you can calculate the size of your mortgage payments based on the amount you want to borrow, the loan's interest rate, and the length (in years) the mortgage payments last. To determine the monthly payment on a mortgage, simply multiply the relevant number from Table 3-1 by the size of your mortgage expressed in (divided by) thousands of dollars. For example, if you will be taking out a $150,000, 30-year mortgage at 6.75 percent, multiply 150 by 6.49 (from Table 3-1) to arrive at a $973.50 monthly payment.

Table 3-1	Monthly Mortgage Payment Calculator	
Interest Rate	*15-Year Mortgage*	*30-Year Mortgage*
4.0%	7.40	4.77
4.5%	7.65	5.07
5.0%	7.91	5.37
5.25%	8.04	5.53

Interest Rate	15-Year Mortgage	30-Year Mortgage
5.5%	8.17	5.68
5.75%	8.31	5.84
6.0%	8.44	6.00
6.25%	8.58	6.16
6.5%	8.71	6.32
6.75%	8.85	*6.49*
7.0%	8.99	6.65
7.25%	9.13	6.83
7.5%	9.27	6.99
7.75%	9.42	7.17
8.0%	9.56	7.34
8.25%	9.71	7.52
8.5%	9.85	7.69
8.75%	10.00	7.87
9.0%	10.14	8.05
9.25%	10.30	8.23
9.5%	10.44	8.41
9.75%	10.60	8.60
10.0%	10.75	8.78

Use this handy-dandy workspace (reproduced throughout the chapter) to track your estimated home-ownership expenses:

Item	Estimated Monthly Expense
Mortgage payment	$ _____
Property taxes	+ $ _____
Insurance	+ $ _____
Improvements, maintenance, and other	+ $ _____
Home-ownership expenses (pre-tax)	= $ _____
Tax savings	– $ _____
Home-ownership expenses (after-tax benefits)	= $ _____

Property taxes

If you live and breathe, escaping taxes is pretty hard. If you buy and own a home, your local government (typically through what is called a County Tax Collector's office) sends you an annual, lump-sum bill for property taxes. Receiving this bill and paying it is never much fun because most communities bill you just once or twice per year. And some homeowners find it aggravating to be paying so much in property taxes on top of all the federal and state income and sales taxes they pay. Why, some people wonder, can't there just be one tax, period? Because of the government's endless tinkering with tax laws.

If you make a small down payment (typically defined as less than 20 percent of the purchase price), many lenders impose property tax and insurance *impound accounts*. These accounts require you to pay your property taxes and insurance to the lender each month along with your mortgage payment.

Property taxes are typically based on the value of a property. Although an average property tax rate is about 1.5 percent of the purchase price of the property per year, you should understand what the exact rate is in your area. Call the Tax Collector's office (you can find the phone number in the government pages section of your local phone directory) in the town where you're contemplating buying a home and ask what the property tax rate is and what additional fees and assessments may apply.

Be careful to make sure that you're comparing apples with apples when comparing communities. For example, some communities may nickel-and-dime you for extra assessments for services that are included in the standard property tax bills of other communities.

Real estate listings, which are typically prepared by real estate agents, may contain information as to what the current property owner is paying in taxes. But relying on such data to understand what your real estate taxes will be if you buy the property can be financially dangerous. The current owner's taxes may very well be based upon an outdated and much lower property valuation. Your property taxes (if you buy the home) are based on the price that you paid for the property. Just as it's dangerous to drive forward by looking in the rearview mirror of your car, you shouldn't buy a property and budget for property taxes based upon the current owner's taxes.

Item	Estimated Monthly Expense
Mortgage payment	$ _____
Property taxes	+ $ _____
Insurance	+ $ _____
Improvements, maintenance, and other	+ $ _____
Home-ownership expenses (pre-tax)	= $ _____
Tax savings	– $ _____
Home-ownership expenses (after-tax benefits)	= $ _____

Insurance

When you purchase a home, your mortgage lender almost surely won't allow you to close the purchase until you've demonstrated that you have proper homeowners insurance. Lenders aren't being paternalistic, but rather self-interested. You see, if you buy the home and make a down payment of, say, 20 percent of the purchase price, the lender is putting up the other 80 percent of the purchase price. So if the home burns to the ground and is a total loss, the lender may care more, at least financially, than you do. In most states, your home is the lender's security for the loan.

Some lenders, in years past, learned the hard way that some homeowners may not care about losing their homes. In some cases, where homes were total losses, homeowners with little financial stake in the property and insufficient insurance coverage simply walked away from the problem and left the lender holding the bag. Because of cases like this, almost all lenders today require you to purchase *private mortgage insurance* (PMI) if you put down less than 20 percent of the purchase price when you buy. (We discuss PMI further later in this chapter, in the section entitled "The 20-percent solution.")

When you buy a home, you should want to protect your investment in the property (as well as cover the not-so-inconsequential cost of replacing your personal property, if it is ever damaged or stolen). In short order, your clothing, furniture, kitchen appliances, and beer-can collection can tally up to a lot of dollars to replace.

When you purchase homeowners insurance, you should buy the most comprehensive coverage that you can and take the highest deductible that you can afford to help minimize the cost. In Chapter 11, we explain how to do all that.

In the meantime, Table 3-2 allows you to estimate what home insurance may cost you.

Table 3-2	What You Can Expect to Pay for Homeowners Insurance
Purchase Price of Home	*Approximate Insurance Cost per Month* *
< $100,000	$40
$150,000	$50
$200,000	$65
$250,000	$85
$300,000	$110
$400,000	$135
$500,000	$160

*Note: As we discuss in Chapter 11, the cost of your insurance policy technically is driven by the cost of rebuilding your home, which is typically less than the total purchase price of the home. Although land has value, it doesn't need to be insured because it wouldn't be destroyed in a fire.

Just as you should do when you shop for a car, get quotes on insuring properties as you evaluate them or ask current owners what they pay for their coverage. (Just remember that some homeowners overpay or don't buy the right kind of protection, so don't take what they pay as the gospel.) If you overlook insurance costs until after you've agreed to buy a property, you could be in for a rude awakening.

Item	*Estimated Monthly Expense*
Mortgage payment	$ _____
Property taxes	+ $ _____
Insurance	+ $ _____
Improvements, maintenance, and other	+ $ _____
Home-ownership expenses (pre-tax)	= $ _____
Tax savings	− $ _____
Home-ownership expenses (after-tax benefits)	= $ _____

Maintenance and other costs

As a homeowner, you *must* make your mortgage and property-tax payments. If you don't, you'll eventually lose your home. Homes also require maintenance over the years. You must do some kinds of maintenance (repairs, for example) at a certain time. Painting and other elective improvements can take place at your discretion. Maintenance is difficult to budget for. You never know precisely when you may need to fix an electrical problem, patch a leaking roof, or replace the washer and dryer — until the problem rears its ugly head.

As a rule of thumb, expect to spend about 1 percent of the purchase price of your home each year on maintenance. So, for example, if you spend $150,000 on a home, you should budget about $1,500 per year (or about $125 per month) for maintenance. Although some years you may spend less, other years you may spend more. When your home's roof goes, for example, replacing it may cost you several years' worth of your budgeted maintenance expenses. With some

---

Tax difference between maintenance and improvements

While you own your home, it is in your interest to track the amount that you spend on improvements. Why? Well, when you go to sell your home someday, the IRS allows you to exclude from taxation that portion of your profit which was spent on capital improvements. So, for example, if you buy a home for $150,000 and sell it five years later for $225,000, you would normally owe tax on the $75,000 profit. (Chapter 15 explains how to *rollover* this gain into another residence so as to avoid taxation.)

But suppose that, during the period you owned this home, you spent additional money on it. For tax purposes, the IRS enables you to add the cost of *improvements* (but not money spent on *maintenance*) to your original purchase price. What's the difference? Well there *is* a difference but, as with all matters on which the IRS has an opinion, that difference isn't always crystal clear.

✔ *Capital improvements* are things that you do to your home that permanently increase its value and lengthen its life. Capital

improvements include such things as landscaping your yard, adding a deck, purchasing new appliances (as long as you leave them when you sell), installing a new heating system or roof, remodeling and adding rooms, and so on.

✔ *Maintenance and repair expenses,* in contrast, include those types of fix-up items that need to be done throughout your home from time to time. Maintenance and repairs include such things as fixing a leaky pipe or toilet, painting, paying someone to cut your lawn and pull weeds, and the like.

So, when you buy a home, be sure to keep handy a file folder into which you can dump receipts for money that you spend on home improvements. If you're in doubt as to whether an expense is an improvement or a maintenance item, keep the receipt and figure it out when it comes time to sell your home. IRS Form 2119 (*Sale of Your Home*) will be waiting for you when you do sell!

types of housing, such as condominiums, you actually pay monthly dues into a homeowners association, which takes care of the maintenance for the complex. In that case, you're only responsible for maintaining the interior of your unit. Check with the association to see what the dues are running. (See Chapter 7 for more information.)

In addition to necessary maintenance, you should also be aware (and beware) of what you may spend on nonessential home improvements. This *Other* category can really get you into trouble. Advertisements, your neighbors, and your coworkers can all entice and peer-pressure you into blowing big bucks on new furniture, endless remodeling projects, landscaping, and you-name-it.

Should you budget for these nonessentials? In general, yes. The potential problem is that your home can become a money pit by causing you to spend too much, not save enough, and (potentially) go into debt via credit cards and the like. (We cover the other dangers of overimprovement in Chapter 7.) Unless you're a terrific saver and can easily accomplish your savings goal and have lots of slack in your budget, be sure not to overlook this part of your home-expense budget.

The amount you expect to spend on improvements is just a guess. It depends upon how *finished* a home you buy and your personal tastes and desires. Consider your previous spending behavior and the types of projects you expect to do as you examine potential homes for purchase.

Item	*Estimated Monthly Expense*
Mortgage payment	$ _____
Property taxes	+ $ _____
Insurance	+ $ _____
Improvements, maintenance, and other	+ $ _____
Home-ownership expenses (pre-tax)	= $ _____
Tax savings	– $ _____
Home-ownership expenses (after-tax benefits)	= $ _____

The tax benefits of homeownership

One of the treasures of homeownership is that the IRS and most state governments allow you to deduct, within certain limits, mortgage interest and property taxes when you file your annual income tax return. When you file your Federal IRS Form 1040, the mortgage interest and property taxes on your home are itemized deductions on Schedule A (see Figure 3-2). On mortgage loans now taken out, you may deduct the interest on the first $1,000,000 of debt as well as all of the property taxes. The good folks at the IRS also allow you to deduct the interest costs on a *home equity* loan (second mortgage) to a maximum of $100,000 borrowed.

Just because mortgage interest and property taxes are allowable deductions on your income tax return does not mean that the government is literally paying for these items for you. Consider that, when you earn a dollar of income and must pay income tax on that dollar, you don't pay the entire dollar back to the government in taxes. The amount of taxes you pay on that dollar is determined by your tax bracket (see Table 3-3).

Table 3-3	1996 Federal Income Tax Brackets and Rates	
Singles Taxable Income	*Married-Filing-Jointly Taxable Income*	*Federal Tax Rate*
Less than $24,000	Less than $40,100	15%
$24,000 to $58,150	$40,100 to $96,900	28%
$58,150 to $121,300	$96,900 to $147,700	31%
$121,300 to $263,750	$147,700 to $263,750	36%
More than $263,750	More than $263,750	39.6%

Technically, you pay federal and state taxes, so you should consider your state tax savings as well when calculating your home-ownership tax savings. However, to keep things simple and still get a reliable estimate, simply multiply your mortgage payment and property taxes by your *federal* income tax rate. This shortcut works well because the small portion of your mortgage payment that is not deductible (because it is for the loan repayment) approximately offsets the overlooked state tax savings.

Item	*Estimated Monthly Expense*
Mortgage payment	$ _____
Property taxes	+ $ _____
Insurance	+ $ _____
Improvements, maintenance, and other	+ $ _____
Home-ownership expenses (pre-tax)	= $ _____
Tax savings	– $ _____
Home-ownership expenses (after-tax benefits)	= $ _____

SCHEDULES A&B
(Form 1040)

Department of the Treasury
Internal Revenue Service   (99)

Schedule A—Itemized Deductions

(Schedule B is on back)

▶ Attach to Form 1040. ▶ See Instructions for Schedules A and B (Form 1040).

OMB No. 1545-0074

19**95**

Attachment
Sequence No. **07**

Name(s) shown on Form 1040

Your social security number

Medical and Dental Expenses		**Caution:** *Do not include expenses reimbursed or paid by others.*		
	1	Medical and dental expenses (see page A-1)	1	
	2	Enter amount from Form 1040, line 32 . ⌊ **2** ⌋		
	3	Multiply line 2 above by 7.5% (.075)	3	
	4	Subtract line 3 from line 1. If line 3 is more than line 1, enter -0-		4
Taxes You Paid (See page A-1.)	5	State and local income taxes	5	
	6	Real estate taxes (see page A-2)	6	
	7	Personal property taxes	7	
	8	Other taxes. List type and amount ▶	8	
	9	Add lines 5 through 8		9
Interest You Paid (See page A-2.)	10	Home mortgage interest and points reported to you on Form 1098	10	
	11	Home mortgage interest not reported to you on Form 1098. If paid to the person from whom you bought the home, see page A-3 and show that person's name, identifying no., and address ▶	11	
Note: Personal interest is not deductible.	12	Points not reported to you on Form 1098. See page A-3 for special rules	12	
	13	Investment interest. If required, attach Form 4952. (See page A-3.)	13	
	14	Add lines 10 through 13		14
Gifts to Charity If you made a gift and got a benefit for it, see page A-3.	15	Gifts by cash or check. If you made any gift of $250 or more, see page A-3	15	
	16	Other than by cash or check. If any gift of $250 or more, see page A-3. If over $500, you **MUST** attach Form 8283	16	
	17	Carryover from prior year	17	
	18	Add lines 15 through 17		18
Casualty and Theft Losses	19	Casualty or theft loss(es). Attach Form 4684. (See page A-4.)		19
Job Expenses and Most Other Miscellaneous Deductions (See page A-5 for expenses to deduct here.)	20	Unreimbursed employee expenses—job travel, union dues, job education, etc. If required, you **MUST** attach Form 2106 or 2106-EZ. (See page A-5.) ▶	20	
	21	Tax preparation fees	21	
	22	Other expenses—investment, safe deposit box, etc. List type and amount ▶	22	
	23	Add lines 20 through 22	23	
	24	Enter amount from Form 1040, line 32 . ⌊ **24** ⌋		
	25	Multiply line 24 above by 2% (.02)	25	
	26	Subtract line 25 from line 23. If line 25 is more than line 23, enter -0-		26
Other Miscellaneous Deductions	27	Other—from list on page A-5. List type and amount ▶		27
Total Itemized Deductions	28	Is Form 1040, line 32, over $114,700 (over $57,350 if married filing separately)? **NO.** Your deduction is not limited. Add the amounts in the far right column for lines 4 through 27. Also, enter on Form 1040, line 34, the **larger** of this amount or your standard deduction. **YES.** Your deduction may be limited. See page A-5 for the amount to enter.	▶	28

For Paperwork Reduction Act Notice, see Form 1040 instructions.

Cat. No. 11330X

Schedule A (Form 1040) 1995

Figure 3-2:
Itemize mortgage interest and property tax deductions on Schedule A of your 1040.

You may also be interested in knowing — but more likely don't care — that the deductibility of the mortgage interest on up to 1 million dollars borrowed covers debt on both your *primary* residence and a second residence. (Buying and maintaining two homes is an expensive proposition and something few people can afford, so don't get any silly ideas!)

Congratulations! You've totaled what your dream home should cost you on a monthly basis after factoring in the tax benefits of homeownership. Don't forget to plug these expected home-ownership costs into your current monthly spending plans (see Chapter 2) to make sure that you can afford to spend this much on a home and still accomplish your financial goals.

Closing Costs

On the day when a home becomes yours officially (known as *closing day*), many people (in addition to the seller) will have their hands in your wallet. Myriad one-time closing costs can leave you poor and destitute or send you running to your parents or your in-laws for financial assistance.

We don't want you to be unable to close your home purchase or be forced to get down on your hands and knees and beg for money from your mother-in-law. (Not only is such groveling hard on your ego, but she will likely charge you 25-percent interest on the borrowed money and expect three grandchildren in the next five years to boot.) Advance preparation for the closing costs saves your sanity and your finances.

Here are some typical closing costs (listed from those which are usually largest to those which are small) and how much to budget for each (exact fees vary by property cost and location):

- ✔ **Loan origination fees (*points*) and other loan charges:** These fees and charges range from nothing to 3 percent of the amount borrowed. Lenders typically charge all sorts of fees for things such as appraising the property, pulling your credit report, preparing loan documents, and processing your application, as well as charging a loan-origination fee, which may be 1 or 2 percent of the loan amount. If you're strapped for cash, you can get a loan that has few or no fees; however, such loans have substantially higher interest rates over their lifetimes. As Chapter 10 explains, you may be able to cut a deal with the seller to pay these loan closing costs.

- ✔ **Escrow fees:** Escrow fees range from several hundred to over a thousand dollars, based on the purchase price of your home. These fees cover the cost of handling all the purchase-related documents and funds. We explain escrows in much more detail in Chapters 8 and 12.

✔ **Homeowners insurance:** This insurance typically costs from several hundred to a thousand dollars plus, depending on the value of your home and how much coverage you want. As we discuss earlier in this chapter, you can't get a mortgage unless you prove to the lender that you have adequate homeowners insurance coverage. Promising to get this coverage isn't enough; lenders insist that you pay the first year's premium on said insurance policy at the time of the closing.

✔ **Title insurance:** This insurance typically costs from several hundred to a thousand dollars, depending on your home's purchase price. Lenders require that you purchase title insurance when you buy your home to make sure that you have clear, marketable title to the property. *Title insurance* protects the lender against the remote possibility that the person selling you the home doesn't actually, legally own it. We discuss title insurance in detail in Chapter 11.

✔ **Property taxes:** These taxes typically cost from several hundred to a couple of thousand dollars and are based upon the home's purchase price and the date that escrow closes. At the close of escrow, you may have to reimburse the sellers for any property taxes that they paid in advance. For example, suppose that (before they sold their home to you) the sellers had already paid their property taxes through June 30th. If the sale closes on April 30, you owe the sellers two months' property taxes — the tax collector won't refund the property taxes they have already paid for May and June.

✔ **Legal fees:** These fees range anywhere from nothing to hundreds of dollars. In some eastern states, lawyers are routinely involved in real estate purchases. In most states, however, lawyers are not needed for home purchases as long as the real estate agents use standard, fill-in-the-blank contracts. Such contracts have the advance input and blessing of the legal eagles.

✔ **Inspections:** Inspection fees can run from $200 to $500. As we explain in Chapter 11, you should never, ever consider buying a home without inspecting it. Because you're likely not a home-inspection expert, you'll surely benefit from hiring someone who inspects property as a full-time job (can you imagine?!). Sometimes, you simply pay these costs directly; at other times, you pay these costs at the closing.

✔ **Private mortgage insurance (PMI):** If you need it, this insurance can cost you several hundred dollars. As we explain in the next section of this chapter, if you put less than 20 percent down on a home, many mortgage lenders require that you take out *private mortgage insurance*. This type of insurance protects the lender in the event that you default. At closing, you need to pay anywhere from a couple of months' premiums to more than a year's premium in advance. If you can, avoid this cost by making a 20-percent down payment.

✔ **Prepaid loan interest:** Lenders charge up to 30 days' interest on your loan to cover the interest that accrues from the date your loan is funded (usually one business day before the escrow closes) up to 30 days prior to your first regularly scheduled loan payment. How much interest you actually have to pay depends on the timing of your first loan payment. If you're smart, and we know that you are, you can work this timing out with the lender so you don't have to pay any advance loan interest.

If you want to avoid paying three useless days of interest charges, *do not schedule your escrow to close on a Monday.* If you do, the lender has to put your mortgage funds into escrow the preceding Friday. As a result, you're charged interest on your loan for Friday, Saturday, and Sunday even though you won't own the home until escrow closes on Monday. This little tip more than pays for this book all by itself. Don't you feel smart now?

✔ **Recording:** The fee to record the deed and mortgage usually runs about $50.

✔ **Overnight/courier fees:** These fees usually cost $50 or less. Remember the times when you sent something via the U.S. Postal Service to a destination that you could have driven to in less than a few hours, and it took them the better part of a week to get it there (or perhaps they lost it)? Well, lenders and other players in real estate deals know that these snafus can occur without warning; and because they don't want to derail your transaction or cost themselves money, they often send stuff the fastest way they can. And why not: It's your money they are spending on the express delivery fees!

✔ **Notary:** Notary fees run from $10 to $20 *per signature per buyer.* At the close of escrow (when you sign all sorts of important documents pledging your worldly possessions and firstborn child, should you renege on your mortgage), you also need to have your signature verified by a notary so everybody in the transaction knows that you are who you say you are.

As you can see, closing costs can mount up in a hurry. In a typical real estate deal, closing costs total 2 to 5 percent of the purchase price of the property. Thus, you shouldn't ignore them in figuring the amount of money you need to close the deal. Having enough to pay the down payment on your loan is just not sufficient.

If you're short of cash, you can take out a mortgage with fewer out-of-pocket fees and points (see Chapter 5) and try to negotiate with the property seller to pay other closing costs (see Chapter 10). Expect to pay a higher ongoing mortgage rate for low-up-front-fee loans. And, all other things being equal, expect to pay and borrow more to entice the seller to pay other closing costs. Also, don't blindly accept all the closing costs come closing time. In Chapter 12, we explain the importance of auditing your closing statement.

Accumulating the Down Payment

Jeremy went house hunting and soon fell in love with a home. Unfortunately, after he found his dream home, he soon discovered all the loan documentation requirements and the extra fees and penalties he would have to pay for having such a small down payment. Ultimately, he couldn't afford to buy the home that he desired because he hadn't saved enough. "If I had known, I would have started saving much sooner — I thought that saving for the future was something you did when you turned middle-aged," he told Eric.

We don't want you to be surprised when you finally set out to purchase a home. That's why now, in the comfort of your rental, commuter train, or bus (or anywhere else you may be reading this book), we'd like you to consider the following:

- ✔ How much money you should save for the down payment and closing costs for the purchase of your home
- ✔ Where your down-payment money is going to come from
- ✔ How you should invest this money while you're awaiting the purchase and closing

The 20-percent solution

Ideally, you should purchase a home and have enough accumulated for a down payment so that your down payment represents 20 percent of the purchase price of the property. Why 20 percent and not 10 or 15 or 25 or 30 percent? For the same reason that Goldilocks, at the residence of the three bears, liked the moderately warm bowl of porridge and disliked the bowls of porridge that were very hot and stone cold.

Twenty percent down is the magic number because it's a big enough cushion to protect lenders from default. If, for example, a buyer puts only 10 percent down, and then property values drop 5 percent, and the lender forecloses, then — *after* paying a real estate commission, transfer tax, and other expenses of sale — the lender will be in the hole. Lenders learned the hard way that buyers are far less likely to default on and walk away from a home on which they *pay* 20 percent down.

If, like most people, you plan to borrow money from a bank or other mortgage lender, be aware that almost all require you to obtain (and pay for) private mortgage insurance (PMI) if your down payment is less than 20 percent of the purchase price of the property. Think of the mortgage lender as Goldilocks — the person who needs to be satisfied. Although PMI typically adds several hundred dollars annually to the cost of your loan, it protects the lender financially if you default. If you buy an expensive home — into the hundreds-of-thousands-of-dollars price range — PMI can add $1,000 or more, annually, to your mortgage bill.

PMI is not a permanent cost. Your need for PMI vanishes when you can prove that you have at least 20 percent *equity* (home value minus loan balance outstanding) in the property. The 20 percent can come from loan paydown, appreciation, improvements, or any combination thereof. Note also that, to remove PMI, most mortgage lenders require that an appraisal be done — at your expense.

Note: If you have (or expect to have) the 20-percent down payment and enough money for the closing costs, skip the next section and go to the section on how to invest your down-payment money.

Ways to buy with less money down

"But I can't save a 20-percent down payment plus closing costs. What do you think I am, a professional athlete, movie star, or founder of a technology company that just went public on the stock exchange?"

Especially if you're just starting to save or are still paying off student loans or worse — digging out from consumer debt — saving 20 percent of a property's purchase price as a down payment plus closing costs can seem like a financial mountain.

Don't panic and don't give up. Here's a grab-bag filled with time-tested ways to overcome this seemingly gargantuan obstacle:

- ✔ **Boost your savings rate.** Say you want to accumulate $30,000 for your home purchase, and you're saving just $100 per month. At this rate, it will take you nearly two decades to reach your savings goal! However, if you can boost your savings rate by $300 per month, you should reach your goal in about five years.

  Being efficient with your spending is always a good financial habit, but efficient saving is a *necessity* for nearly all prospective homebuyers. Without benevolent, loaded relatives or other sources for a financial windfall, you're going to need to accumulate money the old-fashioned way that millions of other homebuyers have done in the past: by gradually saving it. Most people have fat in their budgets. Start by reading Chapter 2 for ways to assess your current spending and boost your savings.

- ✔ **Set your sights lower.** Twenty percent of a big number is a big number, so it stands to reason that 20 percent of a smaller number is a smaller number. If the down payment and closing costs needed to purchase a $150,000 home are stretching you, scale back to a $120,000 or $100,000 home, which should slash your required cash for the home purchase by about 20 to 33 percent.

Buying a home with "no money down"

More than a few books written by (and high-priced seminars led by) real estate salespeople/ gurus claim that not only can you buy property with no money down, but you can also make piles of money doing so. A generation ago, this way of thinking was popularized by Robert Allen in his book *Nothing Down*.

Allen says that the key to buying property with no money down is to find a seller who is a *don't wanter* — that is, someone who "will do anything to get rid of his property." Why would someone be that desperate? Well, perhaps the person is in financial trouble because of a job loss, an overextension of credit, or a major illness.

Perhaps, back when more people used to live in smaller, tight-knit communities where everyone supported one another, this type of *vulture capitalism* may not have flourished. But in these times, Allen says that a don't wanter can offer you the most favorable mortgage terms, such as a small down payment (or none at all) and a low interest rate.

How do you find such downtrodden souls who are just waiting for you to take advantage of them? According to Allen's estimates, 10 percent of the sellers in the real estate market are don't wanters. Simply call people who have property listed for sale in the newspaper or place ads yourself saying that you'll buy in a hurry.

In our experience, finding homes that can be bought with no money down is not easy to do. If you can find such a desperate seller, be aware that the property may have major flaws. If the property were a good one, logic dictates that the seller wouldn't have to sell under such lousy terms. If you have the patience to hunt around and sift through perhaps hundreds of properties to find a good one available with seller financing at no money down, be our guest. Just don't expect the task to be easy or all that lucrative. Better to look for good properties and low-down payment lender financing and to start saving a healthy down payment so that you can qualify for a better loan.

✔ **Check out low-money-down loan programs.** Many lenders offer a number of low-down-payment mortgage programs where you can put down as little as 10 percent, 5 percent, or even 3 percent of the purchase price of a property. In order to qualify for such programs, you generally must have excellent credit and purchase private mortgage insurance. In addition to the extra expense of PMI, expect to get worse loan terms — higher interest rates and more up-front fees — with such low-money-down loans. Check with local lenders and real estate agents in your area. Good agents make a point of knowing about this kind of program.

Unless you're champing at the bit to settle down and purchase a home, try to accumulate a larger down payment. However, if you're the type of person who has trouble saving and may never save a 20-percent down payment, buying with less money down may be your best option. Be sure to shop around for the best loan terms.

✔ **Get family help.** Your folks or grandparents may like, perhaps even love, to help you with the down payment and closing costs for your dream home. Why would they do that? Well, perhaps they had financial assistance from family when they bought a home, way back when. Another possibility is that they have more money accumulated for their future and retirement than they may need. If they have substantial assets, holding onto all these assets until their death could trigger unnecessary estate taxes. A final reason that they may be willing to lend you money is that they are bank-and-bond-type investors and are earning paltry returns.

If your parents or grandparents (or other family members, for that matter) broach the topic of gifting or lending you money for a home purchase, go ahead and discuss the matter. But in many situations, you (as the prospective homebuyer) may need to raise the issue first. Some parents just aren't comfortable bringing up the topic of money or may be worried that you'll take their offer in the wrong way.

✔ **Look into seller financing.** Some homesellers don't need all the cash immediately from the sale of their property. Such sellers may be willing to entertain the idea of offering you a loan, either partial or full. Although some sellers advertise that they are willing to help finance, others must be asked. From a lender's perspective, an 80-10-10 loan is as good as 20 percent down. An *80-10-10 loan* is one in which the buyer puts 10 percent down and the seller extends a 10 percent second mortgage — usually for at least five years, so buyers have time to build up equity or save enough and refinance into a new, larger, 80-percent conventional mortgage.

✔ **Get partners.** With many things in life, there is strength in numbers. You may be able to get more home for your money and may need to come up with less up-front cash if you find partners for a multi-unit real estate purchase. For example, you could find one or two other partners and go in together to purchase a duplex or triplex.

Getting involved in the real estate version of Siamese twins or triplets is not without risk, however. If you go into a partnership to buy a building, be sure to consider all the "what ifs." (What if one of you wants out after a year? What if one of you fails to pay the pro-rata share of expenses? What if one of you wants to remodel and the other doesn't? And so forth.) Have a lawyer prepare a partnership agreement that delineates how issues like these will be dealt with. Otherwise, you could face some major disagreements down the road, even if you go in together with friends or people you know well. We cover the pros and cons of partnerships in Chapter 7.

Where to invest the down payment

As with all informed investing decisions, which investment(s) you consider for money earmarked for your down payment should be determined by how soon you'll need the money back. The longer the time frame during which you can invest, the more growth-oriented and riskier (that is, more *volatile*) an investment you may consider. Conversely, when you have a short time frame — five years or less — during which you can invest, choosing volatile investments is dangerous.

Investments for five years or less

Most prospective homebuyers aren't in a position to take many risks with their down-payment money. The sooner you expect to buy, the less risk you should take. Unless you expect to buy in more than five years, you shouldn't even consider investing in growth investments, such as the stock market.

Although it may appear boring, the first (and likely best) place for accumulating your down-payment money is in a money market mutual fund. As with bank savings accounts, money market mutual funds do not put your principal at risk — the value of your original investment (*principal*) doesn't fluctuate. Rather, you simply earn interest on the money that you have invested. Money market funds invest in super-safe investments, such as in Treasury bills, bank certificates of deposit, and *commercial papers,* which are short-term IOUs issued by the most creditworthy corporations.

Money market funds are one of the three major types of mutual funds — the other two being those which focus on bonds (*bond funds*) and those which focus on stocks (*stock* or *equity funds*). Many people think of mutual funds as being risky investments (partly because they equate funds with stock market investing), but the truth is that, under Securities and Exchange Commission regulations, money market funds can invest only in safe securities, and money funds' investments must have an average maturity of less than 120 days. The short-term nature of these funds eliminates the risk of money market funds being sensitive to changes in interest rates in the way that bonds and bond funds are.

Although some bank savings accounts pay reasonable interest rates, nearly all pay the same amount or less in interest as the best money market funds. Why? Because banks aren't as efficient and low-cost as money markets. Who do you think is paying for the rent in all those bank branches, anyway?

If you really want to save through a bank, shop, shop, shop around. Smaller savings-and-loans and credit unions tend to offer more competitive yields than do the larger banks that spend gobs on advertising and have branches on nearly every corner. Remember, more overhead means lower yields for your money.

In addition to higher yields, the best money market funds offer check writing (so that you can easily access your money) and come in tax-free versions. If you're in a higher income tax bracket, a tax-free money market fund may allow you to earn a higher effective yield than a money fund which pays taxable interest. (Note: You only pay tax on money invested outside of tax-sheltered retirement accounts.) If you're in a high tax bracket, particularly the 31 percent or higher federal bracket (refer to Table 3-2), you should come out ahead by investing in tax-free money market funds. If you reside in a state with high income taxes, consider a state money market fund, which pays interest that's free of both federal and state tax.

The better money market funds also offer telephone exchange and redemption and automated, electronic exchange services with your bank account. Automatic investment comes in handy for accumulating your down payment for a home purchase. Once per month, for example, you can have money zapped from your bank account into your money market fund.

Because a particular type of money market fund (general, Treasury, or tax-free municipal) is basically investing in the same securities as its competitors, opt for a money market fund that keeps lean and mean expenses. A money fund's *operating expenses,* which are deducted before payment of dividends, are the major factor in determining a money fund's yield. As with the high overhead of bank branches, the higher a money fund's operating expenses, the lower its yield. Excellent money funds from the best mutual fund companies are yours for the asking for annual operating expenses of 0.5 percent or less. We recommend good ones in this section.

If you're not in a high federal-tax bracket (that is, you pay 28 percent or less in federal taxes) *and* you're not in a high state-tax bracket (that is, you pay less than 5 percent in state taxes), consider the following taxable money market funds for your home down-payment money:

Fidelity Cash Reserves and Fidelity Daily Income Trust ($2.5K and $5K to open)

Fidelity's Spartan Money Market (higher yields if you have $20K to invest)

Schwab Value Advantage Money Market ($25K to open)

T. Rowe Price Summit Cash Reserves ($25K to open)

USAA Mutual Money Market ($3K to open)

Vanguard's Money Market Reserves Prime Portfolio ($3K to open)

If you sleep better at night after lending your money to an organization with about $5 trillion in debt outstanding, you can invest in a money market fund that invests in U.S. Treasury money market funds, which have the backing of the U.S. federal government (for whatever that's worth). From a tax standpoint, because U.S. Treasuries are state-tax-free but federally taxable, U.S. Treasury money market funds are appropriate if you're not in a high-federal-tax bracket (less than or equal to 28 percent) but you *are* in a high state-tax bracket (5 percent or higher). If you choose to invest in a money market fund that invests in the U.S. Treasury, consider these:

Benham Capital Preservation & Government Agency funds ($1K to open)

Fidelity's Spartan U.S. Treasury Money Market ($20K to open)

USAA's Treasury Money Market ($3K to open)

Vanguard Money Market Reserves U.S. Treasury Portfolio ($3K to open)

Vanguard's Admiral U.S. Treasury Money Market Portfolio (higher yields if you have $50K to invest)

Municipal (also known as *muni*) money market funds invest in short-term debt issued by state and local governments. A municipal money market fund, which pays you federally tax-free dividends, invests in munis issued by state and local governments throughout the country. A state-specific municipal fund invests in state and local government-issued munis for one state, such as New York. So, if you live in New York and buy a New York municipal fund, the dividends on that fund are free of both federal and New York state taxes.

So how do you decide whether to buy a nationwide or state-specific municipal money market fund? Federal-tax-free-only money market funds are appropriate when you're in a high federal-tax bracket (31 percent and up) but *not* a high-state-tax bracket (less than 5 percent).

If you're in a high-state-tax bracket, your state may not have good (or any) state-tax-free money market funds available. You know that this is the case if we omit a fund for your state in the next section. If you live in any of those states, you're likely best off with one of the following national money market funds:

Fidelity Spartan Municipal Money Market ($25K to open)

USAA Tax-Exempt Money Market ($3K to open)

Vanguard Municipal Money Market ($3K to open)

The state-tax-free money market funds in the following list are appropriate when you're in a high federal-tax bracket (31 percent and up) *and* a high state-tax bracket (5 percent or higher). If none is listed for your state, or if you're only in a high federal-tax bracket, remember that you should use one of the nation-wide muni money markets in the preceding list. State- and federal-tax-free money market funds to examine include:

Benham California Tax-Free Money Market ($1K to open)

Fidelity Spartan California Muni Money Market ($25K to open)

Vanguard California Tax-Free Money Market ($3K to open)

Getting in touch with mutual fund companies

Most mutual fund companies don't have many (or any) local branch offices. Generally, this fact helps mutual fund companies keep their expenses low and pay you greater yields on their money market funds.

So how do you deal with an investment company without a location near you? Simple: You open and maintain your mutual fund account via the fund's toll-free 800 phone line and the mail. Some fund providers, such as Fidelity and Charles Schwab, also have a fair number of branch offices.

Here's how to reach, by phone, the major fund companies recommended in this section:

Benham 800-472-3389

Fidelity 800-544-8888

Schwab 800-526-8600

T. Rowe Price 800-638-5660

USAA 800-531-8000

Vanguard 800-662-7447

Fidelity Spartan Connecticut Muni Money Market ($25K to open)

Benham Florida Municipal Money Market ($1K to open)

Fidelity Spartan Florida Muni Money Market ($25K to open)

USAA Tax-Exempt Florida Money Market ($3K to open)

Fidelity Spartan Massachusetts Muni Money Market ($25K to open)

Fidelity Spartan New Jersey Muni Money Market ($25K to open)

Vanguard New Jersey Tax-Free Money Market ($3K to open)

Fidelity Spartan New York Muni Money Market ($25K to open)

USAA Tax-Exempt New York Money Market ($3K to open)

Vanguard Ohio Tax-Free Money Market ($3K to open)

Fidelity Spartan Pennsylvania Muni Money Market ($25K to open)

Vanguard Pennsylvania Tax-Free Money Market ($3K to open)

USAA Tax-Exempt Texas Money Market ($3K to open)

USAA Tax-Exempt Virginia Money Market ($3K to open)

Investments for more than five years

If you expect to hold onto your home down-payment money for more than five years, you can comfortably consider riskier investments, such as longer-term bonds as well as stocks. Eric covers these investments and many others in his books, *Investing For Dummies* and *Mutual Funds For Dummies*.

Short-term bonds and bond funds

You may be thinking, "Five years is an awfully long time to keep my money dozing away in a money market fund."

Well, yes and no. During some time periods, such as during 1996, investors who bought bonds maturing in five years got very little in the way of extra yield versus what they could get in a good money market fund. During other periods, such as the early 1990s, three-year to five-year bonds yielded a good deal more interest than money market funds yielded.

However, deciding to invest in bonds that mature in a few years is not quite as simple as selecting such short-term bonds that are higher-yielding than are money market funds. Here's why. Whenever you invest in bonds that won't mature soon, you are taking on risk. First is the risk that the bond issuer may fall into financial trouble between the time that you buy the bond and the time that it is due to mature. Second is the risk that interest rates in general could greatly increase. If the latter happens, caused more than likely by unexpected inflation, you may end up holding a bond that pays you less interest than the rate of inflation.

Most of the time, bonds that mature in a few years should produce a slightly higher rate of return for you than a money market or savings account. However, if you invest in such bonds, recognize that you may end up earning the same (or perhaps even less) than you would have earned had you stuck with a money market fund. Rising interest rates can deflate the value of an investment in bonds.

Only invest in bonds if you expect to hold them for at least three to five years. If you want to invest in individual bonds and you're not in a high-tax bracket, consider Treasury bonds, which don't require monitoring of credit risk — that is, unless the U.S. government slips into default! Also look at the yield on bank certificates of deposit. You may also consider some high-quality, short-term bond mutual funds which invest in — you guessed it — short-term bonds. A solid one is Vanguard's Short-Term Corporate Portfolio.

If you're in a high-tax bracket, a tax-free money market fund is hard to beat. Some federal-tax-free bond funds to peruse include Vanguard's Municipal Short-Term and Vanguard's Municipal Limited-Term portfolios. Good, double-tax-free, *short-term* bond funds just don't exist.

Chapter 4

Why Home Prices Rise and Fall

*E*ven if you're not an economics or business expert, don't let fear and intimidation deter you from understanding why home prices rise and fall. Consider for a moment what determines the price of a loaf of bread, a car, or any other consumer item you may purchase. Ultimately, you discover that supply and demand influence the price of everything.

Take the overlooked and underappreciated loaf of bread, for example. If bad weather causes a poor grain harvest, grains (a major ingredient in bread) experience price increases. A limited supply of grain now has to meet a normal demand, so higher grain prices drive up the price of bread. Higher prices usually dampen the demand for a product. If the cost of a loaf of bread increases from $1.50 (before the bad weather) to $3.00 per loaf (after the weather problems), all things being equal, people will begin to buy and eat fewer loaves of bread.

Of course, not everyone will eat less bread — real bread lovers, people with large inventories of peanut butter and jelly, and those who can simply afford the extra cost will keep right on buying. But those who are price-conscious and just as happy to eat something else will cut back on their bread purchases.

We're at risk here of making things sound too simple by saying that the price of something is determined by supply and demand. If you stop to think about it, a large number of factors influence supply and demand. Back to our bread example to illustrate this point. On the supply side, the following are but a few of the many factors that influence the supply of bread in the marketplace:

✔ Weather conditions for grain crops

✔ Government regulations that affect land usage, taxation, labor laws, and many other business issues

> ✔ The price of bread ingredients and the myriad factors that affect each of these ingredients
>
> ✔ Trends in the retailing industry and in stores that want to sell bread
>
> ✔ The price of other food items that compete with bread

Experts have written entire textbooks to explain all the factors that influence business and industry. We won't bore you with the details here because those books generally do a terrific job — at boring you, that is.

You may be thinking that we've gone off the deep end. What lunatic talks about the supply and demand of bread in relation to buying a home? Don't abandon us yet, because the supply of and demand for bread is related to the rise and fall of home prices, albeit in an indirect way. If you're contemplating the purchase of a home, you may be concerned about the future direction of home prices. After all, who wants to buy a home just before prices plunge? Conversely, who in their right minds wouldn't love to jump into the real estate market before prices head skyward? To understand what drives home prices, you must examine what drives the supply of and demand for homes.

As we discuss what causes home prices to rise and fall in this chapter, please keep the following in mind: When it comes to buying and owning a home, don't get too hung up on the current state of your local market. If you take the perspective that, after you buy a home, you're likely to own a home for many decades, worrying about timing your purchase is generally not worth the trouble. *Timing* — that is, buying when prices are at rock bottom and getting out when you think that home values are cresting — is extraordinarily difficult to do. We know people who started waiting for lower home prices a generation ago — they are still waiting!

Predicting what's going to happen with real estate prices in a particular neighborhood, town, region, or state over the next one, two, three, or more years is not easy. Ultimately, the demand for and prices of homes in an area are driven largely by the economic health and vitality of that area. With an increase in jobs, particularly ones that pay well, comes a greater demand for housing.

If you first buy a home when you're in your 20s, 30s, or even your 40s, you'll likely end up being a homeowner for several decades or more. Over such a lengthy time, the real estate markets in which you have your money invested will surely experience more than a few ups and downs. History shows that real estate prices experience more and bigger ups than downs over the long term, so don't fret about the cloudiness of your real estate crystal ball.

That said, you may be ambivalent about buying a home at particular times in your life. Perhaps you're not sure that you will stay put for more than three to five years. The shorter the time period you expect to hold onto your home, the more important it is to be careful about when you buy. Thus, part of your home-buying decision may hinge on whether current home prices in your area offer you a good value. Even if you expect to stay put for a while, understanding what causes home prices to rise and fall and knowing ways to maximize your chances of getting a good buy can also be worth your while. This chapter helps you grasp these points.

What Drives Real Estate Markets and Prices?

If you're going to buy a home, you're making a significant investment — perhaps the single biggest investment you've ever made. You can do a mountain of research to decide what, where, and when to buy.

In the rest of this chapter, we explain what to look for, from an investment standpoint, both in a community and in the property that you buy. Some of the information that we provide requires you to think like an investor. Of course, for many people, buying a home is different from buying a piece of investment real estate to rent out. After all, you're going to live in your home.

Note: We discuss different types of properties (single-family homes, condominiums, and the like) and their investment desirability in Chapter 7.

Jobs, glorious jobs

A home provides shelter from the elements and a place to store and warehouse your consumer possessions. Because houses cost money to buy and maintain — and you're likely not a descendant of the Rockefellers, the Gettys, or Bill Gates — you need an ongoing source of money in order to afford your home. Where does this money come from? A job.

Okay, you may call it your *career* or (even better) one of your *passions.* But to be honest, most people work to pay the bills. And a home and its accompanying expenses are one of the biggest sources of expenses that people have (hence, one of the reasons we end up working so many decades as adults)!

So it stands to reason that the demand for housing and the ability to pay for housing is deeply affected by the abundance and quality of jobs in a community or area. From an investment perspective, an ideal area where homes appreciate in value at a relatively high rate has the following characteristics:

✔ **Job growth:** So what if an area has hundreds of thousands or millions of jobs if the number of jobs is shrinking? The New York City metropolitan area had millions of jobs, yet experienced declining real estate prices in the late 1980s and early 1990s due to a deteriorating job base. Job *creation* is the lifeblood of a healthy local real estate market. Check out the unemployment situation and examine how the jobless rate has changed in recent years. Good signs are a declining unemployment rate and increasing job growth.

✔ **Job diversity:** No, we're not talking about political correctness here. If a community is reliant on a paper manufacturer and an underwear maker for half of all its jobs, you should be wary of buying a home there. If these two companies go in the tank, the real estate market will follow. This scenario actually played out in the early 1990s in smaller communities that were badly hurt when large defense manufacturers and military bases lost many employees due to defense cutbacks.

✔ **Job quality:** All jobs are not created equal. Which area do you think has faster appreciating real estate prices: an area with more high-paying jobs in growth industries (such as technology), or an area that's producing mostly low-pay, low-skill jobs (such as those jobs found at fast food joints)? As with food, entertainment, and sex, quality is just as important as (if not more important than) quantity. If most of the jobs in a community come from slow-growing or shrinking employment sectors (such as farms, small retailers, shoe and apparel manufacturers, and government), real estate prices are unlikely to rise quickly in the years ahead. On the other hand, areas with a preponderance of high-growth industries (such as technology) should have a greater chance of experiencing faster price appreciation.

For example, for many decades, people have fretted over high Northern California home prices. Besides being blessed with beautiful geography and weather, this region is far less reliant than other regions on government jobs (less than 10 percent of all jobs, versus more than 15 percent nationally) and the declining sectors of the retailing and manufacturing industries. Northern California's economy is more driven by the fast-growing service and technology sectors.

So how can you get your hands on data that gives you this type of perspective? The U.S. Bureau of Labor Statistics compiles employment and unemployment data for metropolitan areas and counties. A good local library or the Chamber of Commerce should have this data. A real estate agent may be able to help you track it down, as well.

Available housing

Although jobs create the demand for housing, the amount of housing available — both existing and new — is the supply side of the supply-and-demand equation. Even though jobs are being created, housing values may be stagnant if an overabundance of available housing exists. Conversely, a relatively low employment growth rate in an area with a housing shortage could trigger significant real estate price increases.

Start by examining how well the existing supply of housing is being utilized. Vacancy rates, which measure how much or little demand there is for existing rental units, are a useful indicator to investigate. The *vacancy rate* is calculated simply by dividing the number of empty (unrented) rental units by the total number of rental units available. So, for example, if 50 rental units are vacant in Happy Valley, Tennessee, and 1,000 total units are available, the vacancy rate is 5 percent (50 divided by 1,000).

A low vacancy rate (under 5 percent) is generally a good indicator of future real estate price appreciation. If the vacancy rate is low and declining, more competition for few available rental units exists (or will soon exist). This competition tends to drive up rental rates, which makes renting more expensive and less attractive.

On the other hand, high vacancy rates indicate an excess supply of rentals, which tends to depress rents as landlords scramble to find tenants. All things being equal, high (more than 7 to 10 percent) and increasing vacancy rates are generally a bad sign for real estate prices.

In addition to checking out vacancy rates, which tell you how well the existing housing supply is being used, smart real estate investors also look at what's happening with building permits. In order to build new housing, a permit is required. The trend in the number of building permits can tell you how fast or how slowly the supply of real estate properties may be changing in the future.

A significant increase in the number of permits being issued can be a red flag because it may signal a future glut of housing. Such increases often happen after a sustained rise in housing prices in an area. As prices reach a premium level, builders race to bring new housing to market to capitalize on the high prices.

Conversely, depressed prices or a high cost of building (caused, for example, by high interest rates, such as the rates in the late 1970s and early 1980s) can lead to little new housing being developed. Eventually, this trend should bode well for local real estate prices.

The supply of housing is also determined in part by the amount of land available to develop. Unless you think that houseboats or landfill sites are the waves of the future, you'll agree that land is needed to build housing. A limited supply of land generally bodes well for long-term real estate price appreciation in an area. Thus, real estate has appreciated very well over the decades (and is very expensive today) in areas such as Manhattan, San Francisco, Hawaii, Hong Kong, and Tokyo, which are surrounded by water. Conversely, home prices tend to rise slowly in areas with vast tracts of developable land, such as are found in parts of the Midwest and Texas.

Inventory of homes for sale and actual sales

Just as scads of developable land and a barrage of new buildings place a lid on potential real estate price increases in the future, so too do escalating numbers of properties listed for sale. The total number of *listings* (employment agreements between a property owner and a real estate agent) is typically tracked by local associations of real estate agents through their Multiple Listing Service (MLS). Properties that are "for sale by owner" (that is, without an agent) are not included in this total, but such unlisted sales tend to follow the same trends as property listed with agents. (The number of properties for sale by owner is not tracked by anyone or any organization we know.)

In a normal real estate market, the number of homes listed for sale stays at a relatively constant level as new homes come on the market and other homes sell. But as property prices start to reach high levels and some real estate owners/investors seek to cash in and invest elsewhere, the *listing inventory* (number of listings) can increase significantly. When home prices reach a high level relative to the cost of renting (see the next section), increasing numbers of potential buyers choose to rent. Buyer interest also may dry up because of an economic slowdown.

An increase in the number of newly listed houses for sale and a high inventory of unsold homes are two signs that soft home prices likely lie ahead. With many options to choose from, prospective buyers can be pickier about what they buy. This competition among many sellers for few buyers is what begins to exert downward pressure on prices and can create a *buyer's market* — a market that buyers, not sellers, like because prices are soft and mushy as supply far exceeds demand.

If an increasing number of new listings and a high inventory of unsold homes with few sales are red flags for a weakening or weak market, it stands to reason that a decreasing number of new listings and a low inventory of properties listed for sale bode well for home price increases. Few listings, multiple purchase offers, and rapid sales indicate that the demand from buyers exceeds the supply of property listed for sale — a *seller's market.*

If the local economy is strong and housing is not expensive compared to rental rates, more renters elect to (and can afford to) purchase, thus increasing sales activity. If you're a seller, you're in heaven. As a buyer, you can be frustrated by dealing with constant price increases, losing homes in multiple-offer situations, or being beaten by other bidders in the race to a new listing.

Interest rates and home prices

It stands to reason that if the biggest expense of owning a home is the monthly mortgage payment, then the level of interest rates on mortgages should have a big impact on home prices. As interest rates drop, so can payments on mortgages of a given size.

Consider a $100,000, 30-year, fixed-rate mortgage. If the interest rate is 6 percent, the monthly mortgage payment is $600. At an interest rate of 10 percent, the mortgage payment balloons to $878.

It certainly is true that low interest rates enable more renters to become homeowners. So you might think that declining interest rates would cause home prices to rise and, conversely, increasing interest rates would lead to falling home prices. That this isn't the way that the world operates is proven by the fact that many parts of the U.S., in the late 1980s and early 1990s,

experienced falling home prices at the same time that interest rates were plummeting. In addition, when interest rates were higher in the mid-1980s, home prices skyrocketed in major portions of the Northeast and West Coast.

Clearly, other factors do influence home prices, especially the health of the local and national economies and consumer confidence. And, although low interest rates make housing more affordable, low rates also make building more housing at less cost possible. A larger supply of housing tends to dampen housing price increases.

What's the lesson of this story? Don't try to time your housing purchase based upon what is happening, or what you expect to happen, with interest rates. The future change in your home's value could very well disappoint you.

The rental market

Rental rates provide a useful indicator as to the demand for housing. When the demand for rental housing falls behind the supply of rental housing and the local economy continues to grow, rents generally increase. This situation is a plus for future home price increases. As the cost of renting increases, purchasing a home looks all the more attractive to renters who are on the fence and are considering buying.

The trend in rents and the absolute level of rents are not going to tell you all that you need to know. Suppose you know that a two-bedroom, one-bath, 1100-square-foot home in a decent neighborhood in your town is renting for $900 per month. So what? What you also need to know is how this rental cost compares to the cost of purchasing and owning the same home.

Compare the cost of renting a given home with the cost of owning it. Such a comparison is effectively what current renters do when they weigh the costs of buying a home and leaving their landlord behind. Comparing the cost of owning a home to the cost of renting that same property serves as a reality check on home prices.

In order to make a fair comparison between renting and owning, you must compare the monthly cost of renting to the monthly cost of owning. If you compare the cost of renting a home for $1,200 per month to the cost of buying that same home for $250,000, you're comparing apples with oranges. That $250,000 is the total purchase of the home, not your monthly cost of owning it.

And when you calculate home-ownership costs, you must also factor in tax benefits. Your biggest home-ownership expenses — mortgage interest and property taxes — are tax deductible (see Chapter 3).

The following real-life example illustrates how to compare monthly rental and ownership costs. In the mid-1980s, three-bedroom homes on modest lots in popular communities on the San Francisco peninsula were selling for about $250,000. You could rent these same homes for about $1,200 per month. The cost of owning such a home (assuming a 20-percent down payment) amounted to approximately $1,300 per month, factoring in the mortgage interest and property tax write-offs.

Thus, at that time, you could have bought a home in this beautiful, economically robust and diverse area and have had monthly ownership costs about equal to the cost of renting the very same home. Not bad. And don't forget that, over time, the costs of renting would be fully exposed to inflation; whereas, if you had bought your home with a fixed-rate mortgage, the costs of owning would largely be constant (see Chapter 3). Buying a home at this time was a good deal, given these facts.

Now fast-forward to 1990. In the short span of just a few years, home prices in that area skyrocketed. Those $250,000 homes were selling for $400,000. Rents had risen slowly. Thus, the cost of owning such a home amounted to more than $2,400 per month, although the cost of renting remained at $1,300. Thus, in 1990, homebuyers in this area were paying a substantial premium to own (versus renting) a comparable home.

The booming real estate market of the times was also apparent in the increasing numbers of people who formally changed careers or took on a second career as a "real estate investor." Many of these people were buying fixer-uppers (see Chapter 7) and selling them within a year or two after fixing them up. While property values were rising fast, such investors profited. What most of them didn't realize was that they were profiting from the overall market rise and not their fix-up work. Also worth noting is that the number of real estate agents also reaches a high level in that overheated real estate market.

Another indicator that prices were reaching a speculative frenzy was that escalating home prices were making front-page news. In April 1989, *The San Jose Mercury News* ran an article on the front page of the first section: "Why Housing Prices Will Keep Going Up." A real estate agent was quoted in this article as advising her clients at that time to, ". . . act quickly if they see a house they like. If they do not, they will almost surely have to settle for something else." The real estate agent added that she counseled her clients, "If you see something you like, you can't go home and think about it for a week." (Imagine being advised *not* to think about what's likely to be the largest financial transaction of your life!)

Signs abounded that the home-buying market was overheated, but the biggest factor to focus on was that the monthly ownership costs greatly exceeded the monthly rental costs for property. *Guess what happened next?* Well, fewer renters could afford to buy because buying had gotten so expensive. And fewer renters wanted to buy because, by comparison, renting was such a good deal. So the demand for home purchases dropped, which had a depressing effect on home prices. The demand for rentals increased, which ultimately had a buoyant effect on rents. The laws of supply and demand correct a system out of balance. When the economy started to slow, as it eventually does, prospective buyers got very cold feet about spending so much on a home and carrying such a large mortgage.

Now fast-forward five more years. Lo and behold, the market did correct the imbalance. Those $400,000 homes dropped in value to about $350,000 by 1995. Meanwhile, rents increased as the rental market tightened up. If you crunch the numbers, you find that the cost of buying this home in 1995 was about $1,790 per month (versus $1,600 per month in rent). In other words, you could own for just a slightly higher cost than the cost of renting — just like things were back in the mid-1980s! (Over this same time period, interest rates dropped, also helping to reduce ownership costs.)

Comparing the cost of owning a home to the cost of renting that same home is a simple yet powerful indicator of whether real estate in an area is overpriced, underpriced, or priced just right. Buying is generally safer (and a good value) when it costs about the same as renting. However, in some particularly desirable and in-demand communities, homeownership almost always costs more than renting. What's a reasonable premium? There's no simple answer, but if the monthly cost of owning is 20 to 30 percent more than the monthly cost of renting, be cautious. Be especially cautious about buying in such a pricey market if you're expecting to move and sell the property within seven years or less.

After you purchase a home, you'll probably own it for decades to come. So don't worry about timing your first home purchase. Trying to time your purchase has more importance if you may be moving in fewer than five years. In that case, be careful to avoid buying in an overheated market. The level of real estate prices compared to rents, the state of the job market, and the number of home listings for sale are useful indicators of the health of the housing market.

How to Get a Good Buy in Any Market

Well, what if you have to (or want to) buy in a seller's market? Or you're simply frightened that you're going to overpay in any market because you're a home-buying novice. No one, of course, likes to be taken. And most folks like to feel or believe that they are getting a bargain.

Many times, when you purchase products and services through businesses (especially through retailers), the sellers like to tell you how much of a discount or markdown they're offering you:

> 40 PERCENT OFF!
>
> GOING-OUT-OF-BUSINESS SALE — EVERYTHING MUST GO!
>
> SAVE UP TO $2.01 PER POUND!
>
> SPRING CLEARANCE SALE!

Some home sellers and (more often) their agents, like to use the same type of advertising. The following examples are from actual home-for-sale ads:

> HUGE PRICE REDUCTION!
>
> PRICE SLASHED $20,000!
>
> PRICE REDUCTION — OWNER MUST SELL!
>
> REDUCED!

 Whenever you see these types of ads, rather than thinking, "Gee, that might be a good deal," you should instead be thinking, "That home must have been overpriced before."

Now we're not trying to tell you that you can't get a *deal* (in other words, buy a home at less than its fair market value). But doing so isn't easy, and finding just the right situation takes a great deal of work. For most people, not overpaying — in other words, paying *fair market value* (which is not necessarily the asking price) — is a good objective. See Chapter 9 to find out more about determining home values.

But we know that some of you are overachievers. And why not? It's your hard-earned money at stake. Read through our suggestions for finding a good buy even if you are willing to pay fair market value. These ideas can help prevent you from overpaying.

Real estate get-rich-quick schemes

Scores of books have been written (and high-priced seminars conducted) claiming to have the real estate investing approach that can "beat the system." Often, these promoters claim that you can become a multi-millionaire through buying *distressed* property — property with financial, legal, or physical problems. One suggested strategy is to buy property on which a seller has defaulted or is about to default. Or how about buying a property in someone's estate through probate court? Maybe you'd like to try your hand at investing in a property that has been condemned or has toxic-waste contamination!

Getting a "good buy" and purchasing a problem property at a discount larger than the cost of fixing the property *is* possible. But these opportunities are hard to find, and sellers of such properties are often unwilling to sell at a large enough discount to leave you sufficient profit. If you don't know how to thoroughly and correctly evaluate the problems of property, you could end up overpaying. And then you'd have the reward of doing all the fix-up work on a dog of a property!

In some cases, the strategies that these real estate gurus advocate involve taking advantage of people's lack of knowledge. For example, some people don't know that they can protect the equity in their home through filing personal bankruptcy. If you can find such sellers in a dire financial straits, you may be able to get bargain buys on their homes.

Other methods of getting a good buy take a great deal of time and digging. Some involve cold-calling property owners to see whether they are interested in selling. If you phone thousands of people, you may eventually find a good candidate this way. However, when you factor in the value of your time, these deals usually don't appear attractive after all.

Seek hidden opportunities to add value

The easiest problems to correct are cosmetic. Some sellers and their agents are lazy and don't even bother to clean a property. Painting, tearing up dingy carpeting, refinishing hardwood floors, replacing outdated cabinets and appliances, and installing new landscaping need not be difficult projects. And such changes can make some properties look stunningly better.

A somewhat more complicated way to add value is to identify properties not being fully used or developed according to the zoning of the property. Sometimes, you can make more productive use of a property. For example, you may be able to convert a duplex into two separate condominiums. Some single-family residences may incorporate a rental unit if local zoning allows. A good real estate agent, a contractor, and the local planning office in the town or city in which you're looking at property should be able to help you identify properties whose use can be changed.

Identifying, evaluating, buying, and fixing up a property takes valuable time and energy. If you have a talent for finding hidden opportunities and are willing to invest the time required to coordinate the fix-up work, by all means try your hand and money at it! Just be sure to be realistic when you assess how much money you may need to spend to improve the property and how much value your improvements can really add. Also, be sure to hire a competent property inspector (see Chapter 11).

Buy when others are scared to buy

When the economy hits the skids, unemployment rises, and the mood is somber and gloomy, the number of home purchases usually plunges. Prices tend to fall as well. This situation can signal a great time to step up and buy. Buy when homes are "on sale" and when you don't have to compete with many other buyers. Buy when you can have your pick of a larger inventory of homes for sale.

Few people feel comfortable buying an investment that has gone down in value, especially when things look bleak. (For some perverse psychological reason, though, more of us love shopping for bargains in retail stores.) Here are several signs that a soft real estate market is beginning to firm up:

- ✔ The monthly cost of owning a home approximates the monthly cost of renting a similar property. One of the beauties of a major real estate price decline is that it can bring home-ownership costs back in line with rent costs.

- ✔ The inventory of homes listed for sale starts to fall from its peak as home sales pick up.

- ✔ The rental market tightens (as evidenced by increasing rents and a low vacancy rate). Another good sign is that little new housing is being built.

- ✔ The job market improves. Remember that jobs fuel the demand for housing. Home prices tend to rebound when employment increases. Watch for a decrease in the unemployment rate in your region.

Despite lower home prices, an improving economy, and tightening rental and homes-for-sale inventories, prospective homebuyers generally show far less interest in buying a home when things still look bleak. It takes courage to buy during those times when newspaper headlines and the television news reports trumpet the latest round of layoffs. Keep a level head and take advantage of buying opportunities when they occur. Years down the road, you may be glad that you did.

Find a motivated seller

When you take your time and peruse enough properties, you eventually cross paths with a property owner who really needs or wants to sell. The owner may need to relocate to another part of the country for a job, or perhaps the owner is trading up to a larger home and needs the cash from the sale of the current one in order to buy the new home. Sometimes, a property owner simply can't afford to own and maintain a home any longer due to personal financial troubles.

Whatever the reason, buying a home at or below its fair market value is far easier if the seller is what we call *motivated.* How do you find a motivated seller? Simple: You ask questions! The number of prospective buyers who are too shy to (or don't think to) ask why a seller is selling is amazing. Many sellers will be honest, and more than a few real estate agents (especially those who love to talk) have loose lips and share plenty of details. But you gotta ask!

Buy during slow periods

Most local real estate markets go through predictable busy and slow periods like clockwork. Just as it makes good sense to buy when the overall real estate market in an area is depressed, it also can be beneficial to buy during those typical slow periods.

For example, far fewer prospective buyers tend to be looking for homes during the holiday season in the dead of winter. In most markets, the period from Thanksgiving through January or February tends to be quite slow. The colder the region in which you live, the later into the new year this slow period lasts. In the blustery and snowy northernmost regions of the United States, the real estate market doesn't really start to pick up until April. In sunny-and-warm-year-round locales, such as Florida and Southern California, home sales start to pick up as early as February.

Another typically slow period is in the summer months of July and August. Many people take vacations then, and those families who wanted to buy in time for the next school year have likely already bought. The oppressive heat in the southern regions also keeps people indoors and near their air conditioners and iced tea.

The advantage of looking during the slow periods is that you have far less competition from other potential buyers. If you can find a motivated seller, you may really be able to negotiate a great deal without the intrusion of other potential buyers.

We're not saying, however, to look only during slow periods of the year and to expect getting a good buy during these times to be easy. You must be realistic. In most markets, most of the time, fewer properties are for sale during the slow periods. Smart sellers get their properties sold during the more active periods in the spring and fall. Also, be aware that a good portion of those properties on the market during slow periods may be the unwanted leftovers.

Become a great negotiator

Getting a good buy can be as simple as being a good negotiator. Good negotiation skills may enable you to buy a property at less than fair market value, especially if you find a seller who needs to sell soon.

Your negotiating position is also better if you are in a situation where you don't *have* to buy. The more patient you are and the more willing you are to walk away if you don't get a good deal, the better able you will be to negotiate a good buy. Having a backup property in mind (or remembering that many other properties are out there for you to buy) also helps. See Chapter 10 to discover how to be a world-class negotiator.

Buy in a good neighborhood

If you buy a home in a desirable area, you should have a better chance at making a good investment. We explain how to find out whether a neighborhood is good in Chapter 7.

If you buy good real estate and hold it for the long term, you should earn a decent return on your investment. Over the long haul, having bought a property at a discount becomes an insignificant issue. You'll make money from owning a home (and perhaps other real estate investments) as the overall real estate market appreciates.

Part II
Financing 101

The 5th Wave   By Rich Tennant

"I'm well aware that we ask for a lot from our home mortgage applicants, Mr. Harvey. However, sarcasm is rarely required."

In this part . . .

For some people, just the word *mortgage* can bring on a stomach ache. Don't be intimidated. Read these chapters to understand the different types of mortgages, to see how to cut through all the mortgage-related jargon, and to find out how to select the type of mortgage that best meets your needs. In addition to explaining how to get the best deal that you can on a mortgage, we also guide you through the maze of paperwork you face when applying for your mortgage loan.

Chapter 5
Selecting a Mortgage

. . . .

In This Chapter

▶ The difference between fixed-rate and adjustable-rate mortgages

▶ Hybrid loans, balloon loans, and negative amortization (Oh my!)

▶ Choosing the loan that's perfect for you

▶ A look at points, caps, and other mortgage mumbo-jumbo

▶ Finding a lender (or finding someone to find a lender for you)

. . . .

"A bank is a place that will lend you money if you can prove that you don't need it."

–Bob Hope

If you were Oprah Winfrey or Bill Gates, you could skip Chapters 5 and 6, which explain everything that you need to know about mortgages. If you have enough money to pay cash for your home, you can happily thumb your nose at bankers and other mortgage lenders. If you can afford to pay cash for your home, who needs them?!

As for the rest us, we need to take out a mortgage to buy a home for the simple reason that doing so is the only way we can afford a home that meets our needs. This chapter helps all non-wealthy folk to comprehend mortgages and then choose one. (If you *are* wealthy and have a great deal of money to put into a property, this part of the book can also help you to decide how much of your loot to put into your home purchase.)

Start with the basics. What is a mortgage? A *mortgage* is nothing more than a loan that you obtain to close the gap between the cash you have for a down payment and the purchase price of the home that you're buying. Homes in your area may cost $70,000, $170,000, or $370,000. No matter — most people don't have that kind of spare cash in their piggy banks.

Mortgages typically require monthly payments to repay your debt. The mortgage payments are comprised of *interest,* which is what the lender charges for use of the money you borrowed, and *principal,* which is repayment of the original amount borrowed.

Learning how to select a mortgage to meet your needs ensures that you'll be a happy homeowner for years to come. You also need to understand how to get a good deal when shopping around for a mortgage because your mortgage is typically the biggest monthly expense of homeownership (and perhaps of your entire household budget). Paying more for interest on your mortgage than you pay for your humble abode itself is not unusual.

Suppose that you borrow $144,000 (and contribute $36,000 from your savings as the down payment) for the purchase of your $180,000 dream palace. If you borrow that $144,000 with a 30-year, fixed-rate mortgage at 7 percent, you end up paying a whopping $200,892 in interest charges alone over the life of your loan. That $200,892 is not only a great deal of interest — it's also more than the purchase price of the home or the loan amount you originally borrowed!

So that you don't spend any more than you need to on your mortgage, and so that you get the mortgage that best meets your needs, the time has come to get on with the task of understanding the mortgage options out there.

Fixed or Adjustable? That Is the Interest (ing) Question

You may remember the skit from *Saturday Night Live* where Dan Aykroyd and John Belushi worked in a restaurant that served only cheeseburgers, chips, and Pepsi. Customers who tried to order a hamburger, fries, and Coke were out of luck. No hamburgers, just cheeseburgers; no fries, just chips; and no Coke, just Pepsi. At that restaurant, your choices were already made. If only you were so lucky with mortgages.

Like some other financial and investment products, tons of different mortgage options are available for your choosing. The variations can be significant or trivial, expensive or less-costly.

You will note throughout this chapter that two fundamentally different types of mortgages exist. Mortgages differ in terms of how their interest rate is determined. The two types of mortgages are fixed-rate mortgages and adjustable-rate mortgages.

Distinguishing fixed from adjustable mortgages

Before adjustable-rate mortgages came into being, only fixed-rate mortgages existed. Usually issued for 15- or 30-year periods, *fixed-rate mortgages* (as the name suggests) have interest rates that are *fixed* (unchanging) during the entire life of the loan.

With a fixed-rate mortgage, the interest rate stays the same and your monthly mortgage payment amount does not change. No surprises, no uncertainty, and no anxiety for you over interest-rate changes and changes in your monthly payment. Your mortgage interest rate and monthly payment remain locked for the life of the loan. If you like the predictability of your favorite television show airing at the same time daily, you'll probably like fixed-rate mortgages.

On the other hand, *adjustable-rate mortgages* (ARMs for short) have an interest rate that varies (or *adjusts*). The interest rate on an ARM typically adjusts every six to twelve months, but it may change as frequently as every month.

As we discuss later in this chapter, the interest rate on an ARM is primarily determined by what's happening overall to interest rates. If interest rates are generally on the rise, odds are that your ARM will experience increasing rates, thus increasing the size of your mortgage payment. Conversely, when interest rates fall, ARM interest rates and payments generally fall.

If you like change — you enjoy trying different foods and getting up at a different time each day — you may think that adjustable-rate mortgages sound good. Change is what makes life interesting, you say. Please read on, because, even if you believe that variety is the spice of life, you may not like the financial variety and spice of adjustables!

Looking at hybrid loans

If only the world were so simple that only pure fixed-rate and pure adjustable-rate loans were available. But one of the rewards of living in a capitalistic society is that you often have no shortage of choices. Enter *hybrid loans* (or what lenders sometimes call *intermediate ARMs*). Such loans start out like a fixed-rate loan — the initial rate may be fixed for three, five, seven, or even ten years — and then the loan converts into an ARM, usually adjusting every six to twelve months thereafter.

In case you care (and you may not), loans called *7/23s* (which are fixed for the first seven years and then have a one-time adjustment and remain at a fixed rate for the remaining length of the loan term) are also available. We discuss the pros and cons of these loans in the next section.

Making the fixed-rate/adjustable-rate decision

So how do you choose whether to take a fixed-rate or an adjustable-rate loan? Is it as simple as a personality test?

As with many things in life that give you choices, tradeoffs and pros-and-cons apply to each option. In this section, we talk you through the pros-and-cons of your mortgage options; but as we do, please keep one very important fact in

Balloon loans

One type of mortgage, known as a *balloon loan,* appears at first blush to be somewhat like a hybrid loan. The interest rate is fixed, for example, to five, seven, or ten years. However, and this is a big *however,* at the end of this time period, the entire loan balance becomes due. In other words, you must pay off the *entire* loan.

Borrowers are attracted to balloon loans for the same reason that they are attracted to hybrid or ARM loans — because balloon loans start at a lower interest rate than do fixed-rate mortgages. Buyers are sometimes seduced into such loans during high-interest-rate periods or when they can't qualify for or afford the payments of a traditional mortgage.

We don't like balloon loans because they can blow up in your face. You may become trapped without a mortgage if you are unable to *refinance* (obtain a new mortgage to replace the old loan) when the balloon comes due. You may have problems refinancing if, for example, you lose your job, your income drops, the value of your property declines and the appraisal comes in too low to qualify you for a new loan, or interest rates increase and you can't qualify for a new loan at those higher rates.

In the real estate trade, balloon loans are also called *bullet loans.* Why? If the loan comes due during a period of high mortgage rates, industry people say that it's like getting a bullet in the heart.

Remember that refinancing a mortgage is *never* a sure thing. Taking a balloon loan may be a financially hazardous short-term solution to your long-term financing needs.

The one circumstance under which we say that it's okay to *consider* a balloon loan is if you absolutely must have a particular property and the balloon loan is your one and only mortgage option. If that's the case, you should also be as certain as you can be that you'll be able to refinance when the balloon comes due. If you have family members that could step in to help with the refinancing, either by cosigning or by loaning you the money themselves, that's a big back-up plus. Oh, and if you *must* take out a balloon loan, get as long a term as possible, ideally for no less than seven years (and preferably for ten years).

mind: In the final analysis, which mortgage is best for you very much hinges upon your personal and financial situation. *You* are the one who is best-positioned to make the call as to whether a fixed or an adjustable loan better matches your situation and desires.

Fixed-rate mortgages

It stands to reason that, because the interest rate does not vary with a fixed-rate mortgage, the advantage of a fixed-rate mortgage is that you always know what your monthly payment is going to be. Thus, budgeting and planning the rest of your personal finances is easier.

That's the good news. The bad news is that you will pay a premium, in the form of a higher interest rate, to get a lender to commit to lending you money over many years at a fixed rate. The longer the mortgage lender agrees to accept a fixed interest rate, the more risk that lender is taking. A lender who agrees to

loan you money, for example, over 30 years at 8 percent will be hurtin' if interest rates skyrocket (as they did in the early 1980s) to the 15+ percent level. (With the rise of interest rates and inflation at that time, mortgage lenders were paying depositors interest rates that were almost double the levels of the interest that they were charging for mortgages that had commenced a decade before. Not a very profitable way to run a bank!)

In addition to paying a premium interest rate when you take the loan out, another potential drawback to fixed-rate loans is that, if interest rates fall significantly after you have your mortgage, you face the risk of being stranded with your costly mortgage. That could happen if (due to a deterioration in your financial situation or a decline in the value of your property) you don't qualify to *refinance* (get a new loan to replace the old). Even if you do qualify to refinance, doing so takes time and usually costs money for a new appraisal, loan fees, and title insurance.

Here are a couple of other possible minor drawbacks to be aware of with some fixed-rate mortgages:

- ✔ If you sell your house before paying off your fixed-rate mortgage, your buyers probably won't be able to assume that mortgage.

- ✔ Fixed-rate mortgages sometimes have prepayment penalties (explained in the nearby sidebar). The ability to pass your loan on to the next buyer (in real estate talk, the next buyer *assumes* your loan) can be useful if you're forced to sell during a rare period of ultra-high interest rates, such as occurred in the early 1980s. Selling during such a time could reduce the pool of potential buyers for your home if, in order to avoid a prepayment penalty, you don't allow an otherwise qualified buyer who is having trouble obtaining an affordable loan to assume your mortgage.

Adjustable-rate mortgages

Fixed-rate mortgages aren't your only option. Mortgage lenders were intelligent enough to realize that they couldn't foresee interest rates, and thus were born adjustable-rate mortgages (*adjustables* for short).

Although some adjustables are more volatile than others, all are similar in that they *fluctuate* (or float) with the market level of interest rates. If the interest rate fluctuates, then so does your monthly payment. And therein lies the risk: Because a mortgage payment is likely to be a big monthly expense for you, an adjustable-rate mortgage that is adjusting upwards may wreak havoc with your budget.

Given all the trials, tribulations, and challenges of life as we know it, you may rightfully ask, "Why would anyone choose to accept an adjustable-rate mortgage?" Well, people who are stretching themselves — such as some first-time buyers or those *trading up* to a more expensive home — may financially force themselves into accepting adjustable-rate mortgages. Because an ARM starts out at a lower interest rate, such a mortgage enables you to qualify to borrow

Avoid loans with prepayment penalties

Some mortgages come with a provision that penalizes you for paying off the loan balance faster. Such penalties can amount to as much as several percentage points of the amount of the mortgage balance that is paid off early.

Some lenders won't enforce their loan's prepayment penalties when you pay off a mortgage early because you sold the property or because you want to refinance the loan to take advantage of lower interest rates as long as they get to make the new mortgage. Even so, your hands are tied financially unless you go through the same lender.

Many states place limits on the duration and amount of prepayment penalty lenders may charge for mortgages made on owner-occupied residential property. The only way to know whether a loan has a prepayment penalty is to ask and to carefully review the federal truth-in-lending disclosure and the promissory note the mortgage lender provides you with. We think that you should avoid such loans. (Many so-called *no points* loans have prepayment penalties.)

more. As we discuss in Chapter 2, just because you can *qualify* to borrow more doesn't mean that you can *afford* to borrow that much, given your other financial goals and needs.

Other homebuyers who can qualify for both an adjustable-rate and fixed-rate mortgage of the same size have a choice, and some choose the fluctuating adjustable. Why? Because they may very well save themselves money, in the form of smaller total interest charges, with an adjustable-rate loan instead of a fixed-rate loan.

Because you accept the risk of a possible increase in interest rates, mortgage lenders cut you a little slack. The initial interest rate (also sometimes referred to as the *teaser rate*) on an adjustable should be less than the initial interest rate on a comparable fixed-rate loan. In fact, an ARM's interest rate for the first year or two of the loan is generally lower than a fixed-rate mortgage.

Another advantage of an ARM is that, if you purchase your home during a time of high interest rates, you can start paying your mortgage with the artificially depressed initial interest rate. If interest rates then decline, you can capture the benefits of lower rates without refinancing.

Another situation when adjustable-rate loans have an advantage over their fixed-rate brethren is when interest rates decline and you don't qualify to refinance your mortgage to reap the advantage of lower rates. The good news for homeowners who are unable to refinance and who have an ARM is that they probably already capture many of the benefits of the lower rates. With a fixed-rate loan, you must refinance in order to realize the benefits of a decline in interest rates.

TIP

When to consider hybrid loans

If you want more stability in your monthly payments than comes with a regular adjustable, and you expect to keep your loan for no more than from five to ten years, a *hybrid* (or intermediate ARM) loan, which is explained earlier in this chapter, may be the best loan for you.

The longer the initial rate stays locked in, the higher it will be, but the initial rate of a hybrid ARM is almost always lower than the interest rate on a 30-year, fixed-rate mortgage. However, because the initial rate of hybrid loans is locked-in for a longer period of time than the six-month or one-year term of regular ARMs, hybrid ARMs have higher initial interest rates than regular ARM loans.

During periods, such as in 1995 and 1996, when little difference existed between short-term and long-term interest rates, the interest-rate savings in the early years with a hybrid or regular adjustable (versus a fixed-rate loan) were minimal (less than 1 percent). In fact, during certain times, the initial interest rate on a seven- or ten-year hybrid was exactly the same as on a 30-year, fixed-rate loan. During such periods, fixed-rate loans offer the best overall value.

To evaluate hybrids, weigh the likelihood that you'll move before the initial loan interest rate expires. For example, with a seven-year hybrid, if you're saving, say, 0.5 percent per year versus the 30-year, fixed-rate mortgage, but you're quite sure that you will move within seven years, the hybrid will probably save you money. On the other hand, if you think that there's a reasonable chance that you'll stay put for more than seven years, and you don't want to face the risk of rising payments after seven years, you should opt for a 30-year, fixed-rate mortgage instead.

The downside to an adjustable-rate loan is that, if interest rates in general rise, your loan's interest and monthly payment will likely rise, too. During most time periods, if rates rise more than 1 or 2 percent and stay elevated, the adjustable-rate loan is likely to cost you more than a fixed-rate loan.

Before you make the final decision between a fixed-rate mortgage versus an adjustable-rate mortgage, read the following two sections.

What would rising interest rates do to your finances?

Far too many homebuyers, especially first-timers, take out an adjustable-rate mortgage because doing so allows them to stretch and borrow more and buy a more expensive home. Although some of this overborrowing is caused by the modern-day American spendthrift "I gotta have it today" attitude, overborrowing is also encouraged by some real estate and mortgage salespeople. After all, these salespeople's income, in the form of a commission, is a function of the cost of the home that you buy and the size of the mortgage that you take on.

Short-term versus long-term interest rates

When choosing between an adjustable-rate mortgage and a fixed-rate mortgage, many people don't realize that they are making a choice between a mortgage on which the interest rate is determined by either short-term or long-term interest rates.

"What's a short-term versus a long-term interest rate?" you say. Glad you asked. When a mortgage lender quotes an interest rate for a particular type of loan, he should specify (in terms of how many years until the loan is completely paid off) the length of the loan.

Most of the time, borrowers must pay a higher interest rate to borrow money for a longer period of time. Conversely, borrowers generally pay a lower rate of interest for shorter-term loans. So?

Well, the interest rates that are used to determine most adjustable-rate mortgages are *short-term interest rates;* whereas fixed-rate mortgage interest rates are dictated by *long-term interest*

rates. During most time periods, longer-term interest rates are higher than shorter-term rates because of the greater risk the lender accepts in committing to a longer-term rate.

It stands to reason, then, when little difference exists in the market level of short-term and long-term interest rates (such as occurred during 1995), that the rates of fixed-rate mortgages shouldn't be all that different from the rates of adjustable-rate mortgages. Thus, adjustables appear less attractive, and fixed-rate mortgages appear more alluring.

On the other hand, when short-term interest rates are significantly lower than long-term interest rates (such as during the early 1990s), adjustable-rate mortgages should be available at rates a good deal lower than the rates for fixed-rate loans. All things being equal, adjustables appear more attractive during such time periods and save you more money during the early years of your loan.

If you haven't already done so, let your fingers do the walking back to Chapters 2 and 3. Read and digest these chapters in order to understand how much you can really afford to spend on a home, given your other financial needs, commitments, and goals.

If you're at all considering an ARM, you absolutely, positively must understand what rising interest rates (and, therefore, a rising monthly mortgage payment) would do to your personal finances. Only consider taking an ARM if you can answer all of the following questions in the affirmative:

- ✔ Is your monthly budget such that you can afford higher mortgage payments and still accomplish other financial goals that are important to you, such as saving for retirement?

- ✔ Do you have an emergency reserve (equal to at least six-months' living expenses) that you can tap into make the potentially higher monthly mortgage payments?

✔ Can you afford the highest payment allowed on the adjustable-rate mortgage?

The mortgage lender can tell you the *highest possible monthly payment,* which is the payment that you would owe if the interest rate on your ARM went to the lifetime interest-rate cap allowed on the loan.

✔ If you are stretching to borrow near the maximum the lender allows or an amount that will test the limits of your budget, are your job and income stable?

If you expect to be having children in the future, consider now the fact that your household expenses will rise and your income may fall with the arrival of those little bundles of joy.

✔ Can you handle the psychological stress of changing interest rates and mortgage payments?

If you are fiscally positioned to take on the financial risks inherent to an adjustable-rate mortgage, by all means consider taking one — we're not trying to talk you into a fixed-rate loan. The odds are with you to save money, in the form of lower interest charges and payments, with an ARM. Your interest rate starts lower (and stays lower, if the overall level of interest rates doesn't change). Even if rates do go up, as they are sometimes prone to do, they will surely come back down. So, if you can stick with your ARM through times of high and low interest rates, you should still come out ahead.

Also recognize that, although ARMs do carry the risk of a fluctuating interest rate, almost all adjustable-rate loans limit, or *cap,* the rise in the interest rate allowed on your loan. We certainly wouldn't allow you take an ARM without caps. Typical caps are 2 percent per year and 6 percent over the life of the loan. (We cover ARM interest rate caps in detail later in this chapter.)

Consider an adjustable-rate mortgage only if you're financially and emotionally secure enough to handle the maximum possible payments over an extended period of time. ARMs work best for borrowers who take out smaller loans than they are qualified for or who are consistently saving more than 10 percent of their monthly income. If you do choose an ARM, make sure that you have a significant cash cushion that is accessible in the event that rates go up. Don't take an adjustable just because the initially lower interest rate allows you to afford a more expensive home. Better to buy a home that you can afford with a fixed-rate mortgage. (And don't forget hybrid loans if you want a loan with more payment stability but aren't willing to pay the premium of a long-term, fixed-rate loan.)

You can't (nor can the experts) predict where interest rates are headed

All the logicians out there are probably commenting that the choice between an adjustable-rate mortgage and a fixed-rate mortgage is simple. All you need to know in order to make a decision is the direction of interest rates. It's only logical. If interest rates look set to rise, a fixed-rate mortgage would be favorable. Lock in a low rate and smile smugly when interest rates sky-rocket.

Conversely, if you thought that rates were going to stay the same or drop, you would want an ARM. Some real estate books that we've read even go so far as to say that your own personal interest-rate forecast should determine whether to take an ARM or fixed-rate mortgage! "Interest-rate forecasts should be the major factor in deciding whether or not to get an ARM," argues one such book.

Now we don't think that you're stupid, but you are *not* going to figure out which way rates are headed. The movement of interest rates is not logical, and you certainly can't predict it. If you could, you would make a fortune investing in bonds, interest-rate futures, and options.

Even the money-management pros who work with interest rates and bonds as a full-time job can't consistently predict interest rates. Witness the fact that bond-fund managers at mutual fund companies have a tough time beating the buy-and-hold bond-market indexes. If bond-fund managers could foresee where rates were headed, they could easily beat the averages by trading into and out of bonds when they foresaw interest-rate changes on the horizon.

How long do you expect to stay in the home/mortgage?

If you don't plan or expect to stay in your home for a long time, you should consider an ARM. Saving money on interest charges for most adjustables is usually guaranteed in the first two to three years, because an ARM starts at a lower interest rate than a fixed-rate loan does.

Should interest rates rise, however, you can end up paying more interest in subsequent years with the adjustable-rate loan. If you're reasonably certain that you'll hold onto your home for fewer than five years, you should come out ahead with an adjustable.

As we explain earlier in this chapter, a mortgage lender takes more risk when lending money at a fixed rate of interest for many (15 to 30) years. Lenders charge you a premium, in the form of a higher interest rate than what the ARM starts at, for the interest-rate risk that they assume with a fixed-rate loan.

If you expect to hold onto your home and mortgage for a long time — more than five to seven years — a fixed-rate loan may make more sense, especially if you're not in a position to withstand the fluctuating monthly payments that come with an ARM. If you don't plan on keeping your home and mortgage for more than five years, an ARM likely will save you money. However, you should also ask yourself why you're going to all the trouble and great expense of buying a home that you expect to sell so soon. If you're in the intermediate area (expecting to stay seven to ten years, for example), consider the hybrid loans we discuss earlier in this chapter.

If you're still stuck on the fence, go with the fixed-rate loan. A fixed-rate loan is financially safer and easier to shop for than an ARM.

Choosing between a 15-year and a 30-year mortgage

After you've decided which type of mortgage — fixed or adjustable — you want, you may think that your mortgage quandaries are behind you. Unfortunately, they're not. You also need to make another important choice — typically between a 15-year and a 30-year mortgage. (Not all mortgages come in just 15- and 30-year varieties. You may run across some 20- and 40-year versions, but that won't change the issues we're about to tackle.)

If you're stretching to buy the home that you want, the choice of how long-term your mortgage will be may very well not be yours to make. You may be forced (we should say *forcing yourself,* because *you* choose what home to buy) to take the longer-term, 30-year mortgage. Doing so isn't necessarily bad and, in fact, has advantages.

The main advantage that a 30-year mortgage has over its 15-year peer is that it has lower monthly payments that free up more of your monthly income for other purposes, such as saving for other important financial goals (such as retirement). You may want to have more money so that you aren't a financial prisoner to your home and can just have a life! A 30-year mortgage has lower monthly payments because you have a longer time period to repay it (which translates into more payments). A fixed-rate 30-year mortgage with an interest rate of 7 percent, for example, has payments that are approximately 25 percent lower than those on a comparable 15-year mortgage.

What if you can afford the higher payments that a 15-year mortgage requires? Should you take it? Not necessarily. What if, instead of making large payments on the 15-year mortgage, you make smaller payments on a 30-year mortgage and put that extra money to productive use?

 If you do, indeed, make productive use of that extra money, then the 30-year mortgage may be for you. A terrific potential use for that extra dough is to contribute it to a tax-deductible retirement account that you have access to. Contributions that you add to employer-based 401(k) and 403(b) plans (and self-employed SEP-IRAs or Keoghs) not only give you an immediate reduction in taxes but also enable your money to compound, tax-deferred, over the years ahead. Everyone with employment income may also contribute to an Individual Retirement Account (IRA). Your IRA contributions may not be immediately tax-deductible if you (or your spouse's) employer offers a retirement account or pension plan.

If you have exhausted your options for contributing to all the retirement accounts that you can, and if you find it challenging to save money anyway, the 15-year mortgage may offer you a good forced-savings program.

If you elect to take a 30-year mortgage, you retain the flexibility to pay it off faster if you so choose. (Just be sure to avoid those mortgages that have a prepayment penalty.) Constraining yourself with the 15-year mortgage's higher monthly payments does carry a risk. If you fall on tough financial times, you may not be able to meet the required mortgage payments.

Selecting a Fine Fixed-Rate Mortgage

If you decide, based upon our advice and selection criteria, to go with a fixed-rate loan, great! You shouldn't be disappointed. You'll have the peace of mind that comes with stable mortgage payments. And because fixed-rate loans have fewer options, they are a good deal easier to compare than adjustable-rate loans.

However, we don't want to give you the false impression that fixed-rate loans are as simple to shop for as carbonated beverages. Unfortunately, because of the hundreds of lenders in your local area who likely offer such loans and the seemingly never-ending, nit-picky, extra fees and expenses that lenders tack onto loans, you will need to put on your smart-consumer hat and sharpen your No. 2 pencil.

Be sure that you understand the following sections before you attempt to choose the best fixed-rate loan to meet your needs.

The all-important interest rate

If you've ever borrowed money, you know that lenders aren't charities. Lenders make money by charging you, in the form of interest, for the use of their money. Lenders normally quote the *rate of interest* as a percentage per year of the amount borrowed. You may be familiar with rates of interest if you've ever borrowed money through student loans, credit cards, or auto loans. In these cases, lenders may have charged you 8, 10, 12, or perhaps even 18 percent or more for the privilege of using their money. Similarly, mortgage lenders also quote you an annual interest rate.

You've shopped for other products and services by phone, so you may as well get on the horn and call lenders, as well. The first one you call may be offering a fixed-rate loan at an interest rate of 7 percent. Then you call another lender and ask whether they can beat that rate, and that lender says, "Sure, we can get you into a fixed-rate loan at 6.75 percent."

But if you blindly choose the 6.75 percent loan, you could very well be making a very expensive mistake. Perhaps you've heard the expression, "Don't judge a book by its cover." You should not judge a mortgage solely by its interest rate, either. You must also understand the points and other loan fees that the lender assesses.

The finer points of points

Just as Abbott goes with Costello, and Laurel goes with Hardy, and Calvin is inseparable from Hobbes, the interest rate on a mortgage should also go together, in your mind, with the points on the loan. We aren't talking about the kind of points that a basketball player tallies during a game for each successful shot. Points on a mortgage cost you money.

Points are up-front interest. Lenders charge points as a way of being paid for the work and expense of processing and approving your mortgage. When you buy a home, the points are tax-deductible — you get to claim them as an itemized expense on Schedule A of your IRS Form 1040 (see Chapter 3). When you refinance, in contrast, the points must be spread out for tax purposes and deducted over the life of loan.

Lenders quote points as a percentage of the mortgage amount and require you to pay them at the time that you close on your home purchase and begin the lengthy process of repaying your loan. One *point* is equal to 1 percent of the amount that you're borrowing. For example, if a lender says that the loan they are proposing to you has two points, that simply means that you must pay 2 percent of the loan amount as points. On a $120,000 loan, for example, two points cost you $2,400. That's not chump change!

The interest rate on a fixed-rate loan has an inverse relationship to that loan's points. If you are able to (or desire to) pay more points on a mortgage, the lender should reduce the ongoing interest rate. This reduction may be beneficial to you if you have the cash to pay more points and want to lower the interest rate that you'll pay year after year. If you expect to hold onto the home and mortgage for many years, the lower the interest rate, the better.

Conversely, if you want to (or need to) pay fewer points (perhaps because you're cash-constrained when you make the home purchase), you can pay a higher ongoing interest rate. The shorter the time that you expect to hold onto the mortgage, the more sense this strategy of paying less now and more later makes.

Don't get suckered into believing that "no-point" loans are a good deal. There are no free lunches in the real estate world. Remember the points/interest-rate tradeoff: If you pay less in points, the ongoing interest rate will be higher. So if a loan has zero points, it must have a higher interest rate. This does not necessarily mean that the loan is better or worse than comparable loans from other lenders. However, it has been our experience that lenders who aggressively push no-point loans aren't the most competitive lenders in terms of pricing. No-point loans make sense only if you're really tight on cash for your home purchase and expect not to hold onto the home and mortgage for the long term.

Take a look at a couple of specific mortgage options to understand the points/interest-rate tradeoff. Suppose, for example, that you want to borrow $150,000. One lender quotes you 7.25 percent on a 30-year, fixed-rate loan and charges one point (1 percent). Another lender quotes 7.75 percent (a spread of $1/2$ percent is typical) and doesn't charge any points. Which offer is better? The answer depends mostly on how long you plan to keep the loan.

The 7.25-percent loan costs $1,024 per month compared to $1,075 per month for the 7.75-percent mortgage. You can save $51 per month with the 7.25-percent loan, but you'd have to pay $1,500 in points to get it.

To find out which loan is better for you, divide the cost of the points by the monthly savings ($1,500 divided by $51 equals 29.4). This gives you the number of months (in this case, 29) it will take you to recover the cost of the points. Thus, if you don't plan to keep the loan for 30 months, choose the no-points loan. If you plan to keep the loan more than 30 months, pay the points. If you keep the loan for the remaining 27.5 years it takes to repay it, you'll save $16,830 ($51 a month for 330 months).

The 7.25-percent loan costs 0.5 percent less in interest annually than the 7.75-percent loan. Year after year, the 7.25-percent loan saves you 0.5 percent. But, because you have to pay one point up front on the 7.25-percent mortgage, it will take you about 30 months to earn back the savings to cover the cost of that point. So, if you expect to keep the loan more than 30 months, go with the 7.25-percent option.

In order for you to make a fair comparison of mortgages from different lenders, have the lenders provide interest rate quotes at the *same* point level. Ask the mortgage contenders, for example, to tell you what their fixed-rate mortgage interest rate would be at one point. Also, make sure that the loans are of the same term — for example, 30 years.

Other lender fees

If you're paying points with your mortgage, you may think that you won't have to pay any other up-front fees. Well, think again. There is no shortage of up-front loan-processing charges for you to investigate when making mortgage comparisons. Understanding all of a lender's other fees is vital — these fees come out of your pocket, after all. If you don't understand the fee structure, you may end up with a high-cost loan or come up short of cash when the time comes to close on the purchase of your home.

Be sure to ask each lender whose services you are seriously considering for a written itemization of all of these "other" charges. To reduce your chances of throwing money away on a mortgage for which you may not qualify, ask the lender whether your application may be turned down for some reason. For example, disclose any potential problems of the property that were discovered during inspections of the property.

Just as some lenders have no-point mortgages, some lenders also have *no-fee* mortgages. If a lender is pitching a no-fee loan, odds are that the lender will charge you more in other ways, namely in the ongoing interest rate on your loan.

Application and processing fees

Lenders generally charge $200 to $300 up front as an *application* or *processing fee*. This charge is mainly to ensure that you're serious about wanting a loan from them and to compensate them in the event that your loan is rejected. Lenders want to cover their costs to keep from losing money on loan applications that don't materialize into actual loans.

A few lenders don't charge this fee; or if they do, they return it if you take their loan.

Credit report

Your credit report tells a lender how responsibly you've dealt with prior loans. Did you pay all of your previous loans back (and on time)? Credit reports don't cost a great deal, but you can expect to pay from $30 to $50 for the lender to obtain a current copy of yours.

If you know that you have blemishes on your credit report, address those problems *before* you apply for your mortgage. Otherwise, you'll be wasting your time and money applying for a loan for which you'll be denied. You can actually obtain a free copy of your credit report from any lender who recently turned you down for a loan because of derogatory information on your credit file. The lender is legally required to give you a copy of the report. (The credit report provider can provide the report as well.)

Appraisal

Mortgage lenders want an independent assessment to insure that the property that you are buying is worth approximately what you agreed to pay — that's the job of an appraiser. Why would the lender care? Simple — because the lender is likely loaning you a large portion of the purchase price of the property. If you overpay and home values decline or you end up in financial trouble, you may be willing to walk away from the property and leave the lender holding the bag.

The cost of an appraisal varies with the size, complexity, and value of property. Expect to pay a few hundred dollars for an appraisal of most modestly priced, average-type properties.

Arriving at the Absolute Best Adjustable-Rate Mortgage

If you're the calm and collected type of person who is not prone to panicking, can stomach interest rate volatility, and has decided (based on our sage advice in this chapter) to go with an adjustable-rate mortgage (ARM), you'll need to understand a bit more in order to choose a good one. Adjustables are more complicated to evaluate and select than fixed-rate mortgages are.

In addition to understanding points and other loan fees that we cover in the preceding section on fixed-rate loans, you'll also be bombarded with such jargon as *margins, caps,* and *indexes.* If you're a numbers geek, you could spend hundreds of hours comparing different permutations of ARMs and determining how they might behave in different interest-rate environments.

Unlike with a fixed-rate mortgage, ascertaining precisely the amount of money a particular ARM is going to cost you is not possible. As with choosing a home to buy, selecting an ARM that meets your needs and budget involves compromising and deciding what's important to you. So here's your crash course in understanding ARMs.

Where an ARM's interest rate comes from

Most ARMs start at an artificially low interest rate. Selecting an ARM based on this rate is likely to be a huge mistake because you won't be paying this low rate for very long, perhaps for just six to twelve months — or maybe even just one month! Lenders and mortgage brokers are like many other salespeople; they like to promote the low teaser rate. That rate is what they're most likely to tell you about.

The starting rate on an ARM is not anywhere near as important as what the future interest rate is going to be on the loan. How the future interest rate on an ARM is determined is the single most important feature for you to understand when evaluating an ARM.

All ARMs that we've ever seen are based on an equation that includes an *index* and *margin,* the two of which are added together to determine and set the *future interest rate* on the loan. Before we go further, please be sure that you understand these terms:

- ✓ **Index:** The *index* is a measure of interest rates that the lender uses as a reference. For example, the six-month bank certificate of deposit index is used as a reference for many mortgages. Suppose that the going rate on six-month CDs is approximately 5 percent. The index theoretically indicates how much it costs the bank to take in money that it can then lend.

- ✓ **Margin:** The *margin* is the lenders' profit (or *markup*) on the money that they intend to lend. Most loans have margins of around 2.5 percent, but the exact margin depends on the lender and the index that lender is using. When you compare loans that are tied to the same index and are otherwise the same, the loan with the lower margin is better.

- ✓ **Interest Rate:** The *interest rate* is the sum of the index and the margin. It is what you will pay (subject to certain limitations), on your loan.

Putting it all together, in our example of the six-month CD index at 5 percent, plus a margin of 2.5 percent, we get an interest rate sum of 7.5 percent. This figure is known as the *fully indexed rate.* If this loan starts out at 5 percent, for example, the fully indexed rate tells you what interest rate this ARM would increase to if the market level of interest rates, as measured by the CD index, stays constant. Never take an ARM unless you understand this important concept of the fully indexed rate.

Many mortgage lenders know that more than a few borrowers focus on an ARM's initial interest rate and ignore the margin and the index that determine the loan rate. Take our advice and look at an ARM's starting rate *last.* Begin to evaluate an ARM by understanding what index it is tied to and what margin it has. The sections that follow explain common ARM indexes.

Treasury bills

The U.S. federal government is the largest borrower in the universe as we know it, so it should come as no surprise that at least one ARM index is based on the interest rate that the government pays on some of this pile of debt. The most commonly used government interest rate indexes for ARMs are for six-month and twelve-month treasury bills.

The treasury bill indexes tend to be among the faster-moving ones around. In other words, they respond quickly to market changes in interest rates.

Certificates of deposit

Certificates of deposit (CDs) are interest-bearing bank investments that lock you in for a specific period of time. Adjustable-rate mortgages are usually tied to the average interest rate banks are paying on six-month CDs.

As with treasury bills, CDs tend to move rapidly with overall changes in interest rates. However, CD rates tend to move up a bit more slowly when rates rise, because profit-minded bankers like to drag their feet when it comes to paying more interest to depositors. Conversely, CD rates tend to come down quickly when rates decline, so that bankers can maintain their profits.

The 11th District Cost of Funds Index

The 11th District Cost of Funds Index (also known as COFI, pronounced like the stuff you drink in the morning), is published monthly by the Federal Home Loan Bank Board. This index shows the monthly weighted average cost of savings, borrowings, and advances for its member banks located in California, Arizona, and Nevada (the 11th District). Because the COFI is a moving average of the rates that bankers have paid depositors over recent months, it tends to be a relatively stable index.

An ARM tied to a slower-moving index, such as the 11th District Cost of Funds Index, has the advantage of increasing more slowly when interest rates are on the upswing. On the other hand, you have to be patient to benefit from falling interest rates when rates are on the decline. The 11th District is slow to fall when interest rates overall decline.

Because ARMs tied to the 11th District Cost of Funds Index are slower to rise when overall interest rates rise, they generally begin at a higher rate of interest than do ARMs tied to faster moving indexes.

The London Interbank Offered Rate Index

Okay, now for a weirder index. The *London Interbank Offered Rate* index (*LIBOR*) is an average of the interest rates that major international banks charge each other to borrow U.S. dollars in the London money market. Like the U.S. treasury and CD indexes, LIBOR tends to move and adjust quite rapidly to changes in interest rates.

Why do we need an *international* interest-rate index? Well, foreign investors buy American mortgages as investments, and not surprisingly, these investors like ARMs tied to an index that they understand and are familiar with.

How often does the ARM interest rate adjust?

Lenders usually adjust the interest rates on their ARMs every six or twelve months, using the mortgage-rate formula discussed earlier in this section. Some loans adjust monthly. (Monthly adjustments are usually a red flag for negative amortization loans; we explain why to avoid these loans in the nearby sidebar.) In advance of each adjustment, the mortgage lender should send you a notice, spelling out how the new rate is calculated according to the agreed-upon terms of your ARM.

The less often your loan adjusts, the less financial risk you are accepting. In exchange for taking less risk, the mortgage lender normally expects you to pay a higher initial interest rate.

Limits on interest rate adjustments

Despite the fact that an ARM has a system for calculating future interest rates (by adding the margin to the loan index), bankers limit how great a change can occur in the actual rate that you pay. These limits, also known as *rate caps,* affect each future adjustment of an ARM's rate following the end of the initial rate.

Two types of rate caps exist. *Periodic adjustment caps* limit the maximum rate change, up or down, allowed at each adjustment. For ARMs that adjust at six month intervals, the adjustment cap is usually 1 percent. ARMs that adjust more than once annually generally restrict the maximum rate change allowed over the entire year, as well. This *annual rate cap* is usually 2 percent.

Finally, almost all adjustables come with *lifetime caps.* You should never take on an ARM without a lifetime cap. These caps limit the highest rate allowed over the entire life of the loan. ARMs commonly have lifetime caps of 5 to 6 percent higher than the initial start rate.

When you take on an ARM, be sure that you can handle the maximum possible payment allowed, should the interest rate on the ARM rise to the lifetime cap.

Avoid adjustables with negative amortization

Some ARMs cap the increase of your monthly payment but not the increase of the interest rate. The size of your mortgage payment may not reflect all the interest that you actually owe on your loan. So, rather than paying the interest that is owed and paying off some of your loan balance every month, you may end up paying some (but not all) of the interest that you owe. Thus, the extra unpaid interest that you still owe is added to your outstanding debt.

As you make mortgage payments over time, the loan balance you still owe is gradually reduced in a process called *amortizing the mortgage*. The reverse of this process (that is, increasing the size of your loan balance) is called *negative amortization*.

Liken negative amortization to paying only the minimum payment required on a credit card bill. You continue accumulating additional interest on the balance as long as you make only the minimum monthly payment. However, doing this with a mortgage defeats the purpose of your borrowing an amount that fits your overall financial goals (see Chapter 3).

Some lenders try to hide the fact that an ARM that they are pitching you has negative amortization. How can you avoid negative-amortization loans? Simple — Ask!

Also be aware that negative-amortization pops up more often on mortgages that lenders consider risky to make. If you're having trouble finding lenders willing to offer you a mortgage, be especially careful.

Locating the Best, Lowest-Cost Lenders

For those of you out there who abhor shopping, we have some bad news. Unless you enjoy throwing away thousands of dollars, you need to shop around for the best deal on a mortgage. Think of it as "dialing for dollars."

Whether you do the footwork on your own or hire someone competent to help you doesn't matter. But you must make sure that this comparison shopping gets done.

Consider this fact: Given a 30-year, $100,000 mortgage, if (through persistent and wise shopping) you are able to obtain a mortgage that is, for example, 0.5 percent per year lower in interest charges than you otherwise would have gotten, you'll save yourself more than $13,000 over the life of the loan (given approximate current interest rates).

Although we encourage you to find the lowest-cost lenders, we must first issue a caution: If someone offers you a deal that is much better than any other lender's, be very skeptical and suspicious. Such a lender may be baiting you with a loan that doesn't exist or one for which you can't qualify.

INVESTIGATE

Traits of good lenders

Yes, there are thousands of mortgage lenders out there. However, not anywhere near that many mortgage lenders are *good* lenders. Real estate agents and others in the real estate trade, as well as other borrowers that you know, can serve as useful references for steering you towards the top-notch lenders and away from the losers. As you solicit input from others and begin to interview lenders, seek to find lenders with the following traits:

- **Straightforward:** Good loan agents explain their various loan programs in plain English without using double-talk or jargon. They help you compare their loans to their competitors' loans.

- **Approve locally:** Good lenders approve your loan locally. They don't send your loan application to an out-of-town loan committee, where you're transformed from a living, breathing human being into an inanimate loan number. Good lenders actively work with you and your agent to get loan approval.

- **Market savvy:** Good lenders understand the type of property that you want to buy. Here's another big advantage of local loan approval: No deal-breaking, last-minute loan cancellations unexpectedly arise because you inadvertently run afoul of some obscure institutional policy.

This type of snafu generally occurs when a mortgage broker tries to find the loan with the lowest interest rate currently being offered anywhere in the universe. Finding the loan is relatively easy. Getting the money, on the other hand, is nearly impossible, because you don't know what bizarre quirks lie buried deep in the loan documents' fine print.

These quirky loans usually apply to absolutely pristine property. For example, an out-of-state lender once approved a loan subject to having all corrective work completed and the house painted inside and out prior to close of escrow. Given that the loan was approved on Monday and the sale was scheduled to close Friday, there was no way that the work could be completed in four days.

- **Competitive:** Good lenders are competitive. Don't be afraid to ask the lender that you like best to match the interest rate of the lowest-priced lender you find. At worst, the lender will turn you down gently. At best, you'll get the lender you want *and* the loan terms you want. Loan rates and charges *are* negotiable.

- **Detail-oriented:** Good lenders meet contract deadlines. They approve and fund loans on time. Your agent knows which lenders deliver on their promises and which don't. Talk's cheap. You need action, not empty promises. *Missed deadlines may squash your purchase.*

Becoming your own chief mortgage shopper

There's no shortage of mortgage lenders in most areas. Although having a large number of options from which to choose is good for competition, having so many options also makes shopping a drag.

Many different types of companies offer mortgages today. The most common mortgage *originators* (as they are known as in the business) are banks, savings-and-loan associations, and mortgage bankers.

"Who cares?" you ask. Well, mortgage bankers do only mortgages, and the best ones offer very competitive rates. Smaller banks and savings-and-loans can have good deals, as well. As for the big banks whose names are drilled into your head from advertisements, they usually don't offer the best rates.

As you begin your mortgage safari, you don't have to go it completely alone. If you've done a good job selecting a real estate agent to help you with your home purchase, for example, the agent should be able to rattle off a short list of good lenders in the area. Just remember to compare these lenders' rates with the rates of some other mortgage lenders that you find on your own.

Otherwise-good real estate agents may send you to lenders that don't necessarily offer the best mortgage interest rates. Some real estate agents may not be up-to-date with who has the best loans or may not be into shopping around. Others may have simply gotten comfortable doing business with certain lenders or gotten client referrals from said lenders previously.

Another way to find lenders is to look for tables of selected lenders' interest rates in the real estate section of one of the larger Sunday newspapers in your area. However, don't assume that such tables contain only the best lenders in your area. In fact, many of these tables are sent to newspapers for free by firms that distribute information to mortgage brokers. Nonetheless, you can use these tables as a starting point by calling the lenders who list the best rates (realizing, of course, that rates can change daily, and the rates you see in the paper may not accurately reflect what's currently available).

If you're a data hound, HSH Associates (800-873-2837) publishes, on a weekly basis, lists of dozens of lenders' rate quotes for most metropolitan areas. The initial package, which comes with explanatory booklets, costs $20. If you wish to purchase subsequent updates, those go for $10 each.

Working with a mortgage broker

Mortgage brokers can do the mortgage shopping for you. *Mortgage brokers* are middle-men, independent of banks or other financial institutions that actually have money to lend.

Mortgage brokers will tell you that they can get you the best loan deal by shopping among many lenders. They may further argue that another benefit of using their service is that they can explain the multitude of loan choices, help you select a loan, and help you wade through the morass of paperwork that's (unfortunately) required to get a loan.

If your credit history and ability to qualify for a mortgage is marginal, a good mortgage broker can help to polish and package your application and steer you to the few lenders that may make you a loan. Brokers can also help if lenders don't want to make loans on unusual properties that you're interested in

Loan prequalification and preapproval

When you're under contract to buy a property, having your mortgage application denied (after waiting several weeks) may cause you to lose the property after having spent hundreds of dollars on loan fees and property inspections. Even worse, you may lose the home that you've probably spent countless hours searching for and a great deal of emotional energy to secure. Some homesellers won't be willing to wait or may need to sell quickly. If the sellers have other buyers waiting in the wings, you've likely lost the property.

How could you have avoided this heartache? Well, you may hear some people in the real estate business, particularly real estate agents and mortgage folks, advocate that you go through mortgage prequalification or preapproval. In a nutshell, these people are recommending that you get a lender's opinion about your creditworthiness as a borrower before you actually have a property under contract to buy.

Prequalification is an informal discussion between borrower and lender. The lender provides an opinion of the loan amount that you can borrow based solely on what you, the borrower, tell the lender. The lender doesn't verify anything, and is not bound to make the loan when you are ready to buy.

Preapproval is much more rigorous, which is why we prefer it if you have any reason to believe that you'll have difficulty qualifying for the loan you desire. Loan preapproval is based on documented and verified information regarding your likelihood of continued employment, your income, your liabilities, and the cash you have available to close on a home purchase. The only thing the lender can't preapprove is the property you intend to buy because, of course, you haven't found it yet.

Going through the preapproval process is a sign of your seriousness to homesellers — it places sort of a Good Borrowing Seal of Approval on you. A lender's preapproval letter is considerably stronger than a prequalification letter. In a multiple-offer situation where more than one prospective buyer bids on a home at the same time, buyers who have been preapproved for a loan have an advantage over buyers who haven't been proven creditworthy.

Lenders don't charge for prequalification. Given the extra work involved, some lenders do charge for preapproval. Other lenders, however, offer free preapprovals to gain borrower loyalty. Don't choose a lender just because the lender doesn't charge for preapproval. That lender may not have the best loan terms around.

If you do choose to get preapproved with a lender who charges for it, be sure that you're soon going to go through with a home purchase. Otherwise, you'll have thrown good money down the drain.

buying. Many lenders don't like dealing with co-ops and tenancies-in-common (see Chapter 7), borrowers with credit problems, or situations where a homebuyer seeks to borrow a large amount (90 percent or more) of the value of a property.

Good mortgage brokers can deliver on most of these promises, and for this service they receive a cut of the amount that you borrow — typically 0.5 to as much as 2 percent on smaller loans. Not cheap, but given what a headache finding and closing on a good mortgage can be, hiring a mortgage broker may be just what the financial doctor ordered.

Should you apply for more than one mortgage?

When you applied to college or for your last job, you likely didn't only apply to your first choice. You probably had a back-up or two or three. Thus, when it comes time to apply for a mortgage, you may be tempted to apply to more than one mortgage lender. The advantage — if one lender doesn't deliver have a back-up to, well, fall back upon.

However, we believe that if you do your homework and pick a good lender with a reputation for low rates, quality service, and for playing straight and meeting borrowers' expectations, applying for more than one mortgage won't be necessary on most properties. When you apply for a second loan, you must pay additional application fees and spend more time and effort completing extra paperwork.

Applying to more than one mortgage lender makes more sense in special situations where you run a greater risk for having your loan application denied. The first case is when you have credit problems. Read Chapter 2 to whip your finances into shape before you embark on the home-buying journey; read Chapter 6 for tips on completing your loan application in a way that will make lenders salivate.

The second circumstance under which it makes sense to apply to more than one mortgage lender is when you want to buy a physically or legally "difficult" property. It's impossible, of course, to know in advance all the types of property idiosyncrasies that will upset a particular lender. In fact, both of your authors, earlier in our home-ownership days, were denied mortgages because our prospective homes had quirks that a particular lender didn't care for. Minimize your chances for negative surprises by asking your agent and property inspector whether any aspects of the property may give a lender cause for concern.

If you apply for two loans, you should tell both lenders that you're applying elsewhere. When the second lender pulls your credit report, the first lender's recent inquiry will show up. (Less-than-candid borrowers almost always get caught this way.) You should also tell both lenders that you are sincerely interested — just as you would tell all prospective employers.

If you're going to work with a mortgage broker, you must keep in mind that such brokers are in the business of "selling" mortgages and derive a commission from this work, just as do stockbrokers who sell stock and car salespeople who sell cars. A difference, though, is that the interest rate and points that you pay to get most mortgages through a broker are the same as what you would pay a lender directly. Lenders reason that they can afford to share their normal fees with an outside mortgage broker (who is not employed by the bank) because, if you got the loan directly from the bank, you would have to work with and take up more of the time of one of the bank's own mortgage employees.

Some lenders, including those with the lowest rates, don't market through mortgage brokers. And sometimes a loan obtained through a mortgage broker can end up costing you more than if you had gotten it directly from the lender for example, if the mortgage broker is taking a big commission for himself.

The commission that the mortgage broker receives from the lender is not set in stone and is completely negotiable, especially on larger loans. On a $100,000 loan, a 1 percent commission amounts to $1,000. The same commission rate on a $300,000 loan results in a $3,000 cut for the broker, even though this three-times-larger loan doesn't take up three times as much of the mortgage broker's time. You have every right to inquire of the mortgage broker what his take is. Don't become overwhelmed with guilt; remember that your money is filling this person's trough and you have every right to know this information! Ask — and don't hesitate to negotiate.

In addition to understanding and negotiating a commission with the mortgage broker, also get answers to the following questions when choosing a mortgage broker:

- ✔ **How many lenders does the broker do business with and how does the broker keep up to date with new lenders and loans that may be better?** Some mortgage brokers, out of habit and laziness, send all their business to just a few lenders and don't get you the best deals. Ask brokers which lenders have approved the broker to represent them. Some mortgage brokers only represent one or two inconsequential lenders — not the kind of broad representation you need to find the best mortgage.

- ✔ **How knowledgeable is the broker about the loan programs, and does the broker have the patience to explain all of a loan's important features?** The more lenders a mortgage broker represents, the less likely the broker is to know the nuances of each and every loan. Be especially wary of a salesperson who aggressively pushes certain loan programs and glosses over or ignores explaining the important points we discuss in this chapter for evaluating particular mortgages.

All the advice that we give for selecting a good lender applies doubly for choosing a good mortgage broker. Some brokers, for example, have been known to push programs with outrageous interest rates and points, which, not too surprisingly, entail big commissions for them. This problem occurs most frequently with borrowers who have questionable credit or other qualification problems.

Also head for cover if your mortgage broker pushes you toward balloon and negative-amortization loans (discussed earlier in this chapter). Balloon loans, which become fully due and payable several years after you get them, are dangerous because you may not be able to get new financing and could be forced to sell the property.

If you're on the fence about using a mortgage broker, take this simple test: If you're the type of person who dreads shopping and waits until the last minute to buy a gift, a good mortgage broker can probably help you and save you money. A competent mortgage broker can be of greatest value to those who don't bother shopping around for a good deal or who may be shunned by most lenders.

Even if you plan to shop on your own, talking to a mortgage broker may be worthwhile. At the very least, you can compare what you find with what brokers say they can get for you.

Be aware, though, that some brokers only tell you what you want to hear — that they can beat your best find. Later, you may discover that the broker isn't able to deliver when the time comes. If you find a good deal on your own and want to check with a mortgage broker to see what he or she has to offer, it may be wise not to tell the broker the terms of the best deal you've found. If you do, more than a few brokers will always come up with something that they *say* can beat it.

If your mortgage broker quotes you a really good deal (you'll know this if you've shopped a little yourself), be sure to ask who the lender is. (Most brokers refuse to reveal this information until you pay the few hundred dollars to cover the appraisal and credit report.) In most cases, you can check with the actual lender to verify the interest rate and points that the broker quoted you and make sure that you're eligible for the loan. (In some cases, lenders don't market loans directly to the public.)

If you discover, in calling the lender directly, that they don't offer such attractive terms to their customers, don't leap to the conclusion that the mortgage broker lied to you. In rare cases, a mortgage broker may offer you a slightly better deal than what you could have gotten on your own.

If the broker was playing games to get your business, charging the broker's up-front fee on your credit card allows you to dispute the charge and get your money back.

Chapter 6

Mortgage Quandaries, Conundrums, and Paperwork

· ·

In This Chapter

▶ Overcoming common mortgage problems

▶ Handling lower-than-expected appraisals

▶ Getting up close and personal with mortgage forms

· ·

*U*nderstanding and selecting a mortgage (the subject of Chapter 5) is not all that difficult to tackle after you figure out the jargon and know how to think about your overall financial situation and goals.

Unfortunately, when you apply for a mortgage, obstacles may get in your way. In this chapter, we show you how to glide by these irritating and sometimes not-so-trivial challenges. We also answer your queries to other often-perplexing (and, in some cases, desirable) alternatives you may have.

Common Problems

Few things in life are more frustrating than not being able to have something you really want, especially if you perceive, rightly or wrongly, that most other people you know have it. If you want to buy a home and you can't finance the purchase, odds are that your dream will have to be put on hold.

Don't despair if problems stand in your way. You may have to exhibit a bit more patience than usual, but we've never met anyone who was determined to buy a home and was not able to overcome credit or other problems. This chapter shows you how to get the financing you need and deserve! In the last section of this chapter, we explain how to complete those dreaded mortgage application forms.

Lack of down payment

Saving money in America, where *everything* is considered a necessity at one time or another, can be a chore. If you lack sufficient money for a down payment, be sure to turn to Chapter 3 for suggestions about how to get financing.

Insufficient income

Your desired mortgage lender may very well reject your loan application if you appear to be stretching yourself too thin financially. Although getting angry and sticking pins in your little banker doll is a natural first reaction, you should actually be grateful. Why? Because the lender may be doing you a huge favor by keeping you from buying a home that will prevent you from saving money and achieving other financial goals that may be important to you over time.

Please be sure to read Chapters 2 and 3 about getting your financial house in order and determining how much home you really can afford.

If you *know* that you can afford the home that you have your sights set on, here are some keys to getting your loan approved:

✔ **Be patient.** If you have a low income (for example, if you're self-employed and have been deducting everything but the kitchen sink as a business expense), you may very well need to wait a year or two so that you can demonstrate a higher income.

✔ **Put more money down.** If you make a down payment of 25 to 30 percent or more, some mortgage lenders can approve you for their no-income-verification mortgage loan (in rare cases they'll do so for 20 percent down). Generally speaking, such mortgages come with higher interest rates than conventional loans, so recognize that you will be paying a price for this type of loan.

✔ **Get a cosigner.** You always knew that you'd hit your parents up again someday for help and favors. If your folks are in good financial shape, they may be able to cosign a loan to help you qualify. A financially solvent sibling, rich aunt, or wealthy pal can do the same.

Be sure to consider the financial and nonfinancial ramifications of having a relative or buddy cosign a loan with you. If you default on the loan or make payments late, you'll besmirch not only your credit history but also your cosigner's. At a minimum, have a frank discussion about such issues before you enter into such an arrangement and be sure to write up a loan agreement.

Debt and credit problems

When you seek to take out a mortgage, lenders examine your credit history, which is detailed in your personal credit report. Lenders also analyze your current debts and liabilities, which you provide on your mortgage application. Your current debts and credit history can produce a number of red flags that may make lenders skittish about lending you money. This section tells you how to deal with the typical problems that crop up.

Credit report boo-boos

Remember the music club that you joined way back when? Remember the stream of letters that they sent, reminding you that you were delinquent with your payments? That club may get its revenge in a most painful way. Creditors can and will report your loan delinquencies and defaults, and these blemishes show up on your personal credit report.

Here's our suggested plan of attack for dealing with such problems:

✓ **Be proactive.** If you know that there are warts and imperfections on your credit report, write a concise letter to the lender explaining why the flaws are there. For example, maybe you were late on some of your loan payments once because you were out of the country and didn't get your bills processed in time. Or perhaps you lost your job unexpectedly and fell behind in your payments until you located new employment.

✓ **Shop around for understanding and flexible lenders.** Some lenders are more sympathetic to the fact that you're human and have sometimes erred. As you interview lenders, inquire whether your previous credit blemishes may pose a problem. You may also consider enlisting the services of a mortgage broker, who may well be more accustomed to dealing with loan problems.

How to get a copy of your credit report

Getting and retaining a copy of your personal credit report is a good idea. Because your personal credit report contains a history of your use (and abuse!) of credit, it's important that you're aware of what it contains and whether the information is accurate.

If you're applying for a mortgage, you can ask at that time for a copy of your credit report — after all, you're paying for it! You should also know that lenders are required to give you a copy of your credit report *without charge* if they turn you down for a loan.

Another way to obtain a copy of your credit report is to contact one of the major credit bureaus that gather the information and publish these reports. A number of states require credit bureaus to provide you with a free copy of your report if you were denied credit, employment, or rental housing — typically over the most recent 30 to 60 days. TRW (800-392-1122) provides one free report per calendar year per person. Equifax charges a nominal fee of $3 to $8, depending upon the state you reside in (800-685-5111).

✔ **Look to the property seller for a loan.** Property sellers who are interested in playing lender can also be flexible. Surprisingly, some won't even check your credit report. Those who check your credit report may be more willing than banks and other mortgage lenders to forgive past problems, especially if you're financially healthy and strong today.

✔ **Fight and correct errors.** Credit reporting agencies and creditors who report information to the agencies make mistakes. Unfortunately, unlike in our legal system, in the financial world you are guilty until you can convince the credit agencies that you're innocent. Start by identifying the erroneous information on your credit report. If the erroneous information represents an account that you never had, tell the credit bureau to examine the possibility that the derogatory information belongs on someone else's report. If the bad data *is* for one of your accounts but a creditor (for example, First Usury Bank, from which you obtained an auto loan) has made an error, you'll likely have to harass such creditors until they instruct the credit bureau to fix the mistake.

To get these sorts of errors corrected, you must be willing to be persistent and to make a bit of a pain in the creditor's posterior. The process also takes patience. By law, the credit bureaus are supposed to respond to your inquiry within 30 days. If you get the runaround from the frontline customer service representatives you speak with, ask to speak with a supervisor or manager until you get satisfaction. If that technique doesn't work, contact your local Better Business Bureau (see your local phone directory) and file a complaint. You are also allowed to enter a statement of contention on your credit report so that prospective creditors, such as mortgage lenders, who pull your credit report can see your side of the story. But your best strategy is to have the disparaging information removed from your credit report.

✔ **Get a cosigner.** As we suggested earlier, a cosigner, such as a relative, can also help to deal with credit problems that are knocking out your loan application.

✔ **Save more and build a better track record.** If you can continue to rent, buying yourself some more time may do the trick. Why rush buying if lenders avoid you like the plague and reject you or only offer loans with ultra-high interest rates? Spend a couple of years saving more money and keeping a clean credit record, and you'll eventually have lenders chasing you for your business.

If you're having problems getting approved, sit down with your loan officer and make a list of the items that you must rectify to get an approval. Instead of trying to guess what's wrong, you will have a checklist of everything you need to correct.

Excess debt

If you're turned down for a mortgage because of excess debt (such as on credit cards and auto loans), be grateful. The lender has actually done you a favor! Over the long term, such debt is a serious drag on your ability to save money and live within your income.

If you have the cash available to pay off the debt, we emphatically urge you to do so. Mortgage lenders sometimes make this a condition of funding a mortgage, if you have significant debts or are on the margin of qualifying for the loan that you desire. If you lack sufficient cash to pay down the debt and buy the type of home you desire, choose among the following options:

- ✔ **Set you sights more realistically.** Buy a less expensive home for which you can qualify for a mortgage.

- ✔ **Go on a financial diet.** Your best bet for getting rid of consumer debt is to take a hard look at your spending (see Chapter 2) and identify where you can make cuts. Use your savings to pay down the debt. Also explore boosting your employment income.

- ✔ **Get family help.** Another potential option is to have family help you with your borrowing, either by cosigning your loan or by lending or gifting you money to pay down your high interest debt.

Appraisal problems

Your loan application may be sailing smoothly through the loan-approval channels — thanks to your sterling (or at least acceptable) financial condition — and then, all of sudden (like in a Batman and Robin episode):

POW!!! BANG!!! THUMP!!! KABOOM!!!

The property that you've fallen in love with isn't worth what you agreed to pay for it, at least according to the *appraiser* (the person who evaluates property for lenders). If you're a normal person, you may be shocked, dismayed, and perhaps even frightened that the appraiser has given such a low estimate. What course of action you should take depends upon which of the following three issues caused the low appraisal.

You've overpaid

Appraisals don't often come in low, so when they do, more often than not they are low because you (and perhaps your agent) overestimated what the home is worth. If this is the case, be grateful that the appraiser has provided you with a big warning that you're about to throw away money, perhaps thousands of dollars, if you go through with paying what was written up in your purchase contract. It's also possible that the appraised value is low because the home needs a new roof, new foundation, or other major structural repairs. (We cover property inspections in Chapter 11.)

Because you obviously liked the property (after all, you made an offer to buy it), use the appraisal as a tool to either renegotiate a lower purchase price with the seller or get a credit from the seller to do necessary repairs. If the seller won't play, move on to other properties. Also reevaluate your agent's knowledge of property values and motivations — consider finding a new agent if the present agent prodded you into overpaying.

The appraiser doesn't know your area

If you and your agent know local property values and have seen comparable homes that fully justify the price you agreed to pay, it's possible that the appraiser simply doesn't know local property values. One clue that this is the case is if the appraiser doesn't normally appraise homes in your area. Another clue is if the comparable properties that the appraiser chose aren't good, representative comparisons. We get into exactly what is and isn't a comparable property in Chapter 9.

If you have reason to believe that the appraiser may be off base, express your concern to the mortgage lender that you're using. Also, request a copy of the appraisal, which you are entitled to. The lender should be able to shed some light on the appraiser's background and experience with homes in your area. Sometimes, you can have a reappraisal done without an additional charge.

The appraiser/lender is sandbagging you

The least likely explanation for a low appraisal is that your mortgage lender may have come in with a low appraisal to get out of doing a loan that he or she feels is undesirable. In the business, this trick is called *sandbagging.*

Lenders who use in-house appraisals are best able to torpedo loans that they don't want to make. Why, you may reasonably wonder, would lenders sandbag you on a loan for which they've willingly accepted a loan application? Remember that the eager frontline mortgage person at the bank or the mortgage broker who placed your loan with the lender likely works on commission and is not the person who makes mortgage-approval decisions at the lending company.

If you suspect that your loan is being sandbagged, request a copy of your appraisal. If comparable sales data show that the appraisal *is* low, confront your lender on this issue and see what he or she has to say about it. If you get the runaround and no satisfaction, ask for a full refund of your loan application and appraisal fees and take your business to another lender. You may also consider filing a complaint with whatever state organization regulates mortgage lenders in your area.

Those Darn Mortgage Forms

When you finally get to the part of your home purchase where you are applying for a mortgage, you're likely to become so sick of paperwork that you'll yearn for a paperless society. You may be interested in knowing that some lenders around the country are moving to a more computer-driven (and less pen-and-paper oriented) mortgage-application process. No matter; you're still going to have to provide a great deal of personal and financial information.

In this section, we review the forms that you'll commonly be asked to complete in the mortgage-application process. If you're working with a skilled person at the mortgage lender's firm or mortgage brokerage firm that you've chosen, that person can help you to navigate and beat into submission most of this dreaded paperwork.

But we know that you probably have some questions about what kinds of information you're required to provide versus information that you don't have to provide. You also may be uncomfortable revealing certain, how shall we say, less-than-flattering facts about your situation, facts that you feel may jeopardize your qualifications for a mortgage. And finally, no matter how good the mortgage person that you're working with is, the burden is still upon you to pull together many facts, figures, and documents. So here we are, right by your side to coach and cajole you along the way.

The laundry list of required documents

Many mortgage lenders provide you with an incredibly lengthy list of documents that they require with mortgage applications (see Figure 6-1). One quick look at the list is enough to make most prospective homebuyers continue renting!

But don't despair. A close look at the list reveals that not all of the items may pertain to your unique and interesting situation. This list must cover all possible situations, so some of the items won't apply to you. We hope, for example, that you're not simultaneously receiving a diploma, divorcing, being relocated by your employer, and completing bankruptcy papers!

Most of the items on this laundry list are required in order to prove and substantiate your current financial status to the mortgage lender and, subsequently, to other organizations that may buy your loan in the future. Pay stubs, tax returns, and bank and investment-account statements help to document your income and assets. Lenders assess the risk of lending you money and determine how much they can lend you based upon these items.

If you're wondering why lenders can't take you on your word about the personal and confidential financial facts and figures, remember that some people do not tell the truth. Even though *we* know that you're an honest person, lenders have no way of knowing who is honest and who isn't. The unfortunate consequence is that lenders have to treat all of their applicants as though they aren't honest.

WHAT TO BRING TO YOUR LOAN APPLICATION

Use the following checklist to be sure that you bring everything you need to make your loan application an easy, hassle-free experience. **ORIGINALS ARE REQUIRED UNLESS OTHERWISE STATED.**

_____ **Sales Contract** (On the purchase of your new home)

_____ **Original Paystubs For Last 30 Days** (Showing year-to-date earnings, name and Social Security #)

_____ **Most Recent 2 Years Original W-2's**

_____ **Most Recent 2 Years Tax Returns** (With all schedules and signed in blue ink)

_____ **Year-to-Date Profit and Loss Statement and Current Balance Sheet** (If self-employed only)

_____ **Information on Residence History** (For the last 2 years - addresses and dates)

_____ **Coupon Book or Most Recent Statement on All Outstanding Loans and Credit Cards**

_____ **3 Months Bank Statements for All Accounts** (If any recently opened accounts or sizeable deposits, bring documentation to prove the source of the funds.)

_____ **3 Months Statements for IRA/Keogh/401K/Profit Sharing**

_____ **Transcript or Diploma** (If you were a student in the last two years)

_____ **Addresses, Loan Information and Leases (if applicable) on Real Estate You Currently Own**

_____ **Current Landlord's Name, Phone Number and Address or 12 Months Cancelled Checks**

_____ **Copy of Sales Contract** (If you are selling your present home)

_____ **Complete Divorce Papers or Legal Separation Agreement** (If you pay/receive child support or alimony)

_____ **Relocation Agreement** (If you are being transferred into the area)

_____ **Bankruptcy Papers including Schedule of Creditors and Discharge Papers** (If applicable)

_____ **Award Letter and Copy of Most Recent Check** (If you receive Social Security, retirement or disability)

_____ **Pink Slip(s) on Car(s)** (If cars are 5 years old or less)

_____ **Copy of Driver's License and Social Security Card** (FHA only)

_____ **Original Certificate of Eligibility and DD214** (VA only)

_____ $_____**Check for Appraisal and Credit Report Fees**

Figure 6-1:
This is an example of the myriad documents that mortgage lenders ask you to fork over.

Even though lenders require all this documentation, some buyers still falsify information. Worse yet, some mortgage brokers, in their quest to close more loans and earn more commissions, even coach buyers to lie in order to qualify for a loan. One example of how people cheat: Some self-employed people create bogus tax returns with inflated incomes. Although a few people have gotten away with such deception, we don't recommend this wayward path.

If you can't qualify for a mortgage without resorting to trickery, getting turned down is for your own good. Lenders have criteria to ensure that you will be able to repay the money that you borrow and that you don't get in over your head.

Falsifying loan documents is committing perjury and fraud and is *not* in your best interests. Besides the obvious legal objections, you can end up with more mortgage debt than you can really afford. If you're short on a down payment, for example, alternatives are available (see Chapter 3). If the down payment isn't a problem, but you lack the income to qualify for the loan, check out loans that don't require documentation of income. Also, refer to the other ideas for overcoming low income or credit problems discussed earlier in this chapter.

Mortgage lenders can catch you in your lies. How? Well, some mortgage lenders have you sign a document (at the time you close on your home purchase or at the time of your loan application) that allows them to request *directly from the IRS* a copy of the actual return you filed with the IRS. Form 4506 grants the lender permission to get a copy of your tax return. Another document that the lender may spring on you is Form 8821, which lenders give to marginal borrowers. This form asks the IRS to confirm specific information and is more likely to be sent in by a lender to verify your financial information as reported for tax purposes (see Figure 6-2). You'll typically get these documents at closing. You can refuse to sign them — but then again, the lender can refuse to make you a loan!

Permissions to inspect your finances

In order for a mortgage lender to make a proper assessment of your current financial situation, the lender needs to request detailed documentation. Thus, mortgage lenders or brokers ask you to sign a form (like the one shown in Figure 6-3) authorizing and permitting them to make such requests of your employer, the financial institutions that you do business with, and so on.

As we recommend in numerous places throughout this book, you should get, *in writing, before* you agree to do business with a lender, the lender's estimate of what your out-of-pocket expenditures will be in order to close on your home loan. The good news for you is that lenders are required by law to provide, within three days of your application, what's called a *Good Faith Estimate* of closing costs after you've initiated a mortgage with them (see Figure 6-4).

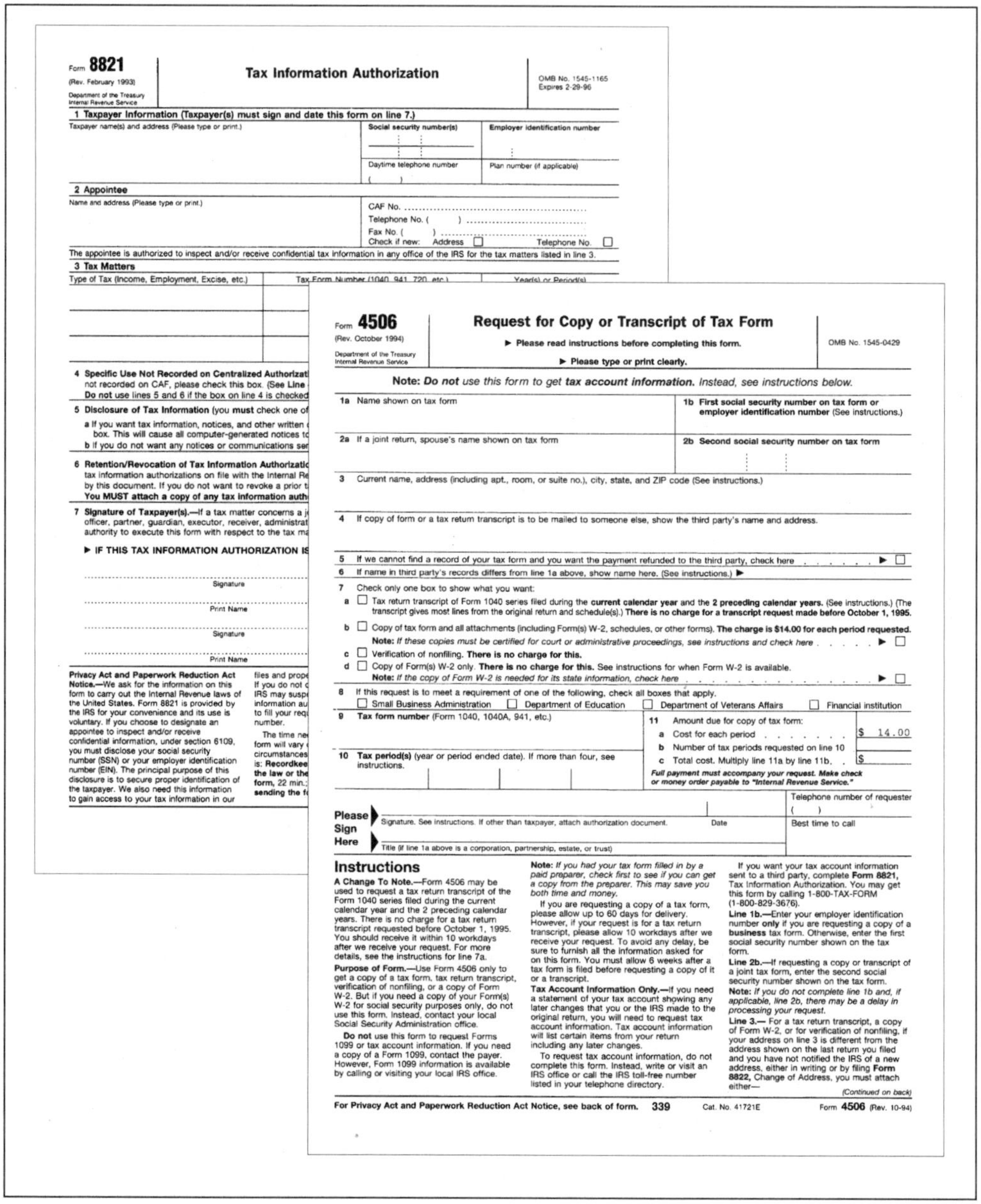

Form **8821** (Rev. February 1993) Department of the Treasury Internal Revenue Service

Tax Information Authorization

OMB No. 1545-1165 Expires 2-29-96

1 Taxpayer Information (Taxpayer(s) must sign and date this form on line 7.)

Taxpayer name(s) and address (Please type or print.) | Social security number(s) | Employer identification number | Daytime telephone number ( ) | Plan number (if applicable)

2 Appointee

Name and address (Please type or print.) | CAF No. | Telephone No. ( ) | Fax No. ( ) | Check if new: Address ☐ Telephone No. ☐

The appointee is authorized to inspect and/or receive confidential tax information in any office of the IRS for the tax matters listed in line 3.

3 Tax Matters

Type of Tax (Income, Employment, Excise, etc.) | Tax Form Number (1040, 941, 720, etc.) | Year(s) or Period(s)

4 Specific Use Not Recorded on Centralized Authorizat… not recorded on CAF, please check this box. (See Line … **Do not** use lines 5 and 6 if the box on line 4 is checked…

5 Disclosure of Tax Information (you **must** check one of…
a If you want tax information, notices, and other written … box. This will cause all computer-generated notices t…
b If you do not want any notices or communications se…

6 Retention/Revocation of Tax Information Authorizatio… tax information authorizations on file with the Internal Re… by this document. If you do not want to revoke a prior t… **You MUST attach a copy of any tax information auth…**

7 Signature of Taxpayer(s).—If a tax matter concerns a j… officer, partner, guardian, executor, receiver, administrat… authority to execute this form with respect to the tax ma…

▶ IF THIS TAX INFORMATION AUTHORIZATION IS…

Signature
Print Name
Signature
Print Name

Privacy Act and Paperwork Reduction Act Notice.—We ask for the information on this form to carry out the Internal Revenue laws of the United States. Form 8821 is provided by the IRS for your convenience and its use is voluntary. If you choose to designate an appointee to inspect and/or receive confidential information, under section 6109, you must disclose your social security number (SSN) or your employer identification number (EIN). The principal purpose of this disclosure is to secure proper identification of the taxpayer. We also need this information to gain access to your tax information in our files and prope… If you do not … IRS may susp… information au… to fill your req… number. The time ne… form will vary … circumstances… is: **Recordkee…** **the law or the…** **form,** 22 min.; **sending the f…**

Form **4506** (Rev. October 1994) Department of the Treasury Internal Revenue Service

Request for Copy or Transcript of Tax Form

▶ **Please read instructions before completing this form.**
▶ **Please type or print clearly.**

OMB No. 1545-0429

Note: ***Do not*** *use this form to get* ***tax account information.*** *Instead, see instructions below.*

1a Name shown on tax form | 1b **First social security number on tax form or employer identification number** (See instructions.)

2a If a joint return, spouse's name shown on tax form | 2b **Second social security number on tax form**

3 Current name, address (including apt., room, or suite no.), city, state, and ZIP code (See instructions.)

4 If copy of form or a tax return transcript is to be mailed to someone else, show the third party's name and address.

5 If we cannot find a record of your tax form and you want the payment refunded to the third party, check here . . . . . . ▶ ☐
6 If name in third party's records differs from line 1a above, show name here. (See instructions.) ▶
7 Check only one box to show what you want:
a ☐ Tax return transcript of Form 1040 series filed during the **current calendar year** and the **2 preceding calendar years.** (See instructions.) (The transcript gives most lines from the original return and schedule(s).) **There is no charge for a transcript request made before October 1, 1995.**
b ☐ Copy of tax form and all attachments (including Form(s) W-2, schedules, or other forms). **The charge is $14.00 for each period requested.** **Note:** *If these copies must be certified for court or administrative proceedings, see instructions and check here* . . . . . ▶ ☐
c ☐ Verification of nonfiling. **There is no charge for this.**
d ☐ Copy of Form(s) W-2 only. **There is no charge for this.** See instructions for when Form W-2 is available. **Note:** *If the copy of Form W-2 is needed for its state information, check here* . . . . ▶ ☐
8 If this request is to meet a requirement of one of the following, check all boxes that apply.
☐ Small Business Administration ☐ Department of Education ☐ Department of Veterans Affairs ☐ Financial institution
9 **Tax form number** (Form 1040, 1040A, 941, etc.)
10 **Tax period(s)** (year or period ended date). If more than four, see instructions.
11 Amount due for copy of tax form:
a Cost for each period . . . . $ 14.00
b Number of tax periods requested on line 10
c Total cost. Multiply line 11a by line 11b. . $
Full payment must accompany your request. Make check or money order payable to "Internal Revenue Service."

Please Sign Here ▶ Signature. See instructions. If other than taxpayer, attach authorization document. | Date | Telephone number of requester ( ) | Best time to call
▶ Title (if line 1a above is a corporation, partnership, estate, or trust)

Instructions

A Change To Note.—Form 4506 may be used to request a tax return transcript of the Form 1040 series filed during the current calendar year and the 2 preceding calendar years. There is no charge for a tax return transcript requested before October 1, 1995. You should receive it within 10 workdays after we receive your request. For more details, see the instructions for line 7a.

Purpose of Form.—Use Form 4506 only to get a copy of a tax form, tax return transcript, verification of nonfiling, or a copy of Form W-2. But if you need a copy of your Form(s) W-2 for social security purposes only, do not use this form. Instead, contact your local Social Security Administration office.

Do not use this form to request Forms 1099 or tax account information. If you need a copy of a Form 1099, contact the payer. However, Form 1099 information is available by calling or visiting your local IRS office.

Note: *If you had your tax form filled in by a paid preparer, check first to see if you can get a copy from the preparer. This may save you both time and money.*

If you are requesting a copy of a tax form, please allow up to 60 days for delivery. However, if your request is for a tax return transcript, please allow 10 workdays after we receive your request. To avoid any delay, be sure to furnish all the information asked for on this form. You must allow 6 weeks after a tax form is filed before requesting a copy of it or a transcript.

Tax Account Information Only.—If you need a statement of your tax account showing any later changes that you or the IRS made to the original return, you will need to request tax account information. Tax account information will list certain items from your return including any later changes.

To request tax account information, do not complete this form. Instead, write or visit an IRS office or call the IRS toll-free number listed in your telephone directory.

If you want your tax account information sent to a third party, complete **Form 8821,** Tax Information Authorization. You may get this form by calling 1-800-TAX-FORM (1-800-829-3676).

Line 1b.—Enter your employer identification number **only** if you are requesting a copy of a **business** tax form. Otherwise, enter the first social security number shown on the tax form.

Line 2b.—If requesting a copy or transcript of a joint tax form, enter the second social security number shown on the tax form.

Note: *If you do not complete line 1b and, if applicable, line 2b, there may be a delay in processing your request.*

Line 3.— For a tax return transcript, a copy of Form W-2, or for verification of nonfiling, if your address on line 3 is different from the address shown on the last return you filed and you have not notified the IRS of a new address, either in writing or by filing **Form 8822,** Change of Address, you must attach either—

(Continued on back)

For Privacy Act and Paperwork Reduction Act Notice, see back of form. 339 Cat. No. 41721E Form **4506** (Rev. 10-94)

Figure 6-2: These documents may be waiting to surprise you in the lender's loan papers at closing.

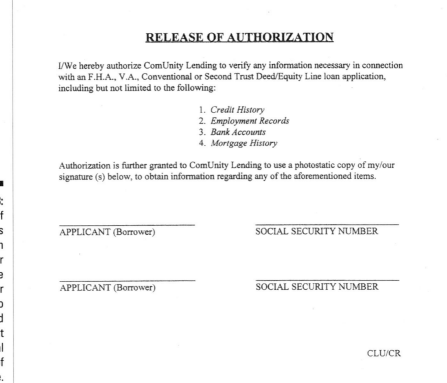

Figure 6-3:
This type of form grants permission to your mortgage lender or broker to verify and document the financial facts of your life.

The Uniform Residential Loan Application

This is the big cheese, the big enchilada, or whatever you want to call it. Mortgage lenders and brokers throughout this vast country use the Uniform Residential Loan Application to collect vital data about home purchases and proposed loans. Many lenders use this standardized document, known in the mortgage trade as *Form 1003,* because they sell their mortgages to investors. When mortgage loans are resold, governmental organizations called *Fannie Mae* and *Freddie Mac* agree (if the mortgage loans meet federal standards) to guarantee the repayment of principal and interest, which makes it easier for lenders to sell the loans and more desirable for investors to buy them.

Some mortgage lenders may toss you a Form 1003 and expect you to return it to them completed. Other lenders and brokers help you fill out the form or even go so far as to complete it all for you.

GOOD FAITH ESTIMATE - BORROWER'S SETTLEMENT COSTS

This list gives an estimate of most of the charges you will have to pay at the settlement of your loan. The figures shown, as estimates, are subject to change. The figures shown are computed based on the sales price and financing indicated.
The numbers listed on the left-handed column of this form correspond to the line number on the HUD-1 form, which will be used in conjunction with the settlement of your loan.
THIS FORM DOES NOT COVER ALL ITEMS YOU WILL BE REQUIRED TO PAY IN CASH AT SETTLEMENT; FOR EXAMPLE, DEPOSITS IN ESCROW FOR REPAIRS OR PEST WORK, YOU MAY BE REQUIRED TO PAY OTHER ADDITIONAL AMOUNTS AT SETTLEMENT.

This estimate was prepared for _____ **on the date of** _____
for the purchase /refi of _____
(property address)

Sales Price / Value
1st Mortgage
2nd Mortgage
Total Financing
Down Payment
Financed VA Funding Fee/MIP

Total Financing including VA Funding Fee / MIP

NONRECURRING CLOSING COSTS
801 Origination Fee Paid To Lender ___ %
802 Discount Points Paid To Lender (Govt. Pts.) ___ %
803 Appraisal Fee
817 Inspection Fee (442)
804 Credit Report Fee
805 Appraisal Review Fee
806 Document Preparation
808 Processing Fee Paid To Lender
809 Underwriting Fee
905 VA Funding Fee
810 Courier Fee
811 Other _____
813 Flood Certification
815 Wire Transfer Fee
816 Warehouse
1101 Settlement or Closing (Escrow Fee)
1102 Title Misc. Fees
1104 (a) Title Insurance Lender's (ALTA)
1105 (b) Title Insurance Owner's (CLTA)
1103 Notary Fees
1201 Recording Fees
1106 Tax Service Fee
1301 Pest Inspection
1202 City Transfer Tax (3.30 x 1,000 of S.P. -split 50-50)
     Subtotal Nonrecurring Closing Costs
ITEMS PAID WHILE ACTING AS A BROKER
821 Commission Paid To Broker ___ %
     Rebate Fee (Premium Pricing and/or Servicing
        Released Premium) Paid To Mortgage Broker ___
825 Processing Fee Paid To Mortgage Broker
     Subtotal Nonrecurring Closing Costs.

RECURRING CLOSING COSTS OR PREPAID EXPENSES
___ Months Taxes
___ Months Insurance
902 PMI Premium (1st Year)
    1 Month [ ] PMI 1 Month [ ] MMI
901* Interest ___ days
     Subtotal: Prepaid Expenses
TOTAL CASH REQUIRED: .TOTAL
Less monies advanced (escrow deposit)
Total cash required at closing

*This interest calculation represents the greatest amount of interest you could be required to pay at settlement. The actual amount will be determined by which day of the month your settlement is conducted. To determine the amount you will have to pay, multiply the number of days remaining in the month in which you settle times $ ___, which is the daily interest charge for your loan.

I hereby acknowledge receipt of a copy of this estimate.
Date: / / _____   Amended Date: / / _____

Borrower _____   Borrower _____
Borrower _____   Borrower _____
Prepared By: 4/5/93   Prepared By: _____

Type of Program _____
P & I @ ___ %
P/MMI
P & I (2nd)
Taxes
Insurance
HOA Dues
Total

CLU/GFE

Figure 6-4: Here's an estimated closing costs worksheet.

If you let someone fill out the Uniform Residential Loan Application for you, be *sure* that the information on the form is accurate and truthful. Ultimately, *you're* responsible for the accuracy and truthfulness of what is on your application. Also, be aware that, in their sales efforts, some mortgage lenders and brokers may invite you to their offices or invite themselves to your home or office to complete this form for you or with you. Although we have no problem with good service, we do want you to keep in mind that you are not beholden or obligated to any lenders or brokers, even if they offer to come over and wash your car and provide you with a pedicure! It's your money and your home purchase, so be sure to shop around for a good loan or mortgage broker.

If, like most people, you take the first whack at completing this form yourself, we trust that you'll find the upcoming sections (in which we walk you through the major items on this application) useful.

I. Type of mortgage and terms of loan

The main items of concern to you in the first section of the application (see Figure 6-5) are the loan amount (Amount), Interest Rate, length of the loan (No. of Months), and the loan type (Fixed Rate or ARM). If at the time that you're applying for your mortgage, you're unsure as to some of these options and what you're going to choose, simply leave the relevant spaces blank.

Your mortgage lender or broker completes the boxes in this section that don't make sense to you — Agency Case Number and Lender Case Number. You are not to fill in these boxes!

Figure 6-5:
In Section I of the Uniform Residential Loan Application, you spell out the type and terms of the loan you want.

I. TYPE OF MORTGAGE AND TERMS OF LOAN					
Mortgage Applied for: ☐ V.A. ☐ Conventional ☐ Other: ☐ FHA ☐ FmHA		Agency Case Number		Lender Case Number	
Amount $	Interest Rate %	No. of Months	Amortization Type:	☐ Fixed Rate ☐ GPM	☐ Other (explain): ☐ ARM (type):

II. Property information and purpose of loan

Your mortgage lender is curious about why you want to borrow the vast sum of money that you listed in Part I. Hence, Part II (see Figure 6-6). In addition to wanting to know the address of the property, the lender also wants to know the legal description of the property. The *legal description* simply means the block

II. PROPERTY INFORMATION AND PURPOSE OF LOAN						
Subject Property Address (street, city, state, ZIP)						No. of Units
Legal Description of Subject Property (attach description if necessary)						Year Built
Purpose of Loan ☐ Purchase ☐ Construction ☐ Refinance ☐ Construction-Permanent		☐ Other (explain):		Property will be: ☐ Primary Residence ☐ Secondary Residence ☐ Investment		
Complete this line if construction or construction-permanent loan. Year Lot Acquired	Original Cost $	Amount Existing Liens $	(a) Present Value of Lot $	(b) Cost of Improvements $	Total (a + b) $	
Complete this line if this is a refinance loan. Year Acquired	Original Cost $	Amount Existing Liens $	Purpose of Refinance	Describe Improvements ☐ made ☐ to be made Cost: $		
Title will be held in what Name(s)			Manner in which Title will be held		Estate will be held in: ☐ Fee Simple ☐ Leasehold (show expiration date)	
Source of Down Payment, Settlement Charges and/or Subordinate Financing (explain)						

Figure 6-6: The property's legal description and what you're going to do with the loan.

and lot number of the property, which come from the preliminary title report. Your real estate agent, your mortgage lender, and you should each have copies of this report soon after you have a signed purchase agreement.

The information you include in the Purpose of Loan section tells the lender whether you plan to use the mortgage to buy a home, refinance an existing loan, or build a new home (Construction). The lender also wants to know, in this section, whether the property is your primary or secondary residence or is an investment property. Your answers to these questions determine which loans your property is eligible for and the terms of the loans. From a lender's perspective, construction loans and investment-property loans are riskier than other loans and generally carry higher interest rates.

You may be tempted (and some mortgage brokers have been, as well) to lie on this part of the mortgage application in order to obtain more favorable loan terms. Be aware that lenders can — and sometimes do — challenge you to prove that you're going to live in the property if they suspect otherwise. Even after closing on a purchase and their loan, lenders have been known to ask for proof that the borrower is living in the property. They may ask you for utility bills (to see whether the bills are in your name), and some lenders have even been known to send a representative around to knock on the borrower's doors to see who is living in the home!

At the time that you apply for your mortgage, you must declare how you will hold title to the property — in other words, how the ownership of the home will be structured for legal purposes. We cover this important decision in Chapter 12.

Mortgage lenders also like to know where your down payment and closing costs are coming from to ensure that this money isn't yet another loan that may burden your ability to repay the money they are lending you. Ideally, lenders want to see the down payment and closing costs coming from your personal savings. Tell the truth — lenders have many ways to trip you up in your lies here. For example, they may ask to see the last several months of your bank or investment account statements to verify that, for example, a relative didn't recently give you the money.

III. Borrower information

The third section of the Uniform Residential Loan Application (see Figure 6-7) is where you get to scribe your name, rank, and serial number. If you're buying the property with someone else, such as your spouse, you have the added thrill of providing information about the other person, as well.

Yrs. School simply means how many total years of formal schooling you have under your belt. If you graduated from high school, you've had 12 years of schooling. Two- or four-year colleges add that many years on top of the 12. If you were silly enough to go to graduate school, add the number of years that you spent toiling away for those additional scraps of paper to hang on your office or den wall.

The lender also wants to know where you've been living recently. If you've been in your most recent housing situation for at least two years, you not only will receive a case of Turtle Wax, but you can also pass on listing your two prior living accommodations.

Lenders are primarily looking for stability here. Most lenders also request a letter from your landlord to verify that you pay rent on time. If you've moved frequently in recent years, most lenders check with more than your most recent landlord. If your application is borderline, good references can tip the scales in your favor. If you've paid what you owed and you've paid on time, you have nothing to worry about. If you haven't, you should explain yourself, either by separate letter to the lender or in the blank space on page four of the application.

Borrower	III. BORROWER INFORMATION	Co-Borrower
Borrower's Name (include Jr. or Sr. if applicable)		Co-Borrower's Name (include Jr. or Sr. if applicable)
Social Security Number · Home Phone (incl. area code) · Age · Yrs. School		Social Security Number · Home Phone (incl. area code) · Age · Yrs. School
☐ Married ☐ Unmarried (include single, divorced, widowed) ☐ Separated · Dependents (not listed by Co-Borrower) no. ages		☐ Married ☐ Unmarried (include single, divorced, widowed) ☐ Separated · Dependents (not listed by Borrower) no. ages
Present Address (street, city, state, ZIP) ☐ Own ☐ Rent ____ No. Yrs.		Present Address (street, city, state, ZIP) ☐ Own ☐ Rent ____ No. Yrs.
If residing at present address for less than two years, complete the following:		
Former Address (street, city, state, ZIP) ☐ Own ☐ Rent ____ No. Yrs.		Former Address (street, city, state, ZIP) ☐ Own ☐ Rent ____ No. Yrs.
Former Address (street, city, state, ZIP) ☐ Own ☐ Rent ____ No. Yrs.		Former Address (street, city, state, ZIP) ☐ Own ☐ Rent ____ No. Yrs.

Figure 6-7: Part III asks, "So tell me about yourself. . . ."

IV. Employment information

Just as they want to know your recent residences, mortgage lenders also want to know your recent work history (see Figure 6-8). If you've been in one position for at least the past two years, that's the only position you need to list. Otherwise, you must list your prior employment to cover the past two-year period. Again, the lender is looking for stability, which can help push a marginal application through the loan-approval channels.

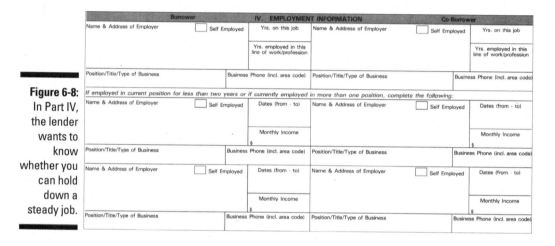

Figure 6-8: In Part IV, the lender wants to know whether you can hold down a steady job.

If you're a detail kind of person, you may be wondering why the application asks for the monthly income from prior jobs but not your current one. The reason is that you provide the monthly income for your current position in the next section (Section V) of the application.

Should you leave a short-term residence or job off your application?

Many people who prepare resumes decide to omit positions that they've held for only a short period of time. The reasons vary, but most people do it to make their resumes look stronger and to avoid being perceived as job hoppers.

If you've had gaps in employment, it's better to show the gap than to be caught with your hand in the cookie jar — lenders often ask for the dates of your employment. Don't lie; lenders who catch you in one lie will scrutinize your loan application twice as carefully, looking for more lies. Lenders don't mind some job hopping.

Another section of the verification-of-employment request, which your current employer receives from the lender, asks what your prospects are for continued employment. The answer to that question is important, too.

In a sense, a mortgage application is like a resume. You want to present your information in its most positive, yet truthful, light.

You may also wonder (and be concerned about) why the lender wants your current and previous employers' phone numbers. Shortly before your loan is ready to close, the lender may call your current employer to verify that you are still employed, but verification of employment is usually done by mail. It is highly unlikely that the lender will call your previous employers.

V. Monthly income and housing expense projections

Section V (see Figure 6-9) makes or breaks many a mortgage application. Here, you list your monthly income, including that derived from investments such as bank, brokerage, and mutual fund accounts. Most people's employment is what qualifies them to borrow money via a mortgage. If your income fluctuates from month to month, simply enter your average monthly income over the past 12 months. (Some lenders use a 24-month average if you're self-employed.)

Figure 6-9: How much do you make and how much will you spend?

V. MONTHLY INCOME AND COMBINED HOUSING EXPENSE INFORMATION						
Gross Monthly Income	Borrower	Co-Borrower	Total	Combined Monthly Housing Expense	Present	Proposed
Base Empl. Income *	$	$	$	Rent	$	
Overtime				First Mortgage (P&I)		$
Bonuses				Other Financing (P&I)		
Commissions				Hazard Insurance		
Dividends/Interest				Real Estate Taxes		
Net Rental Income				Mortgage Insurance		
Other (before completing, see the notice in "describe other income," below)				Homeowner Assn. Dues		
				Other:		
Total	$	$	$	Total	$	$
* Self Employed Borrower(s) may be required to provide additional documentation such as tax returns and financial statements.						
Describe Other Income Notice: Alimony, child support, or separate maintenance income need not be revealed if the Borrower (B) or Co-Borrower (C) does not choose to have it considered for repaying this loan.						Monthly Amount
B/C						$

Net Rental Income refers to the difference between your rental real estate's monthly rents and expenses (excluding depreciation). *Rental property* is property that you've bought for the purpose of renting it out. Therefore, *Net Rental Income* is the profit or loss that you make each month on rental property (excluding depreciation). If you've recently purchased the rental property, the lender only counts 75 percent of the current rent that you are collecting. If you've held your rental property long enough to complete a tax return, then most lenders use the profit or loss (excluding depreciation) reported on your tax return.

If you have other income sources, such as child support or alimony, be sure to list them on the Other line and describe them in the last portion of this section. The more income you can list, the better equipped you are to qualify for a mortgage with the most favorable terms for you.

The Combined Monthly Housing Expense area on the right-hand side of this section enables you to tally up your current and proposed housing expenses. If you're currently renting, simply enter your rent in the relevant box. Your proposed expenses refer to what your estimated expenses would be with the purchase of the home that you're expecting to buy. Your mortgage lender or broker can help you complete this important section.

If you're stretching to buy, make sure that the estimates that your lender or broker plugs into the estimated housing expense section are reasonable and are not inflated. In their efforts to cover their own behinds and to insure that you don't get in over your head, some mortgage lenders make estimates that are too high. If, for example, the mortgage lender estimates that homeowners insurance will cost you $100 per month, but you already have a quote in hand for good coverage at $80 per month, speak up about the discrepancy.

If you're on the borderline between qualifying and not qualifying for a loan, lenders will be less inclined to approve your loan if a big difference exists between your current housing expenses and your proposed expenses as a homeowner. Lenders and mortgage brokers refer to people in this situation as subjecting themselves to *payment shock*. If you're in this situation, you should assess whether you can really afford that significant an increase in your monthly housing expenses (see Chapters 2 and 3).

VI. Assets and liabilities

In Section VI (see Figure 6-10), you present your personal balance sheet, which summarizes your assets and liabilities. Your assets are subdivided into liquid (for example, non-retirement-account) assets and those assets that are not liquid (such as real estate). *Liquid,* in this example, simply means those assets that you can sell quickly to come up with cold hard cash for a home purchase or some other purpose.

Why so many spaces (four) are allotted to checking and savings accounts puzzles us. If you can't squeeze your other non-retirement holdings in brokerage accounts or mutual funds into the small space provided for "Stocks & Bonds," use the extra bank account lines and explain what you're listing there.

Liabilities are any loans or debts you have outstanding. The more such obligations you have, the more reticent a mortgage lender will be to lend you a large amount of money.

If you have the cash available to pay off high-cost consumer loans, such as credit card loans and auto loans, consider doing so now. (If you opted for loan prequalification or preapproval, as we discuss in Chapter 5, the lender likely recommended getting rid of these consumer debts at that time.) Such debts generally carry high interest rates that are not tax-deductible, and they hurt your chances of qualifying for a mortgage (see Chapter 3 for an explanation of this matter).

Note (at the bottom of the liability column) that you are to list child support and alimony payments that you make as well as out-of-pocket expenses related to your job if you aren't self-employed. Such monthly expenses are like debts in the sense that they require monthly feeding.

VI. ASSETS AND LIABILITIES		

This Statement and any applicable supporting schedules may be completed jointly by both married and unmarried Co-Borrowers if their assets and liabilities are sufficiently joined so that the Statement can be meaningfully and fairly presented on a combined basis; otherwise separate Statements and Schedules are required. If the Co-Borrower section was completed about a spouse, this Statement and supporting schedules must be completed about that spouse also.

Completed ☐ Jointly ☐ Not Jointly

ASSETS Description	Cash or Market Value	Liabilities and Pledged Assets. List the creditor's name, address and account number for all outstanding debts, including automobile loans, revolving charge accounts, real estate loans, alimony, child support, stock pledges, etc. Use continuation sheet, if necessary. Indicate by (*) those liabilities which will be satisfied upon sale of real estate owned or upon refinancing of the subject property.	Monthly Pmt. & Mos. Left to Pay	Unpaid Balance
Cash deposit toward purchase held by:	$	LIABILITIES		
		Name and address of Company	$ Pmt./Mos.	$
List checking and savings accounts below				
Name and address of Bank, S&L, or Credit Union				
		Acct. no.		
		Name and address of Company	$ Pmt./Mos.	$
Acct. no.	$			
Name and address of Bank, S&L, or Credit Union				
		Acct. no.		
		Name and address of Company	$ Pmt./Mos.	$
Acct. no.	$			
Name and address of Bank, S&L, or Credit Union				
		Acct. no.		
		Name and address of Company	$ Pmt./Mos.	$
Acct. no.	$			
Name and address of Bank, S&L, or Credit Union				
		Acct. no.		
		Name and address of Company	$ Pmt./Mos.	$
Acct. no.	$			
Stocks & Bonds (Company name/number & description)	$			
		Acct. no.		
		Name and address of Company	$ Pmt./Mos.	$
Life insurance net cash value	$			
Face amount: $				
Subtotal Liquid Assets	$			
Real estate owned (enter market value from schedule of real estate owned)	$	Acct. no.		
Vested interest in retirement fund	$	Name and address of Company	$ Pmt./Mos.	$
Net worth of business(es) owned (attach financial statement)	$			
Automobiles owned (make and year)	$			
		Acct. no.		
		Alimony/Child Support/Separate Maintenance Payments Owed to:	$	
Other Assets (itemize)	$	Job Related Expense (child care, union dues, etc.)	$	
		Total Monthly Payments	$	
Total Assets a.	$	Net Worth (a minus b)	$	Total Liabilities b. $

Freddie Mac Form 65 10/92   Page 2 of 4   Fannie Mae Form 1003 10/92

Figure 6-10:
How much cash and how many assets do you have in reserves for a down payment and closing — and how much do you owe?

VI. ASSETS AND LIABILITIES (cont.)							

Schedule of Real Estate Owned (If additional properties are owned, use continuation sheet.)

Property Address (enter S if sold, PS if pending sale or R if rental being held for income)	Type of Property	Present Market Value	Amount of Mortgages & Liens	Gross Rental Income	Mortgage Payments	Insurance, Maintenance, Taxes & Misc.	Net Rental Income
		$	$	$	$	$	$
Totals		$	$	$	$	$	$

List any additional names under which credit has previously been received and indicate appropriate creditor name(s) and account number(s):

Alternate Name	Creditor Name	Account Number

Section VI continues over onto page 3 and includes space for the details of rental real estate you already own. If you make a profit from such holdings, that profit can help your chances of qualifying for other mortgages. Conversely, *negative cash flow* (property expenses exceeding income) from rentals reduces the amount that a mortgage lender will lend you. Most mortgage lenders want a copy of your tax return (and possibly copies of your rental agreements with tenants) to substantiate the information you put in this space.

VII. Details of transaction

In Section VII (see Figure 6-11), you detail the terms of the proposed home purchase. The purpose of the first part of this section is to total the cost of the home, including closing costs. After subtracting the expected loan amount, this column arrives at how much money you will need to come up with to close on the home purchase. Some prospective buyers find that, after they've successfully completed this section, they must go begging to family or borrow more money to close on the purchase.

VII. DETAILS OF TRANSACTION	
a. Purchase price	$
b. Alterations, improvements, repairs	
c. Land (if acquired separately)	
d. Refinance (incl. debts to be paid off)	
e. Estimated prepaid items	
f. Estimated closing costs	
g. PMI, MIP, Funding Fee	
h. Discount (if Borrower will pay)	
i. Total Costs (add items a through h)	
j. Subordinate financing	
k. Borrower's closing costs paid by Seller	
l. Other Credits (explain)	
m. Loan amount (exclude PMI, MIP, Funding Fee financed)	
n. PMI, MIP, Funding Fee financed	
o. Loan amount (add m & n)	
p. Cash from/to Borrower (subtract j, k, l & o from i)	

Figure 6-11: Time to calculate your closing costs.

VIII. Declarations

Section VIII (shown in Figure 6-12) shouldn't be called "Declarations"; it should be called "Personal interrogation"!

Questions "a" through "i" (above the dotted line) are potential red flags to lenders. If you answer *yes* to any of these questions, explain yourself on a separate page or in the blank space on page four of the application.

The other questions are important details that lenders need to know. Don't worry; a *yes* response here won't kill your loan request.

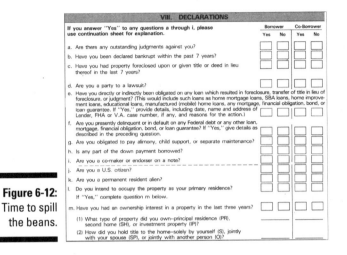

IX. Acknowledgment and agreement

If you haven't been honest on this form, consider Section IX (Figure 6-13) your opportunity to commit perjury.

If you've had a mortgage broker or other person help you with this application, be sure to review for accuracy the answers that they provided before you sign the agreement. This is the time to ask yourself questions (and to review your responses) to ensure that you've presented your information in a positive-but-truthful light.

X. Information for government monitoring purposes

You may skip Section X (Figure 6-14) if you want to. The federal government tracks the ethnicity and gender of borrowers to see (among other things) whether certain peoples are discriminated against by lenders.

X. INFORMATION FOR GOVERNMENT MONITORING PURPOSES

The following information is requested by the Federal Government for certain types of loans related to a dwelling, in order to monitor the Lender's compliance with equal credit opportunity, fair housing and home mortgage disclosure laws. You are not required to furnish this information, but are encouraged to do so. The law provides that a Lender may neither discriminate on the basis of this information, nor on whether you choose to furnish it. However, if you choose not to furnish it, under Federal regulations this Lender is required to note race and sex on the basis of visual observation or surname. If you do not wish to furnish the above information, please check the box below. (Lender must review the above material to assure that the disclosures satisfy all requirements to which the Lender is subject under applicable state law for the particular type of loan applied for.)

BORROWER □ I do not wish to furnish this information

Race/National Origin: □ American Indian or Alaskan Native □ Asian or Pacific Islander □ White, not of Hispanic Origin □ Black, not of Hispanic origin □ Hispanic □ Other (specify) _____

Sex: □ Female   □ Male

CO-BORROWER □ I do not wish to furnish this information

Race/National Origin: □ American Indian or Alaskan Native □ Asian or Pacific Islander □ White, not of Hispanic Origin □ Black, not of Hispanic origin □ Hispanic □ Other (specify) _____

Sex: □ Female   □ Male

To be Completed by Interviewer

This application was taken by:
□ face-to-face interview
□ by mail
□ by telephone

Interviewer's Name (print or type)

Interviewer's Signature   Date

Interviewer's Phone Number (incl. area code)

Name and Address of Interviewer's Employer

Freddie Mac Form 65 10/92   Page 3 of 4   Fannie Mae Form 1003 10/92

Figure 6-14: Big Brother wants to know.

Continuation sheet

Turn over page three of the Uniform Residential Loan Application to reveal a largely blank page 4. This space is for answers that don't neatly fit elsewhere on the application. Here, for example, you may briefly explain why you've changed jobs so often, justify credit problems, list additional assets and liabilities, or explain why you were arrested for streaking during college. If you have nothing else substantive to reveal, you can simply choose to doodle aimlessly in this space with your favorite Crayolas! Perhaps you can even start to sketch out the details of your first home-renovation project.

If you don't have anything to put on page 4, draw a diagonal line across it so the lender knows that you saw it and have nothing to say. Be sure to sign at the bottom of this last page as well, even if you don't write anything on it. Many people don't sign — and no wonder, with the Grand Canyon of space between the top of this page and the signature line at the bottom!

Other typical documents

All mortgage lenders and brokers have their own, individualized package of documents for you to complete. Some documents are standard because they are federally mandated. Covering all these forms here is certainly beyond the scope of this book — and most people's attention span. What follows are some of the other common forms that you're likely to encounter from your mortgage lender or broker.

Your right to receive a copy of appraisal

It was not always the case, but you now have the right to receive a copy of the appraisal report. That borrowers didn't always have this right is a bit absurd — after all, you're the one who's paying for the appraisal!

To make sure you know that you have this right, the government requires that mortgage lenders and brokers present you with the document in Figure 6-15.

Despite the fact that the notice tells you to make your request in writing, try making the request verbally to save yourself time. Then, if your request is ignored, go to the hassle of submitting a written request for your appraisal (within 90 days of the rendering of a decision to approve or reject your loan). Appraisals are good to have in your files — you never know when an appraisal may come in handy. At the very least, you can see what properties were used as comparables to yours in order to discover how good or bad the appraisal is.

Equal Credit Opportunity Act

It is a matter of federal law that a mortgage lender may not reject your loan because of any non-financial personal characteristic, such as race, sex, marital status, age, and so forth (see Figure 6-16). You also do not have to disclose income that you receive as a result of being divorced (although we think that doing so is in your best interest because such income may help get your loan approved).

If you have reason to believe that a mortgage lender is discriminating against you, contact and file a complaint with the Department of Real Estate or whatever government division regulates mortgage lenders in your state. And start hunting around for a better, more ethical lender.

EQUAL CREDIT OPPORTUNITY ACT
(REGULATION B)

RIGHT TO RECEIVE A COPY OF APPRAISAL

You have the right to a copy of the appraisal report used in connection with your application for credit. If you wish a copy, please write to us at the mailing address provided. We must receive your request no later than 90 days after we notify you of the action taken on your credit application, or you withdraw your application. In your letter you must provide us with your name, the address of the subject property, your current address, and the loan number assigned to your transaction.

I (We) have read and understand the aforementioned conditions regarding my right to receive a copy of our appraisal and acknowledge receipt to a copy of this disclosure.

_____   _____
Applicant   Date

_____   _____
Applicant   Date

Figure 6-15:
Exercise your right to your property's appraisal — ask for a copy!

Equal Credit Opportunity Act Notice
(ECOA)

The federal Equal Credit Opportunity Act prohibits creditors from discriminating against Credit Applicant(s) on the basis of race, color, religion, national origin, sex, marital status, age (provided that the applicant has the capacity to enter into a binding contract); because all or part of the applicant(s) income is derived from any public assistance program; or because the applicant has in good faith exercised any right under the Consumer Credit Protection Act. The federal agency that administers compliance with the law concerning this credit is the:

If this loan is to be funded by a Mortgage Banking concern, contact the Federal Trade Commission, Pennsylvania at 6th, Washington, D.C.

If this loan is to be funded by a state chartered Savings and Loan Association, or a Federally chartered Savings and Loan Association contact the Federal Home Loan Bank Board.

Income received from Alimony, Child Support or Separate Maintenance need not be revealed unless you choose to rely on such sources to have it considered as a basis for repaying this obligation. Income from these sources as well as from any other source, including part-time or temporary employment will not be discounted by the lender, because of your sex or marital status; however, the Lender will consider carefully the stability and probable continuity of all income you disclose.

I/WE RECEIVED A COPY OF THIS NOTICE.

Figure 6-16:
It is against
the law for
mortgage
lenders to
discriminate.

_____   _____
Borrower   Date

_____   _____
Borrower   Date

Part III
Property, Players, and Prices

The 5th Wave — By Rich Tennant

"Before we go in, let me ask you — do you like to bowl?"

In this part . . .

In this part, we introduce you to the various types of property you may consider buying and the people you may hire to help you buy a home. In addition to steering you towards winning strategies and winning players, we help you avoid loser properties and, well, losers in general. We close this section by giving you a crash course on how to distinguish good buys from overpriced turkeys so that you won't overpay (and, in fact, may even get a very good deal) when you purchase your dream home.

Chapter 7

Where and What to Buy

*W*hat's your idea of the perfect car, the perfect job, and the perfect way to spend a day? Would you have said the same things ten years ago? Probably not. Perfection is a moving target — it changes as you change.

Where *the* perfect home is concerned, there's no such thing. No one home will be perfect for you from birth to earth, and few people have the financial resources to afford what they think is the perfect home. The home that's perfect in your 20s when you're footloose and fancy-free likely won't cut it when you're 40 if you're married or raising a family. Fast forward 20 more years to when you're nearing retirement. You may want or need to move to a smaller home that's easier to maintain.

Don't fret. Even though no single home stays perfect forever, this chapter shows you how to profitably achieve sequential perfection in your homes. And, because moving is expensive, it also shows you how to minimize the number of times you buy and sell.

You probably know someone who's lost money on a house sale. We're sure that you don't plan to be the next victim of a capricious real estate market. Getting a bargain when you buy a home is a fine initial objective, but don't stop there. Don't you also want your home to appreciate in value while you own it?

The best time to think about how much you'll get for your house when you sell it is before you buy it. Never let your enthusiasm for a house blind you to its flaws. Before you buy, try to look at the property through the eyes of the *next* potential buyer. Anything that disturbs you about the house or neighborhood will probably also bother the next buyer.

We're not suggesting that you should sell your house immediately after buying it. For all we know, you'll live happily ever after in the home you're about to purchase. Then again, an unforeseen life change such as a job transfer, family expansion, or a divorce may force you to sell. If that happens, making a nice profit can take some of the sting out of moving day.

Appreciation is handy for a great deal more than just increasing your net worth. Given that your home increases in value over time, you may someday find that this *equity* (the difference between market value and the mortgage you owe) can help you accomplish important financial and personal goals. You can use the money anyway you wish — add to your retirement, help pay your kids' college education, start your own business, or take the Orient Express from London to Venice to celebrate your 25th wedding anniversary. Nest eggs are extremely versatile financial tools — and completely cholesterol free.

In a world filled with uncertainties, no one can guarantee that your home will increase in value. However, buying a good property in a good neighborhood tremendously increases your odds of making money. This maxim holds true whether the market is strong or weak when you sell.

If you've read Chapter 4, you know that property prices aren't static. They rise and fall due to such factors as the local job market, the supply of and demand for available housing and rental units, interest rates, and yearly cycles of strong versus weak market activity. These things are beyond your control and your ability to predict. But this doesn't mean that your financial destiny as a homeowner is a total fluke of fate. On the contrary, you control three important factors that greatly affect your home's value:

- How much you pay for your home
- Where you buy your home
- What home you buy

The number-one controllable factor is how much you pay for your home. If you grossly overpay for your house when you buy it, you'd be extremely lucky to make a profit when you sell. That's why we devote Chapter 9 to making sure that you know exactly how to spot well priced properties and avoid overpriced turkeys.

This chapter focuses on the other two crucial factors under your control — where and what you buy.

Location, Location, Value

If you're as wealthy as Oprah Winfrey or Bill Gates, you can afford to live anywhere you darn well please. The rest of us have somewhat more limited budgets. Even so, unless you're at the bitter bottom of the housing food chain, you'll have many choices on where to spend your money. Where you ultimately decide to buy is up to you.

You've probably already heard that the three most important things you should look for when buying a home are "location, location, location." That axiom is largely true. People buy neighborhoods every bit as much as houses. Good times or bad, folks pay a premium to live in better neighborhoods. Conversely, rotten neighborhoods ravage home values. You'd have trouble selling the Taj Mahal if it were surrounded by junk yards and chicken farms.

But telling you that the secret of making money in real estate you buy is "location, location, location" is like saying that you'll make a fortune in the stock market if you buy low and sell high. It takes more than glittering generalities to make money. You need specifics.

First off, we don't agree that the three most important factors are location, location, location. Besides, we don't see much point in repeating ourselves three times — it's not like you're a complete idiot or something! *Value* — what you get for your money — is important too.

If, for example, everyone knows Snob Hill Pines is the *best* neighborhood in town, you'll pay a hefty premium to live there. And, although Snob Hill Pines is king of the hill now and may stay that way forever, it's also true that the neighborhood has no place to go except downhill.

Other neighborhoods, ones that aren't held in such high esteem right now, may eventually improve what they offer homebuyers and thus experience far greater property value appreciation. Buying a home in a good location is important, but it shouldn't be your sole home-shopping criterion. If you want to buy a home that is a good investment, you must look for good value. We explain how to do that in this chapter.

Characteristics of good neighborhoods

Good neighborhoods, like beauty, are in the eyes of the beholder. For example, being near excellent schools is important if you have young children. If, on the other hand, you're ready to retire, buying in a peaceful area with outdoor activities may appeal to you, whereas being next to a noisy junior high school is your worst nightmare! Neither neighborhood may suit you if you're the footloose and fancy-free type. Your ideal neighborhood is probably a singles' condo complex downtown, so you can be near the action day or night.

Personal preferences aside, all good neighborhoods have the following characteristics:

- ✔ **Economic health:** Nothing kills property values faster than a forest of "For Sale" signs precipitated by corporate layoffs. See Chapter 4 for ways to evaluate the employers and the job market in a community in which you're contemplating buying a home.

- ✔ **Amenities:** Amenities are special features of a neighborhood that make it an attractive, desirable place to live. Wide streets bordered by stately oak trees, lush green parks, ocean views, quiet cul-de-sacs, proximity to schools, churches, shopping, restaurants, transportation, parking, playgrounds, tennis courts, and beaches are some examples of amenities that add value to a neighborhood. Of course, few people can afford to buy in a neighborhood that has all these amenities, but the more of these perks a neighborhood has, the better from the perspective of most homebuyers.

- ✔ **Quality schools:** You may not care how good or bad the local schools are if you don't have school-age children. However, you had better believe that parents to whom you may later want to sell your home will care a great deal (unless you're buying in a remote retirement or vacation-type community). But you should care about the quality of nearby schools for more than just resale value, because good schools produce better kids, and that clearly impacts the quality of life in the community. Don't rely on test scores or someone's opinion when assessing school quality; visit the schools and speak with parents and teachers to get a handle on the schools in an area.

- ✔ **Low crime rates:** Most folks today are concerned with crime — and well they should be. Crime is far higher in many areas, including the suburbs, than it used to be. As with schools, don't rely on hearsay or isolated news reports. Communities compile crime statistics, generally by neighborhood. Call the local police department or check the town's reference library to get the facts.

- ✔ **Stability:** Some communities are in a constant state of flux. "Out with the old and in with the new," is their motto. Imagine what would happen to property values if a junk yard were replaced by a beautiful park. How about the reverse — an ugly, multi-story, concrete parking garage appears where there was once a beautiful park? Check with the local planning department and a good real estate agent for the inside scoop on proposed developments in neighborhoods that you're considering.

- ✔ **Pride of ownership:** A home's cost has no bearing on the amount of pride its owners take in it. Drive through any neighborhood, posh or modest, and you see in a flash whether the folks who live there are proud of their homes. A neighborhood filled with beautifully maintained homes and manicured lawns shouts pride of ownership.

Property values sag when homeowners no longer take pride in their property. Avoid declining neighborhoods which display the red flags of dispirited owners — poorly kept houses, junk filled yards, abandoned cars on the street, many absentee owners renting houses, high rates of vandalism and crime, and so on. Neighborhood deterioration is a blight which spreads from one house to another.

Selecting the best neighborhood for you

You may get lucky and find the neighborhood of your dreams right away. You're far more likely, however, to end up evaluating the strengths and weaknesses of several neighborhoods while trying to decide which one to favor with your purchase. If you're on a budget — and most people are — you may have to compromise and make tradeoffs.

Suppose that one neighborhood has the schools you like, the second is closest to your office (which would save you an hour a day commuting), and the third neighborhood is in a town with a delightful beach. They're all good neighborhoods. It's a tough decision.

Here are four tie breakers you can use to select the best neighborhood *for you:*

- ✔ **Prioritize your needs.** Buying a home when you have budgetary constraints involves making tradeoffs. For example, if you want to live in the town with great schools and parks, you must settle for a smaller home than if you buy in a more average community. When push comes to shove and you have to choose a place to live, you must decide what is most important to you.

- ✔ **Talk to people who live in the neighborhoods.** Who knows more about a neighborhood than folks who live in it? In addition to asking how they feel about their neighborhood, see what residents say about other neighborhoods you're considering. If you can spark neighborhoodly rivalry, you'll get the dirt about the other neighborhoods' lousy weather, parking problems, unfriendly or snobby owners, and so on. Renters are also a great source of information. Because they don't have a wad of cash invested in a home, renters are generally candid about the shortcomings of a neighborhood. Last, but not least, drive or walk through the neighborhoods at various times of the day and evening to make sure that their charm stays on 24 hours a day.

- ✔ **Get days-on-market (DOM) statistics from your real estate agent.** DOM statistics indicate how long the average house in an area takes to sell after it goes on the market. As a rule, the faster property sells, the more likely it is to sell close to full asking price. Quick sales indicate strong buyer demand, which is nice to have when you're ready to sell.

 ✔ **Get help from a professional.** Ask a real estate agent, lender, or appraiser to compare the upside potential of home values in each neighborhood. As Chapter 8 explains, home buying is a team sport. Get an analysis of each neighborhood's present and future property values from full-time real estate people.

Neither real estate agents nor lenders charge for opinions of value. They both, however, have a vested interest in selling you something. Appraisers, on the other hand, have no ax to grind. True, appraisers charge to analyze neighborhood property values and pricing trends. But if you're going to spend tens of thousands of dollars for a home, paying an additional few hundred dollars to get an *unbiased,* professional analysis of a neighborhood's property values may be money well spent.

Demystifying What's for Sale

Good news. It doesn't matter whether you buy a log cabin, Cape Cod colonial, French provincial, Queen Anne Victorian, or California ranch style house. You can make money on any property if you use the following three fundamental principles to select the home you buy. As you read the following guidelines, remember that they're not hard-and-fast rules — exceptions do exist.

The principle of progression: why to buy one of the cheaper homes on the block

An appraiser will tell you that the *principle of progression* states that property of lesser value is enhanced by proximity to better properties. English translation, please? Buy one of the cheaper homes on the block because the more expensive houses all around yours pull up the value of your home.

For example, your agent shows you a house that just came on the market in a neighborhood you like. At $175,000, it's one of the least expensive home you've seen in the area. The agent says that the other homes around it would sell for anywhere from $225,000 to $275,000. You start to salivate.

Don't whip out your checkbook yet. Do a little homework first. Find out why this house is so cheap. If the right things are wrong with it, write up the offer. If the wrong things are wrong with it, move on to the next property.

Curable defects

If a house is a bargain because it has defects that aren't too difficult or expensive to correct, go for it. For example, maybe the house is an ugly duckling that just needs a paint job, landscaping, and some other minor cosmetic touches in order to be transformed into a swan. Perhaps it's the only two bedroom house on the block, but it has a large storage area that you could convert into a third bedroom for not more than $15,000. For $190,000 ($175,000 for the house plus $15,000 to add the bedroom), you're living in a $225,000 to $275,000 neighborhood. Such a deal!

Problems like these are *curable defects* — property deficiencies you can cure by upgrading, repairing, or replacing the items relatively inexpensively. Painting, modernizing a bathroom, installing new counters and cabinets in the kitchen, and upgrading an electrical system or plumbing are some examples of curable defects.

Incurable defects

If a house has major problems, it's not a bargain at any price. Who'd want a house located next to a garbage dump? Or what about a really ugly home? Just because the seller made a fortune in the sausage business doesn't mean that you (or anyone else) would want to live in a house built in the shape of a giant hot dog. Maybe the house is cheap because a contractor says it's a wreck about ready to fall down — you'd spend at least $125,000 after you bought it for a new roof, new foundation, new plumbing, and complete rewiring.

Enormous deficiencies like these are called *incurable defects.* They aren't economically feasible to correct. There's nothing you can do if a house is poorly located. Nor does it typically make sense to pay $175,000 for the hot-dog house so you can tear it down and build a new home (unless that's what comparable vacant lots sell for). By the same token, if you pay $175,000 for the wreck and then pour in another $125,000 on corrective work, you'll have the dubious honor of owning the most expensive house in the neighborhood.

Don't get us wrong. All rehabs aren't bad. We go into more detail about fixer-uppers later in this chapter.

The benefits of renovating cheaper homes

The less expensive houses on the block are also the least risky ones to renovate, thanks to the principle of progression. For example, suppose that you just paid $175,000 for a house that needs a major rehab. Your construction project is located smack-dab in the middle of a neighborhood of $250,000 homes.

The difference between your purchase price and the value of the surrounding homes approximately defines the *most* you should consider spending on a rehab.

In the preceding example, you should spend no more than $75,000 to bring your home up to the prevailing standard set by the other houses. Of course, this is assuming that you can afford to spend that kind of money (see Chapter 2) and that you have the time and patience to coordinate the rehab work or do it yourself. As long as you improve the property wisely and stay within your budget, you'll probably get most or all the rehab money back when you sell the property.

Use the principle of progression in conjunction with location, location, value. Buying one of the better less-expensive homes in a good neighborhood enhances your likelihood of property appreciation in the years ahead.

The principle of regression: why not to buy the most expensive house on the block

You guessed it. The *principle of regression* is the economic opposite of the principle of progression.

If you buy the most expensive house on the block, the principle of regression punishes you when you sell. The lower value of all the other homes around you brings down your home's value.

If an evil spirit whispers in your ear that you should buy the most expensive house on the block in order to flaunt your high status in life, go to an exorcist immediately. Do not succumb to the blandishments of the evil spirit unless you have a burning desire to lose money when you sell. Satisfy your ego — and make a wiser investment — by purchasing one of the less expensive homes in a better neighborhood.

The most expensive house on the block is also the worst candidate for remodeling. Suppose, for example, that you buy a $250,000 home in a neighborhood of $150,000 houses. From an appraiser's perspective, the home already sticks out like a financial sore thumb. Spending another $50,000 to add a fancy new kitchen to what is already the most expensive house on the block further compounds your problem.

That new kitchen almost certainly won't increase your home's value to $300,000. No one can dispute the fact that you spent $50,000 on the kitchen if you have the receipts to prove your expenditures. But folks who buy $300,000 homes want to be surrounded by other homes worth as much as, or more than, the one they are buying.

Homes are like cups. When you fill a cup too full, it overflows. When you make excessive improvements to your house based upon sale prices of comparable homes in the neighborhood, the money you spend on the rehab goes down the financial drain. This phenomenon is called *overimproving a property*.

Even if you buy the least expensive house in the neighborhood, you can overimprove it if you spend too much money fixing it up. The best time to guard against overimproving your house is *before* you do the work.

If you'll end up with the most expensive house on the block when you finish your project, don't do the project.

The principle of conformity: why unusual is usually costly

The principles of progression and regression deal with economic conformity. If you want to maximize your chances for future appreciation of the home you buy — and we know you do — your home should also conform in size, age, condition, and style to the other homes in your neighborhood. That's the *principle of conformity.*

This principle doesn't mean that your home has to be an identical clone of every other house on the block. It should, however, stay within the prevailing standards of your neighborhood. For example:

- ✔ **Size:** Your home shouldn't dwarf the other houses on the block, or vice versa. If your home is smaller than surrounding houses, use the principle of progression as a guide to bring it into size-conformity with the other houses, and you'll increase your home's value. If, conversely, you have a three bedroom home in a neighborhood of two- and three-bedroom homes, adding a large fourth bedroom to your house would violate the principle of regression.

- ✔ **Age:** You almost never see an older home in the midst of a tract of modern new homes. However, every now and then you find a brand new home incongruously plunked in the midst of older homes. A modern home typically looks out of place in a neighborhood of gracious, older homes. Even if you get a terrific deal on the price, the modern home's lack of conformity with other homes on the block will probably come back to haunt you when you attempt to sell it.

- ✔ **Condition:** The physical condition of your house has a tremendous impact on its value. Not surprisingly, your home loses value if it's a dilapidated dump compared to the rest of the houses on the block.

    Ironically, it's not wise to have your home in far nicer condition than other houses in the neighborhood. Even if your home conforms to all the other houses in size, age, and style, you overimprove your home if the quality of materials, workmanship, and appliances in your home greatly exceeds the prevailing neighborhood quality standards.

- ✔ **Style:** The architectural style of the house you buy isn't critical — as long as it conforms to the prevailing architectural style of other homes in the neighborhood. From an investment standpoint, for example, it's not wise to buy the only Queen Anne Victorian in a block filled with Pennsylvania Dutch Colonial houses, or vice versa. Nor should you buy a three-story home when all the surrounding houses are one story high.

Your home doesn't have to be a bland, boring replica of every other house on the block. You can follow the principle of conformity and still express your individuality by the way you landscape, paint, and furnish your home. You know you've done well when people use words like "tasteful" and "exquisite" to describe your home. On the other hand, your decorating motif is a problem if folks refer to your house as "weird" or "eccentric."

Home Sweet Home

What exactly is a home? When you come right down to it, home is an elusive concept. Everyone knows, for example, that home is where the heart is. That's fine and good if you're a romantic, but not too helpful if you're a homebuyer.

Up until now, we've loosely used the terms "home" and "house" to mean any place where you live or want to live. Under that definition, everything from a studio apartment in Manhattan to a grass hut on a Hawaiian beach qualifies as a home. Now, however, it's time to get precise. We're about to focus on the specific types of property you're most likely to buy — detached homes, condominiums, and cooperative apartments. Each of these options offers homeowners distinct financial and personal advantages and disadvantages that you must understand in order to make a wise buying decision.

Detached residences

If you were raised in New York City, your mental image of home is probably an apartment in a steel and concrete skyscraper, an attached brownstone, or some other type of row house. If, on the other hand, you grew up in Des Moines, when someone says "home" you most likely visualize a brick- or wood-frame residence with a white picket fence, a garden, and a swing set in the yard.

To distinguish the kind of home you see in areas of abundantly cheap land (and programs like *Leave It to Beaver*) from condos, co-ops, and other types of property folks call home, the correct terminology for the white-picket-fence type property is *detached single-family dwelling*. The key operative word is "detached," because such homes aren't attached to any of the surrounding properties. Now that you're properly dazzled by the depth and breadth of our knowledge, we'll just call these "homes" or "houses" like everyone else does.

Detached homes, like cars, come in two basic types — *new* and *used*.

New homes

If you're the type of person who'd never think of buying a used car because you like the new-car smell and don't like buying someone else's problems, you may feel the same way about new homes. They have some very appealing advantages:

- ✔ **A properly constructed new home is built to satisfy the most finicky of buyers.** Choosing a new home gives you the peace of mind of knowing that your home doesn't contain asbestos, lead-based paints, formaldehyde, or other hazardous or toxic substances. Furthermore, you can rest assured that your new home complies with current (and ever-more stringent) federal, state, and local building, fire, safety, and environmental codes. Of course, there's no guarantee that future years won't uncover more hazards!

- ✔ **A properly constructed new home should be cheaper than a used home to operate and maintain.** Operating expenses are minimized because a new home should incorporate the latest technology in energy-efficient heating and cooling systems, modern plumbing and electrical service, energy-efficient appliances, and proper insulation levels. And with a new home, your initial maintenance expenses are practically nonexistent because everything is new — roof, appliances, interior and exterior paint, carpets, and so on. Other than changing the light bulbs, what's to fix?

- ✔ **A properly designed new home won't force you to adjust your lifestyle to its limitations.** On the contrary, new homes have enough wall and floor outlets to accommodate all your high-tech goodies — microwave oven, espresso machine, TV sets, AM-FM receiver, VCRs, CD player, laser disc player, hair dryers, electric razors, electric toothbrushes, and home office gear such as computers, monitors, printers, modems, fax machines, and so on. No unsightly, hazardous tangle of extension cords for you.

New homes are only as good as the developers who build them. Visit several of the developer's older projects. See with your own eyes how well the developments have weathered over the years. Ask homeowners in older developments whether they'd buy another new home from the same developer and what kinds of problems, if any, they've had with their home over the years. Also find out whether the developer amiably fixed defects which occurred, or did homeowners have to take legal action to get problems corrected? Ask real estate agents how much homes in the developments have appreciated in value over time and how that compares with other homes in the general area.

As you might expect, new homes also have some disadvantages. To wit:

- ✔ **What you see usually isn't what you get.** You see a professionally decorated, exquisitely furnished, beautifully landscaped *model* home. You buy a bare bones, unfinished house where nearly everything — appliances, carpets, window coverings, painting, fireplace finishes, landscaping, and so on — is an *extra* that isn't included in the base price.

- ✔ **Prices are less negotiable.** Developers maintain price integrity to protect the value of their unsold inventory of homes and to sustain appraised values for loan purposes. In fact, a developer who cuts prices is warning you that the project is floundering. Rather than reduce asking prices, developers bargain with you by throwing in extras without charge or giving you *upgrades* (that is, more expensive grades of carpet or better appliances) in lieu of a price reduction.

Some developers attract buyers by pricing bare bones houses very close to their actual cost, and then make substantial profits on extras and upgrades. If, upon doing some comparison shopping, you find that these items are outrageously overpriced, don't purchase them from the developer. Instead, buy the bare bones house and purchase extras from outside suppliers.

✔ **On a price-per-square-foot basis, new homes are usually more expensive than used ones.** No surprise. Land, labor, and material costs are higher today than they were years ago when the used homes were built. And you're buying a home without any wear and tear. Although new houses may be more expensive to purchase, remember that they're usually less expensive than used homes to operate and maintain.

✔ **New homes in more developed areas are generally built in areas previously considered undesirable or unbuildable.** It's the old "first come, first served" principle. Earlier developments got better sites. Today's developers take whatever land is available — steep hillsides, flood plains, and land located far away from the central business area. Ten or twenty years from now, today's so-called lousy sites will be considered prime areas. It's all relative.

✔ **New homes may have hidden operating costs.** Developments with extensive amenities usually charge the homeowners dues to cover operating and maintenance expenses of common areas such as swimming pools, tennis courts, exercise facilities, club houses, and the like. Some homeowners associations charge each owner the same annual fee. Others prorate dues based on the home's size or purchase price — the larger or more expensive your home, the higher your dues. If the development has a homeowners association, find out how its dues are structured and what your dues would be.

Sometimes homeowners-association dues are set artificially low to camouflage the true cost of living in the development. When that happens, sooner or later homeowners get slugged with a special assessment to repaint the clubhouse, resurface the tennis court, or whatever. Make sure that the homeowners association you are considering has adequate reserves and that its dues accurately reflect actual operating and maintenance costs. Also check to see whether the historic rate of increase in dues has been reasonable and in line with the overall inflation rate (which, these days, is running about 3 percent per year).

✔ **You may have to use the developer's real estate agent to represent you.** Developers always have their own sales staff and their own purchase contracts. Some developers let you be represented by an outside real estate agent if you wish. Others insist that you use their agent. This is not a negotiable item. If you don't like it, your option is to walk away without buying a home.

If you've fallen in love with a new home but the developer won't let an outside agent represent you, we recommend that you pay for an independent appraisal to get an *unbiased* opinion of the home's value. It's also wise to have your contract reviewed by a real estate lawyer. (See Chapter 9 for how to find one and what they can do for you.)

Just because a home is brand spanking new doesn't mean that it's flawless. People build homes. People are human. To err is human — that's why we have the expression *human error.* Moreover, builders work for profit and may be tempted to cut corners to maximize their short-term profits. Not to mention that some builders simply aren't very good. Thus, even a new, never-been-lived-in home should get a thorough inspection (from foundation to roof) by a professional property inspector to discover possible human errors before you purchase it. We cover property inspections in our usual meticulous manner in Chapter 11.

Used homes

Perhaps you are wondering why we classify all homes as being either new or used. Why not "new and old" instead of "new and used"? Because *old* isn't a precise term. How old is old? Is a home built more than 25 years ago old? or should the cutoff be homes constructed over 50 years ago? If homes built more than 50 years ago are old, what should we call homes built 100 or 200 years ago — decrepit? *Used,* on the other hand, merely means that someone owned the home before you did. (Considering how expensive homes are, you may prefer to call the place you buy a "previously owned" home. If that makes you feel better, go right ahead.)

Regardless of what you choose to call them, used homes have many commendable features:

✔ **Used home are generally less expensive than new homes.** As a rule, folks who bought houses years ago paid less for their homes than developers charge to build comparable new homes today. Furthermore, at any given time, more used homes are on the market than new homes. Good old competition holds the price of used homes down.

Asking prices of used homes are *much* more negotiable than asking prices of new homes. Sellers of used homes don't have to protect the property values of an entire development. They typically just want to get their money and move on to life's next great adventure.

✔ **Used homes are usually located in well established, proven neighborhoods.** With a used home, you don't have to guess what the neighborhood will be like in a few years when it's fully developed. Just look around and you can see what kind of schools, transportation, shopping, entertainment, and other amenities you have.

✔ **Used homes have been field tested.** By the time you buy a used home, its previous owners have usually discovered and corrected most of the problems that developed over time due to settling, structural defects, and construction flaws. You don't have to guess how well the home will age. You can see it with your own eyes.

WARNING!

No matter how well aged a home is, you should still have it thoroughly inspected (inside and out) by qualified professionals *before* you buy it. The last owners may not have had the time, desire, or money to fix problems. They may also not have been aware of hidden problems. Be sure that the home meets today's building codes; doesn't have environmental, health, or safety hazards; is well insulated; and so on. Never try to save money on home inspections just because the house looks fine to you. The only exception to this stern admonishment is if you yourself happen to be a professional property inspector. (See Chapter 11 for more about home inspections and inspectors.)

✔ **Used homes are "done" properties.** When you buy a used home, you don't generally have to go through the hassle and expense of buying and installing carpets, window coverings, and light fixtures; finishing off the fireplace; planting a lawn; landscaping the grounds; building fences and patios; installing sprinkler systems; and the like. The work is already done (unless the used home is a major rehab project), and everything is generally included in the purchase price.

✔ **Buying a used home may be the only way to get the architectural style, craftsmanship, or construction materials you want.** What if your heart is set on owning an authentic 1800's New England farm house or a Queen Anne Victorian? Perhaps you want plaster walls, parquet floors, stained glass windows, or some other kind of materials or craftsmanship that is unaffordable, if not impossible to find, in new homes. If that's the case, buy a used home.

The investment value of detached homes

Americans have always had a deep seated love for detached homes. Like spawning salmon returning to the stream where they were born, many people are drawn to the same kind of house they grew up in when it's their turn to buy a home. Even if you didn't grow up in a detached home, you may desire one because TV shows and advertisements have drilled into your head that such homes are desirable and a sign of success.

Buyer demand for detached homes makes them good investments. Compared to attached residences, such as condominiums and cooperative apartments (which we discuss next), detached homes tend to hold their value better in weak markets and appreciate more rapidly in strong markets. Ask a local real estate agent for a comparison of property value appreciation in detached versus attached residences, and you'll see what we mean.

Like new homes, used homes also have some disadvantages:

- ✔ **Used homes are generally more expensive than new homes to operate and maintain.** Some used homes have been retrofitted with energy-efficient heating and cooling systems. Even so, a used home with 12-foot-high ceilings will always be more expensive to heat than a new home with 9-foot-high ceilings. By the same token, the older a used home's roof, gutters, plumbing system, furnace, water heater, appliances, and so on, the sooner you'll need to repair or replace them.

  Before buying a used home, ask the seller for copies of the last two years' utility bills (gas, electric, water, and sewer) so you can see for yourself exactly how much it costs to operate the house. If the utility bills are horrendous, ask your property inspector how much making the house more energy efficient would cost.

- ✔ **Used homes generally have some degree of *functional obsolescence.*** Examples of functional obsolescence due to outdated floor plans or design features are lack of a master bedroom, one bathroom in a three bedroom house, no garage, inadequate electrical service, and no central heating or air conditioning. How much functional obsolescence is too much? That depends on you. What we think is charming, you may consider an uninhabitable disaster. We deal with extreme functional obsolescence in the fixer-upper section.

- ✔ **Wonderful used homes are sometimes located in less-than-wonderful neighborhoods.** You may be attracted to a charming older home in a lousy neighborhood. Remember: "location, location, value." No matter how stunning the property or how great the deal you're offered on it, don't buy someone else's problem.

Attached residences

If you can't accept the rules and regulations that would, of necessity, be imposed upon you by communal living, don't read any further. You're much too free a spirit to be happy owning an attached residence.

But if you're willing to put up with the constraints of communal living to get the economic and lifestyle goodies associated with it, read on. You may be pleasantly surprised.

Condominiums

What offers first-time buyers their most affordable housing option and gives empty nesters who own detached homes an ideal lifestyle alternative for their golden years? If you said "condominiums," go to the head of the class.

Some folks think that a *condominium* is a type of building. They're wrong. The kind of building in which a condo is located doesn't matter. Condos can be apartments in a Chicago high-rise or split-level townhouses in Dallas or Victorian flats in San Francisco. What makes a condo a condo is the way its *ownership* is structured.

First, a quick break for today's foreign language lesson. In Latin, *con* means "with" and *dominium* means "ownership." Put the two words together, and you get *condominium*, which translates to "ownership with others." You'll definitely dazzle your pals *con* that etymology trivia tidbit.

Suppose, for example, that you buy a condo in a Chicago high-rise. You have a mortgage, property taxes, and a fancy deed suitable for framing to prove that you own unit 603, one of the hundred condos in that building. So far, owning a condominium is pretty much like owning a detached home that floats in the sky.

When you buy a detached home, an invisible line runs along the border of your property to separate what belongs to you from what belongs to your neighbors. When you purchase a condo, on the other hand, your property line is the interior surfaces (walls, floors, ceilings, windows, and doors) of your unit. In other words, with a condo, you get a deed to the air inside your unit and everything filling it — carpeting, window coverings, and all.

Air and interior improvements aren't all you own. You and the other condo owners in the condominium complex share ownership of the *land* upon which the project is located and the high-rise *building* that contains your individual units. Thus, all of you own a portion of the roof, exterior building walls, and foundation — as well as a chunk of the garage, elevators, lobby, hallways, swimming pool, tennis courts, exercise facilities, and so on. All the parts of the complex beyond the individual units are known as *common areas* because you own them *in common* with all the other condo owners.

If you buy a condo, you automatically become a member of the project's homeowners association. You don't have to attend the meetings unless you want to, but you must pay homeowners-association dues. The dues cover common-area operating and maintenance expenses for everything from staff salaries, chlorinating the pool, lighting the lobby, and garbage collection to fire insurance for the building. A portion of your dues goes into a reserve fund to cover inevitable repairs and replacements such as painting the building occasionally and replacing the roof.

Before buying a condo, find out exactly what percentage of joint ownership you'd have in the entire condominium complex. That amount establishes how much you'll be assessed for monthly homeowners-association dues and what percentage you'll pay of a special assessment that may be imposed on owners to cover unforeseen common-area expenses. It also determines how many votes you'd have in earthshaking matters affecting the complex, such as whether to paint the building aqua or tangerine, whether to repair the existing treadmill in the health club or buy a new one, and so on.

Condominiums use several different methods to establish the ownership percentages. The simplest method is to give each owner an equal share of ownership in the entire development. Thus, each owner has one vote and pays an equal amount of the monthly dues and any special assessments.

If the ownership percentage is based on the size or market value of the condo, people who own the larger or more expensive units have more say in what happens in the complex than do owners of the smaller or less expensive condos. However, the heavy hitters also have accordingly higher monthly homeowners-association dues and pay a larger percentage of special assessments.

Why a condo?

Given their complexity, why do folks buy condominiums? Why doesn't everyone stick to simple, straightforward detached homes? Here's why:

- ✔ **Attached residences increase your buying power.** Compare the price of a two-bedroom condo to a two-bedroom detached single-family dwelling in the same neighborhood. On the basis of livable square footage, condos generally sell for at least 20 to 30 percent *less* than comparable detached homes. Owning your very own roof, foundation, and plot of land is much more expensive than sharing these costs with a bunch of other owners.

  For some would-be buyers, the choice is either buying a condo that meets their living-space needs or continuing to rent. Economic necessity explains why the path to the American dream for nearly one out of five first-time real estate buyers is condominium ownership. There's buying power in numbers.

- ✔ **Attached residences cost less to maintain than detached homes.** Suppose, for example, that you're one of 100 condo owners in a Chicago high-rise. Unlike the owner of a detached home, who has to pay the entire cost of maintenance expenses such as installing a new roof or getting an exterior paint job, you can split these maintenance expenses with the other 99 owners. Although replacing the high rise's roof, for example, costs more in absolute terms than with a detached single-family home, the cost per owner should be less. There's economy in numbers.

- ✔ **Attached residences have amenities that you couldn't otherwise afford.** How many people do you know who own detached single-family homes with tennis courts, swimming pools, and fancy exercise clubs? Most homeowners couldn't possibly afford expensive goodies like these. But when the cost is shared among all the owners in a large condo complex, the impossible dream is suddenly your hedonistic reality. There's luxury in numbers.

✔ **Attached residences are ideal homes for some empty nesters.** As you near retirement, you may find yourself rattling around in a detached single-family home like a little ol' pea in a great big empty pod. Perhaps a two-bedroom condo in a building with no maintenance hassles and a doorman who'll forward your mail while you're off on one of your frequent vacations could solve all your problems. There's lifestyle in numbers.

Condo drawbacks

Like detached homes, condos are not for everyone. Judge for yourself how much the following drawbacks may affect you:

✔ **Condominiums offer less privacy.** Shared walls mean you can hear others more easily. Noise is one of the biggest problems with condos and the one area prospective condo buyers frequently overlook. Visit the unit at different times of the day and different days of the week to listen for noise. If possible, spend a few hours or an evening in a unit.

As a rule, the fewer common walls you share with neighbors, the more privacy you have in your unit. That's one reason corner units sell for a premium. And if your unit is on the top floor, you won't have people walking on your ceiling (unless there's a roof deck, of course). The ultimate in privacy, if you can afford it, is a top floor corner unit.

✔ **Condominiums are legally complex.** Prior to buying your condo, you should receive copies of three *extremely* important documents — a Master Deed or Declaration of Covenants, Conditions, and Restrictions (CC&Rs); the homeowners-association bylaws; and the homeowners-association budget. (See the nearby sidebar, "Condominium documents.") *Read these documents from cover to cover.*

The CC&Rs, bylaws, and budget are legally binding on all condo owners. Even though they're bulky, bloated, and boring, you *must* read them very, very, very carefully. If you have questions about what these documents mean, or if you don't understand how they affect you, consult a real estate lawyer. And as long as we're talking legal stuff, find out from your agent or the homeowners association whether the condominium is either currently involved in litigation or plans to be in the foreseeable future. *Lawsuits are expensive.*

✔ **Condominiums are financially complex.** As a prospective owner, check the current operating budget. Be sure that it realistically covers building maintenance costs, staff salaries, utilities, garbage collection, insurance premiums, and other normal operating expenses. If the budget is too low, prepare to get slugged with a massive dues increase sooner or later. By the same token, make sure that the budget includes adequate reserve funds to cover predictable major expenses such as occasional exterior paint jobs and new roofs. How much is adequate? Three to five percent of the condominium's gross operating budget is generally considered a minimally acceptable reserve. If the reserve fund is too low, you're in danger of getting a special assessment in the event of a financial emergency.

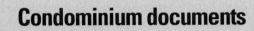

Condominium documents

If you're the type of person who only wants to know what time it is, skip this. If, on the other hand, you're fascinated by how watches are made, you'll love this section. It explains how condominiums are created and operated.

A condo project is born when the project developer records the Master Deed or Declaration of Covenants, Conditions, and Restrictions (CC&Rs) in the county recorder's office, which officially makes this information a matter of public record for all the world to see. CC&Rs establish the condominium by creating a homeowners association, stipulating how the condominiums' maintenance and repairs will be handled, and regulating what can and can't be done to individual units and the condominium's common areas.

Bylaws keep the condominium functioning smoothly. They describe in minute detail the homeowners association's powers, duties, and operation. The bylaws also cover such nitty-gritty items as how the homeowners association officers are elected and grant the association the right to levy assessments on individual condo owners.

Last, but far from least, the developer creates a budget. Unlike our government, the condominium's budget can't (theoretically, at least) operate in the red. The current budget establishes how much the condominium expects to spend this year to operate and maintain itself. Condo owners also receive an annual statement of income and expenses showing precisely how last year's dues were spent and spelling out the condominium's current financial condition.

We recommend that you review the past several years' operating budgets and financial statements for indicators of poor fiscal management.

- One indicator is frequent, large homeowners association dues increases. Dues shouldn't be increasing annually much faster than the rate of inflation (which is running around 3 percent these days).

- Another red flag is special assessments that wouldn't have been necessary if the association had an adequate reserve fund. When discussing the budget and reserve fund, find out whether any dues increases or special assessments are anticipated in the near future to make up operating deficits or cover the cost of a major project.

- A third danger sign you may spot when reading the financial statement is too many homeowners who are delinquent in paying their dues. Operating expenses continue unabated whether or not all the owners pay their dues.

✔ **Some condominiums are overly restrictive.** People who live in close proximity to one another need a smattering of rules to maintain order and keep life blissful. Too many rules, however, can turn your condo into a prison. For example, the condominium may have rules specifying what kind of floor and window coverings you must have in your unit, rules regulating the type or number of pets you can have in your unit, rules limiting your ability to rent your unit to someone else, rules forbidding you to make any alterations or improvements to your unit, rules limiting when or how often you can entertain in your unit, and so on. Before you buy, read the CC&Rs and bylaws *carefully* to find out exactly what kind of usage restrictions they contain.

If you discover the condominium has restrictions you don't like, don't buy the unit. Trying to modify CC&Rs or bylaws to eliminate restrictions after you've bought a unit is usually an expensive exercise in frustration and futility. We know that you have far better things to do with your life than waste a big chunk of it haggling with condominium associations and their lawyers.

Prudent rental restrictions are good. Ideally, all units in the complex will be owner-occupied. If some owners *occasionally* let friends use their units or rent the units for a week or two while they're on vacation, no big deal. However, if most units are owned by investors who rent them to an endless parade of partying strangers, that's bad. You may have trouble getting a mortgage in a complex with too many renters.

- **Brand-new condominium developments have the same advantages and disadvantages as new detached homes, compounded by a condo's added legal and economic complexity.** If you haven't yet read the section about new detached homes earlier in this chapter, now's the time to do so. All our cautionary statements about new detached homes also apply to new condominiums. Like new detached homes, new condo projects are as good or bad as the developers who build them and the lawyers who create them. Because any new project, by definition, doesn't have a track record yet, you must visit earlier projects done by the same developer to see how well they've aged and how satisfied the condo owners are.

Some unscrupulous developers of new condominium projects purposely lowball monthly operating costs to deceive prospective purchasers into thinking that living there costs less than it really does. These developers pay a portion of the monthly expenses out of their own pockets to keep project costs artificially low. The economic ax falls when the developer turns the project over to the homeowners association, which is soon forced to jack up the dues to cover actual operating expenses. When projected operating costs look too good to be true, they probably are. Compare the new project's projected operating expenses with the actual operating expenses of a comparable established project.

- **Where condominium parking and storage is concerned, the obvious isn't.** For example, does your condo deed include a deeded garage or parking space that only you can use, or is parking on a "first come, first served" basis? Are there extra charges for parking, or is parking included in the monthly dues? Are there provisions for guest parking? Is there a parking area for boats or trailers? Do you have a deeded storage area located outside of your unit? If so, where is it? If you need even more storage, is any available and how much does it cost? You're much better off getting answers to these questions before rather than after you buy.

✔ **Some older buildings that have been converted from apartments into condominiums have functional obsolescence problems.** Although older buildings frequently have excellent detailing and craftsmanship, they also often have outdated heating and cooling systems. If you're buying a condo in an older building, find out whether utilities are individually metered or lumped into the monthly homeowners association dues. Does your unit have a thermostat to control its heating and air conditioning, or is the heating and cooling system centrally controlled?

If utilities are included in the monthly dues, other condo owners have no incentive to economize by moderating their use of heat or air conditioning. If you're frugal, you'll just end up subsidizing owners who aren't. By the same token, in a building with central heating and cooling, your climate choices may be limited to roast in the winter and freeze in the summer. Even if *you* can live with utility overcharges and personal discomfort, these factors may deter future buyers from purchasing when you try to sell your unit.

✔ **Size can be a problem.** Large condo complexes usually have a cold, impersonal, hotel-like feeling. And, as a rule, people who live in large complexes tend not to pay as much attention to finances and day-to-day operating details because the homeowners association hires professional property managers to run things for the owners. However, if several owners in a 100-unit complex fail to pay their monthly dues, it's not the end of the world financially. And, socially speaking, the odds of running into an owner you detest diminish as the complex increases in size.

Condos need to be inspected, too

When you buy a condo, you must inspect the entire building — not just your unit. As Chapters 8 and 11 explain, you need a professional property inspector on your real estate team because the structural and mechanical condition of a property greatly affects its value. What's the condition of expensive common area components such as the roof, heating and cooling systems, plumbing and electrical systems, elevators, foundation, and the like? Are amenities such as tennis courts, swimming pool, and health facilities in good shape? Because you're buying part of all the common areas in addition to your individual unit, you need a professional opinion of the entire complex's condition.

Check the building's soundproofing by asking other owners whether they're bothered by noises emanating from units above, below, or beside their unit. The building has a ventilation problem if you can smell other people's cooking odors in your unit or the hallways. If you discover expensive repairs or replacements are needed and the condominium's reserve fund doesn't have anywhere near enough money to cover the anticipated costs, don't buy a unit in this complex. Sooner or later, the owners will be hit with a special assessment and/or a big dues increase.

Don't buy into a small condominium complex unless you enjoy intimate relations with your neighbors. Carefully size up the other owners. Be sure that they're the kind of folks you can trust to carry their fair share of the load financially and operationally. In a small condo, you actively participate in the homeowners association because you must. Every vote has an immediate impact on your finances and the quality of your life. You don't have to love the other owners. BUT (note the big "but"), if some or all of them aren't the type of people you'll be able to get along with, don't buy the unit.

After reading the disadvantages of condo ownership, you may think that only a fool would buy a condo. Not true. We know plenty of content condo owners who'd never consider buying a detached dwelling. In our attempt to protect you, we sometimes go a little overboard on the cautionary side of things. We do so with your best interests at heart.

Condominiums make the most sense for folks who don't want operating and maintenance hassles (remembering that you'll still have the *expense*), want to maximize their bang for the buck spent on living space, and don't need a private yard. Buying a condo for a few years while you save enough money to purchase a detached home doesn't make economic sense. Given the expenses of buying and selling a condo, combined with its likely lack of decent appreciation, you're better off waiting to buy a detached home if you think you can do so within five years.

Cooperative apartments

The two most common types of attached residences are condominiums and cooperative apartments, which are usually called *co-ops*. You can't tell which is which by looking at the building. Like condominiums, what makes a co-op a co-op is its legal structure.

You'll be delighted to know that most of the pros and cons of condominium ownership also apply to co-ops, so you don't have to read a ton of new stuff. (If you haven't read the previous section on condos, do so now.) We'll just focus on the three ways in which condos and co-ops differ: the definition of legal ownership, management, and your financing options.

Definition of legal ownership: deed versus stock

When you buy a condo, you get a deed to your unit. When you buy a co-op, you get a stock certificate (to prove that you own a certain number of shares of stock in the cooperative corporation) and a *proprietary lease,* which entitles you to occupy the apartment you bought. The corporation owns the building and has the deed in its name as, for example, the 10 West 86th Street Corporation. Thus, you are simultaneously a co-owner of the building and a tenant in the building you own.

In most cooperatives, shares are allocated based on a how big a unit is and what floor it's on. Thus, a top-floor apartment usually has more shares than a ground-floor unit of the same size. The more shares you have, the greater your influence in the co-op, because each share gives you one vote. Unfortunately, power has a price. Your pro rata share of the cooperative's total maintenance expenses is based upon the number of shares you own in the corporation. If you own a great many shares, your monthly expenses will be disproportionately high. And, when you're ready to sell, your unusually high monthly expenses may reduce your unit's value.

Management: homeowners association versus board of directors

If you've always fantasized about being the chairman of the board, here's your chance. Buy a co-op apartment and work your way up the corporate ladder. Corporations are run by boards of directors; stock cooperatives are corporations. Because your unit is in a building owned by a corporation, it's governed by a board of directors elected by you and the other owners. Nomenclature aside, just like the homeowners association in a condominium, the board of directors is responsible for the cooperative's day-to-day operations and finances.

Getting in and out of co-ops isn't always easy

Buying and selling co-ops is usually a lot more difficult than buying and selling condos. Most cooperatives stipulate that individual owners can't sell or otherwise transfer their stock or proprietary leases without the express consent of either the board of directors or a majority of owners.

Prospective buyers generally must provide at least four letters of reference regarding their sterling character and Rock of Gibraltar creditworthiness. In addition, they may have to submit to a personal grilling by the board of directors. Given that the owners live in close proximity to one another and depend upon each other financially, having the ability to screen out party animals, deadbeats, and the like is reasonable as long as that power isn't misused to unfairly discriminate against buyers.

Even so, some buyers find the approval process extremely intrusive and strenuously object to giving strangers their financial statements. The approval process also tends to slow down the sale of co-op units on the market.

Owning a co-op is a two-edged sword. As a co-op owner, you have much more control over who your neighbors will (or won't) be than do condo owners. Unfortunately, that control cuts both ways. When you try to sell your unit, people you consider perfect buyers may be turned down by the co-op because your neighbors think that the prospective buyers would entertain too much or can't carry the load financially. Giving up the right to sell your co-op to the highest bidder may be too high a price to pay for the right to choose your neighbors.

Financing your purchase

Getting a mortgage to purchase your co-op may be difficult. Many lenders flat-out refuse to accept shares of stock in a cooperative corporation as security for their mortgage. Conversely, some co-ops absolutely won't permit any individual financing over and above the mortgage the corporation has on the building as a whole. These co-ops believe that one proof of creditworthiness is your ability to pay cash for your unit.

Unless you're richer than Midas, don't buy a co-op if only one or two lenders in your area make cooperative-apartment loans. Odds are you'll pay a higher interest rate due to the lack of lender competition and lender concerns about the greater risks of co-ops. Worse yet, what if these lenders stop making co-op mortgages and no other lenders take their place? You won't be able to sell your unit until you find an all-cash buyer (and they're few and far between) or until you have the financial resources to lend the money yourself to the next buyer.

Deal Properties

If you're like most people, you're cursed with champagne taste and a beer budget. The homes you long for cost far more than you can afford. To buy one of these dream homes, you'd either have to get a really, really good deal or win the lottery.

Good deals *are* out there. The trick is knowing where to find them and how to evaluate them. Some seemingly good deals turn out to be good for the sellers but not for you.

Don't waste time looking at perfect houses if you're searching for a deal. People pay premium prices for perfection. The houses you find great deals on are imperfect properties — houses with either physical or financial problems. The deal you're offered is an inducement to tackle the problem. Whether the deal is ultimately better for you or for the seller is the $64,000 question.

In Chapter 4, we discuss strategies for getting a good buy in any type of housing market. In the rest of this chapter, we cover special property situations that may be good deals or pigs in a poke.

Finding a fixer-upper

Fixer-uppers are houses with physical problems. Real estate agents generally refer to fixer-uppers euphemistically as "needing work" or "having potential."

Fixer-uppers aren't very popular in sluggish real estate markets. Most buyers in such markets don't want to put up with the hassle or financial uncertainties associated with a major rehab, so they buy houses in move-in condition. Such a house is a safe but passive investment. Because its potential has already been fully realized, new owners can't do anything to it to significantly increase its value.

A fixer-upper, on the other hand, offers potentially larger rewards to folks who have the vision to see beyond the mess that is to the wonderful home that could be. A fixer-upper buyer must also have the financial resources and courage to tackle the risks. If you fit that profile, here's what you may be able to look forward to after you've transformed your ugly duckling into a swan:

- ✔ You'll be living in a nicer home and a better neighborhood than you'd have otherwise been able to afford.

- ✔ Instead of buying a home decorated in someone else's idea of good taste, your home will be done the way you like it.

- ✔ You may have increased your home's fair-market value in excess of your out-of-pocket expenses for improvements you made.

For example, if you're handy, you can add thousands of dollars of value to a fixer-upper by doing labor-intensive jobs such as painting, wallpapering, and landscaping yourself. Sweat equity pays big dividends.

If, like us, you're mechanically challenged, forget sweat equity. It's less frustrating and cheaper in the long run to earn money doing what you do best and then hire competent contractors to do what *they* do best. Poor workmanship is a false economy. It looks awful and reduces property values. Doing the project well the first time is easier, faster, and less expensive than doing it badly yourself and then paying someone else to fix your mess. If you're one of those rare people who can do quality work yourself, by all means try your hand and chisel at it — just be realistic about the required time and costs.

Some fixer-uppers are easy to spot. They look like a classic haunted house — peeling paint, shutters falling off, overgrown yard, and so on. Things don't get any better on the inside. These houses may need everything from a good cleaning to electrical system and plumbing overhauls.

Some older houses, condos, and co-ops are subtle fixer-uppers that look fine at first glance but have functional obsolescence. They're livable, but they need improvements, such as adding master bedrooms, bathrooms, or garages and upgrading their electrical systems to bring them up to today's housing standards.

Finding a diamond among the dumps

Finding the right fixer-upper isn't a matter of luck. On the contrary, it takes persistence, skill, and just plain hard work. You spend lots of time tromping through properties, invest more precious time evaluating promising fixer-uppers that ultimately don't make sense economically, and then, just when you're ready to give up, you finally discover a diamond in the rough that you end up buying.

Here's how to separate diamonds from dumps:

- **Read this book.** Everything you need to know is here. Pay special attention to the topics covered in this chapter (good neighborhoods; principles of progression, regression, and conformity; and used homes and condos), Chapter 9 (accurately determining fair market value so you don't overpay) and Chapter 11 (property inspections). Also, be sure that you can financially afford all the necessary outlays after the purchase for the fix-up work (see Chapter 2).

- **Inspect the heck out of the fixer-upper before you buy it.** Every property should be carefully inspected prior to purchase (see Chapter 11). Fixer-uppers need even more scrutiny so that you know *precisely* what you're getting yourself into. Your purchase offer must be conditioned upon your approval of the property inspections and satisfactory resolution of corrective work issues you discover. You can find these clauses in Chapter 10.

Structural repairs versus renovations

Work done on fixer-uppers falls into two broad categories — structural repairs and renovations. *Structural repairs* are changes that a property must undergo to bring it up to local health and safety standards. Such work can include foundation repairs, roof replacements, new electrical and plumbing system installations, and so on — all of which cost big bucks but add relatively little value to property. Ideally, you can get a credit from the seller to do some, if not all, of the necessary structural repairs. The less you have to take out of your pocket for corrective work, the more you have to spend on renovations.

Renovations increase a fixer-upper's value by modernizing the home. Remodeling an old kitchen, installing a second bathroom, and adding a garage are a few examples of major structural renovations that make your home more functional, more pleasant to live in, and more valuable when you sell it.

Cosmetic renovations (painting, carpeting, landscaping, and the like) also add value with far less expense and aggravation. The ideal fixer-uppers to buy are ones that look awful but simply need cosmetic fixes to look their best.

✔ **Get contractors' bids for structural repairs and renovations.** You can use contractors' bids as a negotiating tool to get a corrective-work credit or lower sales price from the sellers for structural repairs such as termite damage repairs and a new roof. You should also get cost estimates for renovations such as bathroom modernization, new kitchen appliances and cabinets, central heating, and anything else required to bring the property up-to-date.

If bids and cost estimates indicate that you'd end up with the most expensive house on the block, don't do the project. Fix-up work has three iron laws:

- It's always more disruptive than you expected.

- It always takes longer to finish than you planned.

- It always costs more than you estimated.

So, if *estimated* fix-up costs would make the property the most expensive house on the block, by the time work is finally completed, the *actual* costs will make it the most expensive house in the state!

Getting financing is usually difficult if corrective work repairs exceed 3 percent of the property value, which is always the case with major fixer-uppers. However, a good real estate agent should know which lenders in your area specialize in fixer-upper loans. Given that one such lender finds you creditworthy and your project feasible, that lender may give you a mortgage to buy the property and a construction loan to make the improvements.

Final thoughts on fixer-uppers

Feeling somewhat overwhelmed by the risks associated with fixer-uppers is normal. Now you understand why most homebuyers avoid them. They fear being sucked into a bottomless bog that utterly disrupts their lives and totally devours their savings. Rent *The Money Pit* at your local video store to preview what may be in your real estate future!

Most novice homebuyers, especially first-time buyers, underestimate the time and cost required to fix up homes. When all is said and done, most people find that it would have cost them the same or less to buy a more finished home and avoid the headaches of doing or coordinating the renovations. Some people have ended up in financial ruin and even divorced over the stresses of such renovations.

If you like challenges and are willing to do a ton of extra detective work, remember these tips to maximize your chances of succeeding with a fixer-upper:

✔ Buy in the best neighborhood you can afford.

✔ Buy one of the cheaper houses on the block.

✔ Make sure that the renovations will more than pay for themselves in increased property value.

✔ Make sure that the purchase price is low enough to allow you to do the corrective work and renovations without turning your property into the most expensive house on the block.

If the real estate gods play fair and square, whoever buys the exquisitely *finished* home you transformed from a dump will pay a bonus for your farsightedness to see the fixer-upper's potential, for your audacity to tackle the financial risk, and for your stamina to put up with the chaos and filth of a rehab. If (and only if) you select wisely, negotiate the price wisely, and renovate wisely, you'll enjoy years of blissful living in the wonderful home you created — and hopefully make a fine profit to boot when you sell it.

Taking over a foreclosure

To get a mortgage, you give the lender the right to take your home away from you and sell it to pay the balance due on the mortgage if you don't make your loan payments, don't pay your property taxes, let your homeowners insurance policy lapse, or do anything else that financially endangers your home.

The legal action to repossess a home and sell it is called a *foreclosure*. Every year, hundreds of thousands of homes end up in foreclosure. These foreclosures often result from misuse of consumer credit. In other cases, however, people fall on hard times — they lose a job, experience unexpected health-care costs, suffer a death in the family, or go through a divorce.

You may have heard stories about people who got good deals buying foreclosures far below the property's appraised value. And, in fact, some people who buy foreclosed property luck out. But for every lucky winner, there are many more people who don't profit or who actually lose money buying foreclosures.

Buyer beware. Foreclosures can be a legal and financial cesspool. Unless you have an expert on your team who will guide you through the entire foreclosure process from beginning to end, don't even think of buying a foreclosure.

If you buy a foreclosed home, you'll most likely also buy the previous owner's problems. Here's a list of risks to ponder:

✔ **Physical:** Some homeowners react to the emotional devastation of a foreclosure with a scorched-earth attitude of "If we can't have it, we'll make sure that nobody else wants it." Before leaving, they take appliances, light fixtures, cabinets, sinks, toilets, and anything else of value. In extreme cases, they break windows, pour concrete down kitchen and bathroom drains, rip wiring out of walls, uproot shrubs, cut down trees, and anything else they can think of to trash the property. What if you're the high bidder for a sabotaged house at an auction of foreclosed properties? Lucky you.

Lenders usually won't let you inspect foreclosed properties prior to their auction. Nor can you make your offer to purchase subject to getting a loan. The risk of buying at an auction a property that you can't first inspect greatly exceeds the possible reward.

✔ **Financial:** Depending on which state the house is located in, a foreclosure can take anywhere from four months to over a year to complete. Suppose that you get what appears to be a good deal from people who are actually selling part way through the foreclosure process to avoid the stigma of forclosure. What if these people lie about how much they owe on their mortgage and property taxes? What if they don't tell you about unrecorded mortgages, court judgments, or federal and state tax *liens* (outstanding tax bills) hanging over the house? One guess who's liable for debts secured by the property. Lucky you.

✔ **Possession:** Suppose that, after buying a foreclosure at an auction, you visit your new home and discover that the previous owners are still living in it with their last remaining possession — a 12-gauge shotgun. They have no intention of leaving peacefully. Who do you think will have the pleasure of evicting them? Lucky you.

Given possible sabotage by the previous owner, buying a foreclosure is never *entirely* safe. The least risky way to purchase one is to buy directly from a lender who got title to the property because no one bought it at auction. Here's why:

✔ Any recorded or undisclosed mortgages, court judgments, or tax liens on the house are either cleared from the house or at least revealed to you prior to your purchase.

✔ You can — *absolutely must,* in fact — have the house minutely scrutinized by professional property inspectors. Where foreclosures are concerned, you've got to find out whether the previous owner left any hidden surprises for you.

✔ The price and terms of sale are negotiable. Even though foreclosures are normally listed at their appraised value, lenders may allowances for corrective work by either reducing the price or giving you a credit to do the work. They'll also, as a rule, offer attractive loan terms (low cash down payments, no loan fees, below-market interest rates) to get rid of these properties quickly. After all, they're in the loan business — not property management.

Think long and hard before buying a foreclosure. Even if you purchase one directly from a lender, you may be buying a house permeated by shattered dreams. Such a house probably hasn't been given the best of care. Do your homework carefully, have the property thoroughly inspected, and understand *fully* what you're getting yourself into before you buy.

Ad Hoc Partnerships

As home prices have escalated in many densely populated parts of the country, so has the frequency of unrelated men and women forming ad hoc partnerships to buy houses. These couples aren't necessarily romantically involved. On the contrary, they're usually folks who decide that a good way of turning the American dream of owning a home into reality is to join forces as partners.

Types of residential partnerships

One type of ad hoc partnership, known as *equity sharing,* involves outside investors who don't live in the property. The investor provides cash to buy a house which the other partner lives in while the property appreciates in value. After a specified period of time, say five years, the partner who lives in the house has the option either to buy out the investor's share of the property or to sell the house and split the proceeds.

In *live-in partnerships,* the other type of residential ad hoc partnership, all partners live together in the jointly purchased property. Pooling their resources gives these individuals a place to call home, a tax shelter, and, if the real estate gods are willing, a profit when they eventually sell and go their separate ways.

Live-in partnerships are the real estate version of Siamese twins. People who live in ultraclose proximity to their partners every day have a relationship that is far more intense than an equity-sharing partnership.

We've seen live-in partnerships that turned out wonderfully. As time passed, the partners became even closer friends than they were before buying the house. Most live-in partnerships, however, are no more than marriages of convenience which the partners suffer through solely to reap economic benefits. Bickering about things like whether to patch a leaky roof or get a new one, who left the sink full of dirty dishes (again!), whether to paint the living room purple or gold, and who gets the backyard for a party next Saturday can strain even the best of relationships.

Structuring a successful partnership

Too many partnerships end up on the rocks unnecessarily. Why? The partners didn't anticipate problems related to co-ownership which arose while they owned the property. Ironically, most of these problems are foreseeable and avoidable. *Proper planning prevents problems.*

WARNING!

The partnership from hell

Unfortunately, partnerships occasionally turn into unmitigated disasters. Irv's sad tale illustrates some pitfalls of residential partnerships.

Irv and Sid, good pals for almost 25 years, bought a condo together. Irv used money inherited from his mother for the condo's down payment and closing costs. Sid, who had a much higher income than Irv but no cash, lived in the condo as his principal residence. Sid covered the monthly mortgage payments, property taxes, and homeowners-association dues and also paid rent to Irv.

It was a perfect partnership. Sid got the tax deductions he needed plus 25 percent of the appreciation when the condo sold. Sid's rent payments gave Irv a good return on the cash he'd invested, and he'd get the lion's share of the condo's appreciation when it sold. Irv and Sid were delighted with their arrangement.

All went well for nearly a year. Then, without warning, Sid filed bankruptcy.

Irv's rent payments stopped, of course. What's more, the bankruptcy court put a lien on the condo to tie up Sid's assets — and inadvertently tied up Irv's money as well. Worst of all, Irv and Sid didn't have a written partnership agreement describing their 75-25 equity split. Without something in writing, Irv was unable to prove this fact to the court's satisfaction.

Before forming a residential partnership, you can do two things to greatly *increase your odds for success:*

- ✔ **Give it a trial run.** If you're considering a live-in partnership, we recommend that you live with your prospective partner for at least six months before buying a home together. You may discover that you've got a major compatibility problem; for example, you may go to bed each night by nine and your roomie may love to party into the wee hours of the morning. Ditto if you, Felix, insist on having everything in its place and your partner-to-be, Oscar, uses the floor for a closet. Imagine the delights of co-ownership if you always pay your bills by the first of the month and your partner's favorite sport is a spirited game of duck-the-bill-collector.

- ✔ **Put it in writing.** We also recommend having a lawyer who handles residential real estate partnerships prepare a written partnership agreement as soon as possible. Don't reinvent the wheel; let an experienced lawyer guide you and your prospective partner through the foreseeable "what ifs" of every partnership.

Ideally, you should have the agreement drawn up well before you make an offer to purchase. Why the rush? To make sure that you and your partner understand precisely how the partnership operates and what your responsibilities to each other are. The agreement should cover important issues such as:

✔ **Financial arrangements:** This section of the agreement deals with the economics of buying, maintaining, and selling the property. It also specifies the tax deductibility of mortgage interest and property taxes for each partner if the partnership involves unequal financial contributions.

What happens if, for example, your partner suddenly dies or goes bankrupt? Should the partners in a live-in partnership give each other first right of refusal to buy the partner's share before it can be sold to an outsider? Planning for the unexpected sure beats reacting to a crisis. Your agreement *must* have equitable provisions for terminating the partnership.

✔ **Dispute resolution:** What if you and your partner come to blows on a critically important issue like whether to plant daisies or roses along the side of the house? If only two partners are involved, how do you break tie votes? Anticipate disputes. Even the best of friends occasionally disagree. That's a fact of life. Provide a method (such as mediation or arbitration) to resolve the problems you can't work out between yourselves.

✔ **Game plan:** If you and your partner intend to improve the property you purchase by, for example, remodeling the kitchen or converting a pair of flats into condominiums, your partnership agreement should be as specific as possible regarding the intended scope of work, project timing, cost, and so on. Plan *now* to avoid arguments later.

Never rush into a partnership — the economic consequences of a mistake are devastating. Carefully weigh the pros and cons. Then get everything in writing with help from a lawyer experienced in covering all the "what if" situations.

Chapter 8

Your Real Estate Team

*W*inston Churchill's description of the Soviet Union also applies to the home-buying process. For the uninitiated, Churchill characterized the Soviet Union as "a riddle wrapped in a mystery inside an enigma."

If you're like most folks who are just starting to look for a home, you're not an expert on property values, financing, or tax and real estate law. And when your life savings are on the line, abject ignorance isn't bliss. Not understanding the process of buying a home can cost you big bucks and make you unhappy with the home that you buy.

How can you find your way through the maze of constantly changing real estate market conditions, local laws, regulations, and tax codes? Where can you sign up for a crash course in home values? Even if you have the aptitude, how will you find the time to become an expert in so many fields?

One way around these problems is to do nothing. You can't get into trouble if you're lying in a corner, curled tightly into the fetal position. Of course, the downside of doing nothing is that nothing gets done. You can never buy a home using this method.

Reading *Home Buying For Dummies* is a far more dynamic course of action. This book shows you how to become a smart homebuyer. However, this book can't do everything for you. You'll probably also need some experts on your side. Don't worry. We explain how to find competent experts who can help you buy a home and who won't charge you an arm and a leg for that help.

Understanding the theory of property values and knowing what your dream home is actually worth are two very different things. Similarly, reading about home buying isn't a slam-dunk guarantee that you'll become an expert homebuyer — there's no substitute for years of practical experience in the field.

The Team Concept

Time and time again, we've seen smart people blunder into horrible situations when they buy a home. What gets them into trouble is usually ignorance of something that they (or their advisors) should have known, but didn't.

Strangely enough, knowing everything isn't important. What *is* important is having good people on your team — people who know what *you* need to know so that you can solve the problems that invariably arise.

You don't have to become an instant expert in home values, mortgages, tax and real estate law, title insurance, escrows, pest-control work, and construction techniques in order to play the home-buying game well. You can choose to hire people who have mastered the skills that you lack.

Home buying is a team sport. Your job is to lead and coach the team, not play every position. After you've assembled a winning team, your players should give you solid advice so that you can make brilliant decisions.

If cost were no object, you'd hire every competent expert you could get your hands on. However, you probably don't have an unlimited budget, so you need to determine which experts are absolutely necessary and which tasks you can handle yourself. In this chapter, we explain which experts are generally worth hiring and which ones you can pass on. Ultimately, of course, you are the one who must determine how competent or challenged you feel with the various aspects of the home-buying process.

Here's a thumbnail sketch of the possible players on your team:

- ✔ **You:** Always remember that you're the most important player on your team. In nearly every home purchase, something goes wrong — one of your players drops the ball or doesn't satisfy your needs. You have every right to politely, yet forcefully, insist that things be made right. Remember that *you* hire the players on your team. They work for you. Bad players may see things the other way around — they'd like to believe (and want you to believe) that *they're* in charge. They may try to manipulate you to act in their interests rather than yours. Don't tolerate this. You're the boss — you can fire as well as hire.

- ✔ **Real estate agent:** Because the home you're about to buy is probably the largest single investment you'll ever make, you must have someone on your team who knows property values. Your agent's primary mission is to help you find your dream home, tell you what the home is worth, and negotiate for it on your behalf to make sure that you don't pay one cent more for it than you absolutely have to.

- ✔ **Real estate broker:** Every state issues two kinds of real estate licenses: a salesperson's license and a broker's license. If your real estate agent is not an independent broker or the broker for a real estate office, then he (or she) must be supervised by a broker who is responsible for everything that your agent does or fails to do. In a crisis, your transaction's success may depend upon backup support from your agent's broker.

- ✔ **Lender:** If you can't pay, you can't play. And because most people can't pay all cash for their homes, you probably need a loan to buy your dream house. A good lender offers competitively priced loans and may even be able to help you select the best type of loan from the financial minefield of loan programs available today.

- ✔ **Property inspectors:** A house's physical condition greatly affects its value. Your dream home should be thoroughly inspected from roof to foundation before you purchase it, to make sure that you actually get what you think you're buying.

- ✔ **Escrow officer:** Mutual distrust is the underlying rule of every real estate deal. You and the seller need a neutral third party, an *escrow officer,* to handle funds and paperwork related to the transaction without playing favorites. The escrow officer is the home-buying game's referee.

- ✔ **Financial and tax advisors:** Before you purchase a home, you should understand how the purchase will fit into the context of your overall financial situation. You should address the issues of what your financial goals are and, given those goals, how much house you can afford. In Chapter 2, we explain how to do that.

- ✔ **Lawyer:** You may or may not need a lawyer on your team, depending on your contract's complexity, your dream home's location, and your personal comfort level. The purchase agreement you sign when buying a home is a legally binding contract. If you have *any* questions about your contract's legality, put a lawyer who specializes in real estate law on your team.

Odds are, you won't win the game unless you have a winning team. But remember that your players are *advisers* — not decision makers. Decision making is your job. You're the boss. The buck stops with you. After all, it's your money on the line.

Reeling in a Real Estate Agent

"What's it worth?"

The wrong answer to this deceptively simple question can cost you *big* bucks! Worse yet, this question has no simple answer because home prices aren't precise. As Chapter 9 explains, home buying isn't a math problem where 2 plus 2 reassuringly equals 4 now and forever more. Home prices aren't fixed — they slither all over the place.

Houses sell for *fair market value,* which is whatever buyers offer and sellers accept. Fair market value is *not* a specific number; it's a price *range.*

For example, suppose that you make an offer on a house worth about $150,000. If the seller has a better agent than you do and you're desperate to buy, you may end up paying $160,000. On the other hand, if you're in no hurry to buy and your agent is a good negotiator, you may be able to buy the home for $140,000. Home sale prices are often directly related both to the agent's knowledge of what comparable houses have sold for and to the agent's negotiating skills. Of course, other factors (such as the buyer's and seller's motivation, needs, and knowledge) are also important.

A good agent can be the foundation of your real estate team. An agent can help you find a home that meets your needs, negotiate for that home on your behalf, supervise property inspections, and coordinate the closing. Agents often have useful leads for mortgage loans. A good agent's negotiating skills and knowledge of property values can save you thousands of dollars.

Some buyers think that "good agent" is a contradiction in terms. Such buyers say that agents have a hidden agenda — to make people buy more expensive homes than they can afford in order to fatten agents' commission checks.

Some agents may try to pressure you to buy sooner rather than later (and to pay more than you should) in order to fatten their commissions. Many well-intentioned-but-inept agents are also out there. In this chapter, you see how to avoid the bad agents — and how to sift through the masses of mediocre agents — in order to narrow the field down to good agents who are worthy of their commissions.

Types of agent relationships

Say that you've been working with an agent named Al who has been showing you property for several months. Yesterday, you finally found a home you like. The house seemed well priced, but you told Al to make a lowball offer anyhow. (What the heck. Everybody knows that prices are negotiable. If the sellers don't like the price, let them make a counteroffer.) But what if your agent blew your cover? Suppose that Al told the sellers all of your innermost secrets — such as how much cash you have for a down payment and how much you're *really* willing to pay for the house. Now the sellers can beat you at your own game. If you discover what Al did to you (many victimized buyers don't), you'd undoubtedly feel hurt, betrayed, and pretty darn angry. You'd ask Al just whose side he's on.

The answer to that question has changed somewhat in recent years. In decades past, buyers thought that they had agents who represented *them.* But, in fact, they didn't. Back then, all agents were legally bound to be either agents or subagents *of the seller.*

Subagents, also called *cooperating agents,* work with one another through membership in a Multiple Listing Service (MLS). Agents use the MLS to promote their own real estate listings, and such agents offer to share their commissions with agents from other offices who actually sell the listed properties. As subagents of the seller, MLS participants are obliged to get top dollar for the sellers' properties.

Unfortunately, most buyers didn't know that the very agents who were working with them were actually representing the interests of the sellers. And the law didn't require agents to tell buyers which party they (the agents) actually represented before preparing offers on behalf of their buyers.

Times have changed somewhat. Some states (such as California) have adopted improved consumer-protection laws. These states passed laws that force agents to give both buyers and sellers a written disclosure regarding their duties as agents. The laws then allow buyers and sellers to select which type of relationship they want to have with their agents.

There are the three different types of relationships that homebuyers and sellers can have with real estate agents. We explain *dual agency* in a nearby sidebar. The other two are both types of *single agency,* which is when the agent only represents one of the two parties (buyer or seller) in the transaction.

- ✔ **Seller's agent:** In this form of single agency, the agent works solely for the seller.
- ✔ **Buyer's agent:** In this type of single agency, the agent works only for the buyer. A buyer's agent isn't an agent of the seller even if the buyer's agent gets a portion of the commission paid by the seller.

Although single agency is an improvement over the old system, buyer's agents still suffer from all the other conflicts of interest inherent in getting a commission that is a percentage of the amount that a buyer spends for a property.

In rare cases, buyer's agents don't accept money from sellers. Instead, a buyer signs a contract to work exclusively with a buyer's agent, and the buyer pays the agent a retainer that is applied toward the fee owed when the buyer's agent finds the buyer a home. Depending on the contract provisions, the retainer may or may not be returned to the buyer if the buyer's agent fails to find the buyer a satisfactory property to purchase.

Here's a way to have the best of both worlds with a buyer's agent. This technique removes the buyer's agent's incentive to get you to spend more, yet it keeps you from paying a fee, even if you don't buy a home. Offer your buyer's agent a lump-sum commission plus a bonus if, *and only if,* the agent gets you a better buy. For example, if the agent typically receives 3 percent of a home's sale price and you expect to buy a home for approximately $100,000, offer the agent a flat $2,500 commission plus an additional $100 bonus for every $1,000 below $100,000 the agent reduces the price for you, up to a maximum $3,000 commission.

Is your agent your ally or your enemy? Because laws regarding an agent's legal responsibility vary from state to state, it's important that you know how the game is played in your state. Be sure that you determine who your agent represents *before* you begin working together.

Dual agency and conflicts of interest

In certain transactions, an agent represents both the seller and the buyer. This type of representation is called *dual agency.*

Dual agency is the most confusing form of agency. Most people think that *dual agency* means that the exact same *agent* represents both the buyer and the seller. Such a situation is possible, but it is highly unusual and highly inadvisable. One agent can't possibly represent your best interests and the seller's best interests at the same time.

In a more common kind of dual agency, transactions involve two different agents who both work for the same real estate broker. For example, suppose that Sam Seller decides one sunny Sunday to list his house for sale with Sarah, an Acme Realty agent. Sarah smiles as she signs the

agreement to represent Sam as the seller's exclusive agent.

Simultaneously, Betty Buyer bumps into Bob, who's also an Acme Realty agent, at a Sunday open house. Betty likes Bob's style and asks him to represent her exclusively as a buyer's agent. Bob enthusiastically agrees.

So far, so good. Sam has Sarah, his exclusive agent. Betty has Bob, her exclusive agent. Things get complicated later that afternoon when Bob shows Betty Buyer the house Sarah just listed for Sam Seller. Betty is bedazzled. She loves the house and tells Bob to write up an offer on it immediately.

When Betty decided to make an offer on Sam's house, the agency relationships that Betty and Sam had with their respective agents changed.

Like it or not, Sarah suddenly represented both Sam and Betty. Similarly, Bob became the agent of both Betty and Sam.

Why? Even though two different agents are involved, both agents work for the same real estate broker, Acme Realty. As soon as Bob started to work on Betty's offer, Acme Realty represented the seller and the buyer of the same property. *That's dual agency.*

Dual agency probably won't be a problem for you if you end up working with an agent in a small office that has only a few agents. The odds that you'll buy a home listed by one of the other agents in your agent's office are slim. However, if the agent that you select works for a large brokerage operation with multiple offices and thousands of agents (such as Coldwell Banker,

Century 21, and the like), your odds of having to deal with dual agency skyrocket.

As a buyer, you should be on guard for two potential problems when confronted with dual agency. First, be careful to ensure that your agent isn't sharing confidential information with one of his peers at his or her real estate company. Second, watch out for agents who push their own company's listings, the sales of which may earn them higher commissions.

Most states permit dual agency relationships as long as the agency status is disclosed to both the sellers and the buyers in advance, and both parties agree to it. Undisclosed dual agency can be used as grounds to have a purchase agreement revoked, and usually permits the injured parties to seek recovery against the real estate agents.

How agents get paid

Real estate brokerage is an all-or-nothing business. As a rule, agents are *only* paid a commission when property sells. If the property doesn't sell, the agents don't get paid.

This payment method can create a conflict of interest between you and your agent. The payment method won't create a conflict of interest with *good* agents, because good agents put your best interests in front of their desire to get paid. You know that you're working with a bad agent, however, if the agent is more interested in quickly closing the sale and having you pay top dollar than in diligently educating you and getting you the best possible deal.

Allow us to answer your burning questions about real estate commissions:

> ✓ **How much do real estate agents get in commissions?** Commissions are calculated as a percentage of the sale price. Depending on local custom, commissions on homes usually range from 4 to 7 percent of the sale price.

> ✓ **Who pays the commission?** Usually sellers. After all, sellers get money when property sells. Buyers rarely have much money left after making the down payment for their dream home and paying loan charges, property inspections fees, homeowners insurance premium, moving costs, and the other expenses of purchase noted in Chapter 3. Because commission is part of the sales price, the effective cost of the commission comes out of both the buyer's and seller's pockets.

✔ **Are commissions negotiable?** Absolutely. *Listing agreements* (the contracts that property owners sign with a broker to sell their property) and purchase agreements usually state that commissions are *not* fixed by law and may be negotiated between sellers and brokers.

✔ **How is the commission distributed?** Suppose that a house sells for a nice, round $200,000. Assuming a 6 percent commission rate, the sale generates a $12,000 commission. That's a lot of money. At least it would be if it all went to one person, but commissions don't work that way as a rule.

Usually, the commission is divided in half at the close of escrow. The *listing broker,* who represents the sellers, gets half ($6,000 in our example) of the commission, and the other half ($6,000) goes to the *selling broker,* who represents the buyers.

If the selling or buying agent works for a broker, the broker typically gets a portion of the commission. The brokerage firm typically takes 30 to 50 percent of the commission, which leaves the agent 50 to 70 percent. In some firms, such as RE/MAX, agents pay a fixed monthly fee to their brokerage firm and end up keeping 80 to 90 percent of the commissions they bring into the firm. Agents who work on their own as independent brokers, of course, don't have to split their commissions with anyone.

Characteristics of good agents

Good agents can be male or female, and they come in a wide assortment of races, colors, creeds, and ages. All good agents, however, have the following characteristics that are beneficial to buyers:

✔ **Good agents educate you.** Your agent knows the home-buying process and explains each step so that you *always* understand what's happening. Agents should be patient, not pushy. A good agent *never* uses your ignorance to manipulate you.

✔ **Good agents never make decisions for you.** Your agent *always* explains what your options are so that *you* can make wise decisions regarding your best course of action.

✔ **Good agents tell you whenever they think that adding other experts (inspectors, lawyers, and the like) to your team is advisable.** Experts don't threaten a good agent. The agent's ego should always be secondary to the primary mission of serving you well.

✔ **Good agents voluntarily restrict themselves geographically and by property type.** Your agent has hopefully learned that trying to be all things to all people invariably results in mediocre service. Different communities can have radically different market conditions, laws, and restrictions. (For more information, see the nearby sidebar "Agents who work outside their areas of expertise are dangerous.")

TECHNICAL STUFF

Where an agent's time goes

Some people think that real estate commissions are disproportionately large relative to the amount of work that agents do. That's a polite way of saying that agents are grossly overpaid.

Justifying a good agent's commission is easier if you understand what we call The Iceberg Theory. As you probably know, 90 percent of an iceberg's bulk is hidden under water. You can't tell how big an iceberg is by the portion you see floating above the waterline. By the same token, you can't tell how much time agents spend working for you based on the amount of time you see them working.

Good agents spend at least nine hours working behind the scene for every hour spent in the presence of their clients. Unfortunately, buyers and sellers don't know this. Buyers and sellers think that commissions are excessive, given the relatively few hours they actually *see* their agents working for them.

Unlike lawyers and other professionals who bill clients by the hour, real estate agents don't itemize the time spent on a transaction from start to finish. If they did, you'd have a better idea of where your agent's time goes.

Good real estate agents spend around 20 hours a week touring new properties and checking up on houses that have been on the market a while in order to see which houses are still available and which have had offers accepted on them. Agents do this legwork, week in and week out, to stay current regarding what's on the market and how property values are changing.

After you select an agent, she starts targeting houses you may want to buy. Good agents screen several properties for each one they eventually show you, which saves you the time of doing the screening yourself. Your agent spends time playing phone tag with listing agents, trying to get instructions about how to show properties, and scheduling showings. Then she spends more hours with you, touring houses and searching for your elusive dream home.

After you've found your dream home, your agent spends time preparing an offer to purchase, presenting the offer, and negotiating counteroffers with the seller's agent regarding the price and terms of sale. After the offer is accepted, a good agent spends more hours helping you with such things as securing a mortgage, coordinating information and paperwork for the escrow, going through the house with your various property inspectors, and reviewing the mandated local, state, and federal disclosure statements from the sellers.

✔ **Good agents are full-time professionals, because serving you properly is a full-time job.** To reduce the financial impact of changing jobs, many people begin their real estate careers as part-timers, working as agents after normal business hours and weekends. That's fine for the agents, but not you.

One of the first questions to ask any agent you're considering working with is, "Are you a full-time agent?" Just as you wouldn't risk letting a part-time lawyer defend you, *don't let a part-time agent represent you.*

Agents who work outside their areas of expertise are dangerous

Many pitfalls await buyers who trust agents who work outside their areas of expertise. Although extreme, here's a real-life example of a disaster caused by an agent who specialized in property located in Sonoma, a town about 40 miles north of San Francisco.

The Sonoma agent represented her friend in the purchase of a small apartment building located in San Francisco. The buyer intended to convert the apartments into condominiums and then sell the condos individually at a profit.

Unfortunately, the Sonoma agent knew nothing about San Francisco's strict rent-control law or its condo-conversion ordinance. The intent of these laws is to discourage people from converting low-rent apartments into upscale condos.

Due to the restrictive nature of these two laws, had the building been converted into condos, the total proceeds from individual sales would've been less than the price the buyer had originally paid for the building. The agent's negligence ultimately led the buyer to lose $125,000 when she later resold the building.

This agent not only made the mistake of working in "foreign territory," she also failed to recommend getting a local expert to advise the buyer on these issues. The buyer could have sued her agent for malpractice. She didn't because the agent was her "friend."

With friends like that, the buyer sure didn't need any enemies. If the Sonoma agent had been a real friend, she'd have referred the buyer to a good San Francisco agent.

Agents who go out of their area of geographical or property expertise do so because they're either greedy or just too darn inept to know better. Whatever the reason, avoid such agents like the plague.

✔ **Good agents have contacts.** Folks prefer doing business with people they know, respect, and trust. You can use your agent's working relationships with local lenders, property inspectors, lawyers, title officers, insurance agents, government officials, and other real estate agents. But watch out: Good agents should refer you to good service providers who offer competitive pricing rather than simply as a return favor to those providers who have referred them business in the past.

✔ **Good agents have time.** Agents earn their living selling time, not houses. Success is a two-edged sword for busy agents. An agent who is already working with several other buyers and sellers probably won't have enough surplus time to serve you properly. Occasional scheduling conflicts are unavoidable. But if you often find your needs being neglected because your agent's time is overcommitted, get a new agent.

Buying without an agent

You may see an *FSBO* (For Sale By Owner) or two during your home search. The sellers may even be friends, neighbors, or work colleagues. Because no real estate agent is involved on the selling side of an FSBO transaction, the sellers don't have to pay a commission. That shaves big bucks off their expenses of sale.

If the FSBO home meets your needs and you found it yourself, you may rightfully wonder whether you need an agent to complete the deal. After all, if the sellers don't have to pay your agent's commission, they should be willing to sell you the home at a lower price.

Some homebuyers have successfully purchased their dream homes without an agent. Others have made big boo-boos that way.

If you're a novice, using an agent usually makes sense. Consider the additional value that an agent brings to the transaction beyond finding you the property — such as negotiating, estimating market value, and helping coordinate property inspections, contingency removals, seller disclosures, financing, opening escrow, and myriad other details.

You may also consider asking an agent to represent you for less than the standard 3 percent commission because you found the property yourself. If you decide not to use an agent, consider hiring an attorney by the hour to review the contract and handle the transaction's important legal details.

Selecting your agent

Now that you know the glittering generalities of a hypothetical good agent, you're ready to get down to the nitty-gritty specifics of choosing an agent of your very own. We recommend that you interview several (at least three) agents before selecting the lucky one.

Referral sources

If you have trouble finding three good agents to interview, here are some referral sources:

- ✔ **Friends, business associates, and members of religious, professional, and social organizations to which you belong:** In short, anyone you know who's either house hunting or who owns a home in your target neighborhood can be a source of agent referrals. Don't just ask for names; find out why these folks liked their agents.

- ✔ **Your employer:** The company you work for may have a relocation service that you can consult.

- ✔ **Professionals in related fields:** Financial, tax, and legal advisors can be good agent-referral sources.

- **The agent who sold your previous home:** If you're a homeowner who's moving into a new area, ask the agent who sold you your home to recommend a good agent in that area. Good agents network with each other.

- **Sunday open houses:** While you're investigating the houses, check out the agents holding them open. These agents have already proved (by their open-house activity) that they work the neighborhood which you want to buy.

Don't take any referral, even if it's from the Pope, as gospel. Most people who make referrals have had limited experience with the recommended agent. Furthermore, the person making the referral is probably not a real estate expert.

Activity list

After you've identified three good agents, the fun begins. To avoid a misunderstanding, tell each agent that you plan to interview several agents before you select the one you'll work with. Ask each agent to bring to the interview a list of *every* property the agent listed or sold during the preceding 12 months. This list, called the *activity list,* is a powerful analytical tool.

Here's what the activity list should include and how you should use the list during the interview:

- **Property address:** Addresses help you zero in on the agent's geographical focus. See how many properties the agent sold and listed in your target neighborhood(s). Eliminate agents who are focused outside your area *and* ones who have no geographical focus.

- **Property type (house, condo, duplex, other):** This information indicates whether the agent works on the kind of property you intend to buy. If, for example, an agent specializes in condos and you want to buy a house, you may have a problem.

- **Sales price:** Does the agent handle property in your price range? An agent who deals in *much* more or less expensive property than you can afford may not be the right agent for you. If, for example, you can't spend more than $150,000, and the cheapest house the agent sold in the past year cost $300,000, you have a mismatch. Such agents probably won't spend much time on you because they have bigger fish to fry.

- **Date of sale:** Sales should be fairly evenly distributed throughout the year. If they aren't, find out why. A lack of recent sales activity may be due to illness or marital problems that may reduce the agent's effectiveness.

- **Whom the agent represented — seller or buyer:** Seasoned agents work about half the time with buyers and the other half with sellers. Newer agents primarily work with buyers. Avoid agents who focus primarily on sellers because such agents likely lack the qualities that you're looking for as a buyer.

✔ **Total dollar value of property sold during the preceding 12 months:**
Comparing the three agents' grand total property sales is a quick way to
measure individual activity and success. There are, however, other equally
important factors to consider when selecting your agent. You don't
necessarily want a "top producer." These agents get to the top by listing
and selling large quantities of property. They usually don't have the time
or patience to do the hand-holding and education you need.

✔ **Name and current phone numbers of sellers/buyers:** You'll use this later
to spot-check references.

Words whisper; actions thunder. The activity list transforms cheap chatter into
solid facts. Good agents willingly give you their lists and encourage you to
check client references. *Eliminate from consideration any agent who won't give
you an activity list.*

Agent interviews

Begin each interview by analyzing the agent's activity list. After you've finished
reviewing the list, get answers to the following questions:

✔ **Are you a full-time agent?** You should have asked this before inviting
the agent to be interviewed. If you didn't, do it now. *Don't work with part-
time agents.*

✔ **Whom do you represent?** This gets back to the fundamental question of
agency. Is the agent representing you exclusively, or is he a dual agent who
represents both you and the seller? *Be sure that you know exactly whom
your agent represents at all times.*

✔ **What can you tell me about your office?** Discuss office size, staff support,
market specialization, and reputation. See whether the agent's broker is
knowledgeable, is available to you if necessary, and is a good problem-
solver. In a crunch, your transaction's success may depend upon the
quality of backup support that you and the agent receive.

Don't select an agent based on the size of the agent's office. Some excellent
agents work as sole practitioners, and other excellent agents prefer the
synergism and support services of a huge office. Although larger offices
tend to have more listings, no one office ever has a monopoly on the good
listings. *Quality of service is more important than quantity of agents or listings.*

✔ **How long have you been an agent?** You want an agent who keeps learning
and growing. After five years in real estate, a good agent has five years'
experience, whereas a mediocre agent has one year's experience five
times. *Time in the saddle is, by itself, no guarantee of competence.*

✔ **Do you have a salesperson's license or a broker's license?** An agent must satisfy more rigorous educational and field sales experience requirements to get a broker's license. Many fine agents have a salesperson's license throughout their entire career. Although a broker's license isn't a guarantee of excellence, *good agents often get a broker's license to improve their professional skills and to give themselves an advantage in agent-selection situations.*

✔ **Do you hold any professional designations? Have you taken any real estate classes recently? What do you read to keep current in your field?** Taking continuing education courses and reading to stay abreast of changes in real estate brokerage are good signs. So is obtaining professional designations, such as the GRI (Graduate, Realtor Institute) and CRS (Certified Residential Specialist) designations through the National Association of Realtors' study programs. *However, credentials in and of themselves are no guarantee of competence or ethics.*

✔ **What is your understanding of my home-buying needs?** You've probably already told the agent what you want to buy, the neighborhood you'd like to live in, and how much you can spend. See whether the agent remembers what you said. If the agent doesn't, watch out. *You need an agent who listens carefully to what you say.*

✔ **What do you think of the other two agents (name them) that I'm interviewing?** To encourage frankness, assure the agents that you won't repeat what they say to you. Good agents don't build themselves up by tearing down other agents. If all three agents are good ones, you won't hear any derogatory comments. If, however, one of the agents (or the agent's firm) has a bad reputation in the real estate community, the other two agents should tell you. *Good or bad, the reputations of your agent and the agent's office rub off on you.*

✔ **How many other buyers and sellers are you currently representing?** If, for example, the agent holds three listings open every weekend and is working with six other buyers to boot, where do you fit in? You shouldn't contort your life to fit the agent's schedule. *A good agent has time to accommodate your schedule.*

✔ **Do you work in partnership with another agent or use assistants?** Some agents team up with another agent to handle buyers and sellers jointly. If this is the case, you must interview both agents. Other agents delegate time-consuming detail work to their assistants, so they themselves can focus on critical points in the transaction. If an agent relies on such assistants, be sure that the assistants are qualified and that you understand exactly how and when during the buying process the agent will work directly with you. *You don't want to hire an agent only to find that you end up working most of the time with an assistant whom you can't stand.*

> ✔ **Is there anything I haven't asked about you or your firm that you think I should know?** Perhaps the agent is planning to change firms or is leaving next week to take an 80-day balloon trip around the world. Maybe the agent's broker is going out of business. *This is the "make sure that I find out everything I need to know to make a good decision" question.*

Checking agents' references

Here's your chance to learn from other people's mistakes, which is infinitely preferable to goofing up yourself. You should have activity lists with names and phone numbers of *every* buyer and seller that the agents represented during the past 12 months. You can pick and choose the people you want to call rather than being restricted to a highly selective list of references who think that these agents are God's gift to real estate.

What's to prevent agents from culling out their worst transactions? Nothing. However, the more deals they delete, the less activity they have to show you — and the worse they look when you compare the agents' overall sales activity.

Any agent who won't give you his or her activity list is trying to hide either a lack of sales or unhappy clients. *Dump the agent.*

Suppose that each agent gives you a list containing 50 transactions. Assuming one buyer or seller for each transaction, 50 clients per agent times three agents interviewed equals 150 phone calls. Not likely. You'd be on the phone forever.

Good news. You don't have to call each and every client to check references — unless you want to. You can get quite an accurate picture of the agents by making six calls per agent.

Here's a fast, easy way to get a representative sampling of client references:

1. **Because you're a buyer, ignore all references from sellers.**

   Doing so probably slices the list in half.

2. **Next, zero in on people who bought property similar in price, location, and property type to what you want to buy.**

3. **Now call two of those representative buyers who purchased a home about 12 months ago, another two buyers who bought 6 months ago, and two buyers whose escrows just closed.**

   By spreading references over the past year, you can find out whether the agent's level of service has been consistently good.

Now that you've identified which buyers to call, here's what to ask when you have them on the phone:

✔ **Is the agent trustworthy? Honest? Did the agent follow through on promises?** Your agent can't be even the tiniest bit untrustworthy, dishonest, or unreliable. A negative answer to any of these questions is the kiss of death.

✔ **Did the agent have enough time to properly serve you? Was the agent available as required to fit your schedule?** Occasional scheduling conflicts are okay. Frequent conflicts are absolutely, flat-out unacceptable.

✔ **Did the agent explain everything that happened during the buying process clearly and in sufficient detail to satisfy you?** What one person thinks is sufficient detail may not be nearly enough for another. You know which type you are — question agent references accordingly.

✔ **Did the agent set realistic contract deadlines and meet or beat them?** "Time is of the essence" is a condition of every real estate contract. Contract time frames for obtaining a loan, completing property inspections, and the like are extremely important and must be strictly adhered to, or the deal will go belly-up. Good agents prepare well-written contracts with realistic time frames and then ensure that all deadlines are met.

✔ **Do the words *self-starter, committed,* and *motivated* describe the agent?** No one likes pushy people. But if you're under the gun to buy quickly, the last thing you want is a lethargic agent. You shouldn't have to jab your agent periodically with an electric prod to make sure that he's still breathing. Find out how energetically the agent in question is prepared to work for you.

✔ **Who found the home you bought — you or the agent?** This question is a double check of the agent's market knowledge. Good agents not only know what's already on the market, but they also know which houses will be coming on the market soon. You shouldn't have to find the house you buy — that's your agent's job.

✔ **Did the agent negotiate a good price for your home?** See whether the agent's buyers still think that they got a good deal. Good agents are very frugal when spending their clients' money. Good agents use their knowledge of property values and their negotiating skills to make sure that their clients pay rock-bottom prices for the homes that they buy. People who bought homes six months or a year ago can tell you how well their purchase prices have stood the test of time.

✔ **Would you use the agent again?** This is the ultimate test of customer satisfaction. If someone says "no," find out why not. The negative answer may be the result of a personality conflict between the buyer and the agent that won't bother you. On the other hand, the negative answer may reveal a horrendous flaw that you haven't yet discovered in the agent.

✔ **Is there anything I haven't asked you about the agent or the agent's office that you think I should know?** You never know what you may find out when you ask the famous catch-all question.

Making your decision

By analyzing all three agents' sales activity, interviewing the agents, and talking to their buyers, you can develop the facts you need to make an informed decision. Here are three final considerations to help you select the paragon of virtue that you need on your real estate team:

- **Will you be proud having the agent represent you?** People who deal with your agent will form opinions of you based upon their impressions of your agent. You can't afford to have anyone on your team who isn't a competent professional.

- **Do you communicate well with the agent?** Good agents make sure that you completely understand everything they say. If you can't understand your agent, you're not stupid — the agent is a poor communicator.

- **Do you enjoy the agent's personality?** Home buying is stressful, even for the coolest of cucumbers. You'll be sharing some extremely intense situations with your agent. Working with an agent you like may transform the home-buying process from a horrible experience into an exciting adventure — or, at least, a tolerable transaction.

Getting the most from your agent

After working so hard to find a great agent, it would be a shame to inadvertently ruin the relationship. Good buyer/agent relationships aren't accidental. Such relationships are based upon pillars of mutual loyalty and trust that develop over time.

Poor relationships, conversely, result from misconceptions of how the game is played. Some buyers act in what they think is their best interests, but they end up shooting themselves squarely in the feet.

More isn't always better

One common fallacy is thinking that five agents are five times better than one agent. The theory sounds so logical. If you work with agents from a variety of offices, you can get better market coverage and first peek at the new listings that each office puts on the market. The more agents you work with, the better your chances of quickly finding your dream home.

Things don't work that way in the real world. When smart agents first meet you, they always ask whether you're working with any other agents. These agents are trying to find out how much you know about the market, to avoid wasting time showing you houses that you've already seen, and to learn what you didn't like about the properties that you saw. Smart agents ask this question in order to avoid making the same mistake that your other agents have made.

One good agent can quickly show you every house on the market that meets your price, neighborhood, size, and condition specifications. If none of the houses is what you want, good agents keep looking until the right home hits the market. Good agents don't limit their searches to just those houses listed by their office. They investigate anything even remotely similar to what you want. Whether you work with one agent or one hundred, you'll see the same houses.

Agents know that they won't get paid if you don't buy. That risk comes with the job. What agents hate is losing a sale after months of hard work because they called you two or three minutes *after* another agent called you about the same house. That risk is unnecessary.

You're free, of course, to work with as many agents as you wish. In fact, working with more than one agent makes sense if you're looking for a home in more than one geographic area.

Don't be surprised, however, if good agents in the same area opt out of a horse race. Their odds of getting paid for their work increase dramatically when they spend their time on buyers who work exclusively with them. Loyalty begets loyalty.

The risk of playing the field is rarely worth the reward. One loyal agent *totally* committed to finding you a home is infinitely better than five agents working for you as a last resort because they consider you just marginally better than Benedict Arnold. Like marriages, the best buyer/agent relationships are *monogamous*.

Your agent is not the enemy

Another fallacy is viewing your agent as your adversary. True, you don't want to tell your innermost secrets to the kind of agent who'll blab them to the seller or seller's agent. Some buyers think that the less their agent knows about them, the better. Such buyers believe that, after agents know why they want to buy and how much cash they have, the agents will somehow magically manipulate them into spending far more than they can afford to spend for the home they eventually buy.

Not true. The reason good agents ask questions about your finances and motivation isn't that they're nosy. Good agents asks such questions because they need to be sure that you're financially qualified in order to avoid wasting your time and theirs by showing you property that you can't afford. If your agent knows that you're under deadline pressure to buy, she'll give your house hunt top priority.

Good agents won't betray your trust. They know that if they take care of you, the commission takes care of itself. If you can't trust your agent, don't play cat-and-mouse games — *get a new agent.*

Strangely enough, smart agents fear you as much as you fear them. They know that you have the power to make or break their careers. If they please you, you'll be a geyser of glowing referrals for them. If they upset you, you'll be a festering thorn in their paw.

Use the immense power of potential referrals to control your relationship with the agent. If your agent does a lousy job, don't get mad — get even. Tell the world every gory detail of your rotten experience. Nothing ruins an agent's career faster than dissatisfied clients.

Bagging a Broker

Selecting a broker is easy. When you choose an agent, your agent's broker goes along for the ride. It's a package deal.

If your purchase rolls merrily along, you may never meet the broker. But if a truly nasty problem rears its ugly head, one guess who you can turn to for a quick fix. Brokers are the invisible grease in problematic transactions.

All states issue two markedly different types of real estate licenses: one for salespeople (agents) and one for brokers. Agents who have broker's licenses must satisfy much more stringent educational and experience standards than agents with a salesperson's license do.

Your agent may have either type of license. Broker licensees have the option either to operate independently or to work for another broker. An agent who has a salesperson's license, on the other hand, *must* work under a broker's direct supervision so that you have access to the broker's higher lever of expertise if you need it.

When Harry Truman was president, he had a sign on his desk that read, "The buck stops here." Like Truman, good brokers don't pass the buck. Here are some of their other characteristics:

- ✔ **Excellent reputation:** The broker's image, good or bad, will be obvious from comments that you hear while checking agent references. You want the seller, lender, and all other people involved in your transaction working with you *because of* your broker's reputation, not in spite of it. You shouldn't have to overcome guilt by association. If an agent's references disparage the agent's broker, dump the agent.

- ✔ **Extensive business relationships:** Good brokers develop and maintain relationships with the people whom their office deals with — other brokers, lenders, title officers, city officials, and the like. This preexisting reservoir of good will is yours to use when the going gets rough. Brokers with strong business relationships can work near-miracles for you in a crisis.

> ✔ **Strong problem-solving skills:** Participants in real estate transactions sometimes get highly emotional. When your life savings are on the line, you may occasionally lash out at the other players. Someone has to handle the resulting quarrels and misunderstandings. That someone is the broker.

Call your broker into the game if your agent is stymied by a tough problem or if you're having problems with the agent. Everything an agent does or fails to do is ultimately the broker's responsibility. The broker's job is to help make your problems go away.

Landing a Lender

Everyone knows that buying a home is likely to be the largest single purchase you'll ever make. Unless you're an all-cash buyer, however, everyone is wrong. Here's why:

Suppose, for example, that your dream home's purchase price is $150,000. You make a 20 percent cash down payment of $30,000 and get a $120,000 fixed-rate loan at 7.5 percent interest from your friendly lender. Over the next 30 years, you repay the loan with payments of about $840 a month. (We show you in Chapters 3 and 5 how to crunch these numbers for yourself.)

Your 360 monthly loan payments total approximately $300,000. If you originally borrowed $120,000, the excess $180,000 is interest on your loan. Total interest charges *exceed* your home's purchase price!

Street-smart versus book-smart

Book-smart people lack hands-on, front-line experience; they have only theoretical experience. They know what should happen in a perfect world based upon what they've read. You're getting book-smart right now.

Street-smart people are tempered by hands-on, practical experience. They know how things work in the real world. If you select a good one, the broker is one of the most street-smart people on your home-buying team.

People learn less from routine deals; real street smarts come from sweaty-palm, turbulent transactions. Most agents have one or two such transactions each year. When these turbulent transactions occur, the broker takes control of the plane, so to speak.

Because the broker participates directly or indirectly in every deal the office handles, your broker's practical experience is directly related to the number of agents in the office. A broker who manages a 25-agent office, for example, gets 25 years' of real estate experience per calendar year. Any broker who can survive five years of handling all the office's gut-wrenching messes becomes a superb problem solver out of sheer necessity.

If you can't pay, you can't play. You need a good lender on your team to transform you from a homelooker into a homeowner. By finding the right lender, you can save yourself big bucks over the life of the loan.

No one loan is right for everyone. A person fresh out of college who's struggling to buy a condo with 5 percent cash down has vastly different loan requirements than an older, cash-rich couple who can put 50 percent cash down on a retirement cottage using equity from the sale of their previous house.

Finding the right loan used to be easy. In the early '70s, you didn't need an advanced degree in math to find a loan. You could get any kind of mortgage you wanted as long as it was a 30-year, fixed-rate loan. All home loans were basically the same, except for minor variations in loan fees and interest rates.

Those kinder, gentler days of yesteryear are long gone. Today, you're confronted by a bewildering array of fixed- and adjustable-rate mortgage (ARM) programs. To understand what lenders say, you must learn the ARM vocabulary: *assumability, periodic cap, life cap, reservation of rights to adjust caps upon assumption, index, margin, negative amortization, adjustment frequency, annual percentage rate,* and the like.

In Chapter 5, We take the mystery out of securing a mortgage and selecting a lender. If you haven't read this chapter yet, now would be a good time to do so.

Procuring Property Inspectors

A home's price is directly related to its physical condition. Homes in top shape sell for top dollar. Fixer-uppers sell at greatly reduced prices because whoever buys them must spend money on repairs to get them back into pristine condition.

Even if you're a smart cookie, you don't know how much work a house may need just by looking at it. You can't see whether the roof leaks, whether the electrical system is shockingly defective, whether the plumbing is shot, whether the furnace's heat exchanger is cracked, whether the chimney is loose, or whether termites are feasting on the woodwork. Invisible defects like these cost major money to repair.

Because you may inadvertently become the owner of such hidden problems, you need property inspectors on your team. None of the other players on your team — including real estate agents, lenders, and brokers — is qualified to advise you about a house's physical condition or the cost of necessary corrective work. In Chapter 11, we cover everything you need to know about property inspections and selecting property inspectors.

Even though a home isn't quite as complicated as a space shuttle, it still has plenty of expensive systems that can go haywire. "Saving" money by foregoing inspections just because a home appears to be in good condition is a false economy. The vast majority of home problems are not visible. *Never buy a house that hasn't been thoroughly inspected from foundation to roof.*

Electing an Escrow Officer

One common denominator crops up in most every real estate deal — mutual distrust. As a buyer, would you give the sellers your hard-earned money before every single condition of the sale is satisfied? Not likely. If your positions were reversed and you were the seller, would you give the buyers the *title* (ownership) to your house before you got their money? No way.

Even the simplest transaction involves myriad details that have to be resolved to everyone's satisfaction before the sale can be completed. Without something to bridge the gulf of mutual buyer-and-seller distrust, deals would grind to a halt.

In order to bridge that gulf of distrust, real estate (like other team sports) has a referee. The *escrow officer* is the referee who keeps the game civilized. Escrow officers aren't on anyone's team — they're neutral. They act as a disinterested third party for buyers and sellers without showing favoritism to either party.

After you and the seller have a signed contract, all the documents, funds, and instructions related to your transaction are given to the escrow holder specified in your purchase agreement. We cover this process, known as *opening an escrow,* in detail in Chapter 12.

Buyers and sellers often select the escrow holder based upon the recommendation of their real estate agents. Depending on where the property you're buying is located, local custom dictates whether your escrow is handled by a lawyer, bank, real estate broker, or the firm that issues title insurance.

Escrow fees range from a few hundred dollars to several thousand dollars and are based on your property's purchase price. Once again, local custom nearly always determines whether the buyer or the seller pays for the escrow, or whether the escrow fees are split 50-50. However, as you see in Chapter 10, this item is often negotiable.

Finding (or Foregoing) Financial and Tax Advisors

The real estate game is played with real money — your hard-earned cash. You've likely scrimped, saved, and done without in order to get the cash for your down payment. When you sell your house someday, its equity will be a major chunk of your net worth. Either way, buying or selling, you have big bucks on the line.

A home purchase has an enormous impact on your personal finances. Before you buy a home, you need to understand how a home purchase will fit within the context of your overall finances and your other goals. Be sure to read Chapters 2 and 3, which deal with these important issues.

You can elect to hire a financial advisor, but most such titled advisors aren't set up to handle home-buying questions objectively. The reason: Financial advisors stand to gain financially from the advice they render. Many so-called financial consultants get commissions from the investments they sell you. If this is the case, how excited will they be to advise you to use your cash to buy a home instead of an investment from them?! Advisors who manage money on a fee (or a percentage) basis have the same conflict of interest.

If you're going to hire an advisor, use one who works by the hour and doesn't have a vested interested in your home-buying decision. Few financial advisors work on this basis. Although tax advisors are more likely to work on this basis, they tend to have a narrower-than-needed financial perspective. A competent tax advisor may be able to help you structure the home's purchase to maximize your tax benefits. For most transactions, however, a tax advisor is unnecessary.

If you want to hire a financial or tax advisor, interview several before you select one. Check with your agent, banker, lawyer, businesses associates, and friends for referrals. As is the case with selecting your agent, you should get client references from each tax advisor and call the references.

Here's what to look for in a good financial or tax advisor:

- ✔ **Is this a full-time job for the advisor?** The realm of personal finances and taxes is too vast for you to trust a part-timer. You need the services of a full-time professional.

- ✔ **Does the advisor speak your language?** Good advisors can explain your options in simple terms. If you don't understand exactly what the tax advisor is saying, ask for clarification. If you still don't understand, get another tax advisor.

- ✔ **Is the advisor objective?** Hire someone who works solely by the hour and doesn't have a vested interest in the advice that they give you as to when to buy and how much to spend. (See the nearby sidebar, "So-called experts don't always give good advice.")

So-called experts don't always give good advice

Ray wasn't very sophisticated about tax advisors when he moved to San Francisco. Several agents that Ray worked with suggested that he use their tax advisor. He selected her based on their recommendations (plus the fact that her office was only two blocks away).

Ray knew that he'd made a mistake when he went over the tax return that she'd prepared for him. Ray asked her how she had arrived at the deductions for auto expenses and professional training. (The deductions were much higher than the totals of the receipts that Ray had given her.)

She explained how these higher deductions reduced his tax bite and said that no one would question the deductions because they were within acceptable guidelines. Ray still didn't understand her concept of deducting more money than he had spent.

Ray's tax advisor went through the tax return again, speaking more slowly and using smaller words. She concluded by saying that everyone overstates expenses.

At the time, Ray knew that she was speaking English because he recognized nearly all the words that she used, but they seemed to be bouncing off his forehead without penetrating his brain. He was getting more and more frustrated. She was getting later and later for her next appointment. In desperation, she finally gave Ray the return and sent him home like a schoolboy to "think it over."

He did.

Ray decided that the problem wasn't that he was stupid. The problem was that he'd been given unethical advice. In her zeal to save Ray money, the tax advisor had falsified Ray's deductions. That falsification was wrong. Worse yet, it was illegal. Ray solved the problem by getting a new tax advisor.

Never blindly follow the advice of experts because you're in awe of their expertise. Experts can be just as wrong as ordinary mortals.

✔ **What is the advisor's fee schedule?** Hourly fees vary widely. Don't pick someone strictly on a cost-per-hour basis. An advisor who's just beginning to practice, for example, may only charge half as much as one with 20 years' experience. If the rookie takes four hours to do what the old pro does in an hour, which advisor is more expensive in the long run? Furthermore, the quality of the seasoned veteran's advice may be superior to the quality of the novice's advice.

✔ **Is the tax advisor a Certified Public Accountant (CPA) or Enrolled Agent (EA)?** These professional designations indicate that the tax advisor has satisfied special education and experience requirements and has passed a rigorous licensing exam. A CPA does general accounting and prepares tax returns. An EA focuses specifically on taxation. Only CPAs, Enrolled Agents, and attorneys are authorized to represent you before the IRS in the event of an audit.

> ✔ **Does the tax advisor have experience with real estate transactions?** Tax practice, like law or medicine, is an extremely broad field. The tax advisors that IBM uses (for example) are undoubtedly wonderful, but IBM's tax advisors are not necessarily the best ones for *you*. You need a tax advisor whose clients have tax problems like yours.

 The best advisors in the world can't do much to change the financial and tax consequences of a transaction *after* the deal is done. If you're going to consult advisors, do so *before* you make significant financial decisions. Plan your financial and tax situation instead of reacting to it after the fact.

Looking for Lawyers

Lawyers are like seat belts. You never know when you may need them. Your deal is rolling merrily along when out of nowhere — slam, bam, wham — you hit a legal pothole and end up in Sue City.

That real estate purchase agreement you sign is meant to be a legally binding contract between you and the seller. If you have *any* questions about the legality of your contract, get a lawyer on your team *immediately*. No one else on the team is qualified to give you legal advice.

Here's what determines whether you need a lawyer on your team:

✔ **Where the property you're buying is located:** In states such as California, lawyers rarely work on deals that only involve filling in the blanks on a standard, preprinted purchase agreement that has been previously reviewed and approved by members of the Bar Association. In other states, however, lawyers routinely do everything from preparing purchase contracts to closing the escrow. Your agent will know the role that lawyers play in your locale.

✔ **The complexity of your transaction:** You need a lawyer if you get into a situation that isn't covered by a standard contract. Unless your agent is also a lawyer, he isn't qualified to do creative legal writing. Complicated issues, such as those that may arise from partnership agreements between unrelated people who buy property together, and the complex legal ramifications of taking title to your home should be handled by a lawyer. (We get into partnership agreements in Chapter 7 and taking title in Chapter 12.)

✔ **When no agent is involved:** Say, for example, that you're buying a home that's for sale by owner. If neither you nor the seller has an agent, get a lawyer to prepare the contract and have the lawyer do the work that an agent would normally handle. Eliminating the agent doesn't eliminate the need for disclosures, inspections, contingency removals, and other details involved in the home-buying process.

✓ **To sleep at night:** You may have the world's easiest deal. Still, if you'd feel more comfortable having a lawyer review the contract, your peace of mind is certainly worth the cost of an hour or two of legal time.

Selecting your lawyer

If, for whatever reason, you decide that you need a lawyer, interview several before making your selection. Real estate law, like medicine, is highly specialized. A corporate attorney or the lawyer who handled your neighbor's divorce isn't the best choice for your real estate team. Get a lawyer who specializes in residential real estate transactions. Your agent and broker are excellent referral sources because they work with real estate lawyers all the time in their transactions.

A good lawyer has the following characteristics:

✓ **Is a full-time lawyer and licensed to practice law in your state:** Of course.

✓ **Is local talent:** Real estate law, like real estate brokerage, is provincial. The law not only varies from state to state, it also changes from area to area within the same state. Rent-control laws, condominium-conversion statutes, and zoning codes, for example, are usually passed by city or county governing agencies. A good local lawyer knows the laws and has working relationships with people who administer the laws in your area.

✓ **Has a realistic fee schedule:** Lawyers' fees vary widely. A good lawyer gives you an estimate of how much it will cost to handle your situation. As with financial and tax advisors, the experience factor comes into play. Seasoned lawyers generally charge more than novice lawyers, but seasoned lawyers also tend to get more done in an hour than inexperienced lawyers can. A low fee is no bargain if the novice is learning on your nickel.

✓ **Has a good track record:** If your case may go to trial, see whether the lawyer has courtroom experience. Some lawyers don't do trial work. Then ask about the lawyer's track record of wins versus losses. What good is a lawyer with a great deal of trial experience if that lawyer never wins a case?

✓ **Is a deal-maker or a deal-breaker (whichever is appropriate):** Some lawyers are great at putting deals together. Others specialize in blowing them out of the water. Each skill is important. Good deal-makers, however, aren't always good deal-breakers, and vice versa. Depending on whether you want the lawyer to get you out of a deal or keep a deal together, be sure that you have the right type of lawyer for your situation.

If your lawyer's *only* solution to every problem is a lawsuit, you may be in the clutches of a deal-breaker who wants to run up big legal fees. Find another lawyer!

✔ **Speaks your language:** Good lawyers explain your options clearly and concisely without resorting to incomprehensible legalese. Then they give you a *risk assessment* of your options in order to help you make a sound decision. For example, the lawyer may say that your first course of action will take longer but will give you a 90 percent chance of success, while the faster option only gives you a 50-50 chance of prevailing.

Getting the most out of a lawyer

Whoever said that an ounce of prevention is worth a pound of cure must have been thinking of lawyers. A two-hour preventative consultation with your lawyer is infinitely better than a two-month trial that could take place just because you "saved" a consulting fee.

If you're not sure whether you'll need a lawyer, Chapter 10 offers a clause that you can put in your contract to get out of any deal that isn't approved by your lawyer. You don't actually need to have a lawyer when you use this clause; it just gives you the option to have the contract reviewed later by a lawyer if you wish.

Good lawyers are excellent strategists. Given adequate lead time, they can structure nearly any deal to your advantage. Conversely, if you bring wonderful lawyers into the game after the deal is done, all they can do is damage control. *The best defense is a good offense.*

Beware of the *awe factor.* People tend to hold lawyers in awe because their word is law. Disobey lawyers and you go to jail. Bologna. Don't blindly follow your lawyer's advice. If you don't understand the advice or if you disagree with it, question it. You may be correct and the lawyer may be wrong. Lawyers are every bit as fallible as everyone else.

Avoiding Gratuitous Advice

We'll say it again: Buying a house is a team sport. Successful transactions result from the coordinated efforts of many different people — agents, brokers, lenders, property inspectors, escrow officers, tax advisors, and lawyers. Each player should make an important contribution to your team.

As long as your experts stick to what they know best, everything goes smoothly. Whenever one of your experts invades another expert's turf, however, war breaks out with a bang.

Unsolicited opinions that deal with property values are one devastating type of gratuitous advice. Such opinions are usually volunteered by tax advisors or lawyers during a review of your transaction. Lawyers and tax advisors don't know property values. Making a lowball offer based on their bad advice, no matter how well-intentioned, could blow the deal on your dream home.

Some buyers foolishly *solicit* gratuitous advice in a misguided attempt to save a few bucks. "Why," buyers ask themselves, "hire a CPA for tax advice if we can get it free from our agent? Why pay for legal advice from a lawyer if our escrow officer gives us free opinions about the best way for us to take title to our home?"

Why? Because, if you're lucky, free advice from the wrong expert is worth exactly what you pay for it. Zip. Zero. Nada. Nothing. If you're unlucky, free advice is very expensive. The IRS, for example, shows no mercy if you make a mistake based upon faulty advice. Ironically, this type of mistake usually ends up costing you far more than a lawyer or tax advisor would have charged you for correct advice.

Given the adverse consequences of bad advice, *good* experts don't offer guidance that they aren't qualified to give. If asked, they categorically refuse to give such advice. Instead, they redirect their clients to the proper expert. Good experts are wise enough to know what they don't know, and humble enough to admit it. On a more selfish level, they don't want to get sued by the clients for giving them lousy advice.

Beware of experts who offer you gratuitous advice outside their field of expertise.

Chapter 9

What's It Worth?

*Y*ou see a house for sale. The asking price is $149,500. Is the house a steal or an overpriced turkey?

If you don't have the faintest idea what the house is worth, don't worry. That's normal. Most buyers don't know property values when they start hunting for a home. To become an *educated buyer,* you need time to familiarize yourself with property values.

When Ray began his real estate career, he spent dozens of hours each week looking at houses. Like all new agents, his appetite for property was boundless and indiscriminate — big houses, tiny condos, old property and new, houses in pristine condition or fixer-uppers, uptown, downtown, and midtown. If a place had a roof and a For Sale sign, Ray toured it inside and out.

Why? The best way to learn property values is to eyeball as many houses as possible, and then monitor the houses until they sell. That's how agents educate themselves.

You don't need to see every house in town get educated. A good agent can accelerate your learning curve by playing the real estate version of show-and-tell. You only need to tour houses that meet your specific budget, size, and neighborhood requirements. After seeing no more than a dozen comparable houses, you'll be an educated buyer.

Uneducated buyers are inadvertent liars

Ray can look into a mirror to see a perfect prototype of a lying uneducated buyer. Like all buyers, Ray believed he was telling his agent the truth when he and his sweet wife, Annie B., began looking for a home in the wine country about 50 miles north of San Francisco. When they first met their agent, Beverly Mueller, Ray wasted no time establishing the ground rules of the house hunt.

"We don't need the Taj Mahal," Ray told Beverly. "I'm in the real estate army, not a civilian like your other buyers. Trust me when I tell you that $300,000 is the flat out, absolute, upper limit of what we'll spend."

"I understand, Ray. We'll only look at places under $300,000," Beverly said.

And look they did. Over the next several months, Beverly showed them every house in their price range on the market in the Sonoma Valley. Ray and Annie rejected each and every one. Either they liked the land and hated the house or vice versa. They were ready to give up when they got lucky.

Ray and Annie found Woodpecker Haven, the home they ended up buying in Glen Ellen, thanks to Karen and Herman Isman, friends of theirs who were also working with Beverly. Karen and Annie drove from San Francisco to Glen Ellen together to see a house that Beverly thought the Ismans would like. It was love at first sight — not for Karen, for Annie.

Why hadn't Beverly shown Ray and Annie the house? Because its asking price was $390,000 — far more than the $300,000 ceiling Ray imposed. Beverly's mistake was believing what Ray told her when they first met.

Why did Ray lie? He didn't intend to. Had he and Annie found what they wanted for less than $300,000, Ray would've been telling the truth. Only after three months of looking at property did it become clear that what Ray and Annie wanted to spend and what they wanted to live in were totally out of whack with market reality.

Many buyers hit the same wall sooner or later during their education process. Ray and Annie belatedly realized that they had to make trade-offs — either reduce their expectations to fit their budget or expand their budget until it satisfied their expectations.

That was when they became educated buyers. They were finally realistic enough to make tough decisions.

What Ray and Annie experienced happens to most people. For example, you decide that you can't afford a home that has both a family room and a pool and that's in the neighborhood you like. Or you opt to keep your wish list intact and buy in a slightly less wonderful neighborhood. Something has to give when you're forced to confront reality.

The other alternative is expanding your buying power. Much as you'd like the security of a 30-year fixed-rate loan, you decide to get an adjustable-rate mortgage instead because the ARM allows you to qualify for a bigger loan. Much as you'd like to buy without financial assistance from your parents, you swallow your pride and ask them for a loan. Again, something has to give.

Groucho Marx once said he'd never belong to any club that would have him as a member. Paraphrasing Groucho, people don't want to live in any house they can afford.

Word Games

Oscar Wilde said a cynic is someone who knows the price of everything and the value of nothing. Neither *cost* nor *price* is the same as *value*. When you understand what these words mean and how they differ, you can replace emotion with objectivity when looking at houses and during price negotiations after you finally make an offer. Out-facting people beats trying to out-argue them.

Value is a moving target

Value is your opinion of what a particular home is worth to you, based on how you intend to use it now and in the future. Value isn't carved in stone. On the contrary, it's pretty darn elusive.

For one thing, opinions are subjective. We, your humble authors, think that we resemble Robert Redford and Paul Newman. You, on the other hand, are of the opinion that we look like Boris Karloff and Bela Lugosi — in full monster makeup. No harm done, as long as we all realize that a big difference exists between opinions and facts.

Furthermore, *internal factors* — things related to your personal situation — have a sneaky way of changing over time. Suppose that you currently place great value on a house with four bedrooms and a large, fenced-in backyard. The home must be located in a town with a good school system. Why? Because you have small children.

Twenty years from now, when the kids are grown and have moved out (you hope!), you may want to sell the house. Why? Because you no longer need such a big home. The house didn't change — what changed were internal factors regarding your use for it and thus its value to you.

External factors are things outside your control that affect property values. If your commute time is cut in half because mass transit rail service is extended into your neighborhood after you buy your home, your home's value may increase. If a garbage dump is built next door to you, you'll have a big problem getting top dollar for your house when you sell it.

The law of supply and demand is another external factor that affects value. If more people want to buy than sell, buyer competition drives home prices up. Conversely, if more people want to sell than buy, home prices drop. See Chapter 4 for a complete explanation of all the factors that influence home prices.

Cost is yesterday

Cost measures past expenditures — for example, what the sellers paid when they bought their house. That was then, and this is now. What the sellers originally paid or how much they spent fixing up the house after they bought it doesn't mean diddlypoo as far as a house's present or future value is concerned.

For example, when home prices began skyrocketing in most parts of both coasts during the mid 1980s, some buyers accused sellers of being greedy. "You paid $175,000 five years ago. Now you're asking $350,000," they said. "If you get your price, you'll make an obscenely large profit."

"So what?" sellers replied compassionately. "If you don't want to pay our modest asking price, move out of the way so the nice buyers standing behind you can present their offer." In a hot sellers' market, people who base their offering price on what sellers originally paid for property waste everyone's time.

The market changed radically in a few short years. By the early 1990s, prices had declined in many areas. Sellers would've been ecstatic to find buyers willing to pay them what they'd paid five years earlier, when home prices peaked. In those areas, sellers who priced their homes based on the inflated purchase prices they'd paid for the houses years earlier learned the same painful lesson buyers were taught in the frenzied '80s: The sellers' profit or loss doesn't matter when determining a home's present value.

Price is what it's worth today

Sellers have *asking prices* on their houses. Buyers put *offering prices* in their contracts. Buyers and sellers negotiate back and forth to establish *purchase prices*. Today's purchase price is tomorrow's cost. Is the purchase price a good value? That depends.

You'll get a bargain if you find a house owned by people who don't know property values or who must sell quickly due to an adverse life change such as divorce, job loss, or a death in the family. Folks who don't have time to sit around waiting for buyers willing to pay top dollar usually take a hit when they sell. Time is the seller's enemy and the buyer's pal.

If, however, you must buy quickly to avoid paying capital gains tax on the sale of your previous house (see Chapter 15) or to get your kids settled before school starts, watch out. You could overpay because you don't have enough time to search for a good deal.

Cost is the past, price is the present, and value (like beauty) is in the eyes of the beholder. What the sellers paid for their house years ago, or what they'd like to get for it today, doesn't matter. Don't squander your hard-earned money on an overpriced house to satisfy an unrealistic seller's fantasy.

Another word game — can't sell versus won't sell

Two weeks of extraordinarily heavy rain in January 1993 undermined the soil of a subdivision in the Anaheim Hills area of Los Angeles. After this drenching, homes in the 25-acre development began slipping downhill at the rate of about an inch a day.

Home foundations and swimming pools cracked. Streets and sidewalks buckled. Local authorities finally ordered everyone in the subdivision to evacuate their homes until the ground stabilized.

Unlike most frustrated sellers we know, these folks really *couldn't* sell their homes. Forces of nature beyond their control reduced their houses' value to zero. Other than salvage value, no market exists for unintentionally mobile homes.

Fortunately, most homeowners who claim that they "can't" sell their houses don't have this problem. They aren't disaster victims whose homes are suddenly rendered valueless by an act of God. On the contrary, they have buyers galore for their houses as well as scads of lenders who'd make loans to those buyers.

If nothing is wrong with their houses, then what's the problem? The homeowners. The problem isn't that they *can't* sell. These homeowners *won't* sell.

As long as homeowners *choose* not to accept what buyers will pay for their houses, they can't sell, and their homes sit on the market. It's a self-fulfilling prophecy. As a prospective homebuyer, beware of such greedy, unrealistic sellers.

Fair Market Value

Natural disasters aside, every home will sell at the right price. That price is defined as its *fair market value* (FMV) — the price a buyer will pay and a seller will accept for the house, given that neither buyer nor seller is under duress. Duress can come from life changes such as divorce or sudden job transfer that put either the buyers or sellers under pressure to perform quickly. If appraisers know that a sale was made under duress, they raise or lower the sale price accordingly to more accurately reflect the house's true fair market value.

Fair market value is more powerful than plain old *value*. As a buyer, you have an opinion of what the house is worth to you. The sellers have a separate, not necessarily equal (and probably higher), opinion of their home's value. These values are opinions, not facts. You can't bank opinions.

Unlike value, fair market value is fact. It becomes a fact when buyers and sellers agree upon a *mutually acceptable price*. Just as it takes two to tango, it takes a buyer and a seller to make fair market value. Facts are bankable.

When fair market value isn't fair — need-based pricing

Whenever the real estate market gets all soft and mushy, many would-be sellers feel that fair market value isn't fair at all. "Why doesn't our house sell?" they ask. "Why can't we get our asking price? It's not fair."

Don't let your highly developed sense of fair play make a sucker out of you. Sellers frequently confuse "fair" with "impartial." Despite its friendly name, fair market value isn't a warm, cuddly fairy godmother. On the contrary, it can be heartless and cruel. Need isn't a component of fair market value. Fair market value doesn't care about any of the following:

- ✔ How much the sellers *need* because they overpaid for their house when they bought it.

- ✔ How much the sellers *need* to recover the money they spent fixing up their house after they bought it.

- ✔ How much money the sellers *need* to pay off their loan.

- ✔ How much money the sellers *need* from the sale to buy their next humble abode, Buckingham Palace.

Here's why a seller's *need-based pricing* doesn't enter into fair market value. Suppose that two identical houses next door to one another are listed for sale. One house was purchased for $32,000 in 1965. The other house sold for $320,000 in 1990, soon after home prices peaked. The first home has no outstanding loan on it. The other still has a big mortgage.

Bill and Mary, who own the house purchased in 1990, *need* more money than Ed, owner of the house purchased in 1965. After all, they paid ten times as much as Ed for their house, and they owe the bank big bucks to pay off their mortgage.

Because the houses are basically identical in size, age, and condition, they have the same fair market value. Not surprisingly, they both sell for $275,000. That gives Ed a nice nest egg for retirement, but barely pays off Mary and Bill's mortgage. Fair? Ed thinks so. Bill and Mary don't.

Fair market value is brutally impartial. It is what it is — not what buyers or sellers want it to be.

Median home prices aren't fair market value

Some folks think that median sale prices for homes indicate fair market values. They don't.

Organizations such as the National Association of Realtors, the Chamber of Commerce, and private research firms generate *median sale-price statistics* by monitoring home sales in a specific geographic region such as a city, county, or state. One function of these organizations is to gather market-research data on home sales activity.

There's nothing magical about the median sale price. It's the midpoint in a range of all the home sales for a reporting period. Half the sales during the reporting period fall above the median, and half fall below it. The median-priced home, in other words, is the one exactly in the middle of the prices of all the houses that sold. Figure 9-1 demonstrates what we mean.

Figure 9-1:
The median sale price is the one smack dab in the middle.

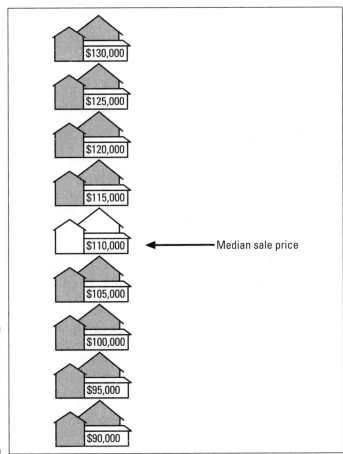

$130,000

$125,000

$120,000

$115,000

$110,000 ◄────── Median sale price

$105,000

$100,000

$95,000

$90,000

When this book went to press, the median sale price of a home in America was $110,000, which tells you that half the homes in America sold for more than $110,000 and half sold for less than $110,000. Unfortunately, all you know about this hypothetical median-priced home is its price.

You don't know how many bedrooms or baths the median-priced home has. Nor do you know how many square feet of interior living space the house has, how old it is, or whether it has a garage or a yard. You don't even know where this elusive median-priced house is located, other than that it's somewhere in the USA.

If median-price information is so vague, why bother with it? Because it tells you two important things:

- **Price trends:** If the median price of a home in America was $80,000 ten years ago and is $110,000 now, you know home prices in general are rising. You don't know why they are, just that they are.

- **Price relativity:** If the median-priced home in Yakima, Washington sells for $75,000 versus $300,000 for the median-priced Honolulu home, you know that you'll get a much bigger bang for your housing buck in Yakima. Honolulu has many redeeming qualities, but cheap housing isn't one of them.

Median home-price statistics make interesting reading, but they aren't any more accurate for determining specific home values than median income statistics are for assessing your paycheck. You need much more precise property-value information before you invest a major chunk of your life's savings in a home.

Zero in on areas you can afford (see Chapter 3) by comparing median home prices on a town-by-town and neighborhood-by-neighborhood basis. When median price statistics indicate that home prices are rising or falling sharply in an area, find out why by reading and talking to players on your real estate team, such as your agent.

Comparable Market Analysis

The best way to accurately determine a home's fair market value is to prepare a written *comparable market analysis* (CMA). A competent real estate agent can and should prepare a CMA for a home that you're interested in *before* you make your purchase offer. Every residential real estate office has its own CMA format. No matter how the information is presented to you, Table 9-1 shows you what good CMAs contain.

Table 9-1 Sample CMA — "Recent Sales" Section

Address	Date Sold	Sale Price	Bedrm/ Bath	Parking	Condition	Remarks
210 Oak	04/30/96	$190,000	3/3	2 car	Very good	Best comp. Approx. same size and cond. as *dream home* (DH), slightly smaller lot. 1867 sq. ft. $102/S.F.
335 Elm	02/14/96	$168,500	3/2	2 car	Fair	Busy street. Older baths. 1805 sq. ft. $93/ S.F.
307 Ash	03/15/96	$185,000	3/3	2 car	Good	Slightly larger than DH, but nearly same size and condition. Good comp. 1850 sq. ft. $100/S.F.
555 Ash	01/12/96	$182,500	3/2.5	2 car	Excellent	Smaller than DH, but knockout renovation. 1740 sq. ft. $105/S.F.
75 Birch	04/20/96	$193,000	3/3	3 car	Very good	Larger than DH, but location isn't as good. Superb landscaping. 1910 sq. ft. $101/ S.F.

These are facts. The CMA's "Recent Sales" section helps establish the fair market value of 220 Oak — your *dream home* that is currently on the market — by comparing it to *all* the other houses that

 ✔ Are located in the same neighborhood

 ✔ Are of approximately the same age, size, and condition

 ✔ Have sold in the past six months

These houses are called *comps,* which is short for *comparables.* Depending on when you began your house hunt, you probably haven't actually toured all the sold comps. No problem. A good real estate agent can show you listing statements, take you on a verbal tour of the houses you haven't seen, and explain how each one compares to your dream home.

Communicating well with your agent about subjective terms such as *large, lots of light, close to school,* and so on is critically important. You must understand precisely what the agent says. Conversely, your agent must understand precisely what you want, need, and can afford.

If you and your agent were to analyze the sale comps in our example, you would find that houses comparable to the home you want to buy — 220 Oak, in Table 9-2 — are selling in the range of $100 or so per square foot. Putting the sale prices into a price-per-square-foot basis makes comparisons much easier. As you can see in Table 9-2, anything that's way above or below the norm really leaps out at you.

Table 9-2		Sample CMA — "Currently For Sale" Section				
Address	*Date Listed*	*Asking Price*	*Bedrm/ Bath*	*Parking*	*Condition*	*Remarks*
220 Oak (*Dream Home*)	04/25/96	$195,000	3/3	2 car	Very good	Quieter location than 123 Oak, good detailing, older kitchen. 1880 sq. ft. $104/S.F.
123 Oak	05/01/96	$199,500	3/2	2 car	Excellent	High end rehab. & priced accordingly. Done, done, done. 1855 sq. ft. $107/S.F.
360 Oak	02/10/96	$175,000	3/2	1 car	Fair	Kitchen & baths need work, no fireplace. 1695 sq. ft. $103/S.F.
140 Elm	04/01/96	$179,500	3/3	2 car	Good	Busy street, small rooms, small yard. 1725 sq. ft. $104/S.F.
505 Elm	10/31/95	$225,000	2/2	1 car	Fair	Delusions of grandeur. Grossly overpriced! 1580 sq. ft. **$142/S.F.**

Address	Date Listed	Asking Price	Bedrm/ Bath	Parking	Condition	Remarks
104 Ash	04/17/96	$189,500	3/2.5	2 car	Very good	Great comp! Good floor plan, large rooms. Surprised it hasn't sold. 1860 sq. ft. $102/S.F.
222 Ash	02/01/96	$219,500	3/2	1 car	Fair	Must have used 505 Elm as comp. Will never sell at this price. 1610 sq. ft. **$136/S.F.**
47 Birch	03/15/96	$209,000	4/3.5	2 car	Good	Nice house, but overimproved for neighborhood. 2005 sq. ft. $104/S.F.
111 Birch	04/25/96	$189,500	3/3	2 car	Very good	Gorgeous kitchen, no fireplace. 1870 sq. ft. $101/S.F.

The "Currently For Sale" section of the CMA compares your dream home (in this case, 220 Oak) to neighborhood comps that are *currently on the market.* These comps are included in the analysis to check price trends. If prices are falling, asking prices of houses on the market today will be lower than sale prices of comparable houses. If prices are rising, you'll see higher asking prices today than comps sold for three to six months ago.

If you've been looking at houses in a specific area for a while, you've probably been in all the comps currently on the market in that area. You don't need anyone to tell you what you've seen with your own eyes. However, you do need an agent's help to compare the comps you've seen to comps you haven't seen because the houses sold before you began your house hunt.

As Table 9-2 shows, your dream house appears to be priced very close to its fair market value based on the actual sale price of 210 Oak (in Table 9-1). Given that 220 Oak has 1880 square feet, it's worth $191,760 at $102 per square foot. Factually establishing property value is easy once you know how.

Your CMA must be comprehensive. It should include *all* comp sales in the past six months and *all* comps currently on the market. Getting an accurate picture of fair market values is more difficult if some parts of the puzzle are missing, especially in a neighborhood where homes don't sell frequently.

Like milk in your refrigerator, comps have expiration dates. Lenders won't accept houses that sold more than six months ago as comps. Their sale prices don't reflect current consumer confidence, business conditions, or mortgage rates. As a general rule, the older the comp, the less likely that it represents today's fair market value.

Why six months? Six months is generally accepted as long enough to have a good cross section of comp sales, but short enough to have fairly consistent market conditions. But six months isn't carved in stone. If a major economic calamity occurred three months ago, for example, six months is too long for a valid comparison. Conversely, if homes in a certain area rarely sell, you may need to examine comparable sales that occurred more than six months ago.

Sale prices are always given far more weight than asking prices, when determining fair market value. Sellers can ask whatever they want for their houses. Asking prices are fantasy. Sale prices are facts — they indicate fair market value. The best proof of what a house is worth is its sale price. Don't guess. Analyze the sale of comparable homes. (Be sure that the comparable sales information factors in price reductions or credits given for corrective work repairs.)

CMA flaws

CMAs beat the heck out of median price statistics for establishing fair market values, but even CMAs aren't perfect. We've seen people use exactly the same comps and arrive at very different opinions of fair market value. Discrepancies creep into the CMA process if you blindly compare comps without knowing all the following details of the subject properties:

- **Wear and tear:** No two homes are the same after they've been lived in. Suppose that two identical tract homes are located next door to one another. One, owned by an older couple with no children or pets, is in pristine condition. The other, owned by a family with several small kids and several large dogs, resembles a federal disaster area. Your guess is as good as ours when figuring out how much repairing the wear-and-tear damage in the second house will cost. A good comparable analysis adjusts for this difference between the two homes.

- **Site differences within a neighborhood:** Even though all the comps are in the same neighborhood, they aren't located on precisely the same plot of ground. How much is being located next to the beautiful park worth? How much will you pay to be seven blocks closer to the bus stop during the rainy season? These value adjustments are a smidge less precise than brain surgery.

✔ **Out-of-neighborhood comps:** Suppose that, in the past six months, no homes were sold in the neighborhood where you want to live. Going into another neighborhood to find comps means that you and your agent must make value adjustments between two different neighborhoods' amenities (schools, shopping, transportation, and so on). Comparing different neighborhoods is far more difficult than making value adjustments within the same neighborhood.

✔ **Noncomp home sales:** What if five houses sold in the neighborhood in the past six months, but none of them were even remotely comparable in age, size, style, or condition to the house you want to buy? You and your agent must estimate value differences for three- versus four-bedroom homes, old versus new kitchens, small versus large yards, garage versus car port, and so on. If the home you want has a panoramic view and none of the other houses have any view at all, how much does the view increase the home's value? Guesstimates like these don't put astronauts on the moon.

These variables are not insurmountable obstacles to establishing your dream home's fair market value. They do, however, greatly increase the margin of error when trying to determine a realistic offering price. You can minimize pricing problems created by these variables if you and/or your agent actually tour comparable homes inside and out.

A valid comparison of your dream home to the other houses is impossible if you and your agent have only read about the comps in listing statements. Seeing is believing. Most *listing statements* (those one-page, house-for-sale advertisements/marketing pieces) are overblown to greater or lesser degrees. You don't know how exaggerated the statement is if you haven't seen the house for yourself. You may find a "large" master bedroom tiny. That "gourmet" kitchen's only distinction may be an especially fancy hot plate. The "sweeping" view from the living room may only exist if you're as tall as Michael Jordan. Of course, you won't know any of these things if you only read the houses' puff sheets instead of visiting the house in person.

Floor plans also greatly affect a home's value. Two houses, for example, may both be approximately the same size, age, and condition, yet vary wildly in value. One house's floor plan flows beautifully from room to room; the rooms themselves are well proportioned with high ceilings. The other house doesn't work well because its floor plan is choppy and the ceilings are low. You can't tell which is which just by reading the two listing statements.

Eyeball. Eyeball. Eyeball. *Eyeballing* — touring houses and noting important details both inside and out — is the best way to ensure which houses are true comps for your dream home.

Appraisals versus CMAs

If you're in no rush to submit an offer and you're the suspicious type, you can double check the opinion of value that you and your agent arrived at before you make an offer on your dream home. You can pay several hundred dollars to get a professional appraisal of the house.

Getting an *unbiased* second opinion of value is always reassuring. An appraiser won't tell you what you want to hear just to make a sale. The appraiser isn't trying to sell you anything. Whether you buy the house or not, the appraiser gets paid.

Unfortunately, the fact that the appraiser charges a fee regardless of whether you buy the house cuts both ways. Suppose that you and the sellers can't reach an agreement on price and terms of sale because the sellers are deluded about how great their home really is. Even if your offer isn't accepted, you still get a bill from the appraiser. Paying for appraisals or property inspections before your offer is accepted generally isn't wise.

If you think a professional appraisal is vastly superior to your agent's opinion of value, think again. A good agent's CMA is usually as good as an appraisal. Conversely, if a professional appraisal is vastly superior because your agent is a lousy judge of property values, get a better agent.

In any given area, appraisers usually don't see as many houses as agents who focus on that area see. Appraisers aren't lazy; they use their time in other ways.

Formal appraisals are time-consuming. An appraiser inspects the property from foundation to attic, measures its square footage, makes detailed notes regarding everything from the quality of construction to the amount of wear and tear, photographs the house inside and out, photographs comps for the house being appraised, writes up the appraisal, and so on. Agents can tour 15-20 houses in the time it takes an appraiser to complete one appraisal.

As a result, appraisers frequently call agents to find out about houses the agents listed or sold that might be comps. No matter how good an agent's description of the house is, personally touring the property is still the best bet. Any appraisal's accuracy suffers if the appraisal is based on comps the appraiser hasn't seen. Agents also call each other about houses they haven't seen, so don't think that appraisers are the only culprits. If your agent hasn't seen most of the comps used in your CMA, get an agent who knows the market.

Unless you're pretty darn unsure about a property's value, and willing to spend the money whether the deal goes through or not, don't waste money on a precontract appraisal.

WARNING!

Phone prices aren't comps

Home sale prices are now just a phone call away in most parts of the country. Depending on the phone service you select, you'll pay $1 per minute (with a $5 or $10 minimum charge) to get a list of addresses, sale dates, and sale prices for houses that sold anywhere from four weeks to ten years ago.

You can do phone searches of towns where you may want to live by specific property, by street, or by price range. If the addresses are short, you can get as many as 12 prices in five minutes. And you can even bill the calls to your credit card.

According to the ads, smart homebuyers use this invaluable sale price data to find areas they can afford. Once they locate the neighborhood, homebuyers use the information to find out what all the other houses on the street sold for so they don't buy the most expensive house on the block.

If this gimmick sounds like a good deal to you, reread the first part of this chapter immediately!

Who cares whether 123 Main Street sold for $75,000 in April 1986? You need a lot more than an address, a sale price, and a sale date to have a comp. What about little details like size, age, condition, yard size, and so on? What good are the sale prices of homes that sold five or ten years ago?

Worse yet, why pollute your mind with misleading information? Save your money and mind for important things like applying these principles to getting a really good deal on your dream home.

Why Buyers and Sellers Often Start Far Apart

We think that the average buyer is brighter than the average seller. How else can you explain why buyers are generally so much more realistic about property prices?

It's not as though there are two different real estate markets: an expensive one for sellers and a cheap one for buyers. Sellers have access to exactly the same comps buyers do. Yet buyers' initial offering prices tend to be far more realistic than sellers' initial asking prices. Why? Figure 9-2 may offer some insight into that question.

Some people believe that the selfish interests of buyers and sellers force them to approach a house's fair market value from opposite directions. Buyers bring their offering price *up* to fair market value because they don't want to overpay. Sellers ratchet their price *down* to fair market value because they hate the thought of leaving any money on the table.

That's logical, but simplistic. This reasoning still doesn't explain why many sellers initially tend to be so much more unrealistic than buyers.

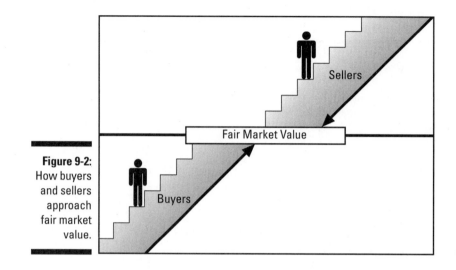

Figure 9-2:
How buyers
and sellers
approach
fair market
value.

The better you understand the warped thought processes of these sellers, the better you can handle their unreasonable objections to your eminently fair offer. To that end, here are three common causes of absurdly high asking prices.

Inept agents

Just because *you* used the information in Chapter 8 to select a great agent doesn't mean that everyone will. In fact, many people do a rotten job of picking an agent.

Perhaps the sellers' agent is an incompetent boob who doesn't know anything about property values. Those poor misguided sellers didn't put a smart asking price on their house because their agents gave them lousy advice.

When your agent discovers that the other agent is inept — either by the poor quality of the comps that the sellers' agent used to establish the asking price or by reputation (these things get around in the real estate brokerage community) — what can you do? That depends.

If the house has been on the market for a month or two and the sellers are open to reason, your agent's brilliant comps will prevail over their agent's fantasy pricing. The sellers will grasp the concept of fair market value and either gratefully accept your offer or make a modest counteroffer because your offering price is so logical, realistic, and fair.

You've got a problem, however, if their house just came on the market. The sellers probably won't believe anything you and your agent say about the asking price being too high. They'll discount your opinion of their house's fair market value because they suspect that you're trying to steal their home. They'll be nearly as suspicious of a formal appraisal done by *your* hand-picked appraiser.

Time cures overpricing by inept agents. The longer the house stays on the market without selling, the more the sellers will doubt their own and their agent's opinion of value.

If the sellers' house isn't priced to sell and they won't listen to reason, move on to the next house on your list. No telling how long the sellers will take to get smart. Don't put your life on hold waiting for them to wise up. They may be very slow learners.

Bidding wars

When home sellers select an agent, the interviewing process may go awry. Bidding wars often develop among the agents competing to list the sellers' house for sale. The concept of fair market value is the bidding war's first victim. If you try to buy such a house, you could be the second victim. Here's what happens when the sellers interview agents:

"Thanks for giving me an opportunity to list your lovely house, Mr. and Mrs. Seller," the first agent says. "As you can see by reviewing the CMA, my fair market value analysis indicates that eight houses sold in your neighborhood in the past six months. Three of them were significantly larger than yours, so they can't be used as comps. The five houses comparable to yours in size, age, location, and condition sold in the range of $150,000 to $170,000. Based on their sale prices, I recommend an asking price of $175,000."

Now the second agent strikes. "Who cares what the comps indicate? Your house is painted a particularly attractive shade of turquoise and your lawn is greener than the lawns of any of those other houses. I suggest starting with a nice, round asking price of $200,000."

Agent three knows that he probably won't get the listing unless he outbids the other two agents. "Our firm's international marketing program is incredibly successful," he says, oozing confidence. "Through our global referral and relocation service, we'll be able to find a buyer in one of those Pacific Rim countries who'll be willing to pay $225,000."

This technique of successive agents giving ever-higher property valuations is known as *buying a listing*. Sellers, when confronted by the choice of market reality versus fantasy, often succumb to fantasy. They rationalize their decision by telling themselves that the highest bidding agent has the most faith in their house.

That's horse-hockey. If the sellers in this example select the highest bidder, it's because that agent dazzled them with the extra $50,000 they'd get by selecting him to sell their house. He told them what they wanted to hear. Greed triumphed over reason.

So who wins the bidding war? Not the folks who own the house. If their asking price has no basis in the real world, you won't purchase it. Nor will any other educated buyer.

How can you avoid becoming the victim of a bidding war? You know what we're going to say. Trust the comps to tell you what the house is worth. If the sellers won't listen to reason, move on. Comps don't fantasize. Neither should you.

Unrealistic sellers

Some sellers get excellent pricing advice from agents — and choose to ignore it. Sellers attempting to sell without an agent make the same mistake — they opt for the ever-popular need-based pricing method (described earlier in this chapter) to set their asking price.

Sellers need time to accept that buyers don't care how much they paid for their house, how much they spent fixing it up, or how much they need to buy their next home. The sellers are stuck with these problems. The buyer isn't.

Unless a house has been on the market long enough to bring the sellers back to reality, move on. Most sellers aren't open to reason until they've tried their price for a couple of months or feel some external pressure to sell. Trying to reason with such sellers prematurely is like trying to teach a pig how to whistle. Your time is wasted, and the pig gets upset.

Overpriced houses aren't wasted

Believe it or not, houses are like red delicious apples. Most houses are green and need more time on the real estate tree before they are ready to pick. A few are ripe for picking right now. The trick is knowing which is which, because houses don't turn red as they ripen.

That's one reason you and your agent must understand fair market values and know the sale prices of comparable homes. Smart homebuyers know which houses are green and which are ripe.

Spotting overpriced turkeys

Many agents show buyers overpriced houses, but their intention is not to sell these houses. One of the tricks agents often adopt early in their careers is using OPTs (overpriced turkeys) to sell well-priced houses.

Suppose, for example, that an agent shows you a three-bedroom, two-bath house with a price tag of $199,500, and then takes you to an even more attractive four-bedroom, three-bath home in the same neighborhood *with the same asking price*. The agent doesn't have to say anything — the difference between price and value is glaringly obvious. The OPT makes the sale.

Here's another way to spot OPTs: They get lots of showings, but no offers.

Part IV
Let the Game Begin

The 5th Wave   By Rich Tennant

"Mr. Johnson, I think we've found your dream home! By the way, how do you feel about ghosts, ancient burial grounds, and curses?"

In this part . . .

*P*lay ball! When you've done all your preliminary homework, you're ready for this part. Here's where we show you how to negotiate a super deal and how to get your home inspected from roof to foundation so that you know whether it's in perfect shape or riddled with expensive defects. Because you can't close the purchase until you get homeowners insurance, we explain what, where, and how to buy the coverage you need. Finally, we describe some of the legal and tax ramifications of your purchase along with ways to make sure that your deal closes smoothly and without unnecessary costs.

Chapter 10

Negotiating to Get What You Want

- -

In This Chapter

▶ Controlling your emotions so they don't control you

▶ Pushing the envelope — if it isn't illegal, it's negotiable

▶ Understanding the characteristics of good offers

▶ Structuring an offer the seller can't refuse

▶ Including contingencies — clauses that protect you financially and structurally

▶ Spotting fake sellers

▶ Lowballing pros and cons

▶ Handling credits in escrow

- -

*W*hen it comes to buying things, most Americans are lousy negotiators. Negotiation is not part of our culture. We've been conditioned for generations to be docile buyers who pay whatever price is marked on a can of beans or a TV set. Instead of negotiating to drive down the price, at best we drive around and comparison shop to find the store with the lowest price. (And many time-starved people don't even do that.)

Sure, we can negotiate when our back is to the wall. We haggle over expensive things like cars and dicker with the boss for a raise, but doing so makes us uncomfortable. We walk away from these encounters with the nagging suspicion that we came out on the short end of the deal — that someone else could've done better.

Realizing our nation's discomfort with negotiating, some car dealers have taken the haggling out of buying a car. Instead of using high-pressure sales tactics, these dealers post a sales price on the car — the *no-dicker sticker*. That's their price; take it or leave it. If you take it, you won't get a low price; but some people think that's a fair tradeoff in order to avoid the unpleasantness of negotiating.

You won't find no-dicker stickers on homes. On the contrary, generally everything from the purchase price to the date that escrow closes is negotiable. Given today's high home prices in most of the densely populated parts of the U.S., buying a home is the ultimate in high-stakes negotiating. Good negotiators come out of a home purchase smiling. Bad negotiators take it in the wallet.

Controlling Your Emotions

Emotion is an integral part of home buying. Real estate transactions are emotional roller-coaster rides for everyone involved.

Sometimes, like San Francisco fog, emotion drifts into transactions so quietly that you hardly notice it. Most of the time, however, it thunders into deals like a herd of elephants having a bad-hair day.

Violent forces at work

Consider the violent forces acting upon you during the home-buying process:

- ✔ **You're dealing with people at their most primal level.** Shelter, food, and security are the three most basic necessities of life. Home is where the heart is. Your home is your castle. People become vicious when their homes are threatened. Speaking of primal urges, now you know why looking for a home is called "house *hunting*."

- ✔ **You're playing for large amounts of real money.** Whether this is your first home or your last, it's probably the largest purchase you've ever made. How much you pay for a home is not the issue. When significant amounts of real money are at risk, the emotional intensity for you and the seller is just as great, no matter whether the house you buy costs $150,000 or $1.5 million.

"Good" depends upon your perspective

Brace yourself. You may be shocked by the sellers' response to your offer to buy their home. From your perspective, you made a really good offer. They, on the other hand, may think that your offer stinks.

Here, for example, is the perspective of first-time buyers who just blew their budget to smithereens to offer $160,000 for a home listed at $175,000: "Honey, I'm so nervous. Do you think that the sellers will accept our offer? I know that the home costs a lot more than we wanted to spend, but it's the best place we've seen in four months of looking. What's taking them so long to get back to us? The suspense is killing me."

And here's the perspective of the retired couple who got their $160,000 offer: "Calm down, dear. Remember your blood pressure. I'm sure that nice young couple didn't mean to insult us. And no matter what you say, I can't believe that they think that we're doddering old fools who don't know how much our house is worth. They probably made the best offer they could. Please don't throw it away."

Two entirely different takes on the exact same offer. Buyers generally think that they're paying too much. Sellers usually think that they're giving their house away. When you're playing for real money, these conflicting perceptions fuel emotional fires that heat up the negotiating process.

✔ **You're probably going through a life change.** Buying a home would be plenty stressful if you only had to deal with the first two forces. Throw in a life change (such as marriage, divorce, birth, death, job change, or retirement), which is often the motivation to purchase a home, and you've created an emotional minefield.

Because eliminating emotions from a home purchase is impossible, the next best thing to do is to control them. Your choice is simple: Either you control your emotions, or they'll control you. People can't upset you unless you let them. The folks who do the best job of controlling their emotions generally end up getting the best deals.

Controlling yourself

Here are five techniques you can use to control your emotions during the home-buying negotiations:

✔ **Put the transaction in perspective.** Which is worse — a failed home purchase or failed open-heart surgery? No matter how badly things go with your real estate transaction, keep reminding yourself that this isn't a life-or-death situation. Tomorrow *is* another day. The sun *will* rise again, roses *will* bloom again, birds *will* sing again, and children *will* laugh again. Life goes on. If worse comes to worst, the deal may die; but you'll live on to find another place that you can call home.

✔ **Don't let time bully you.** Most life changes have predictable time frames. You have plenty of advance notice on marriages, births, retirements, and the like. Don't put yourself under needless pressure by procrastinating or by creating unnecessary, self-imposed deadlines. Allow yourself enough time to buy a home. Allocate time properly, and it will be your friend rather than your enemy.

✔ **Maintain an emotional arm's length.** Keep your options open. Be ready to walk away from a potential house purchase if you can't reach a satisfactory agreement on price and terms. Mentally condition yourself to the prospect that the deal may fall through. Houses are like buses: If you miss one, another will come along sooner or later.

✔ **Accept uncertainty as a part of your transaction.** Much as you'd like to know everything about a property before making an offer on it, that's not how the game is played. You always have far more questions than answers at the beginning of a transaction. Don't worry; you'll be fine as long as you know what things you need to find out and get the answers in a timely manner during your transaction.

First things first

Early in Ray's career, he worked with a buyer who wanted to have every question about the house answered before he'd submit an offer to purchase it. He wanted to structure a flawless offer. Because Ray didn't know any better, he went along with the plan. They spent several weeks fine-tuning the offering price by checking comparable home sales and getting quotes from contractors to do the necessary corrective work that was discovered during the inspections that another prospective buyer had ordered.

Unfortunately, Ray and the buyer got a hard lesson in accepting uncertainty, because they'd overlooked one tiny detail. Ray's "buyer" didn't have a signed offer on the house. The seller got tired of them dithering around, endlessly gathering information, and sold the property to someone else.

If you're smart, you'll do what the successful buyer of this home did. Make a deal first. Condition your offer upon getting your questions answered while you have the house "tied up" with a contract.

That way, if everything goes well, you'll end up the proud owner of a wonderful home. And if you can't get a loan or you don't like the inspection reports, you can bail out of the deal and move on to a more promising home. In the meantime, however, you've removed the property from the competition by getting your offer accepted.

Don't waste time getting answers to secondary questions until you answer the primary question: Can you and the seller agree on price and terms of sale? *Failure to go for the commitment wastes time and money and may cause you to lose the property.*

✔ **Stay objective.** Use a comparable market analysis to factually establish the fair market value of the home that you want to buy (see Chapter 9). A good real estate agent can help with this matter. If you don't plan to use an agent, consider working with a lawyer. If you're like most people, having someone to buffer you from your unavoidable emotional involvement helps. Just make sure that you work with professionals who are patient, not pushy, and who are committed to getting you the best deal.

The Art of Negotiating

Is negotiating like water or ice? If you said "water," go directly to the head of the class.

Negotiating is fluid, not rigid. There is no one-size-fits-all *best* negotiating strategy that you can use in every home-buying situation. Good negotiators adjust their strategy based upon a variety of factors, such as how well priced a property is, how long it's been on the market, how motivated the sellers are, how motivated you are, whether you're dealing from a position of strength (a buyer's market) or weakness (a seller's market), and so on.

Good negotiators, however, apply a few basic principles to every situation. If you understand these principles, you can greatly increase the odds of getting what you want.

Good negotiators are realistic

Good negotiators know that facts are the foundation of successful negotiation. If you want to become a good negotiator, you must see things as they are, rather than as you want them to be. *Wishful thinking makes bad negotiation.*

What's wishful thinking? A common wish in a rising real estate market, for example, is that you can pay yesteryear's price for today's home. You know that you saw a similar house for much less money a while ago. You ignore the fact that prices have increased since then, which eliminates your chance of buying a home today at the old price. Another common (and generally unrealistic) wish is that you can afford to buy a home similar to the one that you were raised in.

How do you eliminate wishful thinking? By replacing fantasy with facts. Unfortunately, that replacement is far easier said than done. Why? Because we all inevitably get emotionally involved whenever we negotiate for something that we intensely desire. Even though that emotional involvement is part of human nature, allowing emotion to seep into a negotiation can cost you dearly.

The importance of objectivity

Unlike you and the seller, good real estate agents don't take things personally. The seller's agent, for example, won't be offended if your agent says that you hate the emerald green paint in the kitchen and the red flocked wallpaper in the den. Your agent, by the same token, won't get upset if the seller's agent says that your offer is ridiculously low.

Agents find it easy to be objective. After all, they're not the ones who spent three weekends painting the kitchen or months looking for just the right wallpaper to put in the den. Nor is it their life's savings on the negotiating table.

Agents listen to what the market says a house is worth. Agents don't allow distracting details (such as how much the seller paid for the house ten years ago or how little you can afford to spend for it today) confuse negotiations. As you know if you've read Chapter 9, no correlation exists between these need-based issues and the fair market value of a home.

Some folks think that agents have calculators for hearts. Not true. The good agents know that if they aren't coldly realistic about property values, the property won't sell, and they won't get paid.

Agent-negotiating red flags

If you follow our advice in Chapter 8 when selecting a real estate agent, you'll choose one that's a good negotiator.

Doing a lousy job of selecting an agent can cost you big bucks. Bad agents don't know how to determine fair market values; as a result, you may pay too much for your home. And why should the bad agent care? After all, the more you pay, the more your agent makes, because agents' commissions are typically a percentage of the purchase price. If your agent pushes you to buy and can't justify the offering price by using comparable home sales, fire your agent and get a good one.

Good negotiators avoid making moral judgments. As long as the seller's position isn't illegal, it's neither fair nor unfair. It's just a negotiating position. Of course, agents are human. Sometimes, even the best agents *temporarily* lose their objectivity in the heat of battle. You know that this has happened if your agent gets red in the face and starts accusing the other side of being unfair.

If your agent snaps out of the funk quickly, no problem. If, on the other hand, your agent can't calm down, you've lost your emotional buffer. Agents who lose their professional detachment are incapable of negotiating well on your behalf.

No matter how satisfying it may be to go on an emotional rampage with your agent about the seller's utter lack of good taste, market knowledge, and scruples, getting angry won't get you the house. If your agent doesn't maintain a level head, ask your agent's broker (see Chapter 8) to negotiate for you, or get another agent.

The negotiating process

Negotiation is an ongoing process — a series of steps without a neatly defined beginning and end. Think of water flowing.

Each step in the negotiating process begins by gathering information. After you read this book, you'll understand the various aspects of buying a home. Then you'll be able to translate your information into action that generates more information that, in turn, leads to further action. Information. Action. Information. Action. Information. Action. And so it goes, until you're the proud owner of your dream home.

One way to begin the first action phase is to get your finances in order, get preapproved for a loan, and select an agent to work with you through the next information-gathering phase. You and your agent then investigate various neighborhoods and tour houses so that you know what's on the market. You also learn the difference between asking prices and fair market values. After you know what houses are really worth, you're ready to focus on the specific neighborhood that you want to live in and begin seriously searching for your dream home.

Making an offer to purchase

After you discover your dream home, you're ready for the next action step in the negotiating process — making an offer to purchase. No standard, universally accepted real estate purchase contract is used throughout the country. On the contrary, purchase contracts vary in length and terms from state to state and, within a state, from one locality to another.

We've included the California Association of Realtors' *Real Estate Purchase Contract* in Appendix A so that you can see what a well-written, comprehensive residential real estate contract looks like. When you're ready to write an offer, your real estate agent or lawyer will provide the appropriate contract for your area.

A carelessly worded, poorly thought out offer can turn what should be a productive negotiation into an adversarial struggle between you and the sellers. Instead of working together to solve your common problem (that is, "you want to buy, and they want to sell — how can *we* each get what *we* want?"), you get sidetracked by issues that can't be resolved so early in the negotiating process.

Although buying a home can be a highly emotional experience, good offers defuse this potentially explosive situation by replacing emotion with facts. Buyers and sellers have feelings that can be hurt. Facts don't. That's why facts are the basis of successful negotiations.

All good offers have three things in common:

- ✔ **Good offers are based upon the sellers' most important concern — a realistic offering price.** You shouldn't pull the offering price out of thin air. Instead, base your offering price on houses (comparable to the seller's house in age, size, condition, and location) that have sold within the past six months. As Chapter 9 explains, sellers' asking prices are often fantasy. The amounts that comparable houses in the area have sold for are facts. *Focus on facts.*

- ✔ **Good offers have realistic financing terms.** Your mortgage's interest rate, loan-origination fee, and time allowed to obtain financing (explained in the upcoming section on contingencies) must be based upon current lending conditions. Some offers get blown out of the water because a buyer's loan terms are unrealistic. *Focus on facts.*

If you've been prequalified or preapproved for a loan (see Chapter 5), you or your agent should stress that advantage when you present your offer. This proves to the sellers that you're a creditworthy buyer who's ready, willing, and *financially able* to purchase their house.

✔ **Good offers don't ask the sellers for a blank check.** Unless property defects are glaringly obvious, neither you nor the sellers will know if any corrective work is needed at the time that your offer is initially submitted. Under these circumstances, it's smart to use property inspection clauses (explained in the next section) that enable you to reopen negotiations regarding any necessary corrective work *after* you've received the inspection reports.

Remember that negotiation is an ongoing process. After the *action* of having your offer accepted, your property inspectors gather *information*. After they've determined what is actually required in the way of corrective work, you and the sellers can renew your negotiations (*action*) armed with hard facts (*information*). This sequence beats wasting time and energy by arguing with the sellers about the cost to complete corrective work before either of you know the precise number of dollars needed to do the repairs. *Focus on facts.*

If the sellers agree with the price and terms contained in your offer, they'll sign it. At that point, you have what's called a *ratified offer* (that is, a signed or accepted offer). This doesn't mean that you own the house. Thanks to contingencies, most ratified offers are only agreements to agree initially.

Contingencies — the homebuyer's escape hatch

Even though your offer has been accepted by the sellers, it should contain extremely important escape clauses known as *contingencies,* which you cleverly built into the contract. A contingency gives you the right to pull out of the deal if some specific future event fails to materialize.

These two contingencies appear in nearly every offer:

✔ **Financing:** You can pull out of the deal if the loan specified in your contract isn't approved.

✔ **Property inspections:** You can pull out of the deal if you don't approve the inspection reports or can't reach an agreement with the sellers about how to handle any necessary repairs.

Other standard contingencies give you the right to review and approve such things as a condominium's master deed, bylaws, and budget as well as a property's title report. You can, if you want, make the contract contingent upon your lawyer's approval of the contract or your parents' inspection of the house. As a rule, no reasonable contingency will be refused by the seller.

Here's a typical loan contingency:

"Conditioned [the magic word] upon buyer getting a 30-year, fixed-rate mortgage secured by the property in the amount of 80 percent of the purchase price. Said loan's interest rate shall not exceed 7.5

percent. Loan fees/points shall not exceed 2 percent of loan amount. If buyer can't obtain such financing within 30 days from acceptance of this offer, buyer must notify seller in writing of buyer's election to cancel this contract and have buyer's deposits returned."

If you want to see a more detailed financing contingency, read paragraph 1 of the California Association of Realtors' purchase contract in Appendix A of this book. We cover property inspections in Chapter 11.

What good is a ratified offer that is riddled with escape clauses you can drive a truck through? Riddled with escape clauses or not, a ratified offer ties up the property. You don't have to worry about the owners selling the property to someone else while you're spending time and money inspecting it.

First get the agreement on price and terms — *then* get answers to all your other questions.

Getting a counteroffer

You'll be relieved to know that counteroffer forms are far less complicated than offer forms in the real estate business. Take a look at the California Association of Realtors' Counter Offer in Figure 10-1, for example, and you'll see that it's only a one-page form.

Sellers use *counteroffers* to fine-tune the price, terms, and conditions of offers they receive. Suppose, for example, that you offer $175,000 for a home that you like and you ask to close escrow 30 days after the sellers accept your offer. Because they had the house listed at $189,500, the sellers think that your offering price is a mite low. Furthermore, they need six weeks to relocate.

Instead of rewriting your entire offer, they give you a counteroffer. It states that they're willing to accept all the terms and conditions of your offer except that they want $185,000 and six weeks after acceptance to close escrow.

The ball's in your court once again. You don't mind a six-week close of escrow, but you don't want to pay more than $180,000, so you give the sellers a *counter-counteroffer* to that effect.

Now only one bone of contention remains — the price. The sellers come back to you with a *firm* $184,000. You grudgingly respond at $181,000 and instruct your agent to make it clear to the sellers that you won't go any higher. Two can play the *firm* game. Negotiations now resemble the trench warfare of World War I.

If you really want the home, this phase of the game can be nerve-racking. You worry about another buyer making the sellers a better offer and stealing the house away while you're trying to get the price down that last $3,000. The sellers are equally concerned that they'll lose you by pushing too hard for the final $3,000. You don't want to pay a penny more than you have to. The sellers don't want to leave any money on the table.

Figure 10-1:
A typical counteroffer form.

You and the sellers are tantalizingly close to agreement on price. Your offering price and the sellers' asking price are both factually based upon recent sales of comparable houses in the neighborhood. So why the deadlock? Because sometimes the same facts can lead to different conclusions (see the nearby sidebar).

An equitable way to resolve this type of impasse is to split the difference 50-50. If the sellers in our example use this technique, they'll come back to you with a $182,500 offer — down $1,500 from their *firm* asking price of $184,000 and up $1,500 from your *firm* offering price of $181,000. The mutual $1,500 concession equals less than 1 percent of the home's fair market value based on a $182,500 sale price. That's pinpoint accuracy in a real estate transaction.

Splitting the difference won't work in all situations. It is, however, a fair way to quickly resolve relatively small differences of opinion (a few percent or less of the home's price) so you can get on with your life.

Fact versus opinion

You and the sellers can use exactly the same facts (that is, recent sale prices of comparable houses) to reach entirely different opinions of fair market value. As we point out in Chapter 9, although houses may be comparable in terms of age, size, and condition, no two homes are identical after they've been lived in.

Furthermore, even though all the houses used in the comparable market analysis are in the same neighborhood, *site differences* (that is, proximity to schools, better view, bigger yard, and the like) usually affect individual property values. Last, but not least, even though all the comparable houses were sold during the previous six months, property values can be affected by changes in mortgage rates and consumer confidence.

For example, your agent thinks that 123 Main Street, which sold two months ago for $180,000, is the best comparison (*comp*) for the home that you're trying to buy. The sellers' agent says that this house is a good comp, but points out that this house has a two-car garage, whereas 123 Main Street has only a one-car garage. Your agent says that 123 Main Street has a larger kitchen with a breakfast nook and is two blocks closer to the park. The sellers' agent says that the property you are considering has higher-quality kitchen cabinets and a new refrigerator and is three blocks closer to the bus stop.

And so it goes. Everyone agrees on 123 Main Street's sale price and date of sale. These are *facts*. They are the same no matter who looks at them. But how much value does a second garage space add to the home that you want to buy? Is being closer to the bus stop worth more to you than proximity to the park? Is an eat-in kitchen more or less valuable to you than fancy kitchen cabinets and a new refrigerator? The answers to these questions are *opinions* that are based on your value judgments. Another person would probably value the amenities somewhat differently.

Pricing is not 100-percent scientific at this level of scrutiny. Each buyer has different needs and different opinions of value.

Negotiating styles

Finding two people who have exactly the same negotiating style is as unlikely as finding two identical 200-year-old houses. All negotiating styles, however, boil down to variations on one of these two basic themes:

- **Combative (I win, you lose):** These negotiators view winning only in the context of beating the other side. To them, negotiation is war. They take no prisoners.

- **Cooperative (we both win):** These negotiators focus on solving problems rather than defeating opponents. Everyone in the transaction works together to find solutions that are satisfactory to both sides.

Which negotiating style is better? That depends on the kind of person you are, what your objectives are, and how much time you have.

Most folks opt for cooperation because they know that the world is round — what goes around nearly always comes back either to haunt you or to help you. Why fight battles in some weird game of mutually assured destruction if you can peacefully work together as allies to solve your common problems?

Brute force versus style

Ray knows a real estate agent who's a superb technician. He is brilliant at determining a home's fair market value, writes flawless contracts, understands financing, and stays current on real estate laws, rules, and regulations. Technically, he's impeccable.

Unfortunately, he has no compassion when it comes to negotiating. He's coldly perfect himself and expects equal perfection from everyone else. He is an ultra-hardball negotiator who gives his opponents no mercy. Some of his own clients don't even like him, but they all respect him because they know that he'll fight ruthlessly on their behalf.

Ironically, other agents hate working with this agent *because* he's such a brutal negotiator. They deal with him only when they have absolutely no alternative. If he represents a buyer in a multiple-offer situation, for example, his buyer's offer won't be selected if the selling agent can find any way to work with another buyer whose agent is less combative.

Ray Jones, a San Francisco agent who died several years ago, was this agent's exact opposite. Jones lacked technical polish, but he was kind, fair, generous, and made folks smile with their hearts. His clients and other agents adored him. In a multiple-offer situation, his buyer's offer was either accepted or at least counter offered, if possible. He made buying a home fun.

Think carefully when selecting an agent to represent you. People do business with you for only two reasons — because they have to or because they want to. The right agent can give you a huge negotiating advantage. The ruthless negotiator may make sense for buyers who are in no hurry to buy and who desire to get a good deal on a property. For others, such a piranha could be bad news.

Combative negotiation is tolerated in a strong buyer's or seller's market. The operative word is *tolerated*. People grudgingly play an "I win, you lose" game when they have no alternative. However, in a balanced market that favors neither buyers nor sellers, combative negotiators are usually told, "I won't play your stupid game because I don't like your style."

Cooperative negotiation, on the other hand, works well under all market conditions because its goal is to scratch everyone's itch. We all enjoy winning and hate losing. People cry when they're defeated. Problems don't cry when they're solved.

Unfortunately, some people are born competitors. The only cooperation they understand is the cooperation of a team that is working together to defeat its opponents. If you're a cooperative negotiator, here are two ways to protect yourself from combative negotiators:

- ✔ **Try switching them from combative to cooperative by finding ways you both can win.** Shift their emphasis from beating you to solving the problem. "You want to sell. I want to buy. How can we do it?"

- ✔ **If that fails, kill the deal.** If you keep negotiating, born competitors strip the money from your bank account and the flesh from your bones. They confuse concessions with weakness. If, for example, you offer to split the difference, they take the 50 percent you give them as their just due and then go for the rest. They won't be happy until they thrill to a victory that is enhanced by your unconditional defeat.

Life's too short to subject yourself to this kind of punishment. No matter how strong a seller's market you must contend with, you can find sellers who are cooperative negotiators — if you try.

Negotiating when the playing field isn't level

President Lyndon Johnson was a consummate politician. He'd cajole, promise, soft-soap, arm-twist, flatter, pressure, sweet-talk, threaten, jawbone, wheedle, bully, or horse-trade other politicians into supporting his legislation.

The late President's negotiating skills were legendary. Once, when accused of using somewhat unethical tactics to get the votes required to pass one of his Great Society programs, LBJ just shrugged. "Sorry you feel that way, son," he supposedly said. *"All I ever wanted was my unfair advantage."*

Don't we all? Unfortunately, no matter how good you are as a negotiator, sooner or later you'll have to negotiate from a position of weakness. The trick in these circumstances is to give yourself every possible advantage.

Buyer's and seller's markets

In the late '80s, many California homebuyers complained bitterly about sellers taking unfair advantage of them. Given the frenzied seller's market at that time, it wasn't unusual for owners of a well-priced house to receive multiple offers on it while their agent was still nailing up the For Sale sign. (Slight exaggeration, but you get the point.)

Five years later, the hobnailed boot was on the other foot. Instead of a supply-demand imbalance, there was a demand-supply imbalance. The anguished screams now came from sellers who were complaining about buyers taking unfair advantage of them.

The playing field usually isn't level. A perfectly balanced market that favors neither buyer nor seller is rare. The market is always in a state of flux.

The party in the weaker position always characterizes the market as "bad." Because you are a seeker of wisdom and truth, don't kid yourself. The market is, in reality, neither good nor bad. The market is impersonal. The market is the market. Moaning and groaning about unfair market dynamics won't help you if you're caught in a seller's market any more than complaining helps sellers caught in the viselike grip of a buyer's market.

Negotiating from a position of weakness

Newly listed homes that are priced to sell often generate multiple offers in a seller's market. But even when the market is not a seller's market, a well-priced, attractive new listing may draw multiple offers.

Unless you absolutely *must* have a particular home, and price is no object, be very careful about entering a bidding war. Such auctions can drive the price of a home above its fair market value. That situation is great for the seller, but it is financially deadly for you. We don't want you to overpay.

If you really want a home and you know that other offers will be made, here's how to improve your chances of winning in a multiple-offer situation:

- ✔ **Use comparable sales data to predetermine the upper limit of what you'll pay.** Don't get caught up by the excitement of a bidding war and let your emotions override your common sense. Be sure that you've read Chapter 9 and you know how to determine fair market value. Set *no matter what* limits on the amount that you'll bid. Otherwise, you could grossly overpay.

- ✔ **Put yourself in the sellers' position.** The sellers don't care how long you've been looking for a home or how little you can afford to pay. Faced with several offers, sellers select the offer that gives them the best combination of price, terms, and contingencies of sale. Find out what the sellers' needs are before making your offer. Their self-interest invariably prevails.

A high purchase price isn't the only way to sweeten a deal. If you have the money, you could make a 25 or 30 percent down payment so the sellers know that your loan will surely be approved. You could offer to give the sellers an extra-long close of escrow so they have plenty of time to find another home. You could also offer to buy the home "as is" so the sellers won't have to pay for any corrective work. If you do this, however, make your offer contingent upon your approval of inspection reports so you can get out of the deal if the house needs too much work.

✔ **Make your best offer initially.** Buyers who win bidding contests, in the words of Civil War General Nathan Bedford Forrest, get there "firstest with the mostest." If you want the house, don't hold back in a multiple-offer situation: You may never get a chance to make your best offer.

✔ **Get preapproved for a loan.** Informed sellers worry about the financial strength of prospective buyers. They don't want to waste their time on buyers who can't qualify for a loan. All other things being equal, if you're preapproved for a loan, you should prevail over buyers who aren't. That way, you also know that *you* aren't wasting your time and money on a house that you can't qualify to buy.

✔ **Don't make your offer subject to the sale of another house.** If you own a house that you *must* sell in order to get the down payment for your new home, you're in trouble. You'll most likely be competing with other buyers who don't have that limitation. The sellers have enough problems selling their house without worrying about you selling yours. Why should they take your offer if they can accept one without a subject-to-sale contingency in it? Offers made subject to the sale of another house get no respect.

✔ **If you must sell in order to buy, put your old house on the market before seriously looking for a new home.** Ideally, you'll have a ratified offer on your old house before making an offer to buy a new place. Then, even with a subject-to-sale clause, your negotiating position will be much stronger. And you won't waste time worrying about how much money you'll have when *and if* your house sells. Stipulate a long close of escrow on the old house and the right to rent it back for several months after the sale so that you'll have adequate lead time to buy your new home.

Spotting fake sellers

Why would anyone want to be a fake seller? That some people would knowingly waste their time and money on an exercise in futility is absurd.

The key word is *knowingly*. All sellers start out thinking that they're sincere. As the quest for a buyer continues, however, circumstances ultimately prove that some sellers are phony.

Sometimes, homes sell for more than the asking price

Amy was a buyer who knew precisely what she wanted. Her dream home didn't have to be large. It did, however, need a light and airy feeling, a gourmet kitchen, nice views, a beautiful garden, and a garage. She'd been house hunting a long time because she refused to settle for anything less than her dream home.

Amy had a good agent. When a house that met all of Amy's specifications was listed at $195,000, Amy and her agent were waiting at the front door on the first day that the house was opened for inspection.

They weren't alone. The home was mobbed with drooling buyers and agents. Everything about the property, including its finely honed price, was flawless. The house was definitely priced to sell.

The listing agent told everyone that offers would be accepted in two days. Given the high level of buyer interest, Amy's agent knew that there would be multiple offers. She suggested that Amy could probably beat the competition by offering $5,000 over the asking price because,

based on the sale price of comparable houses in the neighborhood, the home was priced at (or perhaps slightly below) its fair market value. The extra $5,000 would make Amy's $200,000 offer stand out.

Amy refused. Why, she reasoned, spend an extra $5,000 if she didn't have to? A full-price offer wouldn't insult the sellers. If that wasn't enough money, Amy was sure that the sellers would give her a counteroffer.

She was wrong. The sellers didn't counter any of the many offers they received. Instead, they simply accepted the highest offer, which wasn't Amy's.

Amy took a calculated risk. She could've been right. In fact, we've seen multiple-offer situations where not one of the offers was close to full asking price. Multiple offers are no guarantee that a house will sell at or over its asking price.

Each situation is different and must be evaluated on its own merits. And don't forget to look at the comparable sales data.

Fake sellers usually mimic genuine sellers very cleverly. Like real sellers, counterfeit sellers sign listing agreements, have For Sale signs on their houses, advertise in newspapers, and have open houses on Sundays. They outwardly appear to be the real McCoy. If you don't know how to detect fake sellers, you'll waste your precious time, energy, and money by fruitlessly negotiating to buy a house that isn't really for sale.

Identifying bogus sellers is ridiculously easy once you know how. Here are five simple tests that you can use to spot the fakes:

Are the sellers realistic?

The number-one reason that houses don't sell is that they have unrealistic asking prices. When people categorically state that they "can't" sell a grossly overpriced house, they expose themselves as fakes. What they're actually saying is that they refuse to accept the market's opinion of what their house is worth. People who won't listen to reason aren't sellers — they're property owners masquerading as sellers.

Real sellers may *inadvertently* overprice their homes initially. Unlike fake sellers, however, they eventually wise up. They know that they have a problem if they get no offers (or only lowball offers). Authentic sellers accept the relevance of using recent sales of comparable houses in the neighborhood to establish their house's fair market value. *Genuine sellers are realistic.*

Are the sellers motivated?

Most folks don't sell their homes just to generate commissions for real estate agents. Sellers are usually motivated by a life change, such as wedding bells, a job transfer, family expansion, retirement, or a death in the family. Perhaps the sellers are in contract to buy another home but can't complete the purchase until their house sells. Or their house may be in foreclosure. Whatever. *Real sellers always have a motive for selling.*

In dire situations, such as an impending foreclosure or divorce, sellers often instruct their agents not to tell anyone why they're selling. If possible, however, find out why the house if being sold *before* making your offer. Knowing the sellers' motivation allows you to shape your offer's terms (that is, quick close of escrow, letting the sellers rent back the house after the sale, and the like) to fit the sellers' circumstances.

Lack of motivation is a gigantic red flag. If the sellers or their agent say that they are testing the market, run as fast as you can in the opposite direction. Unmotivated sellers aren't.

Do the sellers have a time frame?

Seller deadlines are established by such things as how much longer the sellers can bear living together when they hate the sight of one another, when the twins are due, when school starts, when they have to begin new jobs in another city, when the escrow is due to close on the new home that they're buying, and so on. Authentic sellers always have a deadline within which they must complete their sale.

Time is a powerful negotiating tool. If you aren't under pressure to buy and the sellers must sell immediately (if not sooner), time is your pal and their enemy. Conversely, if you've sold a previous home at a profit and you have to pay a big capital-gains tax unless you close escrow on another home within ten days, the watch is on the other wrist. Ideally, you know the sellers' deadline but they don't know yours. Most real negotiation occurs at the 11th hour, 59th minute, and 59th second of a 12-hour deadline.

You could be in deep trouble if you have a deadline and the sellers don't. If you reveal this information to the sellers, they may use your deadline to beat you to a pulp. How can you *effectively* negotiate a $10,000 corrective-work credit, for example, if the sellers know that you'll owe the IRS $20,000 in ten days if this deal falls through? You don't have time to buy another home if they refuse to pay for any corrective work. They know that it'll cost you less to do $10,000 worth of repairs than to pay the capital gains tax. Beware of procrastination. Don't let time bully you — and keep your deadlines to yourself.

Are the sellers forthright?

Genuine sellers are disarmingly candid about their house's physical, financial, and legal status. They know that withholding vital information endangers the sale and may lead to a lawsuit. Early disclosure of possible problems, on the other hand, gives everyone the lead time required to solve them. *Real sellers don't have a "buyer beware" mind-set.*

If you keep getting nasty surprises, you're working with fake sellers. Straightforward folks only have one defense against devious sellers who are playing an expensive, and possibly even devastating, game of *I've Got a Secret.* Terminate the transaction.

Are the sellers cooperative?

Real sellers look for ways to make transactions go more smoothly. They work with you to solve problems rather than waste time trying to figure out who's to blame if something goes wrong. Genuine sellers have a let's-make-it-happen attitude. They're deal-makers, not deal-breakers.

Inconsistent behavior is a red flag. If the sellers suddenly start missing contract deadlines or become strangely uncooperative, they may have lost their motivation to sell. Perhaps the wedding was postponed or the new job fell through. Whatever the reason, people sometimes switch from being real sellers to being fakes in mid-transaction. Find out why the sellers are acting strange as soon as you notice the change, and you may be able to head off the problem. If you ignore the danger signs, you'll never know what hit you when the deal blows up in your face.

Lowballing

A *lowball* offer is one that is far, far below a property's actual fair market value. An example of a lowball offer is a $150,000 offer on a house that's worth every penny of $200,000.

Who makes lowball offers? Sometimes, it's a graduate from one of those scuzzy, get-rich-quick real estate seminars. Another lowball offer may come from somebody who is bottom-fishing for sellers in dire financial distress. More often, however, lowballing is a negotiating tactic used by people who state categorically, "No one ever pays full asking price. You always have to start low to end up with a fair price."

Those statements are not true, of course. When you do your homework, you know the difference between well-priced properties and overpriced turkeys. (See Chapter 9 for a brush-up.)

Why lowballing is usually a bad idea

Lowballing a well-priced house breaks the first rule of a good offer — make a realistic offering price based upon the sale price of comparable houses. Because skillful negotiators understand both sides of the issue, imagine that you're the seller of a house that is priced as close as humanly possible to its fair market value.

Several days after your house goes on the market, you receive an offer with an absurdly low purchase price. After the vein in your neck stops pounding, what conclusions can you form about the lowballing buyers?

- ✓ **Taken in the best possible light, the buyers obviously haven't done their homework regarding comparable home sales.** Because they're grossly inept, why waste any more of your valuable time on them?

- ✓ **Maybe the buyers think that you don't know what your house is really worth and are trying to exploit your ignorance.** (That vein starts throbbing again.)

- ✓ **Perhaps the buyers are trying to steal your house based upon a mistaken impression that you're desperate to sell.** There's a name for critters who prey on misfortune — *vultures*.

None of these conclusions is at all favorable. As a seller, you'd probably make one of the following responses to buyers who lowballed your well-priced house:

- ✓ **Let the buyers know that their offer is totally unacceptable by having your agent return it with a message that you wouldn't sell your house to them if they were the last buyers on earth.** Why make a counteroffer to people who are either idiots or scoundrels?

✔ **Make a full-price counteroffer.** To show your contempt for the buyers, you'd hardball them on each and every term and condition in their offer. (Two can play this game.)

Buyers who lowball a well-priced property listed by sellers who can wait for a better offer destroy any chance of developing the mutual trust and sense of fair play upon which cooperative negotiation is based. Bargaining is fine, but you must find a motivated seller and not aim too low. Starting at 25 percent below what the home is worth generally won't work unless the seller is desperate.

When low offers are justified

An enormous difference exists between submitting an offer at the low end of a house's fair market value and lowballing. Suppose, for example, that you offer $180,000 for a home listed at $199,500. You base your offering price on the fact that comparable houses in the neighborhood recently sold in the $180,000 to $195,000 price range. You're at the low end of the range of fair market values. The sellers are at the high end. Both of you are being realistic.

If your offer is based on actual sales of comparable houses, it won't insult the seller. Such a low offer will, however, spark lively debate as both of you attempt to defend your respective prices. Coming in on the low side of a property's fair market value is fine as long as you have plenty of time to negotiate and reason to believe that the seller is motivated.

In situations like the preceding one, your best bet is to have an encyclopedic comparable market analysis and an agent who has *personally* eyeballed all the comps. Follow the guidelines that we cover in Chapter 9.

A low offer is justified only when it isn't a *lowball* offer. Ironically, some sellers provoke low offers by their unwise pricing. These sellers insist on leaving room to negotiate in their price because they "know" that buyers never pay full asking price.

Sound familiar? This practice, unfortunately, becomes a self-fulfilling prophecy. When buyers who know property values make an offer on an overpriced house, their initial offering price is usually on the low side to give them room to negotiate. What goes around, comes around.

Suppose, for example, that a house's fair market value is $200,000. If the sellers put this house on the market at $240,000 to give themselves a 20-percent negotiating cushion and you offer $160,000 for the same reason, you and the sellers start out $80,000 apart. It takes a heap of extra negotiating to bridge a gap that big.

Don't play their silly game unless you have time to squander. Make your initial offer at the low end of the house's fair market value and see how the sellers respond to it. If they refuse to accept the hard evidence of recent comparable home sales in the neighborhood, don't waste valuable time trying to educate them. They aren't sellers yet — they're property owners masquerading as sellers. If you want the house, bide your time. Don't make your move until either they wise up and lower their price or their agent puts the word out that they're motivated sellers who won't turn down any reasonable offer.

Negotiating credits in escrow

Putting a "let's sell it" price on a house isn't always enough to get the house sold. Sellers often find that they have to give buyers money in the form of seller-paid financial concessions in order to close the deal. The two most common concessions are for nonrecurring closing costs and corrective work.

Nonrecurring closing costs

Some sellers come right out and tell you that they'll pay your nonrecurring closing costs if doing so will help put a deal together. *Nonrecurring closing costs* are one-time charges for such things as your appraisal, loan points, credit report, title insurance, and property inspections. If you've read Chapter 3, you know that we're talking big bucks here. Closing costs can amount to 3 to 5 percent of the purchase price.

Even if the sellers don't offer to pay your nonrecurring closing costs, asking for this concession as one of the terms in your offer *usually* won't hurt. Two general exceptions to this rule are when it's a seller's market or when you're in a multiple-offer situation.

Here's how the credit works. Say, for example, that you've signed a contract to buy a $200,000 house. You've got $45,000 in cash, and the escrow officer has just told you that you'll have nonrecurring closing costs totaling 4 percent ($8,000) of the purchase price.

About now, you may be wondering, "Why not just reduce the purchase price to $192,000 instead of asking the sellers for an $8,000 credit?" After all, the sellers' net proceeds of sale are the same either way, and simply reducing the purchase price is less complicated. Not to mention that, because property taxes are often based on the purchase price, a lower purchase price will probably cut your annual tax bite.

The reason: If you're short of cash, as most buyers are, a credit is more helpful than a price reduction. If you have to pay $8,000 in closing costs, you won't have enough cash left to make a 20-percent ($38,400) down payment on your $192,000 home. With less than 20 percent down, your monthly loan costs increase because you have to pay a higher interest rate on your mortgage plus private mortgage insurance costs. Nor will you have any cash left over for emergencies. Under these circumstances, you'd probably decide to buy a less-expensive house.

Contrast that scenario with paying $200,000 for the house and getting a credit from the sellers for nonrecurring closing costs. After putting 20 percent ($40,000) cash down to get the loan with the lowest interest rate, you still have $5,000 in the bank thanks to the $8,000 credit. The credit makes the deal happen.

If you have plenty of cash, get a price reduction rather than a credit. In most areas, the lower your purchase price, the lower your annual property taxes. Just be aware that most agents will lobby for the credit because a price reduction cuts into their commission.

Corrective work

Typically, neither you nor the sellers know how much, if any, corrective work is needed when you submit your offer. Therefore, purchase contracts have provisions for additional negotiations regarding corrective work credits *after* all the necessary inspections have been completed.

If the property inspectors find that little or no corrective work is required, you have little or nothing to negotiate. Suppose, however, that your inspectors discover the $200,000 house you want to buy needs $20,000 of corrective work for termite and dry-rot damage, foundation repairs, and a new roof. Big corrective-work bills can be deal killers.

Seeing is believing. We recommend that you and the sellers' agent be present, if possible, during property inspections, so you both actually see the damage. And when you receive the inspection reports, use them as negotiating tools. Give the sellers copies of the reports for them to review before you meet with them to negotiate a corrective work credit.

This is the moment of truth in most home sales. Sellers usually don't want to pay for the corrective work. Neither do you. The deal *will* fall through if this impasse can't be resolved.

At this point in the negotiations, it's critical that the sellers realize that their house's value has just been reduced by the cost required to repair it. If, for example, comparable houses with no termite or dry-rot damage, with solid foundations, and with good roofs are selling for $200,000, the sellers' house is worth only $180,000 in its present condition. Given its reduced value, an 80 percent loan is $144,000 — not $160,000 based on a $200,000 fair market value. If you can only borrow $144,000 and the sellers refuse to reduce the selling price from $200,000 to $180,000, you have to drop out of the deal.

The sellers may refuse to pay for repairs found by inspectors that you have hired. The sellers may question the impartiality or validity of your inspection reports and order their own inspections to verify or refute yours. The sellers may even threaten to pull out of the contract if you don't back off on your demands.

Sellers who try to kill the messenger are making a big mistake. You didn't bring the damage with you when you came, and (luckily for you) you won't take it with you when you go. Like it or not, the sellers are stuck with it. If they drive you away, they may still have a legal obligation to tell other buyers what you've discovered. That disclosure will obviously lower the price that any future buyer will pay for their house. All things considered, working things out with you will probably be a whole heap faster (and no more expensive) than waiting for another buyer.

Lenders also participate in corrective work problems. They get copies of inspection reports when borrowers tell them that a serious repair problem exists, when their appraisal indicates a property obviously needs major repairs, or when the purchase contract contains a credit for extensive repairs. Whenever the property's loan-to-value ratio exceeds 80 percent, lenders actively help buyers and sellers resolve corrective work problems.

You can solve repair problems in a variety of ways:

- ✔ **Ideally, the sellers leave enough money in escrow to cover the required corrective work with instructions for the escrow officer to pay the contractors as their work is completed.** This strategy has several advantages: You can supervise the work to be sure that it's done properly by contractors of your choice. The sellers don't have to suffer through having the work done while they're living in the house, and they don't have to incur any liability for the workmanship. Last, but not least, the lender knows that the work will be done.

- ✔ **Alternatively, the lender withholds a portion of the full loan amount in a passbook savings account until the corrective work has been completed.** In cases involving major corrective work, the lender may refuse to fund the loan until the problems have been corrected.

- ✔ **The sellers may give a credit for corrective work directly to buyers at the close of escrow.** Lenders usually don't approve of this approach, because it raises uncertainties about whether the corrective work will actually be completed. If it isn't, the security of the lender's loan is impaired.

You can make the sellers feel better by offering to get competitive bids on the work from several reputable, licensed contractors. This effort on your part shows the sellers that you don't want to get rich off their misfortune. All you want is what you thought you were buying in the first place — a well-maintained home with a good foundation and a roof that doesn't leak. Empathy is an excellent negotiating tactic.

Finesse tips

Skillful negotiators get what they want through mutual agreement — not brute force. Brute force is crude, rude, ugly, and decidedly unfriendly. Here are some concepts that you may find useful for negotiating with finesse:

- ✓ **Phones are for making appointments.** Never, never, never let your agent or lawyer present an offer or attempt to negotiate significant issues over the phone. Saying *no* over the phone is too easy for the sellers. Even if they agree with everything you want, they may change their minds by the time they actually have to sign the contract.

- ✓ **Oral agreements are useless.** In our society, we have *written* contracts because people have lousy memories. If you want your deal to be enforceable in a court of law, put everything about it in writing. Get into the habit of writing short, *dated* MFRs (Memos For Record) of important conversations (such as, "June 2 — lender said we'd get 7.5 percent mortgage rate," "June 12 — sellers want to extend close of escrow a week," and so on). Put these notes into your transaction file just in case you need to refresh your memory. Heed the immortal words of Samuel Goldwyn: "A verbal agreement isn't worth the paper it's written on."

- ✓ **Deadline management is essential.** Real estate contracts are filled with deadlines for things like contingency removals, deposit increases, and (of course) the close of escrow. Failure to meet deadlines can have dreadful consequences. Your deal could fall apart — you could even get sued. Most deadlines, however, are flexible — if you handle them correctly. Suppose, for example, that you just found out that completing the property inspections will take longer than anticipated. *Immediately* contact the sellers to explain the reason for the delay and then get a *written* extension of the deadline. Reasonable delays can usually be accommodated if properly explained and promptly handled.

Following the tips in this chapter will give you the negotiating advantage you so richly deserve throughout the home-buying process. And, of course, these tips make getting the keys to your dream home faster, easier, and less expensive for you.

Chapter 11

Protecting Your Home

● ●

In This Chapter

▶ Spotting a pig in a poke

▶ Getting the property inspected

▶ Being present during home inspections

▶ Buying property insurance

▶ Understanding what title insurance does and why lenders make you buy it

● ●

*G*iven how much homes cost today, not having the house you plan to invest in carefully inspected before buying it is idiotic. Skipping inspections to save a few bucks (relatively speaking) could be the most expensive mistake you ever make. Think of your biggest goof ever. Multiply it by a hundred. That gives you some idea of the magnitude of the boo-boo you'd make if you bought a home without first having it *thoroughly* inspected from foundation to roof.

Inspecting Your Property

A home's physical condition greatly affects its value. You'd feel horrible if you paid top dollar for a home that you thought was in tip-top shape and then discovered after you bought it that the house was riddled with expensive defects. And yet, unless you're a professional property inspector, you probably won't have the faintest idea how much corrective work a house needs simply by looking at it.

Buying homes was even riskier 20 years ago. The prevailing attitude then was extremely simple — "buyer beware." Today, the situation has improved. Most states now require that sellers and real estate agents make full, immediate disclosure to prospective buyers of all *known* mechanical, structural, and legal problems associated with owner-occupied residential property. If this trend continues, the time will come when the warning shifts to "seller and agent beware."

Don't let your guard down. Even though the real estate market is a tad more consumer-friendly than it used to be, don't be lulled into a false sense of complacency. *Latent defects* — what sellers and their agents don't know about the home that you're buying — can get you into a heap of budget-busting trouble after your purchase is completed.

If you haven't read Chapter 10 yet, take a quick look at the section about negotiating either a corrective work credit or a price reduction. You'll see how to use property inspections so that they pay for themselves many times over.

Patent and latent defects

Property defects come in two general categories — patent and latent. *Patent defects* are right out in the open for all the world to see. You don't need a professional property inspector to point out glaringly obvious stuff like water stains on the ceiling, cracks in the wall, or a flooded basement. You do, however, need a trained professional to tell you whether the defects are signs of major problems or are inconsequential blemishes.

Latent defects can be even more financially devastating than patent defects because they're hidden. Like playing a high-priced game of hide-and-seek, you must find latent defects or literally pay the consequences.

Latent defects are out of sight — behind walls or concealed in inaccessible areas under the house and up in the attic, away from casual observation. Faulty wiring, termite damage, a cracked heat-exchanger in the furnace, and health- and safety-code problems (such as lead in the water pipes and asbestos insulation) are some examples of latent physical flaws.

Legal blemishes, such as zoning violations and fraudulent title claims, illustrate another kind of invisible latent defect that only experts can detect.

Patent-defect red flags

Even if you've never had any special training, you can spot the danger signs of possibly serious structural problems if you know what to look for as you walk through a property. Although we advocate that you hire a professional property inspector, here's a list of red flags that even a mechanically challenged homebuyer should be able to spot:

✔ **Cracks:** Check the property's foundation, interior walls, exterior retaining walls, fireplace, chimney, concrete floors (basement, garage, and the like), and sidewalk for large cracks. Any crack that you can stick your finger into is a large crack. Watch for vertical cracks on any walls and long, horizontal cracks on exterior walls.

✔ **Moisture:** Look for water stains on ceilings, walls, and floors. Feel basement walls for dampness. Sniff out the source of moldy smells. Check for drainage problems inside and out by looking for standing water. A sump pump in the basement or garage is a red flag waving to get your attention.

✔ **Stickiness:** All doors (exterior, interior, garage, and cabinets) and windows should open and close easily.

✔ **Looseness:** You shouldn't be able to see daylight around windows, doors, or skylights.

✔ **Unevenness:** Floors shouldn't slope, and walls shouldn't bulge.

✔ **Insects:** If the house you're buying is made of wood or wood and stucco, it may have problems with wood-destroying insects or organisms. Mud tubes along a house's foundation or in its basement are a sign of termite infestation. Look carefully at those areas of the property that come into contact with the earth — foundation, decks, garage, and fencing — for signs of decayed or rotted wood.

✔ **Slides:** Check hillsides immediately behind the property to see whether they have netting on them or show evidence of recent earth or mud slides.

Before you have the property inspected, discuss any red flags you discover with your property inspector. Let the pro check them out to see whether they're major problems or only relatively minor flaws that can be quickly and inexpensively corrected. A sticking front door, for example, could indicate either that the house has expensive foundation problems or simply that the door absorbed moisture because it wasn't properly sealed.

All properties should be inspected

Overinspecting a house is much better than underinspecting it. Suppose, for example, that you spend $250 to have the home that you want to buy inspected, and you find out that nothing is wrong with it. Did you waste your money? Nope. You can sleep soundly, knowing that your home doesn't need any corrective work.

If, conversely, you skip the inspection to save $250 and later discover that your house needs $25,000 worth of repairs, you'll end up spending $100 in repairs for every dollar that you "saved." Such a deal! You probably also "save" money by not putting coins into parking meters and categorize walloping parking tickets as a normal driving expense!

Here's a list of properties that *must* be inspected prior to purchase:

✔ **Used houses:** You're most likely to order inspections if your "new" home is someone else's used house. Obviously, the older the house, the greater the likelihood that you'll find defects in its mechanical and structural systems.

✔ **New houses:** Even if you're buying a newly constructed, never-been-lived-in home, having it thoroughly inspected is wise. Just because the building is new doesn't guarantee that it was built properly. Believe it or not, brand-new houses often have construction flaws, sometimes major. Some home builders are not competent, or they cut corners to save some money and boost their profits.

✔ **Condominiums:** You need an inspection before buying a condominium. Don't forget that, when you buy a condo, you also buy into the entire building in which your condo is located (see Chapter 7). As a co-owner of the building, you're assessed your proportional share of the cost for corrective work required in common areas, such as the roof, heating system, or foundation.

✔ **Townhouses, cooperative apartments, and all other forms of co-ownership property:** See the preceding bullet point about condominiums. Shared ownership doesn't get you off the hook. You still need property inspections.

All properties should be inspected. Period. Inspect detached residences, attached residences, single-family dwellings, multifamily dwellings, condos, co-ops, townhouses, and anything else that has a foundation and a roof. If you're spending big bucks for a property, protect your investment by having it inspected.

Types of property inspections

What inspections should you get to protect your investment? That depends on what area of the country you live in, how the building in question is constructed, and what you plan to do to the property after buying it. Here are the three most common inspections — which we recommend be done *after* you have an accepted offer to purchase but *before* removing your inspection contingencies (so that you're able to negotiate the correction of problems discovered by the inspections as we recommend in Chapter 10):

✔ **Prepurchase interior and exterior components inspection:** No matter whether you're buying a wood-frame cottage in the country or an urban condo in a 20-story, steel-and-concrete building, you need a complete inspection of the property's interior and exterior. The inspection should cover such areas as the roof and gutters, plumbing, electrical work, heating and cooling systems, insulation, smoke detectors, kitchen, bathroom, and foundation. The inspection should also point out health, safety, and environmental hazards. This type of inspection usually takes several hours to complete and costs from $200 to $500, depending upon how large the property is and the inspection's length and degree of detail.

Don't be surprised if the property inspector recommends additional inspections. Good property inspectors are generalists who are trained to spot red flags. Like doctors who are general practitioners, good property inspectors refer their clients to specialists, such as roofers, structural engineers, and pest-control inspectors, if they discover a problem beyond their scope of expertise. Property inspectors know that you can't make good decisions unless you have the best possible information.

✔ **Pest-control inspection:** Temperate climates, such as in the South and West, are a mixed blessing. You're not the only one who loves warm, balmy weather. So do termites, carpenter ants, powder-post beetles, dry rot, fungus, and other wood-munching infestations or infections. If these are a problem in your area, you'll also need a pest-control inspection. These inspections generally cost from $75 to $225.

Pest-control inspections are very limited in scope — the inspectors check for property damage caused only by wood-destroying insects (infestations) and organisms (infections, such as dry rot and fungus). Although homes made of wood or wood-and-stucco are the wood-destroyers' primary targets, even brick homes aren't safe. If you get a pest-control inspection, it should be in addition to your prepurchase interior and exterior components inspection — not in lieu of it.

✔ **Architect or general contractor's inspection:** You need an architect or a general contractor on your team if you're buying a fixer-upper, intending to do corrective work, or planning a major property renovation, such as adding rooms or installing a new bathroom. The architect or general contractor can tell you whether what you want to do is structurally possible and meets local planning codes for such things as height restrictions and lot coverage. This inspector can also give you time and cost estimates for the project.

Architects and general contractors usually don't charge for their initial property inspection because they are hoping to get your business. Although these people provide a valuable service, take their so-called reports with a grain of salt. Don't expect them to give you a completely objective assessment as to whether you should buy the property, because they'd probably love to do the work for you.

Inspecting inspectors

Unfortunately, some people who anoint themselves "home inspectors" have neither the background nor the training to do proper prepurchase home inspections. To compound the problem, most states don't certify, license, or regulate home inspectors. If you've got a clipboard, a pickup truck, and a good "houseside manner," you, too, can be a home inspector nearly anywhere in the country.

Worse yet, some contractors inspect houses and then do the corrective work that they discover during their own inspections. That situation ought to start a red flag waving in your mind. Unscrupulous contractors can — and do — manipulate this conflict of interest to their advantage by finding and creating work for themselves.

One way around this problem is to hire someone who only does inspections. Good news. A growing number of property inspectors are exactly that — professional property inspectors, not contractors. This distinction is more than just semantic. Performing property inspections requires a special expertise that not all contractors, engineers, and architects have.

Professional property inspectors are specifically trained to do inspections and only inspections; they make their living solely from inspection fees. They do not do corrective work. This eliminates the temptation to find unnecessary corrective work during their inspections.

Selecting your inspector

How can you find a qualified home inspector? Ask friends and business associates who've recently bought homes whom they used for their property inspections. Get a list of home inspectors from a real estate agent. Be careful, though, of inspectors who are popular with agents — that popularity *may* stem from not killing too many deals by going easy on their inspections. Also check the Yellow Pages of your local phone book under "Building Inspection Services" or "Home Inspection Services." If several sources recommend the same inspector, you've probably found a good one.

The *American Society of Home Inspectors* (ASHI) is a professional association of independent home inspectors. Just because an inspector is an ASHI member doesn't guarantee that you'll get a good inspection, but it certainly increases the likelihood that you'll be working with a qualified professional. You can't just plunk down a membership fee and join. All ASHI-certified members have performed at least 250 property inspections and have passed two written proficiency exams as a prerequisite of membership. ASHI members must also adhere to ASHI's standards of practice, continuing education requirements, and code of ethics. To find members in your area, call ASHI at 800-743-2744.

We recommend that you interview several property inspectors prior to hiring one. Here are questions to help you select the best inspector:

> ✔ **Are you a full-time, professional property inspector?** Only one answer is acceptable — *yes.*
>
> ✔ **What can you tell me about your company?** Discuss the company's size and how long it has been in business.

✓ **Do you carry errors-and-omissions insurance?** Errors-and-omissions insurance covers the possibility that a property inspection could miss some problems. If an inspector makes an error that costs you big bucks, errors and omissions insurance can help to make amends.

✓ **How many inspections do you personally perform each year?** Although the average number of inspections varies from area to area, active inspectors usually conduct between 100 to 300 inspections per year. Find out whether the inspector works primarily in the area in which the property you want to have inspected is located and is thus familiar with *local* codes, *local* regulations, and *local* problems (such as floods, mud slides, earthquakes, tornadoes, and the like).

✓ **Do you hold any special licenses or certifications?** Property inspectors usually have a background in some related field, such as construction, engineering, architecture, electricity, plumbing, or insurance-claim adjusting. This diversity adds extra insights to their inspections. Membership in ASHI or another trade association for property inspectors indicates at least a minimal knowledge of home-inspection procedures.

✓ **What is the scope of your prepurchase inspection?** Make sure that the inspection covers *all* the property's major structural and mechanical systems, inside and out, from foundation to roof. Anything less is unacceptable.

✓ **How long will your inspection take?** Time actually spent at the site is an important consideration. This inspection isn't a race. It usually takes two or three hours to inspect a condo or a home of average size *thoroughly.*

✓ **What type of report will I receive?** Verbal reports, like verbal contracts, are worthless. A boilerplate, checklist-type report is only marginally better. You must have a detailed description of your specific property's mechanical and structural condition. You need a narrative report, written in plain English, which clearly explains the implications of its findings.

Get sample reports from each inspector that you interview. The best way to see whether a company writes good reports is to read one so that you can draw your own conclusion. Figure 11-1 features a superficial inspection report; we've included an example of a thorough inspection report in Appendix B so that you'll know what a good inspection report looks like.

✓ **Do you mind if I tag along during your inspection?** Mind? On the contrary, good inspectors will *insist* that you be present during the property inspection.

✓ **Will your report include an estimate of the cost to do your recommended corrective work?** This is a trick question. If the inspector says *yes,* don't use the inspector. Good professional property inspectors *only* do inspections. They don't do corrective work. Nor do they solicit business for their friends. Good inspectors will help you establish repair costs by referring you to three or four reputable contractors, roofers, electricians,

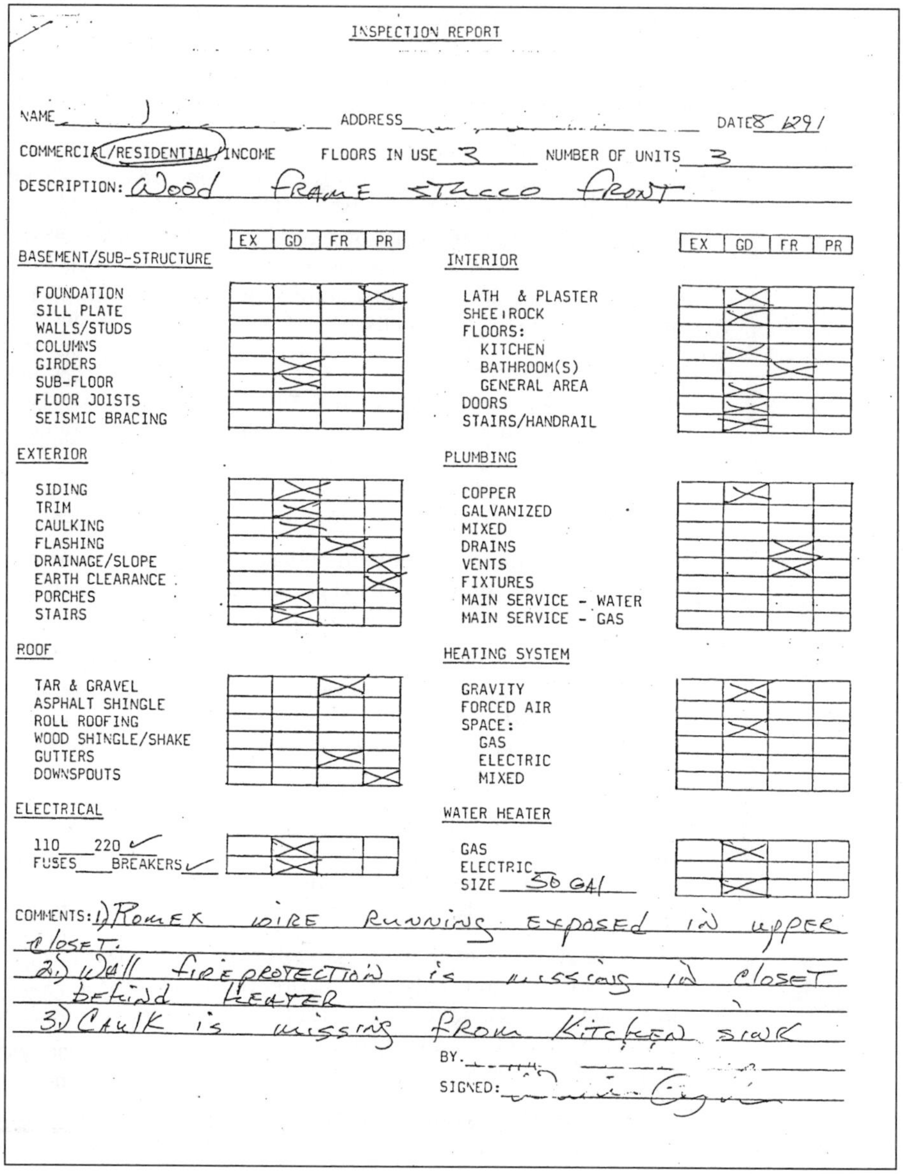

Figure 11-1: This is an example of the type of superficial inspection report that you don't want to waste your money on. For an example of a good inspection report, see Appendix B.

The form reads:

INSPECTION REPORT

NAME _____ ADDRESS _____ DATE 8 /29/

COMMERCIAL/(RESIDENTIAL)/INCOME   FLOORS IN USE 3   NUMBER OF UNITS 3

DESCRIPTION: Wood Frame Stucco Front

BASEMENT/SUB-STRUCTURE (EX GD FR PR)
- FOUNDATION — PR
- SILL PLATE
- WALLS/STUDS
- COLUMNS
- GIRDERS — FR
- SUB-FLOOR
- FLOOR JOISTS
- SEISMIC BRACING

INTERIOR (EX GD FR PR)
- LATH & PLASTER — EX
- SHEETROCK — GD
- FLOORS:
  - KITCHEN — GD
  - BATHROOM(S) — FR
  - GENERAL AREA — GD
- DOORS
- STAIRS/HANDRAIL — GD

EXTERIOR (EX GD FR PR)
- SIDING — GD
- TRIM — GD
- CAULKING — GD
- FLASHING
- DRAINAGE/SLOPE — FR
- EARTH CLEARANCE — PR
- PORCHES — GD
- STAIRS

PLUMBING (EX GD FR PR)
- COPPER — EX
- GALVANIZED
- MIXED
- DRAINS — FR
- VENTS — FR
- FIXTURES
- MAIN SERVICE - WATER
- MAIN SERVICE - GAS

ROOF (EX GD FR PR)
- TAR & GRAVEL — FR
- ASPHALT SHINGLE
- ROLL ROOFING
- WOOD SHINGLE/SHAKE
- GUTTERS — FR
- DOWNSPOUTS

HEATING SYSTEM (EX GD FR PR)
- GRAVITY
- FORCED AIR — EX
- SPACE:
  - GAS — EX
  - ELECTRIC
  - MIXED

ELECTRICAL (EX GD FR PR)
- 110 ___ 220 ✓
- FUSES ___ BREAKERS ✓ — FR

WATER HEATER (EX GD FR PR)
- GAS — EX
- ELECTRIC
- SIZE 50 GAL

COMMENTS: 1) Romex wire running exposed in upper closet.
2) Wall fire protection is missing in closet behind heater
3) Caulk is missing from kitchen sink

BY: _____
SIGNED: _____

and other repair people that you can contact for corrective-work quotes. Because there's usually more than one way to fix a defect, it's up to *you* to decide how best to deal with a problem after you've consulted the appropriate repair people.

TIP

Seeing and reading is infinitely better than just reading

It's important that you and the sellers' agent join the inspector during the property inspection. Reading even the finest of inspection reports is, at best, a mediocre substitute for being at the property and looking at the defects with your own eyes. This may be your best opportunity to question the inspector about the ramifications of a defect and discuss various ways in which the problem can be corrected. By seeing and talking about the defects, you'll gain a better understanding of why some defects are no big deal to fix, whereas others cost megabucks to repair.

From a negotiating standpoint, the sellers are more likely to accept the inspection report's findings if their agent was present when the inspection was performed. They'll *know* that the defects are real — their agent actually saw the defects and can point them out to the sellers before they get a copy of the inspection report. They'll *know* that a skilled professional inspected their house — not some stooge that you hired to defame their property so that you could swindle them out of their hard-earned money. They'll *know* that, even if they drive you away by hardballing you on the corrective work, they'll still be stuck with the problem of selling a defective house.

Even if the house is in perfect condition, you should know where certain things are. If you

attend the inspection, your inspector can show you where to find important stuff like the furnace, water heater, and circuit breakers. The inspector should also show you where the emergency shutoff valves for the house's gas, electric, and water systems are located. By attending the inspection, you'll learn much more about the house's care and maintenance than you'd ever pick up by reading the inspection report.

If it's flat-out impossible to be at the inspection because you're stuck in another city or must be at a command-performance business meeting, make sure to have someone you trust (your agent, a relative or friend, or someone equally as trustworthy) at the inspection to act as your eyes and ears. Ask your surrogate to make an audiotape or videotape recording of the inspection, which you can use to supplement the inspection report. Watching a videotape is not as good as personally being there, but it sure beats just reading a report. You can also call the inspector if you have questions about the report.

Last, but not least, pay attention. Don't bring along a gaggle of kids, relatives, friends, business associates, painters, carpet suppliers, plumbers, electricians, or contractors who'll distract you from the job at hand: learning everything you can about the property that you want to buy. Focus on the inspection.

✔ **How much does your inspection cost?** Unfortunately, this is generally the first question that buyers ask when shopping for a property inspector. This is no time to be penny-wise and pound-foolish. Watch out for unrealistically low, "this week only" promotional fees that may be offered by new inspectors who are just starting in the business. Don't let green inspectors practice on you. Quality inspections cost more than quickie, one-size-fits-all, checklist inspections, but they're worth a lot more. Ultimately, because fees charged by good inspectors are usually pretty much the same (due to competitive pressure) you'll probably end up using the correct criteria to select your inspector — compatibility and competence.

✓ **Would you mind if I call some of your recent customers for references?** Good property inspectors will be happy to give you names and phone numbers of their satisfied customers. Bad inspectors, by definition, don't have satisfied customers. Be sure to check at least three references per inspector. Ask the references whether, after close of escrow, they discovered any major defects that their inspector missed, and whether they'd use their inspector again.

Optimizing your inspection

Here are guidelines for getting the biggest bang out of the bucks that you invest in a prepurchase property inspection:

✓ **Always make your offer to purchase a house subject to your review and approval of the inspection reports.** Doing so gives you the opportunity to either negotiate a credit or price reduction for corrective work that is discovered during the inspections or, if you wish, get out of the deal. We cover this subject extensively in Chapter 10.

✓ **See if the sellers have any presale inspection reports that they ordered or any copies of inspection reports generated by previous prospective buyers.** If so, give the reports to your inspector in order to call the inspector's attention to possible problem areas. Have your agent order a permit search on the property to find out whether electrical, plumbing, or other repairs have been performed.

Suppose that the sellers give you a presale inspection report that they ordered just before putting their house on the market. It says that their house is in perfect condition. You could save money by relying on their report instead of getting your own. Should you? No way. Never let the fox tell you how things are in the hen house. Always pay for your own inspection by an inspector of your own choosing.

✓ **To minimize the cost of corrective repairs, get bids on the job from several reputable, licensed contractors.** Never try to save money by using unlicensed contractors to do the work without permits. Doing so is illegal, can create health and safety problems, and can adversely affect your home's resale value. Many states require that housesellers disclose to prospective purchasers the fact that work on the house was done without permits. If your state doesn't mandate this type of disclosure now, it probably will by the time that you're ready to sell the house.

Prepurchase property inspections are intended to give you a factual basis for negotiating the correction of big-ticket defects — not to nickel-and-dime sellers over credits for stained carpets and worn curtains. If your new home is someone else's used house, let your *offering price* reflect the home's reduced value due to normal wear-and-tear cosmetic defects.

If your agent or the seller offers to pay for a *home warranty plan* or *home protection plan* (that is, a service contract that covers some of your home's major systems and appliances), it wouldn't be gracious of you to turn down a freebie. Never accept such a plan in lieu of an inspection, however, and don't buy this type of plan for yourself. After spending $250 or so for the plan, you'll pay an additional $25 to $50 each time that you need someone to come out and look at a problem. Furthermore, these plans significantly limit how much they'll pay to correct major problems. Hiring a professional property inspector to inspect the home diligently and uncover all existing problems so that you can negotiate their correction with the sellers is a better way to spend your money.

Don't expect your inspections to eliminate all future maintenance problems. In time, the garbage disposal will break. All roofs leak eventually. When these things happen, it isn't part of some hideous plot to defraud you.

Anything in your home that can break or leak will break or leak, sooner or later. Repairs come with homeownership. After closing on your home purchase, normal upkeep is your responsibility — not the sellers'. They'll have repairs of their own to make to their new home.

Insuring Your Home

Nobody likes to spend money for insurance. But if something could cause you a financial catastrophe, you should insure against that risk. The point of insurance is that you spend a relatively small amount of money to protect against losing a great deal of money. For example, if your home burns to the ground and it's not insured, you could be out tens (if not hundreds) of thousands of dollars.

You shouldn't waste money insuring potentially small dollar losses. Suppose, for example, that you mail a package that contains a gift worth $50. If the postal service loses it, you'll be bummed, but the loss won't be a financial catastrophe for you. You shouldn't waste your money on such insurance.

Here are the types of insurance that you do need to have in place *before* you purchase your dream home.

Homeowners insurance

When you buy a home, most lenders require that you purchase homeowners insurance. Even if you're one of those rare people who can buy a home for cash without borrowing money, you should carry homeowners coverage. Why? First, your home and your personal property in your home are worth a pile of money and would cost a small fortune to replace out of your own pocket.

Second, your home can lead to a lawsuit. If someone were injured or killed in your home, you could be sued for tens or hundreds of thousands of dollars, perhaps even a million dollars or more.

The following sections tell how to get the homeowners coverage that you need.

The cost of rebuilding

If your home is destroyed, which most frequently happens from fires, your insurance policy should pay for the cost of rebuilding your home. The portion of your policy that takes care of this loss is the *dwelling coverage* section of the policy. The amount of this coverage should be equal to the cost of rebuilding the home that you own. The cost to rebuild should be based on the square footage of your home. Your policy's dwelling coverage amount should *not* be based on what you paid for the home or the amount of your mortgage. If you're buying a condominium or cooperative apartment, examine the coverage that your building's homeowners association carries.

Get a policy that includes a *guaranteed replacement cost* provision. This provision ensures that the insurance company will rebuild the home, even if the cost of construction is more than the policy coverage. If the insurance company underestimates your dwelling coverage, then the company has to eat the difference.

Ask the insurers that you're speaking with how they define *guaranteed replacement cost coverage* — each insurer defines it differently. The most generous policies, for example, pay for the full replacement cost of the home, no matter how much the replacement ends up costing. Other insurers set limits — for example, they agree to pay up to 120 percent of your policy's total dwelling coverage.

Lawsuit protection

Liability insurance protects you against lawsuits arising from bad things that happen to others while they are on your property. For example, suppose some nice little old lady slips on a banana peel that was left on your driveway. Or perhaps your second-floor deck collapses during a beer-fest and someone breaks a leg or two.

Carry enough liability insurance to protect at least two times the value of your assets. Although the chances of being sued are remote, remember that if you are sued, the financial consequences can be staggering. In fact, if you have substantial assets (worth more than a couple hundred thousand dollars, for example) to protect, you might consider what's called an *umbrella,* or *excess-liability policy.* Bought in increments of $1,000,000, this coverage adds to the liability coverage on your home and car(s). Check for such policies with your home and auto insurers.

Personal property protection

On a typical homeowners policy, the amount of personal property coverage is usually set at about 50 to 75 percent of the amount of dwelling coverage. If you are a condominium or cooperative apartment owner, however, you'll generally need to choose a specific dollar amount for the personal property coverage that you want.

Some policies come with *personal property replacement guarantees* that pay you for the replacement cost of an item rather than for the actual value of a used item at the time that it's damaged or stolen. If this feature is not part of the standard policy sold by your insurer, you may want to purchase it as a *rider* (add-on provision), if such a rider is available.

If you ever need to file a claim, having documentation as to what personal property you had helps. The simplest and fastest way to document your personal effects is to make a videotape of your belongings. Alternatively, you can maintain a file folder of receipts for major purchases and make a written inventory of your belongings. No matter how you document your belongings, be sure to place this documentation somewhere outside your home (and not in the vegetable garden). A list or video isn't going to do you much good if it's in your home and goes up in a puff of smoke during a fire!

Where to get good coverage inexpensively

As with other types of insurance and other financial products, you must shop around. But we know that you've got better things to do with your time than shop, so here's a short list of companies that are known for offering high-quality, low-cost policies:

- ✔ **Allstate:** Check your local phone directory for agents who sell Allstate Insurance policies.

- ✔ **Erie Insurance:** This company does business primarily in states in the Midwest and Mid-Atlantic. Check your local phone directory for agents who sell Erie Insurance policies.

- ✔ **GEICO:** Call the company for specifics at 800-841-3000.

- ✔ **Liberty Mutual:** Check your local phone directory for agents who sell Liberty Mutual's policies.

- ✔ **Nationwide Mutual:** Check your local phone directory for agents who sell Nationwide Mutual's insurance.

- ✔ **State Farm:** Check your local phone directory for agents who sell State Farm Insurance.

- ✔ **USAA:** Insurance through USAA is available to military officers and their family members. Call the company for specifics and to see whether you qualify (800-531-8080).

Other catastrophes to insure against

Depending upon where the home you buy is located, it may be subjected to earthquakes, floods, hurricanes, mud slides, tornadoes, wildfires, or other bad stuff. Standard homeowners policies don't protect against all these vagaries, so you must secure additional riders.

Thousands of communities around the country are at risk for floods. Hence, if you live in one of these areas, you need to purchase a flood insurance rider. Check with prospective homeowners insurance providers. The federal government flood insurance program (800-638-6620) can provide background information on the types of policies made available through private insurance companies.

Earthquakes are another risk to insure against. In addition to California, parts of the Midwest (and even parts of the East Coast) have active fault lines.

Ask people in the area that you're considering what the local risks are. The U.S. Geologic Survey (check your local phone directory) and the Federal Emergency Management Agency

(800-358-9616) offer maps showing, respectively, earthquake and flood risks. Be aware and be informed.

Because the cost of earthquake and flood coverage is based on insurance companies' assessments of the risks of both your area and your property type, you should *not* decide whether to buy these riders based only upon your perception of how small a risk a major quake or flood is. The risk is already built into the price.

You may be able to pay for much of the cost of earthquake or flood insurance by raising the deductibles on the main parts of both your homeowners insurance and the other insurance policies that you carry. Remember — you can more easily afford the smaller claims than the big ones. If you think that flood or earthquake insurance is too costly, compare the costs of the coverage with the expense that you will incur to completely replace your home and personal property. Buy this insurance if you live in an area that has a chance of being affected by these catastrophes.

You may have access to more specific information for your state. Many state insurance departments, which you can locate through the state government listings in your phone book, conduct surveys of insurers' prices and tabulate any complaints received.

As you shop around, be sure to ask about special discounts for such things as homes with a security system or smoke-detection system, discounts for people who have multiple policies with the same insurer, and senior discounts for older folks.

Title insurance

Fast forward to a point several months after you've closed escrow on the purchase of your dream home. Suppose we ask you to prove to us that you actually own the home.

"No problem," you say. You go to the safe deposit box where you keep all your important documents and pull out the fancy deed that the Recorder's Office mailed to you a couple of weeks after your purchase was completed.

Sorry. That deed isn't proof positive.

For example, a man and his "wife" signed a deed that transferred title in their house to another couple. A few weeks later, the buyers were shocked to find that their deed wasn't valid because the real wife's signature had been forged. In fact, the real wife didn't even know that her husband had sold the property.

Title risks

In theory, you can go down to the local County Recorder's Office and find out who owns any piece of property in the county simply by checking the public record. In fact, all sorts of irregularities in the history of the various people who have owned the property since it was originally constructed can affect a property's title — irregularities that are difficult or impossible to find, no matter how diligently you comb the public records. Here are some causes of these hidden risks to titles:

- ✔ **Secret spouses:** A seller may claim to be single when, in fact, he or she is secretly married in another state. Or perhaps the seller was divorced in a community-property state where, through marriage, one spouse obtains a legal interest in property held individually by the other spouse. Whatever the reason, sometimes a present or former spouse no one knew about will show up out of the blue and file a claim against the property. This explains why title-company representatives are so infernally curious about your marital status. They must know whether you're single, married, divorced, or widowed in order to keep ownership records accurate.

- ✔ **Undisclosed heirs:** When property owners die without wills, probate courts must decide whom their rightful heirs are. Court decisions may not be binding on heirs who weren't notified of the proceeding. Even when there's a will, probate courts must sometimes settle questions concerning the will's interpretation. Undiscovered heirs sometimes magically appear and claim that they now own the property in question.

- ✔ **Questionable competency:** Minors and people adjudged to be mentally incompetent can't enter into binding contracts unless the transaction is handled by their court-appointed guardians or conservators. If, for example, the seller was a minor or was mentally incompetent when a deed was signed, the transaction may be voidable or invalid.

- ✔ **Goofs:** This is a highly technical, catchall category for human errors. It covers everything from clerks who overlook liens recorded against property (liens for unpaid federal and state income taxes or local property taxes, for example) and other important documents while doing title searches to surveyors who incorrectly establish property boundaries. Honest mistakes create many title problems.

- ✔ **Forgery and fraud:** As was the case with the fake wife, sellers are sometimes fraudulently impersonated. By the same token, signatures can be forged on documents. That's why escrow officers demand identification (that is, a photo ID, such as a driver's license issued within the last five years, or a current passport) to establish beyond a shadow of a doubt that you are who you claim to be.

- ✔ **Name confusion:** A lot of title problems are caused by people who have names similar (or identical) to the buyer's name or seller's name. Even though you prove that you are who you claim you are, you also have to prove who you *aren't*. If you have a fairly common name, you'll probably have to fill out a Statement of Information to help the title company distinguish you from other people with names like yours. If you've got an ordinary name like Brown, Chen, Garcia, Gonzalez, Johnson, Jones, Lee, Miller, Nguyen, Williams, or the ever-popular Smith, expect to be asked to complete a Statement of Information.

What type of information is requested in a Statement of Information? You (and your spouse if you're married) will have to provide full name, social security number, date and year of birth, birthplace, date and place of marriage (if applicable), residence and employment information, previous marriages, and the like. This information will be used to differentiate good old honest you from the legions of ne'er-do-wells out there with names similar to yours.

What title insurance does

Many people who buy homes spend hundreds of dollars for title insurance without really understanding what they're getting for their money. *Title insurance* assures homeowners and mortgage lenders that property has a marketable (*valid*) title. If, for example, someone makes a claim that threatens your ownership of the home, the title insurance company protects you and the lender against loss or damage, according to the terms and provisions of your respective title insurance policies.

Most of your title insurance premium is spent on research to determine who legally owns the property that you want to buy and to find out whether there are any unpaid tax liens or judgments recorded against it. Because title companies do a good job of eliminating title risks *before* folks buy property, only about 10 percent of the premium goes toward indemnifying homeowners against title claims *after* the close of escrow.

Good news. The title insurance premium that you pay at close of escrow is the one and only title insurance premium that you'll have to pay *unless you refinance your mortgage*.

Title insurance deals with your risk of loss from *past* problems (such as unpaid property tax liens or forgery in the chain of title) that *may* exist at the time that your policy is issued. Because your policy covers the past, which is a fixed event, you only pay one title-insurance premium *as long as you keep your original mortgage.*

If you refinance your mortgage, you'll have to get a new title insurance policy to protect the lender from title risks (such as income tax liens or property tax liens, for example) that may have been recorded against your property between the time your previous policy was issued and the date of the refinance. If you refinance your loan, ask the title company whether you qualify for a *refinance rate* on the new title-insurance policy. Most title companies will give you a big premium reduction — as much as 30 percent off their normal rates — if your previous policy was issued within five years of the new policy's issuance date.

Actual examples of title insurance problems

Folks usually don't pay much attention to title insurance when they are buying a home. Most people only get title insurance because the lender won't give them a mortgage if they don't have it. But homebuyers are mighty glad to have such a policy when a title problem rears its ugly head.

What kind of title problems? For example, a woman spent close to $10,000 to remodel an existing carport and shed and to build a fence along her property line after obtaining her neighbor's permission.

Everything was fine for the woman until her neighbor sold his place several years later. The new owners had their property surveyed and discovered that her carport, shed, and fence extended about two feet onto their land. Instead of tearing everything down, which was the woman's first impulse after getting the bad news, she decided to file a claim on her title insurance policy.

The title company discovered that she was the victim of a faulty land survey. They solved the problem by buying from her new neighbors an *easement in perpetuity* to use the land that she had improved so that she could leave everything (carport, shed, and fence) exactly where it was.

Another example involves a couple whose kitchen was destroyed by fire. The county building department said that to rebuild it, the couple would have to remove a preexisting carport that extended into a five-foot lot setback. The previous owners had gotten all the necessary permits that were required to build the carport, but the local zoning laws had changed since the time that the carport was built in 1970.

The clever couple knew what to do. They called their friendly title company representative. After investigating their problem, the title company paid a contractor $5,000 to have the carport removed. The title company also paid the couple $19,000 to compensate them for the reduced value of their property because it no longer had covered parking.

Two kinds of title insurance

As a homeowner, you have a choice of two different kinds of *owners* title insurance. Depending on the extent of the coverage that you desire, you can either get a standard-coverage policy or an extended-coverage policy.

As you'd expect, *a standard title-insurance policy* is less expensive than an extended policy because its coverage is more limited. Standard policies are limited to certain off-record risks (such as fraud in the chain of title, defective recordings, and competency) plus *recorded* (at the local County Recorder's office) mechanic's liens, tax assessments, judgments, and other property defects that a search of public records can uncover.

Extended title-insurance policies cover everything that standard policies do, plus they provide expanded coverage for off-record risks that could be discovered through an inspection of the property or by making inquiries of people in actual possession of the property, as well as defects such as *unrecorded* (never recorded at the County Recorder's office) mechanics' liens, leases, or contracts of sale. Only an extended title insurance policy would've protected the homeowners in the faulty-land-survey and kitchen-fire examples in the sidebar, "Actual examples of title insurance problems."

Title-insurance costs vary greatly, depending upon the geographic area in which your home is located, the home's purchase price, and the type of coverage that you get. In addition to the owner's policy we recommend you purchase to protect your investment, you'll also need to buy a policy to protect the mortgage lender against loss on the loan amount.

In some eastern states, title companies are barred from doing title searches. If that prohibition exists in your area, you'll have to use a lawyer to handle your title search and escrow. In either case, shop around to see who offers the best combination of competitive premiums and good coverage.

Local custom and practice determine who usually pays for title insurance. In some parts of the country, custom dictates that the buyer pays for it. In other areas, however, the seller pays the title insurance premium, or buyers and sellers split the cost 50-50. As we point out in Chapter 10, the payment for title insurance is a negotiable item. Regardless of local custom, if you're in a strong buyer's market, a seller may offer (or you could ask them) to pay your title insurance costs in order to put the deal together. If, conversely, you're bidding against several other buyers for a particularly desirable house, you'd be smart to sweeten your offer by paying for title insurance, even though local custom prescribes that sellers pay for it.

Chapter 12

It Ain't Over Till the Weight-Challenged Escrow Officer Sings

● ●

In This Chapter

▶ Understanding what the heck escrows are and how they operate

▶ Reviewing closing costs and your closing statement

▶ Discovering why year-end escrows can be tricky

▶ Taking title to your home

▶ Taking possession of your home

▶ Coping with buyer's remorse

● ●

The big day draws near. Soon, if all goes well, you'll plunk down your money, sign on the dotted line, and pick up the keys to your dream home.

For most people, the final throes of buying a home are filled with elephantine incertitude, high anxiety, and flop sweats. You, however, are *not* most people. The tips you find in this chapter will soothe your fevered brow, smooth the yellow brick road to success, and make the endgame downright pleasant and enjoyable.

An Escrow Is a Good Thing

As soon as possible after you and the seller have a *ratified offer* (that is, a signed contract), all funds, documents, and instructions pertaining to your transaction should be delivered to a neutral third party — the *escrow holder* designated in your purchase agreement. The act of giving these funds, documents, and instructions to the escrow holder constitutes the *escrow*. Depending on the local custom in your area, the escrow may be handled by a lawyer, an escrow firm, or a title company. Buyers and sellers generally select an escrow holder based on recommendations from their agents. However, as with other companies you choose to do business with in your home-buying transaction, know that escrow fees and service quality vary.

Real estate deals are characterized by mutual distrust. You and the seller need someone that both of you can trust to hold the stakes while you two meet to work through all the resolved and unresolved details in your contract. The *escrow holder* (also known as the *escrow officer*) is your referee — a neutral third party who won't show any favoritism to either you or the seller.

Know thy escrow officer

Your escrow officer is responsible for preparing and reviewing papers related to the transfer of *title* (a legal document that stipulates ownership of the property); getting them properly signed, delivered, and made a matter of public record; complying with your lender's funding instructions; ordering a title search (explained in Chapter 11); and accounting to you and the seller for your respective money. The escrow officer handles the nitty-gritty paperwork details so that you can concentrate on the deal.

When the escrow is opened, your contract will probably be filled with loopholes known as *contingencies,* or *conditions of sale.* For example, your contract should be written so that you can get out of the deal if you don't approve the property inspection reports, if the seller can't give you clear title to the property, or if you can't get a loan. The escrow officer's job is to receive and follow your instructions. Do not instruct the escrow officer to give your money to the seller until you are *fully* satisfied that the seller has performed under the contract. Chapter 10 goes into great detail about contingencies.

Hopefully, your escrow will go smoothly from start to close. If, however, the escrow officer ever gets conflicting instructions from you and the seller or lender, the escrow will stop dead in its tracks until the argument is resolved. What kind of conflicting instructions? Disputes about whether or not an item of personal property (that is, a refrigerator, a fireplace screen, light fixture, and the like) is included in the purchase price are always popular. So are disagreements about whether corrective work should be done prior to or after close of escrow.

Our friend Kip Oxman, a real estate attorney and broker, has a great saying that works wonders in dispute resolution situations: "When all else fails, RTC." You'll find the answers to most controversies if you **R**ead **T**he **C**ontract. The real estate purchase agreement included in Appendix A is an example of an extremely explicit contract that is intended to eliminate ambiguity.

Good escrow officers are worth their weight in gold in times of crisis when the shouting, tears, and threats of lawsuit begin. At moments like this, often only the escrow officer's incredible patience and crisis-mediation skills keep deals glued together.

Give yourself an unfair advantage by humanizing your escrow. Either call or visit your escrow officer at his or her office to introduce yourself. Ask whether the escrow officer needs any additional information to make the escrow go faster and smoother. Some questions your escrow officer may ask include: What's your middle name? Where can you be reached during the day? What's your insurance agent's name and phone number? Will you need to complete a Statement of Information (covered in the title insurance section of Chapter 11)? What's your social security number (so your deposit can be placed in an interest-bearing account)? A little consideration and respect now will do wonders for you later if the escrow hits a rough patch.

To avoid truly horrible surprises, pay particular attention to the following three areas:

Closing costs

If you have a nice, orderly, sequential mind, you've undoubtedly read the preceding 11 chapters and know that we have a detailed itemization of closing costs in Chapter 3. If you're the kind of person who loves to skip around and sample random chapters that strike your fancy, we suggest that you read that section now, or our tips won't make any sense.

As soon as possible, get a rough idea of how much money you'll have to come up with at the close of escrow. Immediately after opening escrow, ask the escrow officer to prepare a statement of your estimated closing costs. Even though it may take several weeks to get actual costs for inspection fees, repair-work credits, homeowners insurance premiums, and the like, at least you'll have a preliminary number that you can fine-tune as additional information becomes available. Having the knowledge available in this preliminary statement beats getting hammered by unexpected closing costs a couple of days before the close of escrow.

Estimate the closing expenses on the high side. Overestimating expenses and finding, when actual costs come in, that you won't need as much money to close as you first expected is ideal. The sooner that you put a box around your closing costs, the better. Don't react to the situation — control it.

If, like most folks, you must put additional money in escrow just prior to the close of the transaction, use a cashier's check or a money order, or have your funds wired directly to the escrow to avoid delays. Personal checks take time to clear. Credit cards don't cut it in escrows. If you have questions regarding what constitutes *good funds,* ask your escrow officer well in advance of the close of escrow. If your money is out of town, for example, in a high-yielding money market fund (such as is recommended in Chapter 3), check with your investment company about how you can wire money from your account to the escrow company.

Preliminary title report

Shortly after escrow is opened, you should receive an extremely important document — the *preliminary title report* (or *prelim*) from your title company. This report shows who currently owns the property that you want to buy as well as any money claims (such as mortgage liens, income tax judgments, and property tax assessments) that affect the property. Last, but not least, the preliminary title report shows third-party restrictions and interests (such as condominium *covenants, conditions, and restrictions,* CC&Rs, and utility-company or private easements) that limit your use of the property.

Your contract should be contingent upon your review and approval of the preliminary title report. Look it over carefully. Ask your agent, escrow officer, title company representative, or lawyer to explain anything in the report that you don't understand. Don't be shy — there's no such thing as a dumb question.

Under the contract, you should have the right to *reasonably* disapprove of certain claims or restrictions that you don't want on the property and to ask the owner to clear them prior to the close of escrow. For example, asking the seller to pay off all debts secured by liens and judgments against the property is reasonable. Asking the seller of a condo to remove the CC&Rs would be unreasonable because, as noted in Chapter 7, the CC&Rs are an integral part of the property.

A preliminary title report is *not* title insurance. You can find more on the distinction between title insurance and a preliminary title report in the title insurance section of Chapter 11.

Final closing statement

You may believe that the most important piece of paper you get when escrow closes is the deed to your new home. From an accounting standpoint, however, the most important piece of paper is the final closing statement that you get from the escrow officer on the day that your escrow actually closes.

If you think of the escrow as a checking account, the final closing statement is like your checkbook. The final closing statement records all the money related to your home purchase that went through the escrow as either a credit or a debit:

- ✔ **Credits:** Any money that you put into escrow (such as your initial deposit and down payment) appears as a credit to your account. You may also receive credits from the seller for such things as corrective work repairs and property taxes. And, of course, your loan is a credit.

- ✔ **Debits:** Funds paid out of escrow in your behalf are shown as debits. Your debits include modest and not-so-modest expenses, such as what you graciously paid the seller for your dream home, loan fees, homeowners-insurance premiums, and property inspection fees.

You meet with your escrow officer several days before close of escrow to sign the loan documents and other papers related to your home purchase. At that time, you'll be given an estimated closing statement detailing what your closing costs will be if the escrow closes as scheduled. Check the estimated closing statement *extremely* carefully, line-by-line and from top to bottom, to be absolutely certain that it accurately reflects your credits and debits. Escrow officers are human — they sometimes make mistakes. So do other parties in the transaction who may have given the escrow officer incorrect information. And guess what — when mistakes turn up, whose favor do you think they are in? Probably not yours! It's your money on the table. Pay attention to detail. Review the closing statement and question whatever isn't clear or correct.

The final closing statement is extremely important. Keep a copy for your files — it will come in handy when the time comes to complete your income tax return. As detailed in Chapter 3, some expenses (such as loan origination fees and property tax payments) are tax deductible. Furthermore, the closing statement establishes your initial tax (cost) basis in the property. When you're ready to sell your property, you may owe capital gains tax on any profit you've made by selling the property for more than your cost basis (see Chapter 15 for more details).

'Tis the season: December escrows

As a rule, December is a slow month for home sales. A week or two before Thanksgiving, most buyers switch their attention from houses to holidays and family gatherings, and those buyers don't get back onto the home-buying track until around Super Bowl Sunday in late January.

Here are two reasons that you may decide to buck the trend:

- **Bargain hunting:** When the other buyers drop out of the market, you're the only game in town for stubborn sellers who foolishly waited too long to get realistic about their asking price. If they must sell, sellers instruct their agents to put the word out that they're willing to deal. The magic phrase is, "Bring us an offer." If you're a lowballer looking for a deal, now's the time to make your move.

- **Tax deductions:** What you get doesn't matter — what does matter is what you get to *keep*. Buying a home in December gives you tax deductions that you can use to reduce your federal and state income taxes in that calendar year. As we discuss in Chapter 3, owning a home gives you physical shelter *and* tax shelter. On your income taxes, you can, for example, write off your loan origination fee (points), mortgage interest, and property taxes that you pay prior to December 31.

Escrows are perverse creatures under even the best of circumstances. They're proof positive of Murphy's Law, which states that whatever can go wrong will — and always at the worst possible time. Experienced escrow officers know that nasty surprises can rear their ugly heads whenever you least expect them.

What kind of surprises? The list is unpleasantly long: missed deadlines, title glitches, problems paying off existing loans, changes in your loan's terms, insufficient funds to close escrow, and so on.

December escrows are particularly perverse. Partying saps your strength and reduces your effectiveness. People forget to sign papers before leaving on vacation. December 31 is an immutable deadline if you want to close this year for tax purposes. If you end up with a December escrow, here are some things you (and your real estate agent) should do to make sure that you meet your deadline:

- ✔ **Stay in touch with your lender.** Lenders need copious documentation to substantiate loan applications. Be sure that your lender has all the required documents as soon as possible. Lenders say that lack of follow-up on loan document verification is the number-one cause of escrow delays.

- ✔ **Don't leave any blank spaces on your loan application.** Draw a line through any section that doesn't apply to you. If you leave a section blank, the lender will assume that you forgot to complete it. And make a photocopy of everything that you submit, in case the originals get lost.

- ✔ **Stay in touch with your escrow officer.** Don't let your file get buried in a pile of pending escrows stuck on the corner of your escrow officer's desk. You or your agent should check with the escrow officer periodically to make sure that things are going smoothly.

- ✔ **Be available to sign your loan documents.** You may only have 24 to 48 hours after your loan package arrives at the escrow office to sign the documents and return them to the lender. A delay could cost you the loan.

- ✔ **If you're leaving town for the holidays, tell your agent, lender, and escrow officer well in advance of your departure.** Special arrangements can usually be made to close your escrow — no matter where you are — as long as people have advance warning and know how to reach you. The key to success is keeping everyone posted.

- ✔ **Check the calendar.** Many offices are open only till noon on Christmas Eve and New Year's Eve. When Christmas Day and New Year's Day fall on Saturday or Sunday, office hours can really get crazy. Some businesses and public offices close on the preceding Friday, others close on the following Monday, and still others close on both Friday and Monday in order to give their employees a four-day holiday. Be sure to check the holiday office schedule of your agent, lender, escrow officer, and so on. Don't let a holiday office-closing derail your deal.

- ✔ **Allow time between when you'd like to close and when you *must* close.** Give yourself maneuvering room to resolve last-minute problems that *inevitably* appear when you least expect them. Don't schedule your closing on the last business day of the year. You'll have no margin for error if you need to close by year's end.

Follow through

Engagements are to weddings what escrows are to buying houses. Just as wedding bells don't always ring for everyone who gets engaged, all open escrows don't end in home purchases.

Many escrows could've been saved by applying a fundamental principle of winning tennis — follow through. Tennis pros know that there's more to the game than simply making contact with the ball. Pros continue their swing "through the ball" after they hit it, because they know that the last part of the stroke is as important as the initial contact with the ball. If they don't follow through properly, the ball won't end up where they want it to go.

And so it is with real estate deals. Buyers, sellers, and agents often say that a house has been *sold* when the purchase contract is signed. *Not true!* Nothing was sold. The buyer and seller merely ratified an offer. *Big difference!*

If you want to actually buy and move into the home — that is, close your escrow — there must be follow-through on all the details by everyone involved in your transaction. You won't be the proud owner of your dream house until the weight-challenged escrow officer sings!

How You Take Title Is Vital

One of the most important decisions that you can make when buying a home is how you take title in the property. If you're unmarried, your choices are simpler because you take title as a sole owner. When two or more people co-own a property, however, the number of ways to take title multiplies dramatically.

How title is held is critically important. Each form of co-ownership has its own rainbow of advantages, disadvantages, tax consequences, and legal repercussions. You shouldn't make this decision in haste at an escrow office while signing your closing papers. Unfortunately, that's what usually happens.

What's the best form of co-ownership for you? That depends on your circumstances. Here are some forms of co-ownership and the advantages of each type:

- **Joint tenancy:** Suppose, for example, that you and your spouse buy a house together as joint tenants. When your spouse dies 20 years from now, ownership of the house automatically transfers to you without going through probate. This feature of joint tenancy co-ownership is known as the *right of survivorship.*

  Joint-tenancy goodies don't stop there. You also get a *stepped-up basis* on your spouse's half of the house. This stepped-up basis can save you big bucks on the capital gains tax that you'll have to pay if you ever sell the house.

Here's how a stepped-up basis works. Say, for example, that you and your spouse paid $180,000 for the house when you bought it. Immediately after your spouse's death, the house is appraised at $300,000.

Your new cost-of-the-home basis for tax purposes is $240,000 ($90,000 for your half-share of the original purchase price plus $150,000 for your spouse's half of the house at date of death) because no capital gains tax applies to your spouse's $60,000 of appreciation in value.

Even though we used a married couple in our example, you need not be married to use joint tenancy co-ownership. However, a minimum of two people must co-own.

✔ **Community property:** Only married couples can take title as community property. Compared to joint tenancy, the big advantage of community property co-ownership is that both halves of your house get a stepped-up basis upon the death of your spouse. This gives you even bigger tax savings.

Using the same figures as the joint tenancy example, as the surviving spouse, your cost basis is the full $300,000. Capital gains tax is forgiven on every penny of appreciation in value between the date of purchase and time your spouse died.

Another significant advantage of community property co-ownership is the ability to will your share of the house to whomever you wish. Due to the right of survivorship, this choice isn't possible when title is held as joint tenants.

✔ **Tenants-in-common or partnerships:** Holding title as tenants-in-common or in the form of a partnership doesn't give you a stepped-up basis upon the death of a co-owner. This creates an obvious disadvantage from a tax standpoint.

Offsetting legal advantages exist, however, for unrelated persons who take title either as tenants-in-common or as a partnership. Under these forms of co-ownership, you generally have the right to will or sell your share of the property without permission of the co-owners. Furthermore, co-owners don't have to have equal ownership interests in the property — a nice feature for people who just want a small piece of the action.

If you're smart — and we know that you must be or you wouldn't be reading this book — you and your co-owners will have a formal written agreement, prepared by a real estate lawyer, to cover situations likely to arise while you jointly own the property. What kind of situations? Here's a recap of key provisions to include in your written agreement (you can find more on these items in the partnership section of Chapter 7):

✔ Provisions to buy out a co-owner who has to sell when the other owners want to keep the property

✔ Provisions to prorate maintenance and repair costs among co-owners with unequal shares in the property

- Provisions to resolve disputes regarding such things as what color to paint the house

- Provisions for penalties if a co-owner can't cover his or her share of loan payments or property taxes

The preceding information is not intended to be your definitive guide to the subtleties of real property title vesting. This chapter merely points out the most important issues that you should consider. Don't make a decision of this magnitude in haste, especially if your situation is unusual or complicated. In addition to deciding how to hold title, you should also consider estate-planning issues, such as wills and potential trusts (see Chapter 2 to find out more).

Getting Possessive

The day your escrow closes is legally confusing. You don't own the home when the day begins at 12:01 a.m., but you're the owner of record when the day ends at midnight. Sometime during the day, the escrow officer gives the seller your money, notifies you that the deed has been recorded, and officially announces that you're now the proud owner of your dream home. Congratulations!

Moving day

When can you actually take possession of your home and move into it? That depends on the terms of your contract. Look at paragraph 6 of the sample purchase contract in Appendix A to see an example of a "Possession and Keys" clause that specifies date and time of possession and delivery of keys from seller to buyer. Here are your usual options:

- **Move in the same day that escrow closes.** This is fine if the sellers have already moved out. If, however, the sellers haven't moved yet and don't want to deliver possession until they're absolutely, 100-percent certain that escrow has closed, you've got a logistical problem. For two moving vans to occupy exactly the same driveway at exactly the same time borders on the impossible. Moving into a house while someone else is moving out is something you'll *never* attempt more than once. There are easier ways to go crazy.

- **Move in the day after escrow closes.** We recommend this alternative if the sellers won't deliver possession until escrow closes. Let the sellers have the day that escrow closes as their moving day. After all, the sellers are still the owners until title transfers. Moving day is stressful, even under the best of circumstances. Why create unnecessary stress for yourself by trying to move in as the sellers are leaving?

After the sellers vacate, but before your movers bring your belongings into the house, check your new home carefully for damage that may have been caused by the sellers' movers. When movers are involved, accidents can happen. We cover this problem in the next section.

Whether you move into your home the day that escrow closes or the following day, you start paying for utilities and homeowners insurance effective the day that escrow closes. Don't forget to coordinate phone installation and resumption of utility services, if necessary, with the proper companies a couple of weeks prior to the scheduled close of escrow.

✔ **Move in after a seller rent-back.** It's not uncommon for sellers to remain in their house for several weeks after escrow closes while waiting to get into their new home. In that case, you sign a separate rent-back agreement with them that becomes part of your purchase contract. The *rent-back agreement* covers such things as who pays for utilities and maintenance, what happens if there's property damage, how much rent the sellers pay you, and what the penalties are if the sellers don't vacate the property on the date specified in the rent-back.

It's customary for the sellers to pay rent equal to what you're paying for principal and interest on your mortgage, plus property taxes and insurance, so that you break even on what it costs you to own the house during the term of their rental. The amount equaling *principle, interest, taxes,* and *insurance* (known as PITI) is prorated on a per-day basis from close of escrow until the sellers vacate. Suppose, for example, that PITI is $50 per day, and the sellers expect to be out three weeks after escrow closes. You both instruct the escrow officer to hold *four* weeks PITI in escrow to give you a cushion if the sellers encounter a delay in moving into their new place. When the sellers actually move out, you and the sellers jointly instruct the escrow officer to pay you PITI for the actual rental period and to refund to the sellers the unused portion of funds held in escrow.

If the home you're buying is vacant, you may be tempted to ask for permission to start fixing the house up before close of escrow. After all, painting or waxing floors, for example, is much easier and faster when the house is empty. *Don't do it.* If the deal falls through, you've spent your time and money fixing up someone else's house. If the house catches fire, you don't have insurance to cover your losses. The risk exceeds the reward. Instead, allow some time to do these tasks *after* escrow closes and a day or two *before* moving in.

Final verification of condition

Read the "Final Verification of Condition" clause in paragraph 24 of the California Association of Realtors' purchase contract (Appendix A). If your state's contract doesn't have this type of clause in it, instruct your agent or lawyer to write such a clause into your contract. Nearly all contracts have something like paragraph 40 just for this type of supplement to the contract.

We urge you to inspect the property a few days (ideally the day) before escrow closes. Why? To be sure that the property is still in the same general condition that it was in when you signed the contract to buy it. What if the sellers knocked a big hole in the kitchen wall during a wild party? What if they forgot to water the lawn and it turned into a rock garden? What if a sinkhole appeared smack-dab in the middle of the driveway? The "what ifs" are endless.

You'll probably find that everything is hunky-dory. But if it isn't, you can order the escrow officer to stop the escrow while you resolve the problem. Such an action always gets the seller's and real estate agent's attention. If you and the seller can't work out a mutually satisfactory solution, you may have to kill the deal. Killing the deal is better than buying a problem.

Buyer's Remorse

Many home sellers are convinced that they left the family jewels on the table when they sold their houses. The notion that they "gave their house away" is called *seller's remorse*. Seller's remorse is painful, but it generally departs within a month or two after the sale. Sellers are lucky to have such an uncomplicated dementia.

If you're like most buyers, you'll experience the flip side of this nasty psychosis. *Buyer's remorse* is the sinking feeling that you paid way, way, waaaay too much for your new home.

Unfortunately, buyer's remorse is much more complex than seller's remorse. Buyer's remorse is compounded by many other anxieties — that you're getting the world's worst mortgage, that the bottom will fall out of property values in the years after you buy a home, that you'll lose your job, that your health will fail, and that your faithful dog will die.

We're here to help you deal with fear of overpayment. Those other anxieties are absolutely normal reactions to the uncertainties most of us *initially* experience. They *will* go away. If it makes you feel any better, nearly all homebuyers are traumatized by the same irrational concerns while purchasing a home.

In time, you'll discover (as we and millions of others who have gone before you did) that you have a fine mortgage, property values are stable, your continued employment is secure, your health is great, and so is your dog's. Don't take our word for this. Do a little dialing for dollars to verify that you've got a good loan, check the help-wanted ads for jobs like yours, discuss property values with neighbors, get a physical examination, and take your dog to the vet.

So what about the fear that you're paying waaaay too much? If the real estate gods love you, you'll get a light case of buyer's remorse that you can treat by taking a couple of aspirin. Some buyers, however, are so ravaged by it that they try to break their contract.

You can't deal with buyer's remorse until you accept it for what it is — raw, naked fear. You're afraid that you're overpaying for the house. That fear tears some buyers apart. The symptoms of typical, fear-driven buyer's remorse are easy to spot. After you've signed the contract to buy your dream home, you do one or more of the following:

- **Read ads in the real estate section of your local newspaper even more intently than you did before you signed the contract.** You're searching for similar or nicer houses with lower asking prices. (You forget that most houses read a lot better in ads than they eyeball when you tour them.)

- **Spend Saturday and Sunday touring open houses.** Reading ads isn't enough for you. You pound the pavement, looking for better buys than you got. Seeing, after all, *is* believing. (Speaking of seeing, you may see the remorseful sellers making the rounds of the same houses that you're looking at, trying to find less-nice properties with bigger asking prices.)

- **Discuss your purchase with friends, neighbors, business associates, and the guy standing behind you while you wait in line to buy movie tickets.** You ask anyone and everyone if they think that you're paying too much, even though 99.9 percent of the people that you talk to don't have a clue about property values for homes similar to yours. (You accept as gospel any wild guess they make that confirms your suspicions.)

After going through these exercises *during* escrow and for a couple of months *after* the purchase (until you're emotionally and physically exhausted), you'll probably discover that your fears are groundless. There's nothing wrong or unusual about your concerns. What is wrong is letting these fears gnaw away at you secretly instead of openly confronting them.

Facts defeat fear. The faster you get the facts you need, the less you'll suffer.

As Chapter 9 explains, a home can have more than one correct price. Pricing and negotiation are arts, not precise sciences. Don't beat yourself up with *asking* prices. You're okay as long as your home's *purchase* price is in line with the *sale* prices of comparable houses.

If you follow the principles we cover in this book, you'll be just fine! Unlike many homebuyers, you'll know how to get your finances in order before you buy and you'll know how to determine what you can really afford to spend on a home. You'll know how to find a great neighborhood, a great property, a great mortgage, a great agent, and a great property inspector. You'll be able to spot an overpriced turkey and a good value. You'll know about property inspections and negotiating for repair of property defects. You'll know how to avoid nasty people and property surprises.

Knowledge is power. After you've assimilated the advice in this book, you'll be extremely powerful. You'll have nothing to fear. Go for it!

Part V
The Part of Tens

The 5th Wave · By Rich Tennant

"Honey, I thought you checked with the neighborhood committee before having the house painted magenta."

In this part . . .

This part includes such tenfolds as the ten financial musts after you buy, the ten things to know when investing in real estate, and the ten things to consider when selling your house. Looking for a quick and easy reference in nice, even sets of ten? Read on!

Chapter 13
Ten Financial "Musts" After You Buy

● ●

*A*lthough it may have seemed that the day would never come — here you are, *a homeowner*. A homeowner — can you believe it? Go ahead and pinch yourself!

Perhaps you're already correcting your friends who ask how it feels to be a homeowner. Most new owners say, "Well, the bank owns more of the house than I do." Actually, you own 100 percent of the property — you just owe the mortgage lender a bucketload of money. Trust us when we say that, although it may seem like a lot of money now, it won't seem that way decades from now. You'll be glad, then, that you decided to buy rather than continue renting. What you owe today, you'll hopefully own free and clear in 30 years, if not sooner.

If you think that the hard part is over after you buy a home, you may be in for a surprise. Moving probably wasn't a picnic, but moving is just the beginning of your quest to transform your new slag-heap into a beauteous home.

As a new homeowner, you must sidestep the many solicitations that will be winging your way. Unfortunately, when you buy a home, you end up on a zillion or so mailing lists because your home purchase is a matter of public record. Some communities even publish home sales (complete with buyer and seller names and purchase price) in the local newspaper, for goodness' sake!

This chapter can help you become a financially happy new homeowner and can help you avoid the pitfalls to which many new homeowners before you have fallen prey.

Stay on top of your spending and saving

After you buy and move into your home, if you're like most new homeowners, your furniture and other personal possessions seem to take on an even shabbier tinge than before. And because you're now living in the property, you soon discover aspects of it that you don't like as much as when you were looking at it from the outside as a prospective buyer.

If you're like most homebuyers, you can find unlimited furniture, appliances, and remodeling projects that quickly exhaust the incomes of even the rich and famous. Because of these spending temptations, more than a few homebuyers end up not saving any of their hard-earned incomes. Some new homeowners even end up building credit card (and other high interest) consumer debt because their spending outstrips their income.

Feeling a squeeze in the budget when you buy a home is perfectly normal. After all, your housing expenses are probably higher than they were when you were renting. But that's all the more reason that you need to take a lean-and-mean approach to the rest of your budget and spending (see Chapter 2). You can also make your home more energy efficient by doing some simple things such as insulating and installing water-flow restrictors in faucets and shower heads. Also, use your home-inspection report to identify other opportunities for improvement.

Don't neglect saving toward important financial goals, such as retirement. And take your time transforming your new home into a veritable palace. Rejoice and take solace in the fact that you have a roof over your head, a warm and comfortable place to sleep, and adequate living space — things which many people around the world can only dream about.

Consider electronic payment of your mortgage

Mortgage lenders want to be paid and to be paid on time. And you should want to pay them on time. Late payments can cost you dearly — many mortgages have stipulations for penalties equal to 5 percent of the amount of the mortgage payment if your payment is late. If your payment is one whole month late, a 5 percent penalty works out to an annualized interest rate in excess of 60 percent! Even being one day late can trigger this penalty. (And you thought that credit card debt was costly to carry at 18 percent!) Late charges also show up as *derogatories* on your credit report.

Sign up for your mortgage lender's automatic-payment service that allows you to have your mortgage payment zapped electronically from your checking account to the lender on the same day each month. If your mortgage lender doesn't offer this service, you can establish it yourself through one of the many home-banking services (such as CheckFree) or through bill-payment software (such as Quicken or Microsoft Money).

Rebuild your emergency reserve

Most people clean out their emergency reserve (and then some) in order to scrape together enough cash to close on their home purchase. Ideally, you should have ready and available an emergency cash reserve equal to at least three months worth of living expenses. If your employment is unstable and you lack family to lean on financially in a pinch, aim for six months' worth of living expenses. Keep the emergency money in a high yielding money-market mutual fund (see Chapter 3).

As with saving money to accomplish other important financial goals, rebuilding your emergency reserve requires you to go on a financial diet and spend less than you earn. Easier said than done, especially with all the tempting things to spend money on for your home. Avoid the malls, mail-order catalogs, and home-improvement stores until you're back on an even keel.

Keep receipts for all improvements

Sooner or later, you will spend money on your home. Some of what you spend money for should be tracked and documented for tax purposes in order to minimize the capital gain that you may owe tax on in the future. *Capital gain* simply means the difference between what you receive for the house when you sell it less what it cost you to buy the house — with one important modification. The IRS allows you to add the cost of improvements to the original cost of your home in order to calculate what's known as your *adjusted-cost basis*.

In other words:

Capital Gain = Net Sale Price − (Purchase Price + Capital Improvements)

For example, if you buy your home for $150,000 and, over the years, it appreciates so that (after paying the costs of selling) your net selling price is $200,000, your capital gain is $50,000. Remember, though, that the IRS allows you to add the value of the capital improvements that you make to your home to your purchase price.

A *capital improvement* is defined as money you spend on your home that permanently increases its value and useful life — putting a new roof on your house, for example, rather than just patching the existing roof. So if you made $10,000 worth of improvements on the home you bought for $150,000, your capital gain would be reduced to $40,000. Money spent on maintenance, such as fixing a leaky pipe or fixing broken windows, is not added to your cost basis (see Chapter 3 for more details).

Ignore solicitations for mortgage insurance

Soon after you move into your home — often within a matter of just weeks or months — your mailbox becomes flooded with solicitations offering you mortgage life insurance and mortgage disability insurance. Most of the solicitations come from your mortgage lender, but other solicitations may come from insurance firms that picked up on the publicly available information revealing that you recently bought your home.

The fundamental problem with these insurance policies is that, given the amount of insurance protection offered, such policies are usually grossly overpriced and don't provide the right amount of benefits. The amount of life and disability insurance protection that you carry should not necessarily be determined by the size of your mortgage. If you need life insurance protection because you have dependents who rely on your income, buy low-cost, high-quality term insurance. Likewise, if you are dependent on your income, make sure that you have proper long-term disability insurance coverage. See Chapter 2 to find out more about satisfying your insurance needs.

Ignore solicitations to create a faster payoff mortgage

Another type of solicitation that you may receive in the mail extols the virtues — namely, the thousands of dollars in interest savings — that you can reap if you pay your mortgage off faster. For a monthly fee, these services offer to turn your annual, 12-monthly-payment mortgage into 26 biweekly payments, each of which is half of your current monthly payment. Thus, you'll be making 13 months' worth of payments every year instead of 12. Doing so will shave about 8 years off of the repayment schedule of a 30-year mortgage.

There are two problems with these services. First, you are paying the service money for paying off your mortgage faster — something you can do without them and their fees. Second, paying off your mortgage faster than necessary may not be in your best interests.

The question to ask yourself is what you would do with the extra money each month if you didn't pay off the mortgage faster. If you'd spend it on something frivolous that would provide only fleeting, superficial enjoyment, paying off your mortgage faster is probably a better use for the money. Likewise, if you're an older (or otherwise risk-averse) investor, you're unlikely to earn a high enough rate of return by investing your money to make it worth your while *not* to pay off your mortgage faster. On the other hand, if you could (instead) sock more money away into a tax-deductible retirement account, paying off your mortgage faster may actually *cost* you money rather than save you money.

Protest your tax assessment if property values decline

In most communities, real estate property taxes are based upon an estimate of your home's value. If home prices have dropped since you bought your home, you may be able to appeal your assessment and enjoy a reduction in the property taxes that you're required to pay.

Contact your local Assessor's Office to inquire as to the local procedure for appealing your property taxes. Generally, the process involves providing comparable sales data in writing to the assessor to prove the reduced value of your home. If you need help with this exercise, contact the real estate agent who sold you the home. Just be aware that your agent may want to make you feel as though your home hasn't decreased as much in value in order to make you (and perhaps himself) feel better. Explain that you're trying to save money on your property taxes and need comps that sold for less than you paid for your house. See Chapter 9 if you need a quick refresher on establishing property values.

Refinance if interest rates fall

In Chapters 5 and 6, we explain how to select a magnificent mortgage and provide many tips for getting the best mortgage deal you can. But after you're into the routine of making your mortgage payments, if you're like most people, staying on top of strategies to keep your mortgage costs to an absolute minimum is probably as high on your priority list as flossing your teeth three times a day.

Keep half an eye on interest rates. As you may already know, interest rates — like the weather — change. If interest rates decrease from where they were when you took out your mortgage, you may be able to refinance your mortgage and save yourself some money. *Refinancing* (as described in Chapter 5) simply means that you take out another new (lower cost) mortgage to replace your old (higher cost) one.

If rates have dropped at least one full percentage point since you originally took out your loan, start to contemplate and assess refinancing. The key item to calculate is how many months it will take you to recoup the *costs* of refinancing (loan fees, title insurance, and the like). For example, suppose that your favorite mortgage lender tells you that you can whack $150 off of your monthly payment by refinancing. Sounds good, huh? Well, not so quick there, Poindexter. First, you won't save yourself $150 per month just because your payment drops by that amount — don't forget that you'll lose some tax write-offs if you have less mortgage interest to deduct.

As a shortcut to figuring how much you will really reduce your mortgage cost on an after-tax basis, take your tax rate (as delineated in Chapter 3) and decrease your monthly payment savings you expect from the refinance by that amount. If you're a moderate-income earner, odds are that you're in the 28-percent tax bracket. So if you're mortgage payment would drop by $150, and if you were to reduce that $150 by 28 percent (to account for the lost tax savings), then (on an after-tax basis) your savings would actually be $108 per month.

Now $108 per month is nothing to sneeze at, but you still must consider how much refinancing the loan will cost you. If the refinancing costs total, for example, $6,000, it will take you about 56 months ($6,000 divided by $108) to recover those costs. If you plan on moving within five years, refinancing won't save you money — it will actually cost you money. On the other hand, if it costs you just $3,000 to refinance, you can recover those costs within three years. If you expect to stay in your home for at least that long, refinancing is probably a good move.

Ignore solicitations to homestead your home

Another pitch that you, as a new homeowner, may get in the mail is one offering to homestead your home if you pay the friendly firm anywhere from $50 to $100. *Homesteading* means protecting some of your home's equity from lawsuits. A firm may offer to file the appropriate (and quite simple) legal document to protect a portion of your home's equity from lawsuits.

If you live in a state where you need to take action to secure your homestead exemption, by all means do so. Just call the Recorder's Office and ask how to do it. The process is simple (and, in some states, unnecessary) and not worth paying a firm to do for you.

Take time to smell the roses

Okay, so it's a cliché. But too often, people work, work, work to afford a home and don't take the time to enjoy life, family, and friends (or even their home). If you buy a home that's within your financial means and you are resourceful and thrifty with your spending in the years that you live in it, your home should not dictate your finances and your need to work. You should own the home. It shouldn't own you.

No people (that we're aware of) have ever said on their deathbed that they wished that they had spent more time toiling away at work (and therefore less time with family, with friends, and for themselves) so that they could spend more money on their home.

Chapter 14

Ten Things to Know When Investing in Real Estate

· ·

*B*oth owning a home and paying down the mortgage on your home over the years should create *equity* — the difference between what your home is worth and what you owe on it. Even if the unlikely happens and your home does not appreciate in value, you'll build equity as you pay down your mortgage. More than likely, however, your home will also appreciate in value over the years that you own it.

Your home, then, is an investment. You can use the equity in your home down the road for a variety of important purposes including (but not limited to) financing part of your retirement, paying for educational costs, and doing frivolous and fun things, such as traveling. In addition to owning your home, you can invest in real estate in other ways. Here are our top ten tips and things you should know if you're going to invest in real estate.

Real estate is a good long-term investment

In recent years, many people have been swept up in the euphoria of a booming U.S. stock market. Year after year, the market has cranked out easy double-digit returns for investors. Meanwhile, in many parts of the country, real estate prices became stagnant or actually declined. So it seemed to some people, including media pundits, that real estate was yesterday's good investment.

Home values in all locations have always gone through up-and-down cycles. However, the long-term trend is up, and the rises usually are far greater than the subsequent declines. So, if you have a long-term (ideally, a decade or more) investing-time horizon, you should do just fine if you invest in real estate. The average annual returns are comparable to those enjoyed by long-term stock-market investors. The best time to buy a house is always a decade ago. A decade from now, today's prices may look dirt cheap.

Real estate investing isn't for everyone

If you're an impatient, busy person, investing in real estate probably isn't going to be your cup of tea. First, locating, negotiating, and closing on property can take a big chunk of your time if you want to buy good property at a good price. Second come the joys (and the time sinkhole) of managing the property — from finding tenants to keeping the building clean and everything in working order. Your stock and mutual fund investments won't call you in the middle of the night to fix a plumbing problem, but your tenants may!

Even if you have the time to invest in real estate, you may also consider some other important aspects of your personal financial situation. As we discuss in Chapter 2, taking advantage of tax-deductible retirement accounts is vital to your long-term financial health and ability to retire. Buying investment real estate can prevent you from saving adequately in retirement accounts. First, saving for your down payment can hamper your ability to fund these retirement accounts. And second, most of the properties that you buy will require additional out-of-pocket money in the early years.

REITs are good if you hate being a landlord

If you want to place some money in real estate but don't like the thought of being a landlord, consider *real estate investment trusts* (*REITs*). REITs are managed by a company that pools your money with that of other investors to purchase a variety of investment real estate properties these trusts manage.

REITs trade on the major stock exchanges, and some mutual funds also invest in REITs. Both Fidelity (800-544-8888) and Cohen & Steers (800-437-9912) offer good REIT mutual funds.

Don't invest in limited partnerships

You should avoid real estate limited partnerships that are sold through securities brokerage firms. Securities brokers, often operating under the misleading titles of *financial consultant* or *financial advisor,* love to sell limited partnerships because of the hefty commissions that limited partnerships pay to the broker. The broker's take can range as high as 10 percent or more. Guess where this money comes from? If you said, "out of my investment dollars," go to the head of the class!

In addition to the fatal flaw that only 90 cents on the dollar that you invest actually goes to work for you in the investment, broker-sold limited partnerships also typically carry hefty annual operating fees ranging from 2 to 3 percent. So when you add it all up (or, we should say, after all these commissions and fees are subtracted from your hard-earned dollars), limited partnerships are destined to be poor investments for you.

Avoid time-share condos and vacation homes

Another way that smart people lose a great deal of money when investing in real estate is through involvement in time-share condominiums and vacation homes. The allure of both of these purchases is having a place to which you can escape for fun and relaxation.

With a time share, what you're essentially buying, typically, is the ownership of one week's use of a condominium. Suppose that, for this privilege, you pay a one-time fee of $7,000.

Although $7,000 may not sound like a lot, if one week costs $7,000, buying the entire year's rights to use the time-share condo comes to more than $350,000. However, buying a similar condo in the area may set you back only about $125,000! So you're paying a *huge* markup on your week's ownership because of the costs of selling all those weeks and the need for the time share distributor to make a profit. (And you'll be on the hook as well for your share of the annual maintenance fees of a couple of hundred dollars or more.)

A far better idea is to rent a condo that someone else owns — it's cheaper than owning, you can go to a different resort area each year (ski, beach, whatever), and you'll have no ownership and managing headaches. Or you could buy a condo outright, rent it out to others throughout the year, and then rent another one for yourself for the one week or whatever each year when you plan to take a vacation.

Another chilling thought — time-share condominiums are nearly impossible to sell. As we say in Chapter 7, the best time to think about selling is *before* you buy. Real estate is a relatively illiquid form of investment anyhow — why freeze your money solid in a time-share condo?

Vacation homes present a different problem. Most people who purchase a vacation home use it for only a few weeks during the year. The rest of the time, the property is left vacant, thus creating a cash drain. Now, if you are affluent enough to afford this luxury, we're not going to stand in your way and discourage you from owning more than one home. But many people who buy vacation homes aren't wealthy enough to afford them.

Before you buy a vacation property, examine your personal finances in order to determine whether you can still save enough each month after such a purchase to achieve your important financial goals, such as paying for higher education for your children or building your retirement nest egg. If you do buy a vacation home, buy a property that you can rent out during most of the time that you're not using it.

Residential properties are your best investment option

If you're going to invest in real estate, residential property should be your safest and wisest investment.

- First, such types of real estate are probably the most familiar to you because you've lived in (and perhaps bought) such properties already.
- Second, residential property should be easier for you to manage and deal with on an ongoing basis. (Be sure you are knowledgeable of current rent-control laws in your community.)

Commercial or retail real estate has many financial and legal nuances that you probably haven't dealt with (and probably don't want to deal with). Business real estate also tends to be more volatile in value because it is more easily overbuilt; and businesses, unlike people, can shrink in number during poor economic conditions. We're not saying that you should never try investing in this more-complicated type of property, but better for you to first learn to swim in a backyard pool before leaping straight into a shark-infested ocean.

Consider fixer-upper income property

Residential property that has curable defects (see Chapter 7) can be a good investment for people who can manage the repair and rehabilitation of property. You must buy such property at absolute rock-bottom price. To an investor, fixer-uppers can provide an income stream from rentals as well as an appreciation in the value of the property that can result from bringing the property back to its highest and best use.

Consider converting small apartment buildings to condos

In real estate markets like those found in densely populated urban areas, buying a multi-unit building and converting the units into condominiums can be extremely profitable. To make such a transformation succeed, you need a good real estate agent who knows the value of apartments as condos and a good real estate attorney. You also need a wise contractor who can help you estimate the costs of the work and the challenges involved in securing proper building permits.

Consider the property's cash flow

When you're considering the purchase of real estate for investment purposes, you must crunch some numbers. You don't need to remember any calculus (or even any high-school algebra) to do for these calculations — basic addition, subtraction, multiplication, and division will do.

In order to decide how much a specific property is worth (as a prospective buyer) and in order to understand the financial ramifications of your ownership of that property, you should calculate what's called the property's *cash flow*. You determine cash flow by summing the rental income that a property brings in on a monthly basis and then subtracting all the monthly expenses, such as the mortgage payment, property taxes, insurance, utility expenses that you (as the landlord) pay, repair and maintenance costs, advertising expenses, 5 percent (or more) vacancy factor, and so on. Be realistic and add up all the costs. If the property that you're buying is being used as investment real estate by its current owner, ask the sellers for a copy of "Schedule E" (Supplemental Income and Losses) from their income tax return.

Your rental losses are limited for tax purposes

If you purchase rental property that produces a negative cash flow, you should understand before you buy whether you can claim that loss on your personal income tax return. If you're a high-income earner — making more than $100,000 per year — your ability to deduct rental losses may be limited. If you're a really-high-income earner — making more than $150,000 per year — you may not be able to deduct any of your rental losses.

If you want to invest in real estate or stocks, bonds, mutual funds, small businesses, and the like, first invest your time in finding out what makes such investments tick and in learning how you can make informed decisions that fit with your personal financial situation and goals. Pick up a copy of Eric's *Investing For Dummies* to find out more about investing and investments.

Chapter 15

Ten Things to Consider When Selling Your Home

● ●

*1*f you buy a home, the odds are extraordinarily high that, someday, you will sell it — people who live their entire lives in their first home are rare. Selling a home generally is a good deal less complicated than buying one. But just because selling a home is easier than buying one doesn't mean that most people sell their homes properly.

If word gets out that you're considering selling your home, real estate agents will be attracted to you like a swarm of hungry mosquitoes are to the one person on a desert island. And when you sell a home, the IRS and state tax authorities will be waiting with open wallets to attempt to take a nice, large slice of your profits. So, in this chapter, we advise you about some important issues that you should weigh and ponder before you sell. And if you do decide to sell, we want you to do the best possible job of selling your home and avoiding the tax man (legally).

Why are you selling?

Start with the basics. If you're contemplating selling, consider whether your reasons for selling are good ones. For example, who wouldn't like to live in a larger home with more amenities and creature comforts? But if you hastily put your home on the market in order to buy a bigger one, you may be making a major mistake. If your next, more-expensive home stretches you too far financially, you may end up in ruin.

If you need to relocate for your job, or if you have had a major life change, moving may be a necessity. Even so, you should weigh the pros and cons of keeping your property versus selling. Start this analytic process by reading the rest of this chapter.

Can you afford to buy the next home?

If you want to buy a more costly property, such a move is known in the real estate business as *trading up*. Doing an honest assessment of whether you can really afford to trade up is imperative. As we say in Chapter 3, no mortgage lender or real estate agent can objectively answer that question for you. Based upon your income and down payment, the lender and agent can tell you the *most* that you can spend. They can't tell you what you can *afford* to spend and still accomplish your other financial and personal goals.

One of the biggest mistakes that trade-up homebuyers make is overextending themselves with debt to get into a more expensive property. The resulting impact on their budgets can be severe — no money may be left over for retirement savings, for educational expenses, or simply for having fun. In the worst cases, people have ended up losing their homes to foreclosure and bankruptcy when they were hit with unexpected events, such as job losses or the deaths of spouses who had inadequate insurance.

Before you buy your next home, go through the same personal finance exercises we advocate in Chapters 2 and 3. Get a handle on what you can really afford to spend on a home. Unless your income or assets have increased significantly since the time that you purchased your last home, you probably can't afford a much more expensive property. The most important issue for people to consider is how spending more money each month on a home will affect their ability to save for retirement.

What's it worth?

When you're ready to sell your home, you had better have a good understanding of what your home is worth. You (and your agent, if you're using one to sell your home) should analyze what comparable homes are currently selling for in your neck of the woods. For a discussion about comparable market analysis, see Chapter 9.

If you need to sell your home without wasting a ton of time and energy, do what smart retailers do: Price it to sell. We're not advocating that you give your home away, so to speak, but we are suggesting that you avoid inflating your asking price to a point far above what the comparables suggest that your home is worth.

You may be tempted to grossly overprice your home in the hope that an uneducated buyer may pay you more than the home is really worth. The danger in this strategy is that you won't find a fool who will part with all that money for your overpriced property, and no one else will bid on it. Then, as you lower the price closer to what the home is really worth, prospective buyers may be wary of buying your property because of the extended length of time that it's been on the market. In the end, you may have a hard time getting 100 percent of what your property is really worth.

Have you done your homework to find a good real estate agent?

When most people are ready to sell their homes, they enlist the services of a real estate agent to get the property sold. Good agents can be worth their commission if they know how to prepare the property for sale, market it, and get it sold for top dollar. Unlike when you're a homebuyer, your interests (as a seller) are aligned with a good agent's interests — the more you sell the property for, the more you net from the sale, and the more the agent gets paid.

Given how much homes actually cost (and how much they cost to sell and buy), you owe it to yourself to have a good agent representing you in the sale of your house. Be sure that the agent you select is not currently listing so many other properties for sale that the agent lacks enough time to properly service you. Also, the agent you worked with when you bought the home is not necessarily the best agent to hire, because different steps and expertise are required to sell (rather than buy) a home.

Listing agreements cover service, not sale

If you think that a *listing* is a contract between you and a real estate agent to sell your house, you're wrong. A listing isn't a contract of sale — it's a personal service contract. It has nothing to do with actually transferring your property to buyers. It only authorizes a broker to act as your agent in finding people who'll buy your house.

Two basic promises appear in listing agreements. Your broker promises to do his or her best to find buyers for your house. You agree to pay your broker a commission if the broker finds buyers who are ready, willing, and able to purchase your house under the price and terms of the listing agreement.

Here's where things get tricky. The listing doesn't obligate you to sell your house. However, it may obligate you (in rare circumstances) to pay your broker a commission even if you choose not to sell the property.

No matter how much time, energy, and money the broker spends on your behalf, you don't have to pay a commission if your broker can't produce an acceptable offer for you. Selling a house isn't the same as playing horseshoes. Close doesn't count in real estate brokerage.

Avoid signing a listing agreement that commits you to working exclusively with a broker for more than three months. If the broker does a good job and needs to renew the listing because your house hasn't sold yet, you can renew or extend the listing. If, conversely, the broker does a lousy job, you only have to suffer for three months.

Do you have the skills to sell the home yourself?

Some property owners possess the skills and time needed to sell a home themselves. Most don't. The carrot that may entice you to sell a home yourself is the avoidance of the 5- to 7-percent sales commission that agents will ask for before they attempt to sell your property. Don't forget, however, that half of this commission goes to a buyer's agents. Because most buyers work with agents (partly because the agents' services appear to be at no cost to the buyers), you'll only be potentially saving yourself 2.5 to 3.5 percent of the final selling price of your home by selling it without an agent on your side.

Interview several agents who've demonstrated that they know your neighborhood as a result of listing and selling houses in the area and ask them to prepare a comparable market analysis for your home. Avoid selecting the agent with the highest suggested listing price — some agents may try "buying" your listing by telling you what you want to hear regarding what your property is worth. Base your asking price on what comparable houses have sold for in the past six months. As we discuss in Chapter 8, ask each agent for an activity list of all the homes that they have sold over the past 12 months so that you can obtain references from property sellers who have worked with each agent.

Have you properly prepared the property for sale?

The real work of selling a home begins before you ever formally place it on the market for sale or allow the first prospective buyer through the front door. A home should be prepared for sale both inside and out. At a minimum, you should do the sort of cleanup work that you do before your parents (or perhaps the in-laws) visit — you know, scramble around the home cleaning *everything* up (or at least tossing it under beds and into closets!).

But there's more to be done than just running a vacuum (after you pick up the laundry from the floors) and doing the dishes. Have some good-but-brutally-honest friends and prospective agents that you're considering using walk through the house with you to point out defects and flaws that won't cost you an arm and a leg to fix (for example, repairing leaky faucets or painting areas in need of a new paint). Don't be defensive — take good notes! Avoid major projects, such as kitchen renovations, room additions, and the like. Rarely will you get a high enough additional sales price to compensate you for the extra costs of these major projects (not to mention remuneration for the value of the time that you spend in coordinating or doing the work).

Do you understand the property's hot buttons?

People don't buy homes — they buy a *hot button,* and the rest of the house goes with it. Hot buttons vary from house to house. Dynamite kitchens or baths, fireplaces, views, and gardens are often buyer turn-ons. Location is the hot button for people who *must* live in a certain neighborhood.

How can you determine your house's hot buttons? Think back to what appealed to you when you bought it. What you liked then will probably be the same hot buttons that will appeal to the next buyers. After you've identified the hot buttons, emphasize them in your listing statement, multiple-listing writeup, and newspaper ads. Successful sellers know what the buyers will buy before they begin the marketing process.

What are the financial ramifications of selling?

Before you sell your home, you should understand the financial consequences of the sale. For example, how much money will you spend on fix-up work? How much should you be netting from the sale in order to afford your next home? Unless you want to be the proud owner of two homes, we advocate selling your current home before you commit to buying another. You can ask for a long close of escrow and a rent back, if necessary, so that you have time to close the sale of your next home without camping out on the street. Be sure about these things up front so that you won't have nasty surprises along the way or after you sell.

Do you know how to roll over your profits when you sell?

When you sell your home, if it has appreciated since the time that you originally purchased it, you will owe what is called *capital gains tax* on your profit (see Chapter 13 for information about calculating your profit). However, and this is an important *however,* you can legally avoid paying this tax if you follow some relatively simple rules for rolling over your gain.

Basically, the IRS says that you can avoid this tax so long as you purchase your next home within two years — either before or after — of the sale of your present home *and* the next home costs as least as much as the one that you sell. Regardless of whether you're going to roll your gain over or not, you must report the gain to the IRS on Form 2119. Complete this important form for the year that you sell your home.

You may also be interested in knowing that if you're over 55 years old, the IRS allows you a one-time exclusion from taxation for up to $125,000 of capital gains from the sale of your primary residence if you do buy a less-costly replacement home!

Part VI
Appendixes

The 5th Wave   By Rich Tennant

"I'M ENTERING ALL THE BANK'S REQUIREMENTS FOR A MORTGAGE, AND I EITHER HAVE TO BUY A COMPUTER WITH MORE MEMORY OR START LOOKING FOR A SMALLER HOUSE."

In this part . . .

Don't let the word *appendix* scare you. This part includes such priceless goodies as a sample of a comprehensive purchase contract, an example of an excellent inspection report, and a glossary chock-full of the many less-than-intuitive terms tossed around in the real estate business.

Appendix A

Sample Real Estate Purchase Contract

● ●

*B*ecause a real estate purchase contract is a legal document, your real estate agent or lawyer should provide you with the appropriate contract form for your area and help you fill it out. As a rule, these contracts range from somewhat complex to quite complex and sometimes convoluted. Most purchase contracts include a warning that says something like this:

> "This is more than a receipt for money. It is intended to be a legally binding contract. Read it carefully."

Heed the warning!

Purchase contracts vary in length, complexity, and terms from state to state and, within a state, from one locality to another. This appendix includes a sample of the California Association of Realtors' real estate purchase contract. We chose California's contract not just because we live here, but also because it's one of the more comprehensive residential real estate contracts around.

Note that we left no spaces blank in our sample. Blank spaces are open invitations to confusion (at best) and deception (at worst)! Giving someone a contract with blank spaces above your signature is like giving someone a signed blank check. They can fill in whatever they want over your signature, and you may have to pay. Do not leave any spaces blank on your contract.

Another important thing to check is the contract's *revision date* — usually located in the bottom left or right corner of the page. Be sure that you're working on the most recent version of the purchase contract (9/95, in this case).

Here's a trivia question. Why did the buyers' agent sign the purchase contract? After all, the agent is neither the buyer nor the seller. (Hint: Read the bold face print on page 8 of our sample contract just above the agent's signature.) Ann Agent signed to give John and Mary Buyer a receipt for their $500 deposit and to confirm the agency relationship that she represents them exclusively. Now you're one of the very few people in the world who know why agents sign purchase contracts!

See Chapter 10 for a more in-depth discussion of Real Estate Purchase Contracts.

REAL ESTATE PURCHASE CONTRACT AND RECEIPT FOR DEPOSIT
THIS IS MORE THAN A RECEIPT FOR MONEY. IT IS INTENDED TO BE A LEGALLY BINDING CONTRACT. READ IT CAREFULLY.
CALIFORNIA ASSOCIATION OF REALTORS® (C.A.R.) STANDARD FORM
(FOR USE WITH ONE-TO-FOUR FAMILY RESIDENTIAL PROPERTY)

DATE: _JULY 1_ 19_96_ at _UTOPIA_ , California.
RECEIVED FROM _JOHN C. & MARY T. BUYER_ ("Buyer")
A DEPOSIT OF _FIVE HUNDRED AND NO/100_ Dollars $ _500.00_
TOWARD THE PURCHASE PRICE OF _ONE HUNDRED FIFTY THOUSAND AND NO/100_ Dollars $ _150,000.00_
FOR PURCHASE OF PROPERTY SITUATED IN _UTOPIA_ , COUNTY OF _WONDERFUL_ , California,
DESCRIBED AS _555 MAPLE STREET, A SINGLE-FAMILY DWELLING_ ("Property").

1. **FINANCING: THE OBTAINING OF THE LOANS BELOW IS A CONTINGENCY OF THIS AGREEMENT.** Buyer shall act diligently and in good faith to obtain the designated loans.

   A. **LOAN CONTINGENCY** shall remain in effect until: (Check only ONE of the following:)
   ☐ (1) The designated loans are funded and/or the assumption of existing financing is approved by lender and completed.
   OR ☒ (2) _30_ days from acceptance of the offer, by which time Buyer shall give to Seller written notice of Buyer's election to cancel this Agreement because of Buyer's inability to obtain the designated loans, or obtain approval of assumption of existing financing. If Buyer does not give Seller such notice, the contingency of obtaining the designated loans shall be removed by the method specified in paragraph 28.

   B. **BUYER'S DEPOSIT** .... $ _500.00_
   PAYABLE TO _ABC TITLE COMPANY_
   shall be deposited ☒ with Escrow Holder, ☐ into Broker's trust account, or ☐ _____
   by Personal Check, (or, if checked:) ☐ Cashier's Check, ☐ Cash, or ☐ _____
   TO BE HELD UNCASHED UNTIL the next business day after acceptance of the offer, or ☐ _____

   C. **INCREASED DEPOSIT** .... $ _4,000.00_
   within _10_ days from acceptance of the offer, shall be deposited
   ☒ with Escrow Holder, ☐ into Broker's trust account, or ☐ _____

   D. **BALANCE OF DOWN PAYMENT** .... $ _25,500.00_
   to be deposited with Escrow Holder within sufficient time to close escrow.

   E. **FIRST LOAN IN THE AMOUNT OF** .... $ _120,000.00_
   ☒ NEW First Deed of Trust in favor of ☒ LENDER, ☐ SELLER; or
   ☐ ASSUMPTION of Existing First Deed of Trust;
   encumbering the Property, securing a note payable at approximately $ _923.00_ per month, at maximum interest of _8.5_ %
   fixed rate, or ____ % initial adjustable rate with a maximum lifetime interest rate cap of ____ %, balance due in _____ years.
   Buyer shall pay loan fees/points not to exceed _TWO (2) PERCENT OF LOAN AMOUNT_

   F. **SECOND LOAN IN THE AMOUNT OF** .... $ _N/A_
   ☐ NEW Second Deed of Trust in favor of ☐ LENDER, ☐ SELLER; or
   ☐ ASSUMPTION of Existing Second Deed of Trust;
   encumbering the Property, securing a note payable at approximately $ _____ per month, at maximum interest of ____ %
   fixed rate, or ____ % initial adjustable rate with a maximum lifetime interest rate cap of ____ %, balance due in _____ years.
   Buyer shall pay loan fees/points not to exceed _____

   G. **ADDITIONAL FINANCING TERMS:** _N/A_

   H. **TOTAL PURCHASE PRICE,** not including costs of obtaining loans and other closing costs .... $ _150,000.00_

   I. **OBTAINING DEPOSIT, DOWN PAYMENT, AND OTHER CLOSING COSTS** by Buyer is NOT a contingency, unless otherwise agreed in writing.

   J. **FHA/VA FINANCING:** ☐ (If checked:) _N/A_
   (1) Seller shall pay ____ % of loan as discount points.
   (2) Seller shall pay other fees which Buyer is not permitted to pay, not to exceed $ _____ .
   (3) Seller shall pay the cost of repairs required by lender, not otherwise provided for in this Agreement, not to exceed $ _____ .
   (4) All other charges to obtain financing shall be paid by Buyer unless otherwise agreed in writing.
   (5) OTHER: _____

   K. **IF THIS IS AN ALL CASH OFFER,** Buyer shall, within 5 (or ☐ ____) days from acceptance, provide to Seller written verification of sufficient funds to close this transaction. Seller may cancel this Agreement in writing within 5 (or ☐ ____) days (1) after receipt of the verification, if Seller disapproves it, or (2) after the time to provide the verification expires, if Buyer fails to provide it.

   L. **LOAN APPLICATIONS; PREQUALIFICATION:**
   (1) For **NEW and ASSUMED lender financing:** Within 10 (or ☐ ____) days from acceptance, Buyer shall provide to Seller a letter from lender stating that, based on a review of Buyer's written application and credit report, Buyer is prequalified for the NEW and/or ASSUMED loans indicated above. If Buyer fails to provide such letter within that time, Seller may cancel this Agreement in writing.
   (2) For **SELLER financing:** Within 5 (or ☐ ____) days after acceptance: (a) Buyer shall submit to Seller a completed loan application on FNMA/FHLMC Uniform Residential Loan Application; (b) Buyer authorizes Seller and/or Brokers to obtain, at Buyer's expense, a copy of Buyer's credit report; (c) Buyer shall provide any supporting documentation reasonably requested by Seller. Seller may cancel this Agreement in writing if Buyer fails to provide such documents within that time, or if Seller disapproves the application, credit report, or supporting documentation, within 5 (or ☐ ____) days from receipt of those documents.

Buyer and Seller acknowledge receipt of copy of this page, which constitutes Page 1 of _8_ Pages.
Buyer's Initials (_JCB_) (_MJB_) Seller's Initials (_____) (_____)

OFFICE USE ONLY
Reviewed by Broker or Designee _____
Date _____

QUADRUPLICATE
REAL ESTATE PURCHASE CONTRACT AND RECEIPT FOR DEPOSIT (DLF-14 PAGE 1 OF 8)

MR NOV 95

Property Address: <u>555 MAPLE STREET, UTOPIA, CA</u> _____ <u>JULY 1</u> , 19<u>96</u>

M. EXISTING LOANS: For existing loans to be taken over by Buyer, Seller shall, within the time specified in paragraph 28A(4), request and provide to Buyer copies of all applicable notes and deeds of trust, loan balances, and current interest rates. Buyer shall, within the time specified in paragraph 28A(2), provide written notice to Seller of any items reasonably disapproved. Differences between estimated and actual loan balances shall be adjusted at close of escrow by ☐ cash down payment, ☐ seller financing, or ☐ _____. Impound accounts, if any, shall be assigned and charged to Buyer and credited to Seller, (or, if checked:) ☐ _____. IF THIS IS AN ASSUMPTION OF A VA LOAN, THE SALE IS CONTINGENT UPON SELLER BEING PROVIDED A RELEASE OF LIABILITY AND SUBSTITUTION OF ELIGIBILITY, UNLESS OTHERWISE AGREED IN WRITING.

N. LOAN FEATURES: LOAN DOCUMENTS CONTAIN A NUMBER OF IMPORTANT FEATURES AFFECTING THE RIGHTS OF THE BORROWER AND LENDER. READ ALL LOAN DOCUMENTS CAREFULLY.

O. ADDITIONAL SELLER FINANCING TERMS: The following terms apply ONLY to financing extended by Seller under this Agreement. The maximum interest rate specified in paragraphs 1E and/or 1F above, as applicable, shall be the actual fixed interest rate for Seller financing. Buyer's promissory note, deed of trust, and other documents, as appropriate, shall incorporate and implement the following additional terms:

(1) Deed of trust shall contain a REQUEST FOR NOTICE OF DEFAULT on senior loans.

(2) Buyer shall sign and pay for a REQUEST FOR NOTICE OF DELINQUENCY prior to close of escrow and at any future time if requested by Seller.

(3) Note and deed of trust shall contain an acceleration clause making the loan due, when permitted by law, at Seller's option, upon the sale or transfer of the Property or any interest in it.

(4) Note shall contain a late charge of 6% of the installment due, or $5.00, whichever is greater, if the installment is not received within 10 days of the date it is due.

(5) Title insurance coverage in the form of a joint protection policy shall be provided insuring Seller's deed of trust interest in the Property. Any increased cost over owner's policy shall be paid by Buyer.

(6) Tax Service shall be obtained and paid for by Buyer to notify Seller if property taxes have not been paid.

(7) Buyer shall provide and maintain fire and extended coverage insurance, during the period of the seller financing, in an amount sufficient to replace all improvements on the Property, or equal to the total encumbrances against the Property, whichever is less, with a loss payable endorsement in favor of Seller. BUYER AND SELLER ARE ADVISED THAT (a) INSURANCE POLICIES VARY IN THE TYPES OF RISKS COVERED, (b) EARTHQUAKE, FLOOD, AND OTHER OPTIONAL TYPES OF COVERAGE ARE AVAILABLE, and (c) BUYER AND SELLER SHOULD DISCUSS THESE SUBJECTS WITH AN INSURANCE AGENT OR INSURANCE BROKER.

(8) The addition, deletion, or substitution of any person or entity under this Agreement, or to title, prior to close of escrow, shall require Seller's written consent. Seller may grant or withhold consent in Seller's sole discretion. Any additional or substituted person or entity shall, if requested by Seller, submit to Seller the same documentation as required for the original named Buyer. Seller and/or Brokers may obtain a credit report, at Buyer's expense, on any such person or entity.

(9) Buyer and Seller shall each provide to the other, through escrow, their Social Security Numbers or Taxpayer Identification Numbers.

NOTE: If the Property contains 1 to 4 dwelling units, Buyer and Seller shall execute a Seller Financing Disclosure Statement (C.A.R. Form SFD-14) (Civil Code §§2956-2967), if applicable, as provided by arranger of credit, as soon as practicable prior to execution of security documents. ESCROW HOLDER SHALL BE INSTRUCTED BY BUYER AND SELLER TO PERFORM, ARRANGE, OR VERIFY ITEMS 1-9 ABOVE, AS APPLICABLE, PRIOR TO CLOSE OF ESCROW.

2. ESCROW: Escrow shall close ☒ within <u>60</u> days from acceptance of the offer, or ☐ on <u>N/A</u> , 19_____. This Agreement shall, to the extent feasible, constitute escrow instructions of Buyer and Seller. Escrow instructions consistent with this Agreement shall be signed by Buyer and Seller and delivered to <u>ABC TITLE COMPANY</u> , the designated Escrow Holder, ☒ within <u>7</u> days after acceptance of the offer, ☐ at least ___ days before close of escrow, ☐ or _____. Escrow fee to be paid as follows: <u>ACCORDING TO LOCAL CUSTOM</u> . Escrow instructions may include matters required to close this transaction which are not covered by this Agreement. The omission from escrow instructions of any provision in this Agreement shall not constitute a waiver of the provision or the contractual rights or obligations of any party. Any change in terms or provisions of this Agreement requires the mutual, written consent of the Buyer and Seller. Buyer and Seller hereby jointly instruct Escrow Holder and Brokers (a) that Buyer's deposits placed into escrow or into Broker's trust account shall be held as a good faith deposit toward the completion of this transaction, and (b) to pay compensation due Brokers under this Agreement. Release of Buyer's funds will require mutual, signed release instructions from both Buyer and Seller, judicial decision, or arbitration award.

3. TITLE AND VESTING: Buyer shall be provided a current preliminary (title) report covering the Property. Buyer shall, within the time specified in paragraph 28A(2), provide written notice to Seller of any items reasonably disapproved. At close of escrow:

A. Title to the Property shall be transferred by grant deed (or, for stock cooperative, by assignment of stock certificate), and shall include OIL, MINERAL, and WATER rights, if currently owned by Seller, unless otherwise agreed in writing.

B. Title shall be free of liens, except as provided in this Agreement.

C. Title shall be subject to all other encumbrances, easements, covenants, conditions, restrictions, rights, and other matters, which are either:

(1) Of record and shown in the preliminary (title) report, unless disapproved in writing by Buyer within the time specified in paragraph 28A(2); or

(2) Disclosed to or discovered by Buyer prior to the close of escrow, unless disapproved in writing by Buyer within the time specified in paragraph 28A(1) or 28A(2), whichever is later.

D. Buyer shall be provided a California Land Title Association (CLTA) owner's policy issued by <u>ABC TITLE</u> _____ Company, at <u>ACCORDING TO LOCAL CUSTOM</u> expense.

NOTE: (1) A preliminary (title) report is only an offer by the title insurer to issue a policy of title insurance and may not contain every item affecting title. (2) An American Land Title Association (ALTA-R) policy may provide greater protection for Buyer and may be available at the same or slightly higher cost than a CLTA policy. (3) The designated title company can provide information, at Buyer's request, about availability and desirability of various title insurance coverages. (4) If Buyer desires an ALTA-R owner's policy or other title coverage, Buyer shall so instruct Escrow Holder and pay the increased cost, if any, over a CLTA policy. (5) ALTA LENDER'S title insurance policy, if required, shall be paid by Buyer. (6) For Seller financing, paragraph 1O(5) provides for a joint protection policy. (7) Title shall vest as designated in Buyer's escrow instructions. **(THE MANNER OF TAKING TITLE MAY HAVE SIGNIFICANT LEGAL AND TAX CONSEQUENCES. BUYER SHOULD GIVE THIS MATTER SERIOUS CONSIDERATION.)**

4. PRORATIONS:

A. Real property taxes and assessments, interest, rents, Homeowners' Association regular dues and regular assessments, premiums on insurance assumed by Buyer, and payments on bonds and assessments assumed by Buyer, shall be PAID CURRENT and prorated between Buyer and Seller, as of the date of close of escrow, (or if checked:) ☐ <u>N/A</u>

B. Payments on Mello-Roos and other Special Assessment District bonds and assessments which are now a lien, and payments on Homeowners' Association special assessments which are now a lien, shall be PAID CURRENT and prorated between Buyer and Seller as of the date of close of escrow, with payments that are not yet due to be assumed by Buyer WITHOUT CREDIT toward the purchase price, (or if checked:) ☐ <u>N/A</u>

C. County transfer tax or transfer fee shall be paid by <u>ACCORDING TO LOCAL CUSTOM</u>
City transfer tax or transfer fee shall be paid by <u>ACCORDING TO LOCAL CUSTOM</u>
Homeowners' Association transfer fee shall be paid by <u>N/A</u>

D. THE PROPERTY WILL BE REASSESSED UPON CHANGE OF OWNERSHIP. THIS WILL AFFECT THE TAXES TO BE PAID. Any supplemental tax bills shall be paid as follows: (1) for periods after close of escrow, by Buyer (or by final acquiring party, if part of an exchange), and (2) for periods prior to close of escrow, by Seller. TAX BILLS ISSUED AFTER CLOSE OF ESCROW SHALL BE HANDLED DIRECTLY BETWEEN BUYER AND SELLER.

Buyer and Seller acknowledge receipt of copy of this page, which constitutes Page 2 of <u>8</u> Pages.
Buyer's Initials <u>JCB</u> (<u>MJB</u>) Seller's Initials (_____) (_____)

OFFICE USE ONLY
Reviewed by Broker or Designee _____
Date _____

EQUAL HOUSING OPPORTUNITY
MR NOV 95

Property Address: **555 MAPLE STREET, UTOPIA, CA** **JULY 1** 19 **96**

5. **OCCUPANCY:** Buyer ☒ does, ☐ does not, intend to occupy Property as Buyer's primary residence.

6. **POSSESSION AND KEYS:** Seller shall deliver possession and occupancy of the Property to Buyer ☒ on the date of close of escrow at **12:01** AM/(PM) or ☐ no later than ___ days after date of close of escrow at ___ AM/PM, or ☐ _____. Property shall be vacant unless otherwise agreed in writing. If applicable, Seller and Buyer shall execute Interim Occupancy Agreement (C.A.R. Form IOA-14) or Residential Lease Agreement After Sale (C.A.R. Form RLAS-14). Seller shall provide keys and/or means to operate all Property locks, mailboxes, security systems, alarms, and garage door openers. If applicable, Buyer may be required to pay a deposit to a Homeowners' Association (HOA) to obtain keys to accessible HOA facilities.

7. **BUYER'S INVESTIGATION OF PROPERTY CONDITION:** Buyer's acceptance of the condition of the Property is a contingency of this Agreement. Buyer shall have the right to conduct inspections, investigations, tests, surveys, and other studies ("Inspections") at Buyer's expense. Buyer shall, within the time specified in paragraph 28A(1), complete these Inspections and notify Seller in writing of any items disapproved. Buyer is strongly advised to exercise these rights and to make Buyer's own selection of professionals with appropriate qualifications to conduct Inspections of the entire Property. **IF BUYER DOES NOT EXERCISE THESE RIGHTS, BUYER IS ACTING AGAINST THE ADVICE OF BROKERS. BUYER UNDERSTANDS THAT ALTHOUGH CONDITIONS AND DEFECTS ARE OFTEN DIFFICULT TO LOCATE AND DISCOVER, ALL REAL PROPERTY AND IMPROVEMENTS CONTAIN DEFECTS AND CONDITIONS WHICH ARE NOT READILY APPARENT AND WHICH MAY AFFECT THE VALUE OR DESIRABILITY OF THE PROPERTY. BUYER AND SELLER ARE AWARE THAT BROKERS DO NOT GUARANTEE, AND IN NO WAY ASSUME RESPONSIBILITY FOR, THE CONDITION OF THE PROPERTY. BUYER IS ALSO AWARE OF BUYER'S OWN AFFIRMATIVE DUTY TO EXERCISE REASONABLE CARE TO PROTECT HIMSELF OR HERSELF, INCLUDING THOSE FACTS WHICH ARE KNOWN TO OR WITHIN THE DILIGENT ATTENTION AND OBSERVATION OF THE BUYER (Civil Code §2079.5).**

Seller shall make the Property available for all Inspections. Buyer shall keep the Property free and clear of liens; indemnify and hold Seller harmless from all liability, claims, demands, damages, and costs; and repair all damages arising from the Inspections. **No Inspections may be made by any governmental building or zoning inspector or government employee without the prior written consent of Seller, unless required by local law.** Buyer shall provide to Seller, at no cost, upon request of Seller, complete copies of all Inspection reports obtained by Buyer concerning the Property.

BUYER IS STRONGLY ADVISED TO INVESTIGATE THE CONDITION AND SUITABILITY OF ALL ASPECTS OF THE PROPERTY AND ALL MATTERS AFFECTING THE VALUE OR DESIRABILITY OF THE PROPERTY, INCLUDING, BUT NOT LIMITED TO, THE FOLLOWING:

A. CONDITION OF SYSTEMS AND COMPONENTS: Built-in appliances, foundation, roof, plumbing, heating, air conditioning, electrical, mechanical, security, pool/spa, and other structural and non-structural systems and components, any personal property included in the sale, and energy efficiency of the Property.

B. SIZE AND AGE: Square footage, room dimensions, lot size, and age of Property improvements. (Any numerical statements regarding these items are APPROXIMATIONS ONLY, have not been and will not be verified, and should not be relied upon by Buyer.)

C. LINES AND BOUNDARIES: Property lines and boundaries. (Fences, hedges, walls, and other natural or constructed barriers or markers do not necessarily identify true Property boundaries. Property lines may be verified by survey.)

D. WASTE DISPOSAL: Type, size, adequacy, capacity, and condition of sewer and septic systems and components should be checked. (Property may not be connected to sewer, and applicable fees may not have been paid. Septic tank may need to be pumped and leach field may need to be inspected.)

E. GOVERNMENTAL REQUIREMENTS AND LIMITATIONS: Possible absence of required governmental permits, inspections, certificates, or other determinations affecting the Property; limitations, restrictions, and requirements affecting the use of the Property, future development, zoning, building, size, governmental permits, and inspections.

F. RENT AND OCCUPANCY CONTROL: Some cities and counties impose restrictions which may limit the amount of rent that can lawfully be charged, and/or the maximum number of persons who can lawfully occupy the Property.

G. WATER AND UTILITIES; WELL SYSTEMS AND COMPONENTS: Water and utility availability and use restrictions. Adequacy, condition, and performance of well systems and components.

H. ENVIRONMENTAL HAZARDS: Potential environmental hazards including asbestos, formaldehyde, radon, methane, other gases, lead-based paint, other lead contamination, fuel or chemical storage tanks, contaminated soil or water, hazardous waste, waste disposal sites, electromagnetic fields, nuclear sources, and other substances, materials, products, or conditions.

I. GEOLOGIC CONDITIONS: Geologic/seismic conditions, soil and terrain stability, suitability, and drainage.

J. NEIGHBORHOOD, AREA, AND SUBDIVISION CONDITIONS: Neighborhood or area conditions including schools, proximity and adequacy of law enforcement, proximity to commercial, industrial, or agricultural activities, crime statistics, fire protection, other governmental services, existing and proposed transportation, construction, and development which may affect noise, view, or traffic, airport noise, noise or odor from any source, wild and domestic animals, other nuisances, hazards, or circumstances, facilities and condition of common areas of common interest subdivisions, and possible lack of compliance with any Homeowners' Association requirements.

K. PERSONAL FACTORS: Conditions and influences of significance to certain cultures and/or religions, and personal needs, requirements, and preferences of Buyer.

L. VERIFICATION: Brokers have not and will not verify any of the items above, unless otherwise agreed in writing.

BUYER SHOULD MAKE FURTHER INQUIRIES: Buyer is advised to make further inquiries and to consult government agencies, lenders, insurance agents, architects, and other appropriate persons and entities concerning the use of the Property under applicable building, zoning, fire, health, and safety codes, and for evaluation of potential hazards.

8. **CONDITION OF PROPERTY:** No warranties or representations are made regarding the adequacy, condition, performance, or suitability of the Property, or any of its systems or components, except as specifically agreed in writing.
(Check ONLY paragraph A or B; do NOT check both.)

☒ **A. SELLER WARRANTY:** (If A is checked, do NOT also check B.)
Seller warrants that at the time possession is made available to Buyer:
(1) Roof shall be free of leaks KNOWN to Seller or DISCOVERED during escrow.
(2) Built-in appliances (including free-standing oven and range, if included in sale), plumbing, heating, air conditioning, electrical, water, sewer, and pool/spa systems, if any, shall be operative. (Septic/Well systems are **not** covered in this paragraph. Read paragraph 19.)
(3) Plumbing systems, shower pans, and shower enclosures shall be free of leaks KNOWN to Seller or DISCOVERED during escrow.
(4) All fire, safety, and structural defects in chimneys and fireplaces KNOWN to Seller or DISCOVERED during escrow shall be repaired by Seller.
NOTE TO BUYER: This warranty is limited to items specified in this paragraph 8A. Items discovered in Buyer's Inspections which are not covered by this paragraph shall be governed by the procedure in paragraphs 7 and 28.
NOTE TO SELLER: Disclosures in the Real Estate Transfer Disclosure Statement (C.A.R. Form TDS-14), and items discovered in Buyer's Inspections, do NOT eliminate Seller's obligations under this warranty unless specifically agreed in writing.

OR ☐ **B. "AS-IS" CONDITION:** (If B is checked, do NOT also check A.) **N/A**
Property is sold "AS IS," in its present condition, as of the time of acceptance of the offer, without warranty. Seller shall not be responsible for making corrections or repairs of any nature **EXCEPT:**
(1) Property, including pool/spa, landscaping, and grounds, shall be maintained in substantially the same condition as on the date of acceptance of the offer.
(2) SELLER SHALL HAVE WATER, GAS, AND ELECTRICAL UTILITIES ON FOR BUYER'S INSPECTIONS AND THROUGH THE DATE POSSESSION IS MADE AVAILABLE TO BUYER.
(3) This paragraph does not relieve Seller of contractual obligations, if any, under paragraph 13 (Smoke Detector(s) and Water Heater Bracing), paragraph 14 (Retrofit), paragraph 19 (Septic/Sewer/Well System(s)), paragraph 20 (Pest Control), and elsewhere in this Agreement.
(4) _____

NOTE TO BUYER AND SELLER: Buyer retains the right to disapprove the condition of the Property based upon items discovered in Buyer's Inspections under paragraph 7. **SELLER REMAINS OBLIGATED TO DISCLOSE KNOWN MATERIAL DEFECTS AND TO MAKE OTHER DISCLOSURES REQUIRED BY LAW.**

Buyer and Seller acknowledge receipt of copy of this page, which constitutes Page 3 of **8** Pages.
Buyer's Initials (**JCB**) (**M2B**) Seller's Initials (_____) (_____)

OFFICE USE ONLY
Reviewed by Broker or Designee _____
Date _____

EQUAL HOUSING OPPORTUNITY
MR NOV 95

REAL ESTATE PURCHASE CONTRACT AND RECEIPT FOR DEPOSIT (DLF-14 PAGE 3 OF 8)

Property Address: 555 MAPLE STREET, UTOPIA, CA   JULY 1 19 96

9. TRANSFER DISCLOSURE STATEMENT; MELLO-ROOS NOTICE: Unless exempt:

  A. A Real Estate Transfer Disclosure Statement (TDS) (C.A.R. Form TDS-14) shall be completed by Seller and delivered to Buyer (Civil Code §§1102-1102.15). Buyer shall sign and return a copy of the TDS to Seller or Seller's agent. Buyer shall be provided a TDS within 5 (or ☐ ____) days from acceptance of the offer, unless previously provided to Buyer.

  B. Seller shall make a good faith effort to obtain a disclosure notice from any local agencies which levy on the Property a special tax pursuant to the Mello-Roos Community, Facilities Act, and shall promptly deliver to Buyer any such notice made available by those agencies.

  C. If the TDS or the Mello-Roos disclosure notice, or a supplemental or amended disclosure under paragraph 10, is delivered to Buyer after the offer is signed, Buyer shall have the right to terminate this Agreement within three (3) days after delivery in person, or five (5) days after delivery by deposit in the mail, by giving written notice of termination to Seller or Seller's agent.

  D. Disclosure in the TDS, or exemptions from providing it, do not eliminate Seller's obligation to disclose known material defects, or to meet Seller's other obligations under this Agreement.

10. SUBSEQUENT DISCLOSURES: In the event Seller, prior to close of escrow, becomes aware of adverse conditions materially affecting the Property, or any material inaccuracy in disclosures, information, or representations previously provided to Buyer (including those made in a Real Estate Transfer Disclosure Statement (TDS) pursuant to Civil Code §1102, et seq.), Seller shall promptly provide a supplemental or amended disclosure, in writing, covering those items. If Buyer disapproves of any conditions so disclosed, Buyer may terminate this Agreement under the procedure in paragraph 9C.

11. PROPERTY DISCLOSURES: When applicable to the Property and required by law, Seller shall provide to Buyer, at Seller's expense, the following disclosures and information. Buyer shall then, within the time specified in paragraph 28A(2), investigate the disclosures and information, and provide written notice to Seller of any item disapproved pursuant to paragraphs 11A-11D(2) below.

  A. **GEOLOGIC, EARTHQUAKE AND SEISMIC HAZARD ZONES DISCLOSURE:** If the Property is located in an Earthquake Fault Zone (Special Studies Zone) (EFZ), (Public Resources Code §§2621-2625), Seismic Hazard Zone (SHZ) (Public Resources Code §§2690-2699.6), or in a locally designated geologic, seismic, or other hazard zone or area where disclosure is required by law, Seller shall, within the time specified in paragraph 28A(3), disclose to Buyer in writing these facts and any other information required by law. (GEOLOGIC, SEISMIC AND FLOOD HAZARD DISCLOSURE (C.A.R. Form GFD-14) SHALL SATISFY THIS REQUIREMENT.) Construction or development of any structure may be restricted in such zones. Disclosure of EFZs and SHZs is required only if maps, or information contained in such maps, are "reasonably available" (Public Resources Code §§2621.9(c)(1) and 2694(c)(1)).

  B. **SPECIAL FLOOD HAZARD AREAS:** If the Property is located in a Special Flood Hazard Area designated by the Federal Emergency Management Agency (FEMA), Seller shall, within the time specified in paragraph 28A(3), disclose this fact to Buyer in writing. (GEOLOGIC, SEISMIC AND FLOOD HAZARD DISCLOSURE (C.A.R. Form GFD-14) SHALL SATISFY THIS REQUIREMENT.) Government regulations may impose building restrictions and requirements which may substantially impact and limit construction and remodeling of improvements in such areas. Flood insurance may be required by lender. In addition, Seller will notify Buyer if Seller has received federal flood disaster assistance on the Property, in which case, Buyer will be required to maintain flood insurance.

  C. **STATE FIRE RESPONSIBILITY AREAS:** If the Property is located in a State Fire Responsibility Area, Seller shall, within the time specified in paragraph 28A(3), disclose this fact to Buyer in writing (Public Resources Code §4136). Disclosure may be made in the Real Estate Transfer Disclosure Statement (C.A.R. Form TDS-14). Government regulations may impose building restrictions and requirements which may substantially impact and limit construction and remodeling of improvements in such areas. Disclosure of these areas is required only if the Seller has actual knowledge that the Property is located in such an area or if maps of such areas have been provided to the county assessor's office.

  D. **EARTHQUAKE SAFETY:**

  (1) **PRE-1960 PROPERTIES:** If the Property was built prior to 1960 and contains ONE TO FOUR DWELLING UNITS of conventional light frame construction, Seller shall, unless exempt, within the time specified in paragraph 28A(3), provide to Buyer: (a) a copy of "The Homeowner's Guide to Earthquake Safety," and (b) written disclosure of known seismic deficiencies (Government Code §§8897-8897.5).

  (2) **PRE-1975 PROPERTIES:** If the Property was built prior to 1975 and contains RESIDENTIAL, COMMERCIAL, OR OTHER STRUCTURES constructed of masonry or pre-cast concrete, with wood frame floors or roofs, Seller shall, unless exempt, within the time specified in paragraph 28A(3), provide to Buyer a copy of "The Commercial Property Owner's Guide to Earthquake Safety" (Government Code §§8893-8893.5).

  (3) **ALL PROPERTIES:** If the booklets described in paragraphs 11D(1) and 11D(2) are not required, Buyer is advised that they are available and contain important information that may be useful for ALL TYPES OF PROPERTY.

  E. **ENVIRONMENTAL HAZARDS AND ENERGY EFFICIENCY BOOKLETS:** "Environmental Hazards: Guide for Homeowners and Buyers" booklet, and a home energy rating booklet, when available, contain useful information for ALL TYPES OF PROPERTY.

  F. **LEAD-BASED PAINT:** For residential property constructed prior to 1978, when effective, Buyer and Seller are required to sign a lead-based paint disclosure form(s). (DISCLOSURE AND ACKNOWLEDGMENT OF LEAD-BASED PAINT BEFORE SALE (C.A.R. Form FLS-14), when applicable, and/or NOTICE TO PURCHASERS OF HOUSING CONSTRUCTED BEFORE 1978 (C.A.R. Form LPD-14) for FHA-financed property, shall satisfy this requirement.) In addition, when effective, Buyer shall be furnished a copy of "Protect Your Family From Lead in Your Home" booklet.

12. CONDOMINIUM/COMMON INTEREST SUBDIVISION: If the Property is a unit in a condominium, planned development, or other common interest subdivision:

  A. The Property has _____ parking spaces assigned to it. N/A

  B. The current regular Homeowners' Association (HOA) dues/assessments are $ _____ ☐ Monthly, ☐ _____

  C. Seller shall, within the time specified in paragraph 28A(4), request and provide to Buyer any known pending special assessments, claims, or litigation; copies of covenants, conditions, and restrictions; articles of incorporation; by-laws; other governing documents; most current financial statement distributed (Civil Code §1365); statement regarding limited enforceability of age restrictions, if applicable; current HOA statement showing any unpaid assessments (Civil Code §1368); any other documents required by law; and the most recent 12 months of HOA minutes, if available. Buyer shall, within the time specified in paragraph 28A(2), provide written notice to Seller of any items disapproved. Cost of obtaining those items shall be paid by Seller.

  D. No warranty is made regarding the Property's compliance with any governing document or HOA requirements, unless agreed in writing.

13. SMOKE DETECTOR(S) AND WATER HEATER BRACING: State law requires that residences be equipped with operable smoke detector(s), and that all water heaters must be braced, anchored, or strapped to resist falling or horizontal displacement due to earthquake. Local law may impose additional requirements. Unless exempt, Seller shall, prior to close of escrow, provide to Buyer a written statement of compliance and any other documents required, in accordance with applicable state and local laws. (SMOKE DETECTOR AND WATER HEATER STATEMENT OF COMPLIANCE (C.A.R. Form SDC-14) SHALL SATISFY THE STATE PORTION OF THIS REQUIREMENT.) Additional smoke detector(s) and water heater bracing, anchoring, or strapping, if required, shall be installed at Seller's expense prior to close of escrow.

14. RETROFIT: ☐ Buyer, ☒ Seller, shall pay the cost of compliance with any minimum mandatory government retrofit standards and inspections required as a condition of closing escrow under local, state, or federal law, including, but not limited to, repairs required for mandatory compliance with building and safety requirements, and energy and utility efficiency requirements, EXCEPT: NONE , and except as otherwise agreed in writing.

15. GOVERNMENTAL COMPLIANCE:

  A. Seller represents that Seller has no knowledge of any notice, filed or issued against the Property, of violations of city, county, state, or federal building, zoning, fire, or health: laws, codes, statutes, ordinances, regulations, or rules, EXCEPT: NONE

  B. Seller shall promptly disclose to Buyer any improvements, additions, alterations, or repairs ("Repairs") made by Seller or known to Seller to have been made without required governmental permits, final inspections, and approvals.

  C. If Seller receives notice or is made aware of any of the above violations prior to close of escrow, Seller shall immediately notify Buyer in writing. Buyer shall, within the time specified in paragraph 28A(2), provide written notice to Seller of any items disapproved.

  D. Nothing in this paragraph relieves Seller of any other obligations in this Agreement. Neither Buyer nor Seller shall be required to make Repairs to the Property for any purpose, unless agreed in writing between Buyer and Seller, or required by law as a condition of closing escrow. No warranty is made concerning the presence or absence of building permits or inspections, or compliance or lack of compliance with building codes, unless agreed in writing.

Buyer and Seller acknowledge receipt of copy of this page, which constitutes Page 4 of __8__ Pages.

Buyer's Initials (JCB) (MJB)   Seller's Initials (____) (____)

OFFICE USE ONLY
Reviewed by Broker or Designee ____
Date ____

EQUAL HOUSING OPPORTUNITY
MTR NOV 95

QUADRUPLICATE
REAL ESTATE PURCHASE CONTRACT AND RECEIPT FOR DEPOSIT (DLF-14 PAGE 4 OF 8)

Property Address: _555 MAPLE STREET, UTOPIA, CA_ _JULY 1_, 19_96_

16. FIXTURES: All EXISTING fixtures and fittings that are attached to the Property, or for which special openings have been made, are INCLUDED IN THE PURCHASE PRICE (unless excluded below), and shall be transferred free of liens. These include, but are not limited to, existing electrical, lighting, plumbing and heating fixtures, fireplace inserts, solar systems, built-in appliances, screens, awnings, shutters, window coverings, attached floor coverings, television antennas, satellite dishes and related equipment, private integrated telephone systems, air coolers/conditioners, pool/spa equipment, water softeners (if owned by Seller), security systems/alarms (if owned by Seller), garage door openers/remote controls, attached fireplace equipment, mailbox, in-ground landscaping including trees/shrubs, and _____

ITEMS EXCLUDED: _NONE_

17. PERSONAL PROPERTY: The following items of personal property, free of liens and without warranty of condition (unless provided in paragraph 8A) or fitness for use, are included: _ALL APPLIANCES NOW IN HOME, ENTRY HALL MIRROR & SWING SET IN BACKYARD_

18. HOME WARRANTY PLANS: Buyer and Seller are informed that home warranty plans are available to provide additional protection and benefit to Buyer and Seller.
☐ (If checked:) Buyer and Seller elect to purchase a one-year home warranty plan with the following optional coverage: _N/A_
to be paid by _____, and to be issued by _____, at a cost not to exceed $_____ Company.

19. SEPTIC/SEWER/WELL SYSTEMS: Prior to close of escrow: _N/A_
A. (If checked:) ☐ Buyer, ☐ Seller, shall pay to have septic system inspected and certified as operative.
B. (If checked:) ☐ Buyer, ☐ Seller, shall pay to have septic system pumped if required by inspector for certification.
C. (If checked:) ☐ Buyer, ☐ Seller, shall pay for sewer connection, if required by local law in effect prior to close of escrow.
D. (If checked:) ☐ Buyer, ☐ Seller, shall pay to have wells tested for potability.
E. (If checked:) ☐ Buyer, ☐ Seller, shall pay to have wells tested for productivity to produce a minimum of ____ gallons per minute (GPM).
F. All testing shall comply with any local laws pertaining to testing. Buyer shall, within the time specified in paragraph 28, provide written notice to Seller of any items disapproved under paragraph 19D or 19E.
NO WARRANTY is made as to the appropriate type, size, adequacy, or capacity of the septic, sewer, or well systems, unless agreed in writing.

20. PEST CONTROL:
☒ (If checked, the following PEST CONTROL terms apply:)
A. Seller shall, within the time specified in paragraph 28A(3), provide to Buyer a current written Wood Destroying Pests and Organisms Inspection Report ("Report") covering the main building and attached structures (and, if checked: ☒ detached garages or carports, ☒ decks, ☐ the following other structures on the Property: _NONE_).
If the Property is a unit in a condominium, planned development, or residential stock cooperative, the Report shall cover only the separate interest and any exclusive-use areas being transferred, and shall NOT cover common areas.
B. ☒ Buyer, ☐ Seller, shall pay for the Report, which shall be prepared by _ACE PEST CONTROL COMPANY_, a registered structural pest control company.
C. If no infestation or infection by wood destroying pests or organisms is found, the Report shall include a written Certification.
D. If requested by Buyer or Seller, the Report shall separately identify each recommendation for corrective work as follows:
"Section 1" — Infestation or infection which is evident.
"Section 2" — Conditions which are present and deemed likely to lead to infestation or infection.
E. ☐ Buyer, ☒ Seller, shall pay for work recommended to correct conditions described in "**Section 1.**"
F. ☐ Buyer, ☒ Seller, shall pay for work recommended to correct conditions described in "**Section 2,**" if requested by Buyer.
G. Nothing in this **paragraph 20** shall relieve Seller of the obligation, if any, to repair or replace shower pans and shower enclosures, if required by paragraph 8. A WATER TEST OF SHOWER PANS MAY NOT BE PERFORMED ON UNITS ON AN UPPER LEVEL WITHOUT THE CONSENT OF THE OWNERS OF PROPERTY BELOW THE SHOWER.
H. **Work to be performed at Seller's expense** may be performed by Seller or through others, provided that:
(1) All required permits and final inspections are obtained; and
(2) Upon completion of repairs a Certification is provided to Buyer.
I. **If inspection of inaccessible areas** is recommended in the Report, Buyer has the option to accept and approve the Report, or request in writing, within 5 (or ☐ ____) days of receipt of the Report, that further inspection be made. BUYER'S FAILURE TO NOTIFY SELLER IN WRITING OF SUCH REQUEST SHALL CONCLUSIVELY BE CONSIDERED APPROVAL OF THE REPORT. If further inspection recommends "Section 1" and/or "Section 2" corrective work, such work, and the inspection, entry, and closing of the inaccessible areas, shall be paid for by the party designated in paragraphs 20B, 20E, and/or 20F. If no infestation or infection is found, the inspection, entry, and closing of the inaccessible areas shall be paid for by Buyer.
J. **Inspections, corrective work, and Certification** under this paragraph shall not include roof coverings. Read paragraph 7A concerning inspection of roof coverings.
K. **Certification shall be issued prior to close of escrow.** However, if Buyer and Seller agree in writing that work to be performed at Seller's expense will be done after close of escrow, funds equal to one and one-half times the amount of the approved estimate shall be held in escrow unless otherwise agreed in writing. Such funds shall be disbursed upon Buyer's receipt of Certification. Any remaining balance shall be returned to Seller.
L. **"Certification"** means a written statement by a registered structural pest control company, that on the date of inspection or re-inspection, the Property is "free" or is "now free" of "evidence of active infestation in the visible and accessible areas." (Business and Professions Code §§8519(a) and 8519(b).)

21. RENTAL PROPERTY: ☐ (If checked:) Buyer shall take the Property subject to the rights of existing tenants. Seller shall, within the time specified in paragraph 28A(3), deliver to Buyer copies of all leases, rental agreements, outstanding notices sent to tenants, and current income and expense statements ("Rental Documents"). Seller shall, within the time specified in paragraph 28A(4), request from tenants and provide to Buyer any tenant estoppel certificates. Buyer shall, within the time specified in paragraph 28A(2), provide written notice to Seller of any items disapproved. Seller shall make no changes in leases and tenancies, and shall enter into no new leases or rental agreements, during the pendency of this transaction, without Buyer's prior written consent. Seller shall transfer to Buyer, through escrow, all unused tenant deposits. No warranty is made concerning compliance with governmental restrictions, if any, limiting the amount of rent that can lawfully be charged, and/or the maximum number of persons who can lawfully occupy the Property, unless otherwise agreed in writing.

22. SELECTION OF SERVICE PROVIDERS: If Brokers give Buyer or Seller referrals to professional persons, service or product providers, or vendors of any type, including, but not limited to, lending institutions, loan brokers, title insurers, escrow companies, inspectors, structural pest control companies, contractors, and home warranty companies ("Providers"), the referrals are given based on the following disclosures:
A. Brokers do not guarantee the performance of any Providers.
B. Buyer and Seller are free to select Providers other than those referred or recommended by Brokers.

23. REPAIRS: Repairs under this Agreement shall be completed prior to close of escrow, unless otherwise agreed in writing, and shall be performed in compliance with applicable governmental permit, inspection, and approval requirements. It is understood that exact restoration of appearance or cosmetic items following all such Repairs may not be possible. Repairs shall be performed in a skillful manner with materials of quality comparable to that of existing materials.

24. FINAL VERIFICATION OF CONDITION: Buyer shall have the right to make a final inspection of the Property approximately 5 (or ☒ _ONE_) days prior to close of escrow, NOT AS A CONTINGENCY OF THE SALE, but solely to confirm that: (a) Repairs have been completed as agreed in writing by Buyer and Seller, (b) Seller has complied with Seller's other obligations, and (c) the Property is otherwise in substantially the same condition as on the date of acceptance of the offer, unless otherwise agreed in writing.

Buyer and Seller acknowledge receipt of copy of this page, which constitutes Page 5 of _8_ Pages.
Buyer's Initials (_JCB_) (_MJB_) Seller's Initials (_____) (_____)

OFFICE USE ONLY
Reviewed by Broker or Designee _____
Date _____

EQUAL HOUSING OPPORTUNITY
M/R NOV 95

QUADRUPLICATE
REAL ESTATE PURCHASE CONTRACT AND RECEIPT FOR DEPOSIT (DLF-14 PAGE 5 OF 8)

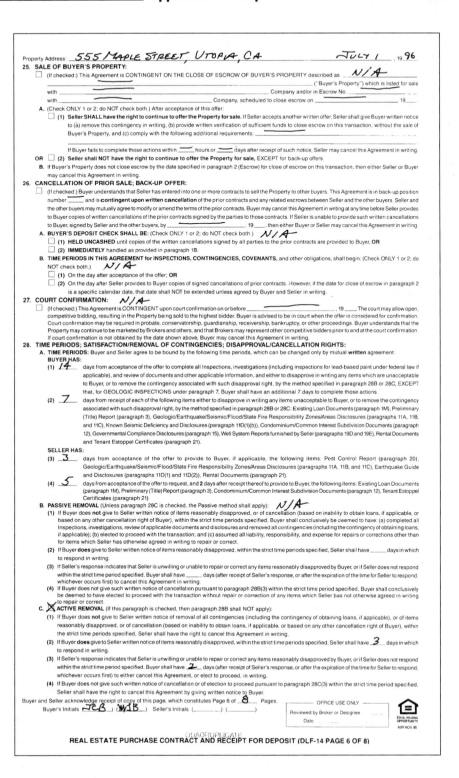

Property Address: _555 MAPLE STREET, UTOPIA, CA_ _JULY 1_, 19 96

25. SALE OF BUYER'S PROPERTY:

☐ (If checked:) This Agreement is CONTINGENT ON THE CLOSE OF ESCROW OF BUYER'S PROPERTY described as _N/A_

_____ ("Buyer's Property") which is listed for sale

with _____ Company and/or in Escrow No. _____

with _____ Company, scheduled to close escrow on _____, 19 ___

A. (Check ONLY 1 or 2; do NOT check both.) After acceptance of this offer:

☐ (1) **Seller SHALL have the right to continue to offer the Property for sale.** If Seller accepts another written offer, Seller shall give Buyer written notice to (a) remove this contingency in writing, (b) provide written verification of sufficient funds to close escrow on this transaction, without the sale of Buyer's Property, and (c) comply with the following additional requirements: _____

If Buyer fails to complete those actions within ____ hours or ____ days after receipt of such notice, Seller may cancel this Agreement in writing.

OR ☐ (2) **Seller shall NOT have the right to continue to offer the Property for sale,** EXCEPT for back-up offers.

B. If Buyer's Property does not close escrow by the date specified in paragraph 2 (Escrow) for close of escrow on this transaction, then either Seller or Buyer may cancel this Agreement in writing.

26. CANCELLATION OF PRIOR SALE; BACK-UP OFFER:

☐ (If checked:) Buyer understands that Seller has entered into one or more contracts to sell the Property to other buyers. This Agreement is in back-up position number ____ and is **contingent upon written cancellation** of the prior contracts and any related escrows between Seller and the other buyers. Seller and the other buyers may mutually agree to modify or amend the terms of the prior contracts. Buyer may cancel this Agreement in writing at any time before Seller provides to Buyer copies of written cancellations of the prior contracts signed by the parties to those contracts. If Seller is unable to provide such written cancellations to Buyer, signed by Seller and the other buyers, by _____, 19 ___, then either Buyer or Seller may cancel this Agreement in writing.

A. BUYER'S DEPOSIT CHECK SHALL BE: (Check ONLY 1 or 2; do NOT check both.) _N/A_

☐ (1) **HELD UNCASHED** until copies of the written cancellations signed by all parties to the prior contracts are provided to Buyer, **OR**

☐ (2) **IMMEDIATELY** handled as provided in paragraph 1B.

B. TIME PERIODS IN THIS AGREEMENT for INSPECTIONS, CONTINGENCIES, COVENANTS, and other obligations, shall begin: (Check ONLY 1 or 2; do NOT check both.) _N/A_

☐ (1) On the day after acceptance of the offer; **OR**

☐ (2) On the day after Seller provides to Buyer copies of signed cancellations of prior contracts. However, if the date for close of escrow in paragraph 2 is a specific calendar date, that date shall NOT be extended unless agreed by Buyer and Seller in writing.

27. COURT CONFIRMATION: _N/A_

☐ (If checked:) This Agreement is CONTINGENT upon court confirmation on or before _____, 19 ___. The court may allow open, competitive bidding, resulting in the Property being sold to the highest bidder. Buyer is advised to be in court when the offer is considered for confirmation. Court confirmation may be required in probate, conservatorship, guardianship, receivership, bankruptcy, or other proceedings. Buyer understands that the Property may continue to be marketed by Brokers and others, and that Brokers may represent other competitive bidders prior to and at the court confirmation. If court confirmation is not obtained by the date shown above, Buyer may cancel this Agreement in writing.

28. TIME PERIODS; SATISFACTION/REMOVAL OF CONTINGENCIES; DISAPPROVAL/CANCELLATION RIGHTS:

A. **TIME PERIODS:** Buyer and Seller agree to be bound by the following time periods, which can be changed only by mutual **written** agreement:

BUYER HAS:

(1) _14_ days from acceptance of the offer to complete all Inspections, investigations (including inspections for lead-based paint under federal law if applicable), and review of documents and other applicable information, and either to disapprove in writing any items which are unacceptable to Buyer, or to remove the contingency associated with such disapproval right, by the method specified in paragraph 28B or 28C, EXCEPT that, for GEOLOGIC INSPECTIONS under paragraph 7, Buyer shall have an additional 7 days to complete those actions.

(2) _7_ days from receipt of each of the following items either to disapprove in writing any items unacceptable to Buyer, or to remove the contingency associated with such disapproval right, by the method specified in paragraph 28B or 28C: Existing Loan Documents (paragraph 1M), Preliminary (Title) Report (paragraph 3), Geologic/Earthquake/Seismic/Flood/State Fire Responsibility Zones/Areas Disclosures (paragraphs 11A, 11B, and 11C), Known Seismic Deficiency and Disclosures (paragraph 11D(1)(b)), Condominium/Common Interest Subdivision Documents (paragraph 12), Governmental Compliance Disclosures (paragraph 15), Well System Reports furnished by Seller (paragraphs 19D and 19E), Rental Documents and Tenant Estoppel Certificates (paragraph 21).

SELLER HAS:

(3) _3_ days from acceptance of the offer to provide to Buyer, if applicable, the following items: Pest Control Report (paragraph 20), Geologic/Earthquake/Seismic/Flood/State Fire Responsibility Zones/Areas Disclosures (paragraphs 11A, 11B, and 11C), Earthquake Guide and Disclosures (paragraphs 11D(1) and 11D(2)), Rental Documents (paragraph 21).

(4) _5_ days from acceptance of the offer to request, and **2** days after receipt thereof to provide to Buyer, the following items: Existing Loan Documents (paragraph 1M), Preliminary (Title) Report (paragraph 3), Condominium/Common Interest Subdivision Documents (paragraph 12), Tenant Estoppel Certificates (paragraph 21).

B. **PASSIVE REMOVAL** (Unless paragraph 28C is checked, the Passive method shall apply): _N/A_

(1) If Buyer does **not** give to Seller written notice of items reasonably disapproved, or of cancellation (based on inability to obtain loans, if applicable, or based on any other cancellation right of Buyer), within the strict time periods specified, Buyer shall be deemed to have: (a) completed all Inspections, investigations, review of applicable documents and disclosures and removed all contingencies (including the contingency of obtaining loans, if applicable); (b) elected to proceed with the transaction; and (c) assumed all liability, responsibility, and expense for repairs or corrections other than for items which Seller has otherwise agreed in writing to repair or correct.

(2) If Buyer **does** give to Seller written notice of items reasonably disapproved, within the strict time periods specified, Seller shall have ____ days in which to respond in writing.

(3) If Seller's response indicates that Seller is unwilling or unable to repair or correct any items reasonably disapproved by Buyer, or if Seller does not respond within the strict time period specified, Buyer shall have ____ days (after receipt of Seller's response, or after the expiration of the time for Seller to respond, whichever occurs first) to cancel this Agreement in writing.

(4) If Buyer does not give such written notice of cancellation pursuant to paragraph 28B(3) within the strict time period specified, Buyer shall conclusively be deemed to have elected to proceed with the transaction without repair or correction of any items which Seller has not otherwise agreed in writing to repair or correct.

C. ☒ **ACTIVE REMOVAL** (If this paragraph is checked, then paragraph 28B shall NOT apply):

(1) If Buyer does **not** give to Seller written notice of removal of all contingencies (including the contingency of obtaining loans, if applicable), or of items reasonably disapproved, or of cancellation (based on inability to obtain loans, if applicable, or based on any other cancellation right of Buyer), within the strict time periods specified, Seller shall have the right to cancel this Agreement in writing.

(2) If Buyer **does** give to Seller written notice of items reasonably disapproved, within the strict time periods specified, Seller shall have _3_ days in which to respond in writing.

(3) If Seller's response indicates that Seller is unwilling or unable to repair or correct any items reasonably disapproved by Buyer, or if Seller does not respond within the strict time period specified, Buyer shall have _2_ days (after receipt of Seller's response, or after the expiration of the time for Seller to respond, whichever occurs first) to either cancel this Agreement, or elect to proceed, in writing.

(4) If Buyer does not give such written notice of cancellation or of election to proceed pursuant to paragraph 28C(3) within the strict time period specified, Seller shall have the right to cancel this Agreement by giving written notice to Buyer.

Buyer and Seller acknowledge receipt of copy of this page, which constitutes Page 6 of _8_ Pages.

Buyer's Initials (_JCB_) (_WJB_) Seller's Initials (_____) (_____)

——— OFFICE USE ONLY ———
Reviewed by Broker or Designee
Date _____

EQUAL HOUSING OPPORTUNITY
MJR NOV 96

QUADRUPLICATE
REAL ESTATE PURCHASE CONTRACT AND RECEIPT FOR DEPOSIT (DLF-14 PAGE 6 OF 8)

Property Address: 555 MAPLE STREET, UTOPIA, CA   July 1, 1996

D. CANCELLATION OF SALE/ESCROW; RETURN OF DEPOSITS: If Buyer or Seller provides written notice of cancellation pursuant to rights duly exercised under paragraphs 1A. 1L, 3, 7, 9, 11, 12, 15, 21, 25, 26, 27, or 30, the deposits, less costs and fees, as applicable, shall be returned to Buyer. Buyer and Seller understand that, in such event: (1) Buyer and Seller are each required to sign mutual instructions to cancel the transaction and escrow, and release deposits, as provided by law; (2) A party may be subject to a civil penalty of up to $1,000 for refusal to sign such instructions (Civil Code §1057.3) if no good faith dispute exists as to who is entitled to the deposited funds; (3) Fees and costs may be payable to service providers and vendors for services and products provided during escrow.

29. **TAX WITHHOLDING:**

A. Under the Foreign Investment in Real Property Tax Act (FIRPTA), IRC §1445, every Buyer must, unless an exemption applies, deduct and withhold 10% of the gross sales price from Seller's proceeds and send it to the Internal Revenue Service, if the Seller is a "foreign person" under that statute.

B. In addition, under California Revenue and Taxation Code §18662, every Buyer must, unless an exemption applies, deduct and withhold 3⅓% of the gross sales price from Seller's proceeds and send it to the Franchise Tax Board if the Seller has a last known address outside of California or if the Seller's proceeds will be paid to a financial intermediary of the Seller.

C. Penalties may be imposed on a responsible party for non-compliance with the requirements of these statutes and related regulations. Seller and Buyer agree to execute and deliver any instrument, affidavit, statement, or instruction reasonably necessary to carry out these requirements, and to withholding of tax under those statutes if required. (SELLER'S AFFIDAVIT OF NON-FOREIGN STATUS AND/OR CALIFORNIA RESIDENCY (C.A.R. Form AS-14), OR BUYER'S AFFIDAVIT (C.A.R. Form AB-11), IF APPLICABLE, SHALL SATISFY THESE REQUIREMENTS.)

30. **PROPERTY DESTRUCTION OR DAMAGE:** This paragraph applies only to destruction or damage that occurs after acceptance of the offer.

A. In the event of destruction or damage through no fault of Buyer or Seller, **before** Buyer receives either title or possession:

(1) If such destruction or damage totals 1% or less of the purchase price, Seller shall repair such destruction or damage and the transaction shall go forward.

(2) If such destruction or damage exceeds 1% of the purchase price, Buyer shall have the right only to elect to either (a) terminate this Agreement by giving written notice of cancellation to Seller, or (b) purchase the Property in its then-present condition. If Buyer elects to purchase the property in its then-present condition, Seller shall credit Buyer 1% of the purchase price, and shall assign to Buyer all rights to any insurance claims and proceeds covering the destruction or damage.

B. In the event of destruction or damage through no fault of Buyer or Seller, **after** Buyer receives possession but before title has transferred to Buyer:

(1) If such destruction or damage totals 1% or less of the purchase price (a) Seller shall be under no obligation to repair such destruction or damage, (b) the transaction shall go forward, and (c) Seller shall assign to Buyer all rights to any insurance claims and proceeds covering the destruction or damage.

(2) If such destruction or damage exceeds 1% of the purchase price, Buyer shall have the right only to elect to either (a) terminate this Agreement by giving written notice of cancellation to Seller, or (b) purchase the Property in its then-present condition. If Buyer elects to purchase the property in its then-present condition, Seller shall assign to Buyer all rights to any insurance claims and proceeds covering the destruction or damage.

C. Destruction or damage after title has transferred to Buyer shall be borne by Buyer.

D. In the event the transaction is terminated under this paragraph, any expenses paid by Buyer or Seller for credit reports, appraisals, title examination, inspections of any kind, or other items, shall remain that party's responsibility.

IF TRANSFER OF TITLE AND POSSESSION DO NOT OCCUR AT THE SAME TIME, BUYER AND SELLER ARE ADVISED TO SEEK ADVICE OF THEIR INSURANCE ADVISORS AS TO THE INSURANCE CONSEQUENCE THEREOF.

31. **MULTIPLE LISTING SERVICE (MLS):** Brokers are authorized to report the terms of this transaction to any MLS, to be published and disseminated to persons authorized to use the information on terms approved by the MLS.

32. **EQUAL HOUSING OPPORTUNITY:** The Property is sold in compliance with federal, state, and local anti-discrimination laws.

33. **MEDIATION OF DISPUTES:** BUYER AND SELLER AGREE TO MEDIATE ANY DISPUTE OR CLAIM ARISING BETWEEN THEM OUT OF THIS CONTRACT OR ANY RESULTING TRANSACTION BEFORE RESORTING TO ARBITRATION OR COURT ACTION. Mediation is a process by which parties attempt to resolve a dispute or claim by submitting it to an impartial, neutral mediator, who is authorized to facilitate the resolution of the dispute, but who is not empowered to impose a settlement on the parties. Mediation fees, if any, shall be divided equally among the parties involved. In addition, Buyer and Seller agree to mediate disputes or claims involving either or both Brokers, consistent with this provision, provided either or both Brokers shall have agreed to such mediation prior to or within a reasonable time after the dispute or claim is presented to Brokers. Any election by either or both Brokers to participate in mediation shall not result in Brokers being deemed parties to the purchase and sale Agreement. IF ANY PARTY COMMENCES AN ARBITRATION OR COURT ACTION BASED ON A DISPUTE OR CLAIM TO WHICH THIS PARAGRAPH APPLIES WITHOUT FIRST ATTEMPTING TO RESOLVE THE MATTER THROUGH MEDIATION, THEN IN THE DISCRETION OF THE ARBITRATOR(S) OR JUDGE, THAT PARTY SHALL NOT BE ENTITLED TO RECOVER ATTORNEY'S FEES, EVEN IF THEY WOULD OTHERWISE BE AVAILABLE TO THAT PARTY IN ANY SUCH ARBITRATION OR COURT ACTION. This mediation provision applies whether or not the Arbitration of Disputes provision is initialled. Exclusions are listed in paragraph 35.

34. **ARBITRATION OF DISPUTES: (If initialled by all parties:) Buyer and Seller agree that any dispute or claim in law or equity arising between Buyer and Seller out of this contract or any resulting transaction, which is not settled through mediation, shall be decided by neutral, binding arbitration and not by court action, except as provided by California law for judicial review of arbitration proceedings. In addition, Buyer and Seller agree to arbitrate disputes or claims involving either or both Brokers, consistent with this provision, provided either or both Brokers shall have agreed to such arbitration prior to or within a reasonable time after the dispute or claim is presented to Brokers. Any election by either or both Brokers to participate in arbitration shall not result in Brokers being deemed parties to the purchase and sale Agreement.**

The arbitration shall be conducted in accordance with the rules of either the American Arbitration Association (AAA) or Judicial Arbitration and Mediation Services, Inc./Endispute (JAMS/Endispute). The selection between AAA and JAMS/Endispute rules shall be made by the claimant first filing for arbitration. The parties to an arbitration may agree in writing to use different rules and/or arbitrator(s). In all other respects, the arbitration shall be conducted in accordance with Part III, Title 9 of the California Code of Civil Procedure. Judgment upon the award rendered by the arbitrator(s) may be entered in any court having jurisdiction thereof. The parties shall have the right to discovery in accordance with Code of Civil Procedure §1283.05. Exclusions are listed in paragraph 35.

"NOTICE: BY INITIALLING IN THE SPACE BELOW YOU ARE AGREEING TO HAVE ANY DISPUTE ARISING OUT OF THE MATTERS INCLUDED IN THE 'ARBITRATION OF DISPUTES' PROVISION DECIDED BY NEUTRAL ARBITRATION AS PROVIDED BY CALIFORNIA LAW AND YOU ARE GIVING UP ANY RIGHTS YOU MIGHT POSSESS TO HAVE THE DISPUTE LITIGATED IN A COURT OR JURY TRIAL. BY INITIALLING IN THE SPACE BELOW YOU ARE GIVING UP YOUR JUDICIAL RIGHTS TO DISCOVERY AND APPEAL, UNLESS THOSE RIGHTS ARE SPECIFICALLY INCLUDED IN THE 'ARBITRATION OF DISPUTES' PROVISION. IF YOU REFUSE TO SUBMIT TO ARBITRATION AFTER AGREEING TO THIS PROVISION, YOU MAY BE COMPELLED TO ARBITRATE UNDER THE AUTHORITY OF THE CALIFORNIA CODE OF CIVIL PROCEDURE. YOUR AGREEMENT TO THIS ARBITRATION PROVISION IS VOLUNTARY."

"WE HAVE READ AND UNDERSTAND THE FOREGOING AND AGREE TO SUBMIT DISPUTES ARISING OUT OF THE MATTERS INCLUDED IN THE 'ARBITRATION OF DISPUTES' PROVISION TO NEUTRAL ARBITRATION."

Buyer's Initials   Seller's Initials
JCB / MJB   /

35. **EXCLUSIONS FROM MEDIATION AND ARBITRATION:** The following matters are excluded from mediation and arbitration hereunder: (a) a judicial or non-judicial foreclosure or other action or proceeding to enforce a deed of trust, mortgage, or installment land sale contract as defined in Civil Code §2985, (b) an unlawful detainer action, (c) the filing or enforcement of a mechanic's lien, (d) any matter which is within the jurisdiction of a probate or small claims court, and (e) an action for bodily injury or wrongful death, or for latent or patent defects to which Code of Civil Procedure §337.1 or §337.15 applies. The filing of a court action to enable the recording of a notice of pending action, for order of attachment, receivership, injunction, or other provisional remedies, shall not constitute a violation of the Mediation of Disputes and Arbitration of Disputes provisions.

Buyer and Seller acknowledge receipt of copy of this page, which constitutes Page 7 of **8** Pages

Buyer's Initials (JCB) (MJB)   Seller's Initials (_____) (_____)

OFFICE USE ONLY
Reviewed by Broker or Designee ___
Date ___

EQUAL HOUSING OPPORTUNITY
M/R NOV 95

REAL ESTATE PURCHASE CONTRACT AND RECEIPT FOR DEPOSIT (DLF-14 PAGE 7 OF 8)

Property Address: *555 MAPLE STREET, UTOPIA, CA*   *JULY 1*, 19 *96*

36. LIQUIDATED DAMAGES: (If initialed by all parties:)

Buyer's Initials   Seller's Initials

JCB / MJB / _____

Buyer and Seller agree that if Buyer fails to complete this purchase by reason of any default of Buyer:
- A. Seller shall be released from the obligation to sell the Property to Buyer.
- B. Seller shall retain, as liquidated damages for breach of contract, the deposit actually paid. However, the amount retained shall be no more than 3% of the purchase price if the Property is a dwelling with no more than four units, one of which Buyer intends to occupy as Buyer's residence. Any excess shall promptly be returned to Buyer.
- C. Buyer and Seller shall sign RECEIPT FOR INCREASED DEPOSIT/LIQUIDATED DAMAGES (C.A.R. Form RID-11) for any increased deposit.
- D. In the event of a dispute, funds deposited in trust accounts or escrow are not released automatically and require mutual, signed release instructions from both Buyer and Seller, judicial decision, or arbitration award.

37. ATTORNEY'S FEES: In any action, proceeding, or arbitration between Buyer and Seller arising out of this Agreement, the prevailing party between Buyer and Seller shall be entitled to reasonable attorney's fees and costs from the non-prevailing Buyer or Seller, except as provided in paragraph 33.

38. DEFINITIONS: As used in this Agreement:
- A. "DAYS" means calendar days, unless otherwise required by law.
- B. "DAYS FROM ACCEPTANCE" means the specified number of calendar days after acceptance of the offer or final counter offer is communicated to the other party as specified in paragraph 42, not counting the calendar date on which acceptance is communicated.
- C. "CLOSE OF ESCROW" means the date the grant deed or other evidence of transfer of title is recorded.
- D. "LOCAL LAW" means any law, code, statute, ordinance, regulation, or rule, adopted by a city or county.
- E. "REPAIRS" means alterations, repairs, replacements, or modifications of the Property.
- F. SINGULAR and PLURAL terms each include the others, when appropriate.

39. TIME OF ESSENCE; ENTIRE CONTRACT; CHANGES: Time is of the essence. All agreements between the parties are incorporated in this Agreement which constitutes the entire contract. Its terms are intended by the parties as a final, complete, and exclusive expression of their agreement with respect to its subject matter and may not be contradicted by evidence of any prior agreement or contemporaneous oral agreement. The captions in this Agreement are for convenience of reference only and are not intended as part of this Agreement. **This Agreement may not be extended, amended, modified, altered, or changed in any respect whatsoever except in writing signed by Buyer and Seller.**

40. OTHER TERMS AND CONDITIONS; ATTACHED SUPPLEMENTS:
- A. *NONE*
- B. The following ATTACHED supplements are incorporated in this Agreement:
  - ☐ *NONE*   ☐ _____

41. AGENCY CONFIRMATION: The following agency relationships are hereby confirmed for this transaction:

Listing Agent: *ABLE BROKER* _____ is the agent of (check one):
(Print Firm Name)

☒ the Seller exclusively; or ☐ both the Buyer and Seller.

Selling Agent: *BEST BROKER* _____ (if not same as Listing Agent) is the agent of (check one):
(Print Firm Name)

☒ the Buyer exclusively; or ☐ the Seller exclusively; or ☐ both the Buyer and Seller.

Real Estate Brokers are not parties to the purchase and sale Agreement between Buyer and Seller. **(IF THE PROPERTY CONTAINS 1-4 RESIDENTIAL DWELLING UNITS, BUYER AND SELLER MUST ALSO BE GIVEN ONE OR MORE DISCLOSURES REGARDING REAL ESTATE AGENCY RELATIONSHIPS FORMS (C.A.R. Form AD-14).)**

42. OFFER: This is an offer to purchase the Property. **All paragraphs with spaces for initials by Buyer and Seller are incorporated in this Agreement only if initialed by all parties. If at least one, but not all parties initial, a counter offer is required until agreement is reached. Unless acceptance is signed by Seller and a signed copy delivered in person, by mail, or facsimile, and personally received by Buyer or by** _____ who is authorized to receive it, by *JULY 3*, 19*96* at *12:01* AM/**PM** the offer shall be deemed revoked and the deposit shall be returned. Buyer and Seller acknowledge that Brokers are not parties to the purchase and sale Agreement. Buyer has read and acknowledges receipt of a copy of the offer and agrees to the above confirmation of agency relationships. If this offer is accepted and Buyer subsequently defaults, Buyer may be responsible for payment of Brokers' compensation. This Agreement and any supplement, addendum, or modification, including any photocopy or facsimile, may be signed in two or more counterparts, all of which shall constitute one and the same writing.

BUYER *John C. Buyer*

BUYER *Mary J. Buyer*

Receipt for deposit is acknowledged, and agency relationships are confirmed as above. Real Estate Brokers are not parties to the purchase and sale Agreement between Buyer and Seller.

Real Estate Broker (Selling) *BEST BROKER*   Date *JULY 1, 1996*
(Print Firm Name)

By _____

Address *201 MAIN STREET, UTOPIA, CA*

Telephone *(555) 555-5555*   Fax *(678) 444-4444*

ACCEPTANCE

The undersigned Seller accepts the above offer, agrees to sell the Property on the above terms and conditions (If checked: ☐ **SUBJECT TO ATTACHED COUNTER OFFER**), and agrees to the above confirmation of agency relationships. Seller agrees to pay compensation for services as follows:

_____ to _____, Broker, and _____ to _____, Broker.

payable (a) on recordation of the deed or other evidence of title, or (b) if completion of sale is prevented by default of Seller, upon Seller's default, or (c) if completion of sale is prevented by default of Buyer, only if and when Seller collects damages from Buyer, by suit or otherwise, and then in an amount equal to one-half of the damages recovered, but not to exceed the above compensation, after first deducting title and escrow expenses and the expenses of collection, if any. Seller hereby irrevocably assigns to Brokers such compensation from Seller's proceeds and irrevocably instructs Escrow Holder to disburse those funds to Brokers at close of escrow. Commission instructions can be amended or revoked only with the consent of the Brokers. In any action, proceeding, or arbitration relating to the payment of such compensation, the prevailing party shall be entitled to reasonable attorney's fees and costs, except as provided in paragraph 33. The undersigned Seller has read and acknowledges receipt of a copy of this Agreement, and authorizes Brokers to deliver a signed copy to Buyer.

SELLER _____ Date _____

SELLER _____ Time _____

Agency relationships are confirmed as above. Real Estate Brokers are not parties to the purchase and sale Agreement between Buyer and Seller.

Real Estate Broker (Listing) _____ Date _____
(Print Firm Name)

By _____

Address _____

Telephone _____ Fax _____

(___/___) **ACKNOWLEDGMENT OF RECEIPT:** Buyer, or the person authorized in paragraph 42, acknowledges receipt of signed acceptance on
(Initials) (date) _____, at _____ AM/PM.

This form is available for use by the entire real estate industry. The use of this form is not intended to identify the user as a REALTOR®. REALTOR® is a registered collective membership mark which may be used only by real estate licensees who are members of the NATIONAL ASSOCIATION OF REALTORS® and who subscribe to its Code of Ethics.

Page 8 of **8** Pages.

QUADRUPLICATE

OFFICE USE ONLY

Reviewed by Broker or Designee _____

Date _____

EQUAL HOUSING OPPORTUNITY

MR NOV 95

REAL ESTATE PURCHASE CONTRACT AND RECEIPT FOR DEPOSIT (DLF-14 PAGE 8 OF 8)

Appendix B
Example of a Good Inspection Report

. . . .

*I*n Chapter 11, we show you an example of a lousy inspection report. This appendix gives an example of what you should expect to see in a good inspection report.

Like our sample, your report should paint a vivid word picture of the home you may purchase. The inspection report should be brimming with in-depth explanations — not merely a list of checkmarks, a generic boilerplate, and hastily scribbled notes.

Get the most out of your inspection dollar. Find a professional inspection company that will thoroughly inspect the property's mechanical and structural systems inside and out from foundation to roof and present you with a solid report on which you can make an informed home-buying decision (see Chapter 11 for advice on finding a great home inspector).

Camp Brothers Inspection Services, Inc.

One Glenview Drive, San Francisco, CA 94131

(415) 641-1006

- **Inspection Date:** _____ xx, 1996 · **Report Number:** 96 - _____
- **Date of Report:** _____ xx, 1996 · **Inspector:** Warren Camp, ASHI®
  Certified Member, #732
- **Report:** Prepurchase Inspection at: x x x x _____ Street, San Francisco
- **Dwelling Description:** Single-family dwelling
- **Present During Inspection:** · **Weather:** No rain within 10 days
  Buyer: Red E. Toobuy
  Buyer's Agent: Ken B. Elpful; Manny Elpful Associates
  Seller's Agent: A. Frank Lister; Frank & Company
  Others: Bugzie O. Bliterate; Nuke 'em, Heat 'em, Treat 'em Pest Control Company
- **The inspected unit was furnished at inspection.**
- **A Structural/Pest Control Report was not provided.**
- **The Seller's Disclosure form was provided.**

As requested by the buyer or buyer's agent, this report is being prepared for the exclusive use of the buyer to accompany the on-site verbal presentation. In no way is it to be used by, nor are we obligated to review it with, any third parties. Because Camp Brothers Inspection Services (CBIS) has not personally described the extent and nature of its findings to anyone but those present for the entire inspection, CBIS strongly discourages third parties from using this report. Interested parties should arrange with CBIS for an inspection that meets their more individualized needs.

This report provides a professional opinion of general features and major deficiencies of the building and its systems at inspection. It does not necessarily analyze or report on adjacent properties, nor does it cover environmental / neighborhood concerns. It summarizes observations on components inspected in accordance with customary property-inspection standards. The scope of our inspection is limited only to items discussed. It is not technically exhaustive. Because certain findings are variable (separations and cracking lengths that increase in time, levelness and plumbness readings that may change over time, erosion and corrosion levels that do not remain static, and so on), no one should rely on any reported findings for more than 60 days.

This is not a code compliance report; a home, product, or system guarantee of any kind; nor is it an evaluation of the property's saleability. It includes only items accessible to visual inspection; no furniture relocation, dismantling, demolition, or other manual handling, etc., would have occurred in its preparation. It does not fulfill the requirements set forth in California Civil Code Section 1102 as to the required disclosures of a transferor of real property.

The CBIS inspector explained to the client the two types of reports CBIS prepares. Rather than selecting the in-depth, narrative report with extensive recommendations, the client selected the present standard report. Findings and recommendations that would normally have been included in the extensive narrative report would be excluded from this report. Please call CBIS with your questions.

TABLE OF CONTENTS

SECTION	PAGE NUMBER

- Prepurchase Inspection Report

x x x x _____ Street, San Francisco, California   _____ x x, 1996

INTRODUCTION

The inspected property was a single-family dwelling. Most interior spaces were unfurnished. Low-voltage wiring, heat exchangers, gardens, fences, retaining walls, underground piping and storage tanks, and sprinklers are not included in the scope of CBIS inspection reports.

CBIS inspections are designed to meet or exceed recent "Standards of Practice" established by the American Society of Home Inspectors (ASHI) of which the CBIS inspector is a certified member. A copy of the Standards is available upon request.

For the most part, the building was a single-level, framed structure built over a crawl space. Built around 1954, the original structural work of this wood-framed building appeared customarily constructed. No unusual or extensive damage was apparent, however, several items need attention.

Portions of this single-family dwelling have been recently remodeled. Alteration of the plumbing and electrical work throughout the property and structural installations at the rear addition were made in a nonprofessional manner. These concerns are brought up in other sections of this report. Because many of the walls and ceilings were closed, it was not possible to ascertain the full extent of renovation. If more information about these remodeled areas is needed, (a) consult with a licensed structural engineer, (b) review copies of permits and remodeling contracts that may be made available, and (c) examine the seller's disclosure form for additional information.

The building interior and exterior were adequately maintained. But of course, *all* buildings have flaws. We'll discuss a number of these flaws, but we cannot discover and report on every one. This inspection and report is not technically exhaustive, and CBIS does not provide a thorough or fully detailed analysis of problem areas. With only a few hours to inspect the entire property, CBIS provides, at best, a professional opinion based upon experience. The inspector is not a licensed engineer or expert in every trade or craft. Only representative sample-checks of various exposed-to-view segments of this property were made. If additional items or conditions are found when repairs or improvements begin, call CBIS immediately before further work resumes.

All the main points of this report were fully discussed with Red E. Toobuy and his agent, Ken B. Elpful, at inspection. The following sections describe the findings discussed. Please call with questions.

Repairs, corrections, and other follow-up items to consider. (Note: Check-marked concerns are merely highlights of the inspector's findings. Read the entire report to fully appreciate this effort. Where you have interest, follow these and the following recommendations and have specialists address those items excluded from this inspection and report.)

> ✔ Check with the building inspection department about permits and inspections for building alterations and additions.

EXTERIOR
Building Exterior

This building, with board-and-batten on the facade, and stucco on the balance, needs maintenance on the rear addition. Surfaces should be weathersealed in the not-too-distant future to prevent moisture entry. When references are made to front, rear, left and right, they are made facing the building from _____ Street.

Other items not yet painted or waterproofed were found. They include five or six louvered wall vents, the garage door, one new door, and various window trim pieces.

At the rear of the garage, soil or pavement was close to the top of the foundation. This condition can cause wood decay and deterioration. Because CBIS is not qualified as structural/pest-control inspectors, refer to a current report for findings and corrective recommendations.

Wood-to-earth contacts were found at various posts and sills. Contacts encourage wood decay, entry of pests, and moisture retention. All contacts should be properly separated and appropriate grade levels maintained.

Rust deterioration was found on several exposed nails on the rear addition's roof eave. Prior to painting, these surfaces should either be fully prepared for paint or removed.

A few cracks in the stucco were evident at inspection. The cracking is likely due to material shrinkage or expansion or ordinary building movement. Cracks should be caulked and weathersealed. Contact a painting and waterproofing contractor to replenish and seal exterior surfaces to prevent water entry.

Stucco siding on rear and side yard walls extended downward over the foundation and made contact with grade (ground covering). This is conducive to entry of wood-destroying pests or organisms from behind the stucco. As an upgrade, raise the base of stucco siding a few inches to expose the foundation.

Aluminum windows on the rear addition appeared sound. CBIS suggests that exposed wooden frames, sills, and trim adjacent to the metal window frames be caulked and painted and routinely maintained to prevent possible water entry. A sampling of these windows was operational at inspection.

Wood-sash windows elsewhere were generally in satisfactory condition, however, nearly all of the painted, wood-sash windows were unable to be opened when tested, and some rooms have not have been provided with adequate ventilation. Routine maintenance is recommended for exposed wooden sashes, adjacent window trim, and glazing putty to also eliminate potential water seepage and extend lifespan.

The garage entry door was a tilt-up type without open-vent screens.

The door's spring balances were not equipped with the safety device that prevents catapulting that might occur if the springs were to actually break under pressure. Contact a professional garage door installer for appropriate replacement/correction.

Excessive changes in the height of pavement and steps at the kitchen-to-driveway landing could prove hazardous. Exercise caution in these areas.

Pavement and Drainage

This building sits on a steep hillside and erosive grooves were visible in several locations. Not being engineers of any kind, CBIS is unable to represent or evaluate this condition. Contact a qualified engineer regarding stability of the building and hillside and any past, present, or future soil embankment or building movement.

The sloped rear yard was in disrepair. Soil and rock had slipped, fallen, or crept in such a manner as to make use of this yard possibly unsafe. No guardrails, fencing, or retaining walls were in place. No further examination or findings within the yard areas were included in today's inspection. Red can contact a soil engineer for further examination if desired.

Adequate soil drainage for Bay Area homes is imperative because soil types in this area swell when saturated and may damage a building's foundation. Grade at the front was adequately sloped, providing adequate drainage away from the foundation during rainstorms.

A drainage pattern at the sides and rear yard was not as easy to predict. Water entry appears probable into the at the subarea possibly because the soil and pavement was not significantly sloped away from the building but should be. Because calcification and/or staining was found on the inside a few foundation walls, grading and drainage could be improved.

Moisture and drainage conditions vary with specific soil types, landscape/hardscape designs, and weather changes. Consequently, a report on seepage and ponding conditions, or representations regarding soil stability, could not be made by this inspection company. Refer to a seller's disclosure and/or a soil engineer's report to fully appreciate the potential for water entry—whether caused by light rains, natural springs, prolonged heavy rains, or other causes. Routinely keep all drains, patios, and walkways clean and well maintained.

Underground Piping

Understandably, inspection of inaccessible, underground perimeter drainage systems could not be inspected. Neither could CBIS inspect other underground devices like conduits, gas and water piping, waste and vent lines, and so on, as well as under-slab components.

CBIS detected no outward signs of presently existing or previously placed underground fuel storage tanks (USTs) within the inspected areas. There were no fill spout, vent pipe, supply tubing and return line, or a fuse box—typical indicators of USTs. Interested parties may wish to explore further since such exploration is not within the scope of ASHI standard inspection practices.

- ✔ Free and service windows, trim, and hardware.
- ✔ Refer to a current Structural/Pest Control Inspection Report.
- ✔ Paint or waterproof all raw materials.
- ✔ Repair needed areas.
- ✔ Regrade landscape and hardscape surfaces away from building.
- ✔ Contact a soil engineer regarding erosion and hillside stability.

FOUNDATION

The foundation was only partially accessible because of low headroom throughout the subarea. No ratproofing membranes were yet placed beneath the family room or the main building's crawl space areas which might be a thoughtful consideration.

Visible foundation stem walls at the main building have been installed according to customarily practiced standards. The crawl space at the family room addition was not accessible.

Garage and crawl space legs were made of continuous concrete, which is often reinforced with internally placed steel bars.

There was hairline or minor cracking on foundation sections at the side of the family room addition. Such cracking in a building of this type and age is not uncommon and should be routinely monitored. If the cracking increases, or new cracks develop, contact a qualified engineer for an evaluation. Looking for any direct and current transference of foundation movement to adjacent finished family room walls, ceilings, and floors of the room above, no outward sign was detectable. It was not possible to determine if this cracking was a current condition. Determining whether foundations shift or rotate or cracks will appear, or if existing cracks will extend further, is not within the scope of ASHI® inspections. Neither can CBIS predict the likelihood of future foundation failures, shifting, or settlement. If more information is needed, a qualified structural engineer, experienced in similar structures, should be contacted to fully inspect and evaluate findings on these and any other structural concerns (like earthquake-preparedness measures).

Where CBIS had access throughout open walls of the garage and subarea, a few foundation bolts were visible. In the name of earthquake preparedness, CBIS always suggests that foundation bolts, along with any other mechanical treatments that a structural engineer might specify (e.g., T-bracing, angle clips, hold downs, shear walls, etc.), be considered for seismic resistance.

✔ Routinely monitor the foundation.

STRUCTURAL FRAMING
Substructure

New and original framing was seen at the rear addition. The lower areas of partially accessible, exposed framing were limited to portions of the crawl space. Framing, for the most part, was customary with no visible sign of critical sags, cracks, deterioration, or movement.

Wood posts in the crawl space below the family room were in unsatisfactory condition. The support posts under the center girder were not connected to embedded concrete piers. The number and/or size of fasteners at the tops and bottoms of posts was small. *No* fastening devices (screws or nails) were yet in place! Plywood was also used in a nonconforming manner as a shim. Corrective work is needed and would be easy to do at the direction of a structural engineer.

The exposed header over the driveway was some cause for concern because of the nonconforming sizes of fasteners used. The header had rotated; the post moved out of plumb; and the nailing connections have become weak. Structurally, connections made between one structural member and another are essential. Post bases and tops, and beam connections to each other, and to joists, here and throughout the subarea and attic, were minimal but could easily be supplemented.

Cripple-wall studs at the garage door or subarea were tied together customarily, however, they were not yet benefited with supplemental fasteners or plywood shearwall panels known today to strengthen wooden structures located in earthquake country. Many structural posts, beams, and studs had not yet been retrofitted for earthquake preparedness. As a standard recommendation, these measures should be taken. Corrective recommendations should come from a qualified, licensed, structural engineer.

Moisture staining was found on garage walls. These stains looked and felt dry, and, when tested with the biprobe electric moisture meter, were dry. Because the cause of water staining, and the determination of its currentness, is difficult to determine, refer to a seller's disclosure statement to learn what efforts were made in each of these areas.

Rodent dropping was throughout the subarea next to the garage. Contact a pest control company for an evaluation.

Portions of the main building's crawl space ceilings were installed with thermal insulation, however, a calculated "energy inspection" is not within this industry's Standards of Practice. Several sections had separated and were lying on subarea soil.

• Prepurchase Inspection Report

x x x x _____ Street, San Francisco, California ⎯⎯⎯⎯⎯⎯⎯ x x, 1996

Main Structure

No evidence of *current* structural movement was noted during inspection of samplings of doors, windows, floors, walls, and ceilings. The tops of some doors were taper-cut to allow for wall shifting over the years. Any separations on walls, molding, or ceilings, or sagging or sloping of floors appeared to be the result of ordinary shifting and/or expansion within framing and supporting soils. In CBIS's opinion, the findings do not represent significant, current movement.

Attic Area

An attic had its access door in the hallway ceiling. Floor boards were not yet sitting on joists in this area. Insulation covered many of the ceiling joists. Walls and ceilings below could possibly be damaged by crawling or walking in these areas. A limited inspection was made by ladder from the access door opening.

Joists had runs of electrical wiring laid through and over their tops. Care must be taken whenever access is required.

Ceiling insulation was installed throughout much of the attic floor. Reporting on adequacy of building insulation is not within inspection-industry standards. Neither would we be able to examine or suspect any failures or hazards beneath or amid insulation. An electrical contractor could inspect the embedded wiring fully for a safety evaluation.

Insulation baffles, required around most heat-producing elements like exhaust fans, lighting fixtures, and flues, were not visible in expected locations and should be provided.

Visually accessible roofing supports were customarily framed. A representative number of purlins (supporting members) and/or collar ties (members connecting two roof sections) were found. No access was available for the family room addition's attic inspection.

There were beneficial vent openings at overhanging roof eaves. Ventilation was customarily provided.

> ✔ Hire a structural engineer to evaluate family room framing.
> ✔ Seismically retrofit some or all structural posts, beams, plates, and studs for earthquake preparedness.
> ✔ Correct the rotated header and fasten it appropriately.
> ✔ Refer to a current Structural/Pest Control Inspection Report for findings and corrective recommendations.
> ✔ Provide insulation baffles where needed. Refasten fallen crawl space insulation.

SECURITY AND FIRE SAFETY

CBIS has some fire-safety concerns about this property. Garage wall surfaces, adjacent to habitable rooms, were not completely fire-resistant. Currently, there is risk of potential flame spread, as well as radon infiltration, into habitable spaces. Fully separate mechanical rooms from habitable rooms (e.g., by patching all openings with drywall, plaster, sheet metal, etc., or undertaking fire-resistant construction where appropriate). CBIS was unable to locate any smoke detectors or sprinklers in this area. A monitored alarm system with adequate smoke and heat detectors could be installed.

A few smoke detectors were installed on three bedroom walls and one hallway wall. Because state and local codes change frequently, consult the building department for direction on optimal number, type, and location of units. Be certain to replace batteries every year with fresh batteries. Providing appropriately specified and located fire extinguishers also improves fire safety.

The building's front door was equipped with a lock, deadbolt, and large glass pane. Glazing did not have a label certifying specification (e.g., tempered or safety). Door and window panes without safety glazing can be hazardous when broken, so current building code requires safety-labeled glass to minimize possible injury. Replacement of this glazing may not now be required; however, exercise caution and common sense in this area to prevent accidental breakage and possible bodily injury.

The front entry door lock required minor adjustment for security as well as for quick and easy operation.

It was a solid-core door which is more resistant to breaking and entering, as well as to flame spread, than a hollow-core door. (Not all solid-core doors are fire-resistant unless label-certified.)

The glass-and-panel door from the garage to the side entry was a weak door offering little in the way of security.

Front and rear hinge-type garage doors were without at least a 1-inch-throw lock or deadbolt. At all exterior doors, deadbolts are the recommended auxiliary locking devices.

The side entrance (kitchen) deadbolt was a "double-keyed" type — a key for the inside as well as outside lock cylinder is required. If these keys are not easily accessible, emergency egress could be impossible, and bear serious safety consequences. Conversion to single-keyed bolts is easy, affordable, and should be considered. Contact a locksmith.

Family room addition windows were installed close to the floor. Unfortunately, each glass pane lacked glazing labels certifying specification. Replacement glazing or barrier installation may not now be required, but exercise caution and common sense in these areas.

Means of egress was a concern. When attempting to freely operate various fire-exit windows leading outside from each of the bedrooms, the windows were painted shut and not easy to open.

Interior and exterior lighting should be supplemented for overall security and safety. And, as a reminder before taking possession of your new home, rekey all existing door-lock cylinders to improve overall security and provide peace of mind.

✔ Provide and install needed fire-protection, separations, devices, or systems.
✔ Improve door-lock safety.
✔ Make fire egress windows freely operable.

PLUMBING
Water Supply

The shutoff valve for the main water-service line was located on the building's front wall. It was operable; no leakage was detected. A 3/4-inch copper waterline joined the building from the street. Domestic hot- and cold-water-supply lines were mostly made of copper.

CBIS found a combination of galvanized iron and copper waterlines at the front of the building. The seller should provide information about the extent of copper piping replacement. Galvanized iron water piping is subject to corrosion from mineral build-up that can restrict water flow to fixtures.

Measured at the main valve, static pressure on the waterline was 89 pounds per square inch (PSI), which is a moderate-to-high level. Prescribed water-pressure-ratings are set at 55 to

65 PSI to prevent leakage from excessive pressures. A water-pressure regulator, pressure gauge on the incoming waterline, and routine water-pressure monitoring are recommended.

Part of the hot-water piping in the subarea had no thermal insulation. Full insulation would reduce energy consumption and improve hot-response time for each water fixture.

Copper water piping was without proper or sufficient wall and floor fasteners. This omission might contribute to hammering noises in these lines, like those detected in both bathrooms.

Vents, Drains, and Traps

Throughout much of this structure, visible waste and vent piping were made of cast iron. A 2-inch cast-iron waste or vent line beneath the crawl space access door was cracked and patched, requiring replacement of this piping in the not-to-distant future.

A waste/vent line in the garage was incomplete, lacking a cap or clean-out plug. Located to the right of the furnace, a plumber should simply install a cap.

A number of drains were inspected and maintaining an effective water trap-seal.

Traps for bathroom washbasins were problematic because they were not fastened to a tail piece and *they leaked*. Competent plumbing connections are required.

Gas Supply

The main gas-shutoff valve, located on the exterior wall of the building, was tight. If a shut-off valve is not now, or in cases of emergency, accessible or operable, PG&E could be contacted for correction.

✔ Install a water-pressure regulator and pressure gauge on the incoming water line.
✔ Cap the open waste/vent line.
✔ Fasten water lines throughout.

WATER HEATER

The hot water heater in the garage was the gas-fueled type and was operating during inspection. It had no fiberglass thermal jacket.

The water heater also lacked adequate cross-strapping and restraining blocks designed to resist movement during an intense earthquake.

It was apparently a recently installed model. With a fiberglass tank, an identification plate indicated that this A.O. Smith appliance had a 40-gallon capacity, a setting of 38,000 BTUs, and a 40.4-gallon-per-hour recovery rating.

The tank bottom was free of rust. No leaks were evident.

A safety valve on water heater tops, referred to as a "temperature and pressure relief valve," is necessary to the operation of these appliances. The T&PR valve was properly located. A water overflow tube was connected to the valve according to accepted trade practices.

The shutoff valve on the cold-water supply piping was operational and no leakage was evident.

Hot-water piping immediately adjacent to the water heater had some thermal wrapping, however, an "energy inspection" is not within the scope of our inspections.

The drain valve at the base of the tank, when opened, showed minimal sludge deposits.

The gas-shutoff valve was difficult to operate and should be adjusted.

Fresh air needed for complete combustion was minimal in this area. Additional, continuous ventilation is suggested. Open air-vents and windows provide such ventilation.

Gas-fueled heaters must always be vented safely. Visible portions of the exhaust vent flue were installed in a questionable and possibly unsafe condition (inaccessible portions of piping were not inspected). Flue connections were inappropriately "taped over" with asbestos-like materials. The mere presence of asbestos in a building material does not necessarily represent a health hazard. Many factors must be considered before making such determination (e.g., percentage of asbestos make-up, exact type of asbestos, and current physical condition). Considering the age of this building, other asbestos-containing materials that may not be visibly detectable or identified in this report may be present. Contact specialty contractors to conduct a lab-test for asbestos presence and analysis, and if found to be positive, provide estimates for removal or encapsulation of these materials following the U.S. Environmental Protection Agency's standards of practice.

The flue was also stained, suggesting either leakage at the roof line or condensation from a lack of fresh air in this area, however, no moisture was evident at inspection.

As a standard earthquake-preparedness consideration, some or all of the following installations should always be undertaken:

   a. Flexible water-supply piping to water heaters
   b. Fully functional seismic cross-strapping (see enclosed CBIS brochure)
   c. Flexible gas-supply piping to heaters and all gas-fueled appliances

   ✔ Provide and install bracing and strapping.
   ✔ Verify the correct size of gas supply tubing (to furnace as well).
   ✔ Provide required fresh-air circulation.

LAUNDRY

The garage-area laundry was no longer operational. Water-supply hoses were not connected.

Air chambers on the water lines had not yet been installed. Because they benefit the circulation of hot and cold water within these lines, air chambers should be installed by a qualified plumbing contractor.

Neither a sewer vent line nor trap seal had been installed. Contact a licensed plumbing contractor for such installation when the fixtures are made operable.

The gas shutoff valve was tight and requires adjustment.

"Fresh air exchange" was minimal in this area. Provide and install sufficient sources of fresh air ventilation.

   ✔ Improve air circulation for the laundry by a fan, vent grill, or window.
   ✔ Install air chambers on the water lines before operating the washing machine.

ELECTRICAL
Service and Main Disconnect

Electrical wiring for this building was fed from overhead and provided approximately 240 volts to the meter. No main disconnect circuit breaker was in place within the electric panel as expected. To shut the entire building's electric service off, five circuit breakers would need to be disconnected which might inhibit a timely shut-down of power in the event of an emergency. Installation of a single, main disconnect device would be a thoughtful upgrade.

The main disconnect panel, located on the right exterior wall, had an approximately 60-amp service size for the building. Conductors that had had their gauge marks either taped over or unmarked were estimated as #8 wire gauge.

Ampacity (the service entrance capacity) was marginal, based on the building's current load-demands. To comfortably handle the current wiring loads, the main service capacity should be increased.

The main electrical panel was fastened to the building exterior, protected from weather. However, the main panel was rusted and extremely dirty. Caution must be exercised in this location because such foreign matter can allow arcing which can lead to shorting.

Subpanel Distribution

The building's main disconnect device was combined in a panel with other circuits. No other panels were easily located or inspected.

Protected by circuit breakers, the combined main-distribution panel had the following circuitry distribution:

> 1 @ 120-volt circuit at 15 amps
> 4 @ 120-volt circuits at 20 amps

This subpanel was not fully circuit-labeled and should be. It was a panel benefited by a closed-front protection cover.

"Double-tapping" (connecting two conductors to one circuit breaker) occurred within the panel. *Such wiring should be corrected immediately* because double-tapping increases the possibility and frequency of tripping the overcurrent protection device.

As a part of regular property maintenance, all circuit breakers should be trip-tested and reset to insure that they are, and will remain, fully operational.

Grounding and Polarity

Of course, all electrical systems should be safely and properly grounded. An appropriately driven grounding rod was not easily located beneath the main panel. When sample testing outlets requiring adequate grounding, *little or no grounding protection was found.*

Furthermore, nearly every recently installed, 3-hole receptacle was *wired with a weak, faulty, or "open ground"* and needs immediate attention. At all three bedrooms, living room, and family room, "open ground" conditions with three-slot receptacles were found. *This situation should be immediately corrected.*

"Open ground" conditions were also on garage wall receptacles. *This is potentially dangerous and should be corrected immediately for maximum personal safety.*

In a random sampling of receptacles, "reverse polarity" was present in a few locations (at both bathrooms and the kitchen sink). This condition, hazardous in certain instances, can be easily corrected and should be. What's more, the toilet outlet in the master bathroom was not GFCI protected as expected.

Wiring

Electrical wiring for this building was comprised of original as well as supplemental wiring. Much of the exposed wiring was the Romex type.

The following is only a sampling of wiring concerns and is not intended to take the place of an electrical contractor's findings:

a. A defective light switch for the kitchen's above-sink fixture needs to be corrected.
b. Bathroom light switches were extremely loose which compromises grounding protection and must be adequately refastened.
c. Detection or evaluation of electromagnetic fields (EMFs) is not a part of our industry's Standards of Practice and is not included.
d. Some Romex wiring at garage walls was less than 8 feet high and unprotected, and this may permit damage to the cable. This exposed wiring should be piped into metal conduit or covered with approved protective material like drywall.
e. Extension cord wiring at the kitchen counter and stapled cord wiring in the garage was inappropriately used as a substitute for permanent wiring and should be properly wired if it is to remain in use.
f. Light fixtures throughout the garage and master bathroom were without lamps (bulbs). One bath fixture lacking lamps was extremely close to the shower. Because mistaken contact with hot sockets can be dangerous, replacement lamps should be provided in every such location.

In summary, safety concerns have arisen with interior wiring as well as the service entrance feeding the building. Hire a licensed electrician to examine the entire electrical system to its fullest and correct immediately wherever needed.

Camp Brothers always recommends the installation of ground-fault circuit-interruption-type receptacles in kitchens, bathrooms, and other wet locations as an added safety measure.

✔ Correct the panel's "double tapping."
✔ Remedy immediately *all* grounding and wiring problems.
✔ Provide panel with complete circuit identification.

HEATING
Heat Source Types and Condition
The Borg Warner brand gas-fueled, forced-air furnace in the garage was operational and had an estimated 64,000-BTU-output-capacity rating. Installed several years ago, it may be approaching the end of its "useful life." If a life-expectancy determination is needed, contact a heating specialist.

The following conditions are noted:
a. The gas-shutoff valve was tight and requires adjustment.
b. Presence of a natural gas leak was detected at the front shelf. *Such leakage could be extremely hazardous and must be corrected immediately.* Contact a licensed plumber or a PG&E representative for thorough testing.
c. No service calendar was visible. A current record of scheduling visits would suggest maintenance history of the heating system.
d. This appliance did not have benefit of pilotless ignition. A thermocouple device, which would shut off the gas supply if the pilot were not lit, would be a thoughtful pilot-safety upgrade.
e. An electrical disconnect switch was located near the furnace to facilitate shutting down electrical power to this furnace for maintenance and repairs.
f. Some warm air attic ducts were loosely connected or already separated and require competent transition fittings and fasteners to join rigid ducting to flex ducting.

g. No thermal insulation was presently installed on the return-air duct. Because the duct is in an unconditioned or cold area, such omission lends itself to higher energy consumption than on insulated ducts.

h. The metal return-air duct was in direct contact with crawl space soil and should be separated to prevent corrosion and future contamination.

i. The warm-air ducts and plenum were wrapped with crumbly asbestos-like material.

Circulation and Ventilation

The return air duct, flame ports, shelf, and furnace bottom were dirty and should be vacuumed regularly. The supply register on the hall floor was extremely dirty.

The filter box allows for 14 x 25 x 1-inch filters. Furnace filters need to be changed every two to four months. Dirty filters actually block air flow to the heat exchanger causing it to overheat. Improper filter maintenance is a primary cause of premature cracking.

Oxygen sources necessary for combustion were minimal.

Vent and Flue Piping

A cement-asbestos flue pipe was found. (See the discussion of asbestos elsewhere in this report.)

Heat Exchanger

This heater's gas burners appeared to be out of balance with unusual flame characteristics. Unevenness is difficult for anyone but a heating contractor or utility company technician to analyze. Such a check-up should be made.

There was corrosion and pitting around the frontal entry of the heat exchanger area.

The firebox (heat exchanger) of this furnace separates and redirects hot air from ambient air, which it also warms and circulates. A full inspection of a heat exchanger is not possible without dismantling a furnace which was not done. There was also no access for an inspection mirror. Ask PG&E or a heating contractor to conduct a standard safety check of this and all gas appliances, supply lines, and flues at every change of occupancy.

    ✔ Correct the gas leak at once.
    ✔ Address the nature and risk of asbestos-like material.
    ✔ Clean the ventilation and circulation components.
    ✔ Refasten all separated warm-air ducts.
    ✔ Separate the return-air duct from soil.
    ✔ Ask PG&E or a heating contractor to conduct a standard test and safety check of all gas-fueled appliances, supply lines, and flues.

INTERIOR

Generally, walls, ceilings, and floors were adequately maintained. The inspection industry does not report on cosmetic details.

Because the number of operable windows throughout has been reduced by painting, sources for fresh air have been diminished. Windows should be opened routinely.

Much of the family room and bedroom flooring was carpeted. Uncovered hardwood flooring in the living room was adequately maintained.

Windows in a number of rooms should be repaired. Some window locks and hardware need adjustment. Some double-hung sashes had broken wires. Five or six windows were not easily openable and need minor service work. Generally, any broken, deteriorated, and/or missing door and window locks and components, even though not specifically called out in this report, should be replaced or repaired.

> ✔ Repair windows, doors, and hardware as needed.

FIREPLACE

The living room fireplace had a sound firebox. Little cracking of bricks or mortar joints was detected. The firebox was empty.

Needing attention was the matter of cleanliness of the firebox, damper throat, and full extent of the chimney. Contact a professional chimney-sweep contractor to fully examine, repair, and clean all areas needed, as well as those areas that were not readily accessible for this inspection. This will insure continued safe and efficient fireplace operation.

The chimney had a screen-type spark arrester on its top.

The fireplace damper door was operational and well fitted. However, neither a protective ember screen nor a glass-door assembly was present.

The mantle, breastplate, and outer hearth were well maintained.

A full professional chimney inspection should be performed with each property's change in ownership and, thereafter, on a regular basis with the system maintenance of the building.

> ✔ Hire a professional chimney-sweep inspector/contractor.

KITCHEN

The kitchen was well maintained. The sink, faucet, trap and drain, and shutoff valves were working when tested. Water pressure was adequate.

Leakage at the faucet ball needs *immediate correction*.

The disposer was operational.

Inner surfaces of the dishwasher were clean. It did not yet have an anti-siphoning device but was well secured to the underside of the counter. An anti-siphoning device, installed above the sink rim, prevents backflow of waste products into the clean dishwasher appliance if the sewer system is blocked. A licensed plumber should be contacted for this installation.

Stained-wood cabinetry was in satisfactory condition.

Plastic laminated counters were also in satisfactory condition, however, the backsplash cap was missing and should be replaced.

Joints in all counter and sink areas should be continuously sealed with a good quality flexible caulking to help prevent moisture penetration.

A ducted exhaust fan in the overhead appliance was operational. The greasy exhaust filter should be cleaned and maintained regularly.

Resilient sheet flooring was recently installed and well maintained.

> ✔ Install an anti-siphoning device for the dishwasher.
> ✔ Complete the countertop's backsplash installation.
> ✔ Clean, repair, or replace exhaust fan components.

BATHROOM

This building had two bathrooms. Both were recently remodeled.

Water pressure was adequate; however, measurement is only a relative comparison rating. New owners should personally test each fixture to become familiar with each and make desired modifications.

Testing "dynamic water flow" (running two or more cold water fixtures concurrently) showed some drop in volume. Red was shown how to perform a "homeowner's dynamic water flow and temperature test" with each fixture on the property to prevent scalding if a toilet is flushed while someone is taking a shower.

No evidence of significant or unusual deterioration was evident on visible drain lines and trap piping. Tested drains ran freely, however, water leakage occurred quickly at the traps of both vanity wash basins, the shower pan, and the tub overflow fittings. All of these need *immediate repairs and/or corrections*, performed with permit, by a licensed plumbing contractor.

Toilets were secured to the floor.

Shower glass in both bathrooms did have a glazing label certifying composition.

✔ Correct the leaking traps, drains, lines, and fittings.

ROOFING

Membrane Types and Condition

Multiple layers of roofing materials appear to have been laid over this structure. The actual number or combined weight placed on structural members could not be determined. Multiple layers concern roofers and inspectors for different reasons: they create an uneven surface; retain moisture and/or gas vapors between membranes; may transfer decay to structural members in their contact; and may add excessive weight to the structure. Whenever multi-layered roofs receive their next membrane, all existing roofing materials should be torn off and discarded. Consider installing appropriately specified plywood sheathing at that time.

Although they were not fresh, each of the composition shingle sections appeared sound.

There was little or no evidence of unusual or significant roof deterioration, however, wooden sub-shingles had deteriorated edges.

Roof sections revealed vapor blisters, lumps, and patches. Debris was found on the roof. Roofing must be promptly and regularly maintained.

If a life-expectancy determination for the roofing system is needed, a licensed roofing contractor should be contacted to examine as well as estimate costs for maintenance repairs or complete replacement.

Chimneys, Gutters, and Flashing

Step-shingle flashing at sides of the fireplace chimney had rusted edges and may not be fastened securely to the chimney. Further exploration should be made by a sheet metal specialist.

A few gutter locations were severely rusted, especially on three unpainted interior sections.

Sheet metal gutters at the mitered corner of the rear patio, were damaged and need replacement soon. Several runs had separated from the building and/or had rusted spikes.

No counterflashing was in place between the roof and gutters which is needed to effectively collect and divert rain water to downspouts.

Gutters were laden with organic debris. Keep gutters and all other drain openings free of debris for proper drainage throughout the year. Outlets at the tops of downspouts should have mesh screening installed to prevent clogging.

Gutter installations were questionable. Gutters at sides and rear did not appear to be adequately sloped to provide proper drainage and should be resloped.

The downspout system was, for the most part, customarily installed. Unfortunately, a number of downspouts likely dump water directly onto various foundation areas below, which can cause erosion. Splash blocks or extenders can be placed at the base of such downspouts to divert collected water. Outlets at the tops of downspouts should also have mesh screening to prevent clogging.

Roofs are seldom, if ever, regularly inspected. Regardless of whether a Camp Brothers roof inspection was made, roofing problems are often subtle and difficult to evaluate. Because property inspectors don't often have the hands-on training and accessibility roofers have, whenever questions of roofing adequacy arise, a licensed roofing contractor should be asked to provide a thorough inspection and evaluation.

Biennially, before the rainy season, roofs should be examined by a qualified roofing contractor, and routinely maintained.

- ✔ Clean the roof system of debris.
- ✔ Have step shingle flashing examined by a qualified sheet metal contractor.
- ✔ Replace the gutter system with one that is fully primed and has counterflashing between gutters and shingles.

SEISMIC MAPS NOTATIONS (Optional Evaluation)

Map #1 — **Intensity of Ground Shaking:** "E" (the least intense rating in the city)
Map #2 — **Landslide Locations:** "Within such location(s)—three blocks from active slide"
Map #3 — **Building Damage:** "Minimal damage during a major (having an 8 or greater Richter rating) earthquake."
Map #4 — **Reservoir Failure:** "Outside such location(s)"
Map #5 — **Geologic Make-Up:** "Unsheared Franciscan Rock, KJU—highest stability"
Map #6 — **Liquefaction:** "Outside such location(s)"
Map #7 — **Subsidence:** "Outside such location(s)"
Map #8 — **Tsunami:** "Outside such location(s)"

• Prepurchase Inspection Report
x x x x _____ Street, San Francisco, California   _____ x x, 1996

Additional articles/pamphlets provided:

All-Points Bulletin newsletter; PG&E utilities pamphlets; "House Doctor" TV schedule; smoke detectors and asbestos articles; the NARI membership directory; an earthquake hardware catalogue, Beat the Quake, and a CBIS year-round home maintenance checklist.

Copies to:	deliver	mail	pick-up	fax	messenger
Buyer:	[ ]	[1]	[ ]	[ ]	[ ]
Buyer's Agent:	[ ]	[ ]	[ ]	[1]	[ ]
Seller's Agent:	[ ]	[ ]	[ ]	[ ]	[ ]

• Page 15

Appendix C

Glossary

● ●

*T*he terms that appear in *italic type* within the definitions are defined in this glossary.

acceleration clause: Watch out for an *acceleration clause* in your mortgage contract. This provision gives the lender the right to demand payment of the entire outstanding balance if you miss a monthly payment, sell the property, or otherwise fail to perform as promised under the terms of your mortgage. (See also *due-on-sale clause*.) Ouch!

adjustable-rate mortgage (ARM): An *adjustable-rate mortgage* is a mortgage whose *interest rate* and monthly payments vary throughout its life. ARMs typically start with an unusually low interest rate (see *teaser rate*) that gradually rises over time. If the overall level of interest rates drops, as measured by a variety of different indexes (see *index*), the interest rate of your ARM generally follows suit. Similarly, if interest rates rise, so does your mortgage's interest rate and monthly payment. The amount that the interest can fluctuate is limited by *caps* (see also *periodic caps* and *lifetime caps*). Before you agree to an adjustable-rate mortgage, be sure that you can afford the highest payments that would result if the interest rate on your mortgage increased to the maximum allowed.

adjusted cost basis: For tax purposes, the *adjusted cost basis* is important when you sell your property, because it allows you to determine what your profit or loss is. You can arrive at the adjusted cost basis by adding the cost of the *capital improvements* that you've made to the home to the price that you paid for the home. Capital improvements increase your property's value and its life expectancy.

adjustment period or adjustment frequency: This term has nothing to do with the first few weeks after you've broken up with your sweetheart; it refers to how often the *interest rate* for an *adjustable-rate mortgage* changes. Some adjustable-rate mortgages change every month, but it is more typical to have one or two adjustments per year. The less frequently your loan rate shifts, the less financial uncertainty you may have. But less frequent adjustments in your mortgage rate mean that you will probably have a higher *teaser* or initial interest rate. (The initial interest rate is also called the "start rate.")

annual percentage rate (APR): This figure states the total yearly cost of a mortgage as expressed by the actual rate of interest paid. The *APR* includes the base *interest rate*, *points*, and any other add-on loan fees and costs. The APR is thus invariably higher than the rate of interest that the lender quotes for the mortgage.

appraisal: You must pay for the mortgage lender to hire an appraiser to give an "opinion of value" (that is, the appraiser gives a measure of the market value) of the house you want to buy. This professional opinion helps to protect the lender from lending you money on a home that is worth less than what you've agreed to pay for it. For typical homes, the *appraisal* fee is in the $200 to $300 range.

appreciation/depreciation: *Appreciation* refers to the increase of a property's value. *Depreciation* (the reverse of appreciation) is when a property's value decreases.

arbitration of disputes: A method of solving contract disputes which is generally less costly and faster than going to a court of law. In *arbitration,* buyers and sellers present their differences to a neutral arbitrator who, after hearing the evidence, makes a decision that resolves the disagreement. The arbitrator's decision is final and may be enforced as if it were a court judgment. Consult a real estate lawyer if you are ever a party in an arbitration. (Also see *mediation.*)

assessed value: The *assessed value* is the value of a property (according to your local county tax assessor) for the purpose of determining your *property taxes.*

assumable mortgage: Some mortgages allow future buyers of your home to take over the remaining loan balance of your mortgage. If you need to sell your house but *interest rates* are high, having an *assumable mortgage* may be handy. You may be able to offer the buyer your assumable loan at a lower interest rate than the current going interest rate. Most assumables are *adjustable-rate mortgages — fixed-rate, assumable mortgages* are nearly extinct these days because lenders realize that they lose a great deal of money on these types of mortgages when interest rates skyrocket.

balloon loans: These loans require level payments just as a 15- or 30-year *fixed-rate mortgage* does. But well before their *maturity date* (the date when they'd be paid off) — typically three to ten years after the start date — the full remaining balance of the loan becomes due and payable. Although *balloon loans* can save you money because they charge a lower rate of interest relative to fixed-rate loans, balloon loans are dangerous. Being able to *refinance* a loan is never a sure thing. Beware of balloon loans!

bridge loan: If you find yourself in the inadvisable situation where you have closed on a new home before you have sold your old one, you may need a short-term *bridge loan* that enables you to borrow against the *equity* that is tied up in your old home until your old home sells. We say "bridge" because such a loan is the only thing keeping you above water financially during this period when you own two houses. Bridge loans are expensive compared to other alternatives, such as using a *cash reserve,* borrowing from family or friends, or using the proceeds from the sale of your current home. In most cases, you need the bridge loan for only a few months in order to tide you over until you sell your house. Thus, the loan fees can represent a high cost (about 10 percent of the loan amount) for such a short-term loan.

broker: Real estate *brokers* are one level higher on the real estate professional totem pole than *real estate agents* (or salespeople). Real estate agents cannot legally work on their own — they must be supervised by a broker. To become a broker in most states, a real estate salesperson must have a number of years of full-time real estate experience, meet special educational requirements, and pass a state licensing exam. See also *real estate agent* and *Realtor.*

buydown: A *buydown* is a *Veterans Administration* loan plan that is available only in some new housing developments and is aimed at veterans with low or modest incomes. Buydown simply means that a builder agrees to pay part of the homebuyer's mortgage for the first few years. Sellers also sometimes do interest rate buydowns to create attractive financing for buyers of their houses by paying lenders a predetermined amount of money so lenders will reduce their mortgage interest rates.

buyer's brokers: Historically, real estate *brokers* and *agents* worked only for sellers. The *buyer's broker* only owes allegiance to the buyer and does not have an agent relationship with the seller. Although this may be viewed as an improvement for all the buyers in the world, don't be too ecstatic. Buyer's brokers are still paid on *commission* when you buy, so don't expect them to be supportive of you if you habitually lollygag. Also keep in mind that the higher the purchase price of the house, the more money the buyer's broker makes.

capital gains: For tax purposes, a *capital gain* is the profit that you make when you sell a home. For example, if you buy a home for $125,000 and then (a number of years later) you sell the house for $175,000, your capital gain is $50,000. You can avoid paying tax on this profit by purchasing another home that costs at least as much as the one that you sold, but you must buy the new home within two years of the sale of the home that you previously owned.

capital gains rollover: *Capital gains rollover* is not a passing dance fad. Instead, capital gains rollover refers to certain tax privileges you have if and when you sell, for a profit, the house that is your primary residence. If you have a *capital gain* when selling your primary residence, you can roll over (or defer) paying tax on the profit if you buy a new home of equal or greater value within two years before or after the sale of your previous house.

caps: Real estate *caps* having nothing to do with dental work. There are two different types of caps for *adjustable-rate mortgages.* The *life cap* limits the highest or lowest *interest rate* that is allowed over the entire life of your mortgage. The *periodic cap* limits the amount that your interest rate can change in one *adjustment period.* A one-year *ARM,* for example, may have a start rate of 7.5 percent with a + or − 2 percent periodic adjustment cap and a 6 percent life cap. On a worst-case basis, the loan's *interest rate* would be 9.5 percent in the second year, 11.5 percent in the third year, and 13.5 percent (7.5 percent start rate plus the 6 percent life cap) forevermore, starting with the fourth year.

cash reserve: Most mortgage lenders require that homebuyers have sufficient cash left over after closing on their home purchase in order to make the first two mortgage payments or to cover a financial emergency.

closing costs: After you've passed every home-buying obstacle and reached the safe clearing in order to buy your home, one final potential land mine appears in the form of *closing costs.* These costs generally total from 2 percent to 5 percent of the home's purchase price and are completely independent of (and in addition to) the *down payment.* Closing costs include such things as *points* (that is, loan *origination fee* to cover lender's administrative costs), an *appraisal* fee, a *credit report* fee, mortgage interest for the period between the closing date and the first mortgage payment, *homeowners insurance* premium, *title insurance,* pro-rated *property taxes,* and recording and transferring charges. So when you are finally ready to buy, you need to have enough cash to pay all these costs in order to buy your dream home.

commission: The *commission* is the percentage of the selling price of a house that is paid to the *real estate agents* and *brokers.* Because most agents and brokers are paid by commission, understanding how the commission can influence the way that agents and brokers work is important for homebuyers. Agents and brokers make money only when you make a purchase, and they make more money when you make a bigger purchase. Choose an agent carefully and take your agent's advice with a grain of salt because this inherent conflict of interest can often set an agent's visions and goals at odds with your visions and goals.

community property: Along with *joint tenancy* and *tenancy-in-common, community property* is a way that married couples may take title to real property. Community property offers two major advantages over joint tenancy and tenancy-in-common. First, community property ownership allows spouses to transfer interests, by Will or otherwise, to whomever they wish. The second advantage of holding title to a home in community property is that the surviving spouse gets favorable tax treatment. The market value of the entire house as of the spouse's date of death (such market value is also called the house's "stepped-up basis") is used rather than the house's original cost, which reduces the taxable profit (assuming that the home has appreciated in value) when the house is sold.

comparable market analysis (CMA): Buying a Ford Taurus from the first dealer that you visit would be impulsive and foolish. You need to shop around to find out where the best deal on that type of car is. The same is true with home buying. If you are interested in buying a home, you need to find out how much money houses in the area have been selling for. You must identify "comparable" homes that have sold within the last six months, are in the immediate vicinity of the home that you desire to purchase, and are as similar as possible to the one that you're interested in buying in terms of size, age, and condition. You must do the same thing for comparable houses currently on the market to see if prices are rising, flat, or falling. A written analysis of comparable houses currently being offered for sale and comparable houses sold in the past six months is called a *comparable market analysis (CMA).*

condominiums: *Condominiums* are housing units that are contained within a development area in which you own your actual unit and a share of everything else in the development (lobby, parking areas, land, and the like, which are known as *common areas).* Condominiums are a less-expensive form of housing than single-family homes are. For this reason, condominiums are mistakenly seen as good starter houses. Unfortunately, condominiums generally don't increase in value as rapidly as single-family houses do because the demand for condos is lower than the demand for houses. And, because condominiums are far easier for builders to develop than single-family homes are, the supply of condominiums often exceeds the demand for them.

contingencies: *Contingencies* are conditions contained in almost all home purchase offers. The seller or buyer must meet or waive all contingencies before the deal can be closed. These conditions are related to such things as the buyer's review and approval of property inspections or the buyer's ability to get the mortgage financing that is specified in the contract.

convertible adjustable-rate mortgages: Unlike conventional *adjustable-rate mortgages, convertible adjustable-rate mortgages* give you the opportunity to convert to a *fixed-rate mortgage,* usually between the 13th to 60th month of the loan. For this privilege, convertible adjustable-rate mortgage loans have a higher rate of interest than conventional adjustable-rate mortgages, and a conversion fee (which can range from a few hundred dollars to one percent or so of the remaining balance) is charged. Additionally, if you choose to convert to a fixed-rate mortgage, you will pay a slightly higher rate than what you can get by shopping around for the best rates available at the time you convert.

cooperatives (co-ops): *Cooperatives* are apartment buildings where you own a share of a corporation whose main asset is the building that you live in. In high-cost areas, cooperatives (like their cousins, *condominiums* and *townhouses*) are cheaper alternatives to buying single-family houses. Unfortunately, cooperatives also resemble their cousins in that they generally lag behind single-family homes in terms of *appreciation.* Co-ops are also, as a rule, harder to sell and obtain loans for than condominiums.

cosigner: If you have a checkered past in the credit world, you may need help securing a mortgage, even though you are financially stable. A friend or relative can come to your rescue by co-signing (which literally means being indebted for) a mortgage. A *cosigner* cannot improve your *credit report* but can improve your chances of getting a mortgage. Cosigners should be aware, however, that co-signing for your loan will adversely affect their future creditworthiness since your loan becomes what is known as a contingent liability against their borrowing power.

cost basis: See *adjusted cost basis.*

covenants, conditions, and restrictions (CC&Rs): *CC&Rs* establish a condominium by creating a homeowners association, by stipulating how the *condominium's* maintenance and repairs will be handled, and by regulating what can and can't be done to individual units and the condominium's common areas. These restrictions may apply to lawn maintenance, window curtain colors, and the like. Some CC&Rs put community decision-making rights into the hands of a homeowners association.

credit report: A *credit report* is the main report that a lender uses to determine your creditworthiness. You must pay for the lender to obtain this report, which the lender uses to determine your ability to handle all forms of credit and to pay off loans in a timely fashion.

debt-to-income ratio: Before you go out home buying, you should determine what your price range is. Lenders generally figure that you shouldn't spend more than about 33 to 40 percent of your monthly income for your housing costs. The *debt-to-income ratio* measures your future monthly housing expenses, which include your proposed mortgage payment (debt), property tax, and insurance, in relation to your monthly income.

deed: A *deed* is the document that conveys title to real property. Before you receive the deed, the *title insurance* company must receive the mortgage company's payment and your payments for the *down payment* and *closing costs.* The title insurance company must also show that the seller holds clear and legal title to the property for which title is being conveyed.

default: *Default* is the failure to make your monthly mortgage payments on time. You are officially in default when you have missed two or more monthly payments. Default also refers to other violations of the mortgage terms. Default can lead to *foreclosure* on your house.

delinquency: At first you are *delinquent;* then you are in *default.* Delinquency occurs when a monthly mortgage payment is not received by the due date.

down payment: The *down payment* is the part of the purchase price that the buyer pays in cash, up front, and does not finance with a mortgage. Generally, the larger the down payment, the better the deal that you can get on a mortgage. You can usually get access to the best mortgage programs with a down payment of 20 percent of the purchase price of the home.

due-on-sale clause: A *due-on-sale clause* contained in the mortgage entitles the lender to demand full payment of all money due on your loan when you sell or transfer title to the property.

earthquake insurance: Although the West Coast is often associated with earthquakes, other areas are also prone to earthquakes. An *earthquake insurance* rider on a homeowners policy pays to repair or rebuild your home if it is damaged in an earthquake. If you live in an area with earthquake risk, get earthquake insurance coverage!

equity: In the real estate world, *equity* refers to the difference between the market value of your home and what you owe on it. For example, if your home is worth $200,000 and you have an outstanding mortgage of $140,000, your equity is $60,000.

escrow: *Escrow* is not an exotic dish; it's the holding of important documents and money (related to the purchase/sale of a property) by a neutral third party (the escrow officer) prior to the close of the transaction. After the seller accepts the buyer's offer, the buyer does not immediately move into the house. A period where *contingencies* have to be met or waived exists. During this period, the escrow service holds the buyer's *down payment* and the buyer's and seller's documents related to the sale. "Closing escrow" means that the deal is completed. Among other duties, the escrow officer makes sure that the previous mortgage is paid off, your loan is funded, and the *real estate agents* are paid.

Fannie Mae: See *Federal National Mortgage Association.*

Federal Home Loan Mortgage Corporation (FHLMC): The *FHLMC* (or *Freddie Mac*) is one of the best known institutions in the *secondary mortgage market.* Freddie Mac buys mortgages from banks and other mortgage-lending institutions and, in turn, sells these mortgages to investors. These loan investments are considered safe because Freddie Mac buys mortgages only from companies that conform to its stringent mortgage regulations, and Freddie Mac guarantees the repayment of *principal* and interest on the mortgages that it sells.

Federal Housing Administration mortgage (FHA): *Federal Housing Administration mortgages* are marketed to people with modest means. The main advantages of these mortgages is that they require a small *down payment* (usually between 3 percent and 5 percent). FHA mortgages also offer competitive *interest rates* — typically $1/2$ to 1 percent below the interest rates on other mortgages. The downside is that, with an

FHA mortgage, the buyer must purchase mortgage *default* insurance (see *private mortgage insurance*).

Federal National Mortgage Association (FNMA): The *FNMA* (or *Fannie Mae*) is one of the best known institutions in the *secondary mortgage market*. Fannie Mae buys mortgages from banks and other mortgage-lending institutions and, in turn, sells them to investors. These loan investments are considered safe because Fannie Mae buys mortgages only from companies that conform to its stringent mortgage regulations, and Fannie Mae guarantees the repayment of *principal* and interest on the loans that it sells.

fixed-rate mortgage: The *fixed-rate mortgage* is the granddaddy of all mortgages. You lock into an *interest rate* (for example, 8.5 percent), and it never changes during the life (term) of your 15- or 30-year mortgage. Your mortgage payment will be the same amount each and every month. Compare fixed-rate mortgages with *adjustable-rate mortgages.*

flood insurance: "When the flood waters recede, the poor folk start from scratch." (Richard Wright) They start from scratch unless they have *flood insurance.* In federally designated flood areas, flood insurance is required. If there's even a remote chance that your area may flood, having flood insurance is prudent.

foreclosure: *Foreclosure* is the legal process of the mortgage lender taking possession of and selling the property to attempt to satisfy indebtedness. When you *default* on a loan and the lender deems that you are incapable of making payments, you may lose your house to foreclosure. Being in default, however, does not necessarily lead to foreclosure. Some lenders are lenient and help you work out a solution if they see that your problems are temporary. Foreclosure is traumatic for the homeowner and expensive for the lender.

formula: We're not talking about baby food here. In real estate lingo, the *formula* is how you calculate interest rates for *adjustable-rate mortgages.* Add the *margin* to the *index* to get the *interest rate* (margin + index = interest rate).

Freddie Mac: See *Federal Home Loan Mortgage Corporation.*

graduated-payment mortgage: A rare bird these days, the *graduated-payment mortgage* gives you the opportunity to cut your total interest costs. With a graduated-payment mortgage, your monthly payments are increased by a predetermined formula (for example, a 3 percent increase each year for seven years, after which time payments no longer fluctuate). If you expect to land a job that may allow you to make these higher payments, you may want to consider this option.

home-equity loan: A *home-equity loan* is technical jargon for what used to be called a *second mortgage.* With this type of loan, you borrow against the *equity* in your house. If used wisely, a home-equity loan can help people pay off high-interest consumer debt, which is usually at a higher *interest rate* than a home-equity loan and is not tax-deductible; or a home-equity loan can be used for other short-term needs, such as for payments on a remodeling project.

homeowners insurance: Required and necessary. No ifs, ands, or buts about it; you need "dwelling coverage" that can cover the cost to rebuild your house. The *liability insurance* portion of this policy protects you against accidents that occur on your property. Another essential piece is the *personal property coverage* that pays to replace your lost worldly possessions and usually totals 50 to 75 percent of the dwelling coverage. Finally, get *flood or earthquake insurance* if you are in an area susceptible to these natural disasters. As with other types of insurance, get the highest deductibles with which you are comfortable.

home warranty plan: A *home warranty plan* is a type of insurance that covers repairs to specific parts of the home for a predetermined time period. Because home warranty plans typically cover small-potato items, such plans are not worth buying. Instead, spend your money on a good *house inspection* before you buy the home in order to identify any major problems (electrical, plumbing, or structural).

house inspection: Like *homeowners insurance,* we think that a *house inspection* is a necessity. The following should be inspected: overall condition of the property, inside and out; electrical, heating, and plumbing systems; foundation; roof; pest control and dry rot; and seismic/slide risk. A good house inspection can save you money by locating problems. With the inspection report in hand, you can ask the seller to either do repairs or reduce the purchase price. Hire your own inspectors. Never be satisfied with a seller's inspection reports.

hybrid loans: Combining the features of *fixed-rate* and *adjustable-rate mortgages* is the objective of *hybrid loans.* The initial *interest rate* for a hybrid loan may hold at the same rate for the first three to ten years of the loan (as opposed to only six to twelve months for a standard adjustable-rate mortgage), and then the interest rate adjusts biannually or annually. Remember that the longer the interest holds at the

same initial rate, the higher the interest rate will be. These hybrid loans are best for people who plan to own their house for a short time (fewer than ten years) and who do not like the volatility of a typical adjustable-rate mortgage.

index: The *index* is the measure of the overall level of *interest rates* that the lender uses as a reference to calculate the specific interest rate on an adjustable-rate loan. The index plus the *margin* is the *formula* for determining the interest rate on an *adjustable-rate mortgage.* One index used on some mortgages is the six-month treasury bill. If the going rate for these treasury bills is 5.5 percent and the margin is 2.5 percent, your interest rate would be 8 percent. Other common indices used are certificates of deposit index, 11th District Cost of Funds index, and LIBOR index.

interest rate: Interest is what lenders charge you to use their money. The higher the rate of interest, the higher the risk. For *fixed-rate mortgages,* remember that the *interest rate* has a seesaw relationship with the *points.* A high number of points is usually associated with a lower interest rate, and vice versa. For an *adjustable-rate mortgage,* make sure that you understand the *formula* (the *index* plus the *margin*) that determines how the interest rate is calculated after the *teaser rate* expires.

investment property: Real estate is a good long-term investment — it has produced returns similar to those from diversified stock portfolios over the years. In practice, investment in real estate is different from investment in stocks. You can also *leverage* your real estate investment — that is, you can make a profit on your investment as well as on borrowed money. Investing in real estate is time intensive (although investing in stocks can be, too, if you don't use a professional money manager). You also need to be adept at managing people and money if you are to bear fruit with real estate investments. One drawback of *investment property* is that you cannot shelter your investment-property profits in a retirement account the way you can shelter profits earned through stock investments.

joint tenancy: *Joint tenancy* is a form of co-ownership that gives each tenant equal interest and rights in the property, including the right of survivorship. At the death of one joint tenant, ownership automatically transfers to the surviving joint tenant. This form of ownership is most appropriate for unmarried people in a long-term relationship. Some of the limitations of joint tenancy are (first) that each person must own an equal share of the house and (second) the right of survivorship is terminated if one person transfers his *deed* from joint tenancy to *tenancy-in-common*.

late charge: A *late charge* is a fee that is charged if a mortgage payment is received late. A late charge can be steep — as much as 5 percent of the amount of your mortgage payment. Ouch! Get those payments in on time!

lease-option: A *lease-option* is something of which syndicated real estate columnist Robert J. Bruss is a big fan. A property that you can lease with an option to purchase at a later date has a lease-option contract. These contracts usually require an up-front payment (called "option consideration") to secure the purchase option. The consideration is usually credited toward your down payment when you exercise your option to buy the home. An important factor in a lease-option agreement is what portion of the monthly rent payments (typically one-third) is applied toward the purchase price

if you buy. You'll usually pay a slightly higher rent because of the *lease-option* privilege.

leverage: *Leverage* refers to exerting great influence with little effort. Buying a house allows you to leverage your cash in two ways. Suppose, for example, that you make a 20 percent *down payment* on a $100,000 house — thus investing $20,000. The first leverage is that you control a $100,000 property with $20,000. If your house *appreciates* to a value of $120,000, you've made a $20,000 profit on a $20,000 investment — a 100-percent return thanks to leveraging. However, leverage works both ways, so if your house depreciates. . . .

lien: A *lien* is a legal claim against a property for the purpose of securing payment for work performed and money owed on account of loans, judgements, or claims. Liens are encumbrances, and they need to be paid off before a property can be sold or title can be transferred to a subsequent buyer. The *liens* that exist on a property for sale appear in a property's preliminary title report.

life cap: The total amount that your *adjustable-rate mortgage interest rate* and monthly payment can fluctuate up or down during the duration of the loan is determined by the *life cap*. The life cap is different from the *periodic cap* that limits the extent to which your interest rate can change up or down in any one *adjustment period*.

liquidated damages: In most real estate contracts, buyers and sellers may agree at the beginning of the transaction regarding how much money would be awarded to one party if the other party violates the terms of the contract without good cause. *Liquidated damages* confines and defines how much money the injured party may recover.

Buyers, for example, generally limit their losses to the amount of their deposit. You should discuss the advisability of using the liquidated damages provision with a lawyer or real estate agent.

lock-in: A *lock-in* is a mortgage lender's commitment and written agreement to guarantee a specified *interest rate* to the homebuyer, provided that the loan is closed within a set period of time. The lock-in also usually specifies the number of *points* to be paid at closing. Most lenders will not lock-in unless you have made an offer on the property and the property has been appraised. For the privilege of locking in the rate in advance of the closing of a loan, you may pay a slight interest rate premium.

margin: The *margin* is the amount that is added to the *index* in order to calculate your *interest rate* for an *adjustable-rate mortgage.* Most loans have margins around 2.5 percent. Unlike the *index* (which constantly moves up and down), the margin never changes over the life of the loan.

mediation of disputes: *Mediation* is a fast, inexpensive way to resolve simple contract disputes. In mediation, buyers and sellers present their differences to a neutral *mediator* who does *not* have the power to impose a settlement on either party. Instead, the mediator helps buyers and sellers work together to reach a mutually acceptable solution of their differences. It is probably in your best interests to mediate your problem before going to an arbitrator or suing in a court of law. (Also see *arbitration*.)

mortgage broker: A *mortgage broker* is a person who can help you find a mortgage. Mortgage brokers buy mortgages wholesale from lenders and then mark the mortgages up (typically from 0.5 to 1 percent) and sell them to buyers. A good mortgage broker is most helpful for people who will not shop around on their own for a mortgage or for people who have blemishes on their *credit reports.*

mortgage life insurance: *Mortgage life insurance* guarantees that the lender will receive its money in the event that you meet an untimely demise. Many people may try to convince you that you need this insurance to protect your dependents and loved ones. We recommend that you do not waste your time or money with this insurance! Mortgage life insurance is expensive. If you need life insurance, buy low-cost, high-quality term life insurance instead of mortgage life insurance.

multiple listing service: A *multiple listing service* (or *MLS*) is a *real estate agents'* cooperative service that contains descriptions of most of the houses that are for sale. Real estate agents use this computer-based service to keep up with property they are listing for sale in their area.

negative amortization: Although it may sound like science fiction jargon, *negative amortization* occurs when your outstanding mortgage balance increases despite the fact that you're making the required monthly payments. Negative amortization occurs with *adjustable-rate mortgages* that *cap* the increase in your monthly payment but do not cap the *interest rate.* Therefore, your monthly payments do not cover all the interest that you actually owe. If you have ever watched your credit card balance snowball as you made only the minimum monthly payment, then you already have experience with this phenomenon. Avoid loans with this feature!

origination fee: See *points.*

partnership: A *partnership* is a way for unmarried people to take title of a property. *Partnerships* most often occur among people who have a business relationship and who buy the property as either a business asset or for investment purposes. If you intend to buy property with partners, have a real estate lawyer prepare a written partnership agreement for all the partners to sign *before* making an offer to purchase.

periodic cap: This *cap* limits the amount that the *interest rate* of an *adjustable-rate mortgage* can change up or down in one *adjustment period*. See also *caps*.

points: Also known as a loan's "origination fee," *points* are interest charges paid up-front when you close on your loan. Points are actually a percentage of your total loan amount (one point is equal to 1 percent of the loan amount). For a $100,000 loan, one point costs you $1,000. Generally speaking, the more points that a loan has, the lower its *interest rate* should be. All the points that you pay on a purchase mortgage are deductible in the year that you pay them. If you *refinance* your mortgage, however, the points that you pay at the time that you refinance must be amortized over the life of the loan. If you get a 30-year mortgage when you refinance, for example, you can deduct only one-thirtieth of the points on your taxes each year.

prepayment penalty: One advantage of most mortgages is that you can make additional payments to pay the loan off faster if you have the inclination and the money to do so. A *prepayment penalty* discourages you from doing this by penalizing you for early payments. Some states prohibit lenders from penalizing people who prepay their loans. Avoid mortgages which penalize prepayment!

principal: The *principal* is the amount that you borrow for a loan. If you borrow $100,000, your principal is $100,000. Each monthly mortgage payment consists of a portion of principal that must be repaid plus the interest that the lender is charging you for the use of the money. During the early years of your mortgage, your loan payment is primarily interest.

private mortgage insurance (PMI): If your *down payment* is less than 20 percent of your home's purchase price, you will likely need to purchase *private mortgage insurance* (also known as "mortgage default insurance"). The smaller the down payment, the more likely a homebuyer is to *default* on a loan. Private mortgage insurance can add hundreds of dollars per year to your loan costs. After the *equity* in your property increases to 20 percent, you no longer need the insurance. Do not confuse this insurance with *mortgage life insurance*.

probate sale: A *probate sale* is the sale of a home that occurs when a homeowner dies and the property is to be divided among inheritors or sold to pay debts. The executor of the estate organizes the probate sale, and a probate court judge oversees the process. The highest bidder receives the property.

property tax: You will have to pay a *property tax* on the home you own. Annually, property tax averages 1 to 2 percent of a home's value, but property tax rates vary widely throughout this great land.

prorations: Certain items such as property taxes and homeowners association dues are continuing expenses that must be prorated (distributed) between the buyers and sellers at close of escrow. If the buyers, for example, owe the sellers money for property taxes that the sellers paid in advance, the prorated amount of money due the sellers at close of escrow is shown as a debit (charge) to the buyers and a credit to the sellers.

real estate agent: *Real estate agents* are the worker bees of real estate sales. Also called "salespeople," agents are supervised by a real estate *broker*. Agents are licensed by the state; their pay is typically based totally on *commissions* generated by selling property.

real estate investment trust (REIT): *Real estate investment trusts* are like a mutual fund of real estate investments. Such trusts invest in a collection of properties (from shopping centers to apartment buildings). REITs trade on the major stock exchanges. If you want to invest in real estate while avoiding the hassles inherent in owning property, real estate investment trusts may be the right choice for you.

Realtor: A *Realtor* is a real estate *broker* or *agent* who belongs to the National Association of Realtors, a trade association whose members agree to its ways of doing business and code of ethics. The National Association of Realtors offers its members seminars and courses that deal with real estate topics.

refinance: *Refinance*, or "re-fi," is a fancy word for taking out a new mortgage loan (usually at a lower *interest rate*) to pay off an existing mortgage (generally at a higher interest rate). Refinancing is not automatic, nor is refinancing guaranteed. Refinancing can also be a hassle and expensive. Carefully weigh the costs and benefits of refinancing.

return on investment: The *return on investment* is the percentage of profit that you make on an investment. If you put $1,000 into an investment, and one year later your account is worth $1,100, you have made a profit of $100. Your return is the profit ($100) divided by the initial investment ($1,000) — 10 percent. See also *leverage*.

reverse mortgage: A *reverse mortgage* enables elderly homeowners, typically who are low on cash, to tap into their home's *equity* without selling their home or moving from it. Specifically, a lending institution makes a check out to you each month, and you can use the check as you want. This money is really a loan against the value of your home; because the money that you receive is a loan, the money is tax-free when you receive it. The downside of these loans is that they deplete your equity in your estate, the fees and *interest rates* tend to be on the high side, and some require repayment within a certain number of years.

second mortgage: See *home-equity loan*. A *second mortgage* is a mortgage that ranks after a first mortgage in priority of recording. In the event of a *foreclosure,* the proceeds from the sale of the home are used to pay off the loans in the order in which they were recorded. You can have a third (or even a fourth) mortgage, but the further down the line the mortgage is, the higher the risk of *default* on the mortgage — hence, the higher *interest rate* that you'll pay on the mortgage.

The 72-hour clause: The *72-hour clause* is commonly inserted into real estate purchase offers when the purchase of a home is contingent upon the sale of the buyer's current house. The seller accepts the buyer's offer, but reserves the right to accept a better offer if one should happen to come along. However, the seller cannot do this arbitrarily. If the seller receives an offer that he wants to accept, he must notify the buyer of that fact in writing. The buyer then usually has 72 hours (though the alloted amount of time can vary) from the seller's notification to remove the contingency-of-sale clause and move on with the purchase; otherwise, the buyer's offer is wiped out.

shared-equity transaction: In a *shared-equity transaction,* a private investor contributes money toward the purchase of a house and subsequently shares *equity* as a co-owner. When the house is sold, the investor takes a share of the profit or loss. These shared-equity transactions can become fairly complicated because the investor co-owner and the resident co-owner may have conflicts of interest. For example, the investor co-owner may want to sell the property to make a profit, but the resident co-owner may want to stay put. If you intend to participate in an equity-sharing transaction, have a lawyer who works with residential real estate *partnerships* prepare a written partnership agreement for all parties to sign prior to purchasing the property.

tax deductible: *Tax deductible* refers to payments that you may deduct against your federal and state taxable income. The interest portion of your mortgage payments, loan *points,* and *property taxes* are tax deductible; your employment income is not!

teaser rate: Otherwise known as the *initial interest rate,* the *teaser rate* is the attractively low interest rate that most *adjustable-rate mortgages* start with. Don't be sucked into a mortgage because it has a low teaser rate. Look at the mortgage's *formula (index + margin = interest rate)* for a more reliable method of estimating the loan's future interest rate — the interest rate that will apply after the loan is "fully indexed."

tenancy-in-common: *Tenancy-in-common* is probably the best way for unmarried co-owners to take title to a home (except for those unmarried co-owners who are involved in close, long-term relationships — see *joint tenancy*). Co-owners do not need to own equal shares of the property that is held as a tenancy-in-common. A tenancy-in-common also does not provide for the right of survivorship that automatically passes the deceased partner's ownership to the survivor without *probate.* The deceased's share of the property involved in a tenancy-in-common passes to the person named to receive that share of the property in the deceased's will or living trust.

title insurance: *Title insurance* covers the legal fees and expenses necessary to defend your title against claims that may be made against your ownership of the property. The extent of your coverage depends upon whether you have an owner's standard coverage or extended-coverage title insurance policy. To get a mortgage, you also have to buy a lender's title insurance policy to protect your lender against title risks.

top producers: People remark that 20 percent of all *real estate agents* account for 80 percent of all real estate sales. Be cautious. Why is that agent a *top producer?* Some agents get to the top by being pushy and selling a great deal of property without patiently educating buyers — not the kind of agent that you want! If, however, the agent is a top producer because she works hard to meet the needs of her clients, then being a top producer is a good thing.

townhouses: *Townhouse* is the decorative name for a row (or attached) home. Townhouses are cheaper than single-family homes because they use common walls and roofs and save land. In terms of investment appreciation potential, townhouses lie somewhere between single-family homes and *condominiums.*

Veterans Administration loans: *Veterans Administration loans* are *fixed-rate mortgages* for veterans of the American military services. The rules to obtain these mortgages are less stringent in certain respects than are the rules for conventional mortgages. Veterans Administration loans require no *down payment* as long as the appraised value of the house is below a certain threshold level, and the *interest rate* on Veterans Administration loans typically falls 0.5 to 1 percent below the rate that is currently being charged on conventional loans.

Index

financial advisors, real estate teams, 189–191
fixed-rate mortgages, 86–87
  defined, 42, 325
  home ownership, 12
  interest rate considerations, 94–95
  points, 95–96
  selecting, 94–98
  versus adjustable rate, 84–94
fixer-uppers, 158–162
  as good investments, 280
  risks and opportunities of, 161–162
  structural repairs versus renovations,
    160–161
flood insurance, 325
FNMA (Federal National Mortgage
    Association), 44, 325
foreclosures, 162–163
  buying directly from lenders, 163
  defined, 325
  risks of, 162–163
Form 1003. *See* Uniform Residential Loan
    Application
forms (mortgage), 115–132
  estimated closing costs worksheet, *120*
  falsifying caveat, 117
  permissions to inspect finances, 117–119
  required documents, 115–117
  Uniform Residential Loan Application
    (Form 1003), 119–130
formulas, defined, 325
Freddie Mac, FHLMC (Federal Home Loan
    Mortgage Corporation), 324
FSBO (For Sale By Owner), buying without
    agents, 177, 286

• G •

general contractor inspections, 243
get-rich-quick schemes, real estate, 77
Ginnie Mae, GNMA (Government National
    Mortgage Association), 44
graduated-payment mortgages, 325

• H •

health insurance, 37
home ownership
  advantages of, 10–15
  affordability, 21, 39–66
  appreciation, 136
  cost of, 41–55
  equity, 13, 136
  evaluating, 9–21
  fair market value, 170, 199–202
  financing, 23–38
  fixed-rate mortgages. *See* fixed-rate
    mortgages
  individualizing, 13–14
  inflation and, 12, 20–21
  insurance, 34–38, 49–50
  job security and, 17–18
  landlord avoidance, 14–15
  location, 137–140
  logistics and, 18–19
  net worth, 13
  overbuying, 19
  realities of, 10–16
  reverse mortgages, 13
  tax benefits of, 52–55
  ten pitfalls of rent-versus-buy decisions,
    16–21
  trading down, 13
  trading up, 284
  underbuying, 19–20
  value, 197
  vested interests and, 18
  worth considerations, 195–212
home prices, 67–80
  adding value with hidden opportunities,
    77–78
  affordability, 39–66
  available housing and, 70–72
  bidding wars, 211
  buying during slow periods, 79–80
  buying when others are scared to, 78
  comparable market analysis (CMAs),
    202–209
  cost overview, 198

• N •

perspective and, 216
process of, 220–225
selling for more than asking price, 230
styles, 226–227
unfair advantages, 227–229
violent forces and, 216–217
weak positions, 228–229
net worth, home ownership and, 13
new homes
    detached residences, 144–147
    inspecting, 242
"no-point" mortgages, 96
nonrecurring closing costs, negotiating credits
        in escrow, 235–236
notary fees, closing costs, 57

• O •

offers to purchase, negotiations, 221–222
oral agreements and negotiations, 238
origination fees. *See* points
out-of-neighborhood comps, comparable
        market analysis (CMAs), 207
overbuying, home ownership, 19
overimproving properties, principle of
        regression, 142
overnight fees, closing costs, 57
overpriced homes, 212
ownership advantages of home purchases,
        10–15
    See also home ownership
    inflation and, 11–12
    renting comparison, 11–13, 17, 73–75

• P •

partnerships, 164–166
    defined, 329
    down payments and, 61
    equity sharing, 164
    live-in, 164
    risks, 165
    titles and, 264
    types of residential, 164

patent defects, inspections, 240–241
periodic adjustment caps, adjustable rate
        mortgages, 101, 329
permissions to inspect finances, mortgage
        forms, 117–119
personal property insurance, 251
pest-control inspections, 243
phone listings, home prices, 209
PMI (private mortgage insurance)
    closing costs and, 56
    defined, 329
    down payments and, 58–59
points
    closing costs, 55
    defined, 95, 329
    fixed-rate mortgages, 95–96
    "no-point" mortgages, 96
preliminary title reports, escrow and, 260
prepaid loan interest, closing costs, 57
prepayment penalties
    avoiding loans with, 88
    defined, 329
prepurchase interior and exterior components
        inspections, 242–243
prequalification and preapproval,
        mortgages, 105
prices. *See* home prices
principal, defined, 329
principle of conformity, 143–144
principle of progression, 140–142
    benefits of renovating cheaper homes,
        141–142
    curable defects, 140–141
    incurable defects, 141
principle of regression, 142
private mortgage insurance. *See* PMI
probate, living trusts and, 37
probate sales, 329
profits, rolling over, 287
progression, principle of, 140–142
property inspectors, real estate teams,
        187–188
property taxes, 48–49
    closing costs, 56
    defined, 329

10/31/95

Fun, Fast, & Cheap!™

NEW!

The Internet For Macs® For Dummies® Quick Reference
by Charles Seiter

ISBN:1-56884-967-2
$9.99 USA/$12.99 Canada

NEW!

Windows® 95 For Dummies® Quick Reference
by Greg Harvey

ISBN: 1-56884-964-8
$9.99 USA/$12.99 Canada

SUPER STAR

Photoshop 3 For Macs® For Dummies® Quick Reference
by Deke McClelland

ISBN: 1-56884-968-0
$9.99 USA/$12.99 Canada

SUPER STAR

WordPerfect® For DOS For Dummies® Quick Reference
by Greg Harvey

ISBN: 1-56884-009-8
$8.95 USA/$12.95 Canada

Title	Author	ISBN	Price
DATABASE			
Access 2 For Dummies® Quick Reference	by Stuart J. Stuple	ISBN: 1-56884-167-1	$8.95 USA/$11.95 Canada
dBASE 5 For DOS For Dummies® Quick Reference	by Barrie Sosinsky	ISBN: 1-56884-954-0	$9.99 USA/$12.99 Canada
dBASE 5 For Windows® For Dummies® Quick Reference	by Stuart J. Stuple	ISBN: 1-56884-953-2	$9.99 USA/$12.99 Canada
Paradox 5 For Windows® For Dummies® Quick Reference	by Scott Palmer	ISBN: 1-56884-960-5	$9.99 USA/$12.99 Canada
DESKTOP PUBLISHING/ILLUSTRATION/GRAPHICS			
CorelDRAW! 5 For Dummies® Quick Reference	by Raymond E. Werner	ISBN: 1-56884-952-4	$9.99 USA/$12.99 Canada
Harvard Graphics For Windows® For Dummies® Quick Reference	by Raymond E. Werner	ISBN: 1-56884-962-1	$9.99 USA/$12.99 Canada
Photoshop 3 For Macs® For Dummies® Quick Reference	by Deke McClelland	ISBN: 1-56884-968-0	$9.99 USA/$12.99 Canada
FINANCE/PERSONAL FINANCE			
Quicken 4 For Windows® For Dummies® Quick Reference	by Stephen L. Nelson	ISBN: 1-56884-950-8	$9.95 USA/$12.95 Canada
GROUPWARE/INTEGRATED			
Microsoft® Office 4 For Windows® For Dummies® Quick Reference	by Doug Lowe	ISBN: 1-56884-958-3	$9.99 USA/$12.99 Canada
Microsoft® Works 3 For Windows® For Dummies® Quick Reference	by Michael Partington	ISBN: 1-56884-959-1	$9.99 USA/$12.99 Canada
INTERNET/COMMUNICATIONS/NETWORKING			
The Internet For Dummies® Quick Reference	by John R. Levine & Margaret Levine Young	ISBN: 1-56884-168-X	$8.95 USA/$11.95 Canada
MACINTOSH			
Macintosh® System 7.5 For Dummies® Quick Reference	by Stuart J. Stuple	ISBN: 1-56884-956-7	$9.99 USA/$12.99 Canada
OPERATING SYSTEMS:			
DOS			
DOS For Dummies® Quick Reference	by Greg Harvey	ISBN: 1-56884-007-1	$8.95 USA/$11.95 Canada
UNIX			
UNIX® For Dummies® Quick Reference	by John R. Levine & Margaret Levine Young	ISBN: 1-56884-094-2	$8.95 USA/$11.95 Canada
WINDOWS			
Windows® 3.1 For Dummies® Quick Reference, 2nd Edition	by Greg Harvey	ISBN: 1-56884-951-6	$8.95 USA/$11.95 Canada
PCs/HARDWARE			
Memory Management For Dummies® Quick Reference	by Doug Lowe	ISBN: 1-56884-362-3	$9.99 USA/$12.99 Canada
PRESENTATION/AUTOCAD			
AutoCAD For Dummies® Quick Reference	by Ellen Finkelstein	ISBN: 1-56884-198-1	$9.95 USA/$12.95 Canada
SPREADSHEET			
1-2-3 For Dummies® Quick Reference	by John Walkenbach	ISBN: 1-56884-027-6	$8.95 USA/$11.95 Canada
1-2-3 For Windows® 5 For Dummies® Quick Reference	by John Walkenbach	ISBN: 1-56884-957-5	$9.95 USA/$12.95 Canada
Excel For Windows® For Dummies® Quick Reference, 2nd Edition	by John Walkenbach	ISBN: 1-56884-096-9	$8.95 USA/$11.95 Canada
Quattro Pro 6 For Windows® For Dummies® Quick Reference	by Stuart J. Stuple	ISBN: 1-56884-172-8	$9.95 USA/$12.95 Canada
WORD PROCESSING			
Word For Windows® 6 For Dummies® Quick Reference	by George Lynch	ISBN: 1-56884-095-0	$8.95 USA/$11.95 Canada
Word For Windows® For Dummies® Quick Reference	by George Lynch	ISBN: 1-56884-029-2	$8.95 USA/$11.95 Canada
WordPerfect® 6.1 For Windows® For Dummies® Quick Reference, 2nd Edition	by Greg Harvey	ISBN: 1-56884-966-4	$9.99 USA/$12.99/Canada

For scholastic requests & educational orders please call Educational Sales at 1. 800. 434. 2086

FOR MORE INFO OR TO ORDER, PLEASE CALL ▶ 800. 762. 2974

For volume discounts & special orders please call Tony Real, Special Sales, at 415. 655. 3048

Order Center: **(800) 762-2974** *(8 a.m.–6 p.m., EST, weekdays)*

3/26/96

Quantity	ISBN	Title	Price	Total

Shipping & Handling Charges

	Description	First book	Each additional book	Total
Domestic	Normal	$4.50	$1.50	$
	Two Day Air	$8.50	$2.50	$
	Overnight	$18.00	$3.00	$
International	Surface	$8.00	$8.00	$
	Airmail	$16.00	$16.00	$
	DHL Air	$17.00	$17.00	$

*For large quantities call for shipping & handling charges.

**Prices are subject to change without notice.

Ship to:

Name _____

Company _____

Address _____

City/State/Zip _____

Daytime Phone _____

Payment: ☐ Check to IDG Books Worldwide (US Funds Only)

☐ VISA   ☐ MasterCard   ☐ American Express

Card # _____ Expires _____

Signature _____

Subtotal _____

CA residents add
applicable sales tax _____

IN, MA, and MD
residents add
5% sales tax _____

IL residents add
6.25% sales tax _____

RI residents add
7% sales tax _____

TX residents add
8.25% sales tax _____

Shipping _____

Total _____

Please send this order form to:

IDG Books Worldwide, Inc.
Attn: Order Entry Dept.
7260 Shadeland Station, Suite 100
Indianapolis, IN 46256

Allow up to 3 weeks for delivery.
Thank you!